IMPULSE TO REVOLUTION IN LATIN AMERICA

Jeffrey W. Barrett

PRAEGER

PRAEGER SPECIAL STUDIES • PRAEGER SCIENTIFIC

New York • Philadelphia • Eastbourne, UK
Toronto • Hong Kong • Tokyo • Sydney

Library of Congress Cataloging in Publication Data

Barrett, Jeffrey W.
  Impulse to revolution in Latin America.

  1. Latin America—Politics and government—
1948- —Philosophy. 2. Latin America—Economic
conditions—1945- . 3. Latin America—Social
conditions—1945- . 4. National characteristics,
Latin American. 5. Failure (Psychology) 6. Totalitarianism
I. Title.
F1414.2.B32 1985   980'.03   84-26297
ISBN 0-03-001558-8 (alk. paper)

Published in 1985 by Praeger Publishers
CBS Educational and Professional Publishing, a Division of CBS Inc.
521 Fifth Avenue, New York, NY 10175 USA

© 1985 by Praeger Publishers

56789 052 987654321

Printed in the United States of America on acid-free paper

INTERNATIONAL OFFICES

Orders from outside the United States should be sent to the appropriate address listed below. Orders from areas not
listed below should be placed through CBS International Publishing, 383 Madison Ave., New York, NY 10175 USA

Australia, New Zealand
Holt Saunders, Pty, Ltd., 9 Waltham St., Artarmon, N.S.W. 2064, Sydney, Australia

Canada
Holt, Rinehart & Winston of Canada, 55 Horner Ave., Toronto, Ontario, Canada M8Z 4X6

Europe, the Middle East, & Africa
Holt Saunders, Ltd., 1 St. Anne's Road, Eastbourne, East Sussex, England BN21 3UN

Japan
Holt Saunders, Ltd., Ichibancho Central Building, 22-1 Ichibancho, 3rd Floor, Chiyodaku, Tokyo, Japan

Hong Kong, Southeast Asia
Holt Saunders Asia, Ltd., 10 Fl, Intercontinental Plaza, 94 Granville Road, Tsim Sha Tsui East, Kowloon,
Hong Kong

**Manuscript submissions should be sent to the Editorial Director, Praeger Publishers, 521 Fifth Avenue,
New York, NY 10175 USA**

To Shirley

Preface

In the early 1970s a leading Latin American journalist, Carlos Rangel Guevara, wrote a book about the history and people of his continent and came to the following rather remarkable conclusion:

> Almost five hundred years have elapsed since 1492, half a millennium. If we try to summarize those five centuries of Latin American history, going to the heart of the matter and leaving analysis, anecdotes, controversies, and influences for later, the most certain, most truthful, and most general observation we can make about it is that *up to the present day, it has been a story of failure.*
>
> This statement may seem shocking but it is a truth that Latin Americans carry in their conscience, usually silently due to the pain, but which comes out into the open in moments of sincerity.[1]

Guevara was quite correct when he maintained that this is an idea that persistently recurs to Latin Americans despite its painful consequences. Westerners, in contrast, are not at all used to thinking in terms of entire nations or continents as "failures." The difference in the two perspectives is the result of two very distinct historical experiences. For the past two hundred years, Westerns have seen their modern industrial culture become dominant throughout the world—dominant in the sense that they have contributed more to foreign peoples than they have borrowed from them. Westerners have been prone to take this state of affairs for granted, to accept it as the natural order of things. Latin Americans, however, have looked at the imbalance of exchange from the position of borrowers; and as Rangel suggests, they have frequently interpreted it as evidence of national failure.

The theme of national failure is an important one throughout this book. In Part I we first explore the most conspicuous form of national failure in Latin America, economic underdevelopment, and pay particular attention to the cultural and political factors that have retarded economic growth. From there we will move on to what will be considered the heart of the book: how Latin Americans react to the multitude of economic, social, and political problems that beset them, and how they evaluate themselves in relation to other peoples. Once this ground is covered, we will be in a position to examine from a new perspective two subjects of particular interest to U.S. readers: Latin American anti-Westernism and Latin American revolution.

The second section of the book deals with a far less obvious feature of Latin American life: the great potential that exists in that area of the world for totalitarian political solutions. This is such an unexplored and unappreciated subject that most of Part II is devoted to examining it in depth. It is necessary first to gain some understanding as to what totalitarianism actually is, and we do this by looking at totalitarian theory in Fascist Italy and Bolshevik Russia. We then study totalitarian practices in Cuba, the only country in Latin America where totalitarianism has fully matured. Finally, in the last chapter, we discuss other Latin American countries where the urge to totalitarianism has clearly revealed itself yet failed to grow to fruition. The end result of this line of inquiry is to show how the physical and psychological conditions found in contemporary Latin American culture tend to nurture totalitarian ambition in highly nationalistic political leaders who aspire to revolutionary social change.

The subject matter of this book requires from time to time that adjustments be made to commonly understood definitions of certain words and phrases. The most important of these—the term *Western*—has already appeared in this essay, and so its meaning might best be clarified at this point. When Americans speak of the West or the Western world, they are normally referring to countries in Europe and to other countries around the world like the United States and Australia whose populations are largely made up of descendants of Europeans. By this definition Latin America, a child of Spain and Portugal, might also be considered part of the West. Latin Americans, however, tend to use the term *West* to refer to that group of countries with European cultural backgrounds that have become successfully modernized. Although Latin Americans fully recognize their own European heritage, they do not normally see themselves as part of the West because they do not yet have the second qualification: membership in that rather exclusive club of modernized nation-states. Because this book is about Latin America and its problems, we need a term that conveniently designates those areas of the world Latin Americans commonly think of when they talk about the West. For this reason we adopt the general Latin American usage of the word *West*. The reader should bear in mind that it is a relative and flexible term broadly referring to the most prosperous and successful nation-states populated by Europeans or descendants of Europeans.

In recent decades Westerners have been confronted with the need to try to look at themselves and at the world through the eyes of peoples less successful than themselves. Traditionally Westerners have not paid a great deal of attention to peoples left behind in the process of modernization. Instead, they have been fascinated with each other, with that small family of nation-states where the technological advances were made, the age-old diseases conquered, the great armies fielded. Since the end of World War II, however, Westerners have been rapidly entering an era where the world is so interconnected by technology that previously distant and obscure peoples can have a substantial impact upon their lives. Thus, Westerners have arrived at a point where they can no longer ignore the nationalistic feelings and anxieties stirred up in other peoples by the enormous influence of their example and culture. The focus of this study is upon Latin Americans and their particular concerns, but to one degree or another, the conclusions drawn from it are valid for other peoples whose fate has placed them in a similar historical dilemma.

CONTENTS

PART I
UNDERDEVELOPMENT AND NATIONAL IDENTITY

1
THE DEBATE
OVER UNDERDEVELOPMENT

When the problem of underdevelopment is viewed historically, it is not difficult to see why many peoples of today's world are burdened by poverty. For almost the entire span of human history, all peoples lived at or just above the subsistence level. In contemporary times most peoples continue to do so. About two hundred years ago, the peoples living in Western Europe began to rise above the condition of mass poverty that had been the fate of humanity for thousands of years. This decisive break with the past could have happened among any people in the world—or among none at all. It happened among the inhabitants of Western Europe. It was these peoples who set a new standard for adequate living conditions; and it was these peoples who, by their example, informed the peoples living in non-European cultures that they were "underdeveloped."

If other peoples wished to match the Europeans in their success, they had to do more than simply acquire Western mechanical and organizational skills. They also had to acquire the values, attitudes, and customs that prompted the Europeans constantly to innovate and build upon those skills. What the Europeans accomplished through an unplanned, glacial *evolution*, other peoples had to manage through a quick, deliberate *revolution*. But to transform over a span of mere decades the basic human values, beliefs, and ways of thinking of an enormous human mass numbering in the millions is the most profound and difficult of all revolutions. Of all non-European cultures, only the Japanese have surmounted the obstacles and broken into the small circle of prosperous "modern" peoples.

The close relationship between modernization and the "modern" values that have distinguished European culture is made evident by the example of the European emigrants who, in the greatest population migration of human history, departed from their homelands and fanned out into the undeveloped territories of the earth. Wherever large numbers of Europeans have gone, they have flourished. The British,

3

who led the way into the industrial age, were especially prolific colonizers; and transplanted offshoots of this island people built up highly developed economies in the remote wilds of North America, Australia, and New Zealand.

The ethnic makeup of the population in Latin America, as well as the patterns of economic prosperity on that continent, tends to further verify the intimate connection between modern values and modernization. It was Latin America's historic destiny to be populated mainly by American Indians, Africans, and Iberians (the Spanish and Portuguese). The first two of these peoples were, of course, beyond the influence of modernizing European civilization; and the Iberians, almost as if they were sealed off by the Pyrenees mountain range, were among the Europeans least affected by the developments pioneered by the Dutch, French, and British. Shifting attention from the continent as a whole to the regions of Latin America, we also find that traditionally the most advanced belt of industrial and agricultural development (Uruguay, southern Brazil, and the Río Plata region of Argentina) was located precisely in that area which received the greatest influx of European immigration during the latter nineteenth and early twentieth centuries. Also worthy of attention are the economic achievements of smaller groups of European immigrants scattered over the rest of the continent who performed outstandingly well in relation to the rest of the population.

Swayed by this kind of evidence, Latin America's first modernizers readily acknowledged the close relationship between cultural values and economic development. For approximately a century after independence, leading political and intellectual figures used what may be termed a "values approach" when they sought to analyze the causes of underdevelopment. For example, Juan Bautiste Alberdi, possibly the most influential South American thinker of the nineteenth century, opened a major investigation of his continent's social ills with the following statement, which, while frank and unsparing, was very typical of the period: "South America is occupied by a poor people who inhabit a rich land, just the opposite of Europe, which is occupied mainly by a rich people who inhabit a poor land."[1] Theorists like Alberdi attributed what at that time was commonly termed Latin American "backwardness" mainly to an unfortunate heritage of values. Their solution was to change those values through educational efforts and the promotion of European immigration.

Because this perspective on economic development appeals to elementary common sense, it is widely used by Latin Americans today.[2] Either explicitly or implicitly, it repeatedly manifests itself in the conversations of Latin Americans, particularly when they are discussing specific economic problems. Not infrequently Latin Americans can be heard to wonder aloud what their continent would be like if Latin America had originally been settled by the British and not by the Spanish or Portuguese. Less articulate Hispanic Americans, even illiterate peasants, will sometimes attribute their society's woes to an inheritance of "bad Spanish blood."

But contemporary Latin America also wears another face on how it evaluates its condition of underdevelopment. In highly visible sectors of Latin American life, the values explanation has given way to another approach, which generally asserts itself in the writings of intellectuals, the rhetoric of politicians, and other areas where the assessment of national poverty is more formal and public. In the last 50 years something that can be called a structuralist approach has gradually supplanted the older wisdom among Latin American intellectuals and political elites; why this should happen in opposition to the prevailing common sense will be discussed in Chapter 5.

Focusing on concerns that scarcely consider values, a structuralist analysis preoccupies itself with such items as the "structure" of international trade (for example, favoring rich imperialist nations), the structure of agricultural ownership (for example, feudal and unproductive), the structure of industry (for example, capitalist, producing for profit and not for people), and the structure of the internal market (for example, maldistribution of income). In general, a structuralist perspective views the purchasing and productive power of society as controlled by the "wrong" social groups, and its "revolution" consists of their redistribution to the "right" groups. For example, it is frequently hostile to foreign or private ownership of income-producing property, and its solution would be to transfer control of this property to the state (nationalization) or sometimes to worker cooperatives (socialization). Its basic assumption is that the structure of wealth and power that exists in underdeveloped countries is actually the cause of the underdevelopment. Its basic failing is demonstrating how the shifting of control of national resources to some other sector of the population will, in itself, bring about economic modernization.

While important in Latin America, structuralist concepts have not been overly influential among mainstream Western economists whose preoccupation with the challenge of underdevelopment in the post-World War II era has evolved into still another major approach to the study of national poverty. For scholars of this school, economic development, or more precisely the enlargement of a country's gross national product, is primarily a process of saving and investing capital. The problem of underdevelopment is, therefore, basically a problem of a scarcity of capital.

Western economists are understandably encouraged toward this perspective by their own theoretical training, which isolates capital and labor as the heavy engines of economic growth; and since impoverished lands are generally overflowing with unemployed and underemployed labor, capital accumulation is left as their paramount concern.

The viewpoint of these developmental economists is also strengthened by their great interest in designing rather imposing-looking mathematical formulas (in technical language known as "economic models") which governments of poor countries can use to "plan" the growth of their economies. The hope is that these formulas are mathematical representations of an economy and will allow planners to predict how the economy will respond under different kinds of government intervention. Obviously, such formulas can be devised only if the factors affecting economic development are quantifiable and not so numerous as to make the whole exercise impossibly unwieldy. Factors that influence the availability of investable capital and presumably economic growth (balance of trade, interest rates, money supply, foreign aid, and so forth) have the advantages of being familiar to the economist, limited in number, and easily translatable into numbers.

Many of the economists under consideration are willing to acknowledge that certain noneconomic factors, including cultural values, affect economic development and even give generous reference to them. But as more and more of their colleagues have complained, they don't know quite what to do with these observations when it comes to drawing up their strategy for modernization.[3] They can deal with hinderances to modernization such as government nepotism or corruption only by ignoring them or, more specifically, by assuming they will change under the impact of increasing capital investment. Thus, even when they recognize noneconomic factors as significant obstacles, they continue to put capital at the center of their planning methods and their theory of development.

A growing number of economists have been stressing that capital cannot remain the exclusive or even primary focus of their labors because capital behaves differently in different cultures.[4] They sometimes point out as an example how foreign aid in the form of the Marshall Plan helped to rebuild a war-devastated Europe in a decade while foreign aid to underdeveloped countries is consumed as rapidly as it arrives, with considerably less impressive results. Because they feel that many of the standard theoretical tools of their profession do not work well when applied to underdeveloped societies, they have moved on to untraditional areas of study such as research into the cultural mores that influence economic leadership. Upon this new terrain they have met sociologists, anthropologists, and political scientists interested in the same problem of national poverty. No hoped-for conceptual scheme has been worked out suitable to the needs of government planners, but their activity in this area is most certainly a vindication of the wisdom of the nineteenth-century Latin American theorists who toiled in these same intellectual fields many years ago.

To recognize the primacy of the values approach to underdevelopment does not signify that many of the insights of the structural and scarcity-of-capital theorists cannot be accepted as valid. It does mean that any assumption that holds that capital investment alone or structural change alone is sufficient to precipitate the needed value reform must be regarded as unrealistic. Of course, a scarcity of investment capital, a traditional structure of society, and *modernization-impeding values*, that is, those values found in Latin American culture that tend to retard economic progress, interrelate, reinforce, and influence one another. The disappearance of the first two developmental obstacles will therefore have an effect on prevailing values, but only in hesitant, gradual, and unpredicatable fashion. To put this into concrete terms, the Israelis, who are essentially European colonists on an arid strip of desert in the Middle East, are far more prepared to transform their land into a modernized nation-state than are a nonmodern people with all the structural revolution they can bear and all the petrodollars they can spend.

The problem of modernization-impedeing values is especially important to Latin American revolutionaries who desire rapid economic progress. Their modernization revolution, to be sure, will have to impose structural reforms and sharply augment the rate of capital accumulation and investment. But with these revolutions executed, the real revolution will have just begun—a revolt against the values and attitudinal heritage of the past.

If, then, modernization-impeding values are of such importance to our understanding of underdevelopment, it is necessary to start by examining their features, their evolution, and the forces that nourish their tenacious hold upon a human society.

2
MODERNIZATION-IMPEDING VALUES

THE CULTURAL LEGACY

At a point along his famous travels in America, Alexis de Tocqueville paused to record in his notebook the following observation: "One cannot but be astonished at the influence which the point of departure has on the good or ill destiny of peoples."[1] For the Latin American peoples, the point of departure was the Iberian Peninsula, a fist of the European land mass that jutted into the stormy Atlantic. It was from this soil that the cultural seeds of the Old World were carried and transplanted in lands that are known today as Latin America.

During the initial phase of modern European exploration and expansion, the Spanish and Portuguese of this period produced some of the greatest explorers and conquerers in history. They were not, however, in the vanguard of the commercial, scientific, and industrial developments that brought about the vastly more productive economic systems that have distinguished modern times. Instead, their northern neighbors led the way into the new era. The Iberians remained behind, continuing to live in an older age where the medieval aristocratic outlook and the "rightness" of the aristocratic way of life were firmly rooted.

While many explanations might be offered for this, scholars have traditionally placed great emphasis on the social attitudes fostered by the *Reconquista* (Reconquest). The Reconquista was a series of wars lasting for centuries in which Christian nobles grappled with Moslem Moors and gradually pushed them from Iberian territory. Even after these wars were over, the Spanish monarch Philip II kept battling for his version of the true religion with endless crusades against Protestants, Jews, heathens, infidels, crypto-Moslems and lukewarm Catholics. During this period of interminable warfare, fighting feudal nobles had critically important roles to perform and so were able to strengthen their social position and enhance their social prestige. They

8

also greatly expanded their numbers because kings, often hard pressed for money and soldiers, were willing to stoop to the debased practice of selling titles of nobility. The trading and artisan classes, meanwhile, fared poorly. Jews and Moslems made up a large percentage of these, and the steady intensification of religious fanaticism cast them into the roles of aliens and enemies. Literally hundreds of thousands of the most productive inhabitants of Iberia were driven from the peninsula for not being Catholic, or in the case of converts, for not being Catholic enough. The cumulative effect of the centuries of crusading was, in short, the relative increase in the prestige of an aristocratic class that was generally idle and contemptuous of work, and a relative increase in their numbers to where they were conspicuous enough to impress upon the larger population their haughty indifference to productive endeavors.

After the discovery of America, Iberians sailed forth to the New World, conquered the indigenous peoples there, and set themselves up as new elites. Because the values of these new elites were influential in shaping colonial society, it is important to examine their beliefs, ideals, and customs with some care. To begin with, the Iberian conquerers were thoroughly imbued with the hierarchical values of their homeland. Although most of them came from lowly social origins, they were excited by the knowledge that with the right combination of audacity, courage, and luck, even a humble peasant could become a noble in the faraway colonies. To them the ideal way of life was to pass their days as great independent feudal grandees, lords of all they surveyed and absolute masters of the lesser human beings who were placed on earth to serve their every need.

In addition to traditions of aristocracy and hierarchy, the Iberian conquerers of the New World encouraged traditions of violence and exploitation. They did this, in part, by means of the social structure they set up for themselves and their descendants. The Iberians in America patterned their system on the familiar hierarchical model with overlords on top and either serfs or slaves toiling at the bottom. The problem with such an arrangement is that whenever a social system affords its elites unrestricted power over lesser human beings, it fosters the corruption of those who wield that power; that is, it encourages the brutalization of those who have the capacity to brutalize. The masters of the agricultural estates in Iberian America enjoyed power that was far less restrained by custom and tradition than was the case with the feudal lords of medieval Europe.[2] Nor could their ability to tyrannize be effectively checked by the Spanish monarchs. Spain was simply too far away, and the will to enforce royal decrees designed to protect the Indians diminished with every mile of the long journey. Indeed, the eighteenth-century voyager Antonio de Ulloa found that some of the most vicious oppressors of the Indians were those sent to ensure their protection.[3]

A look at the Brazilian plantation system offers some insights as to how a situation where an elite has unrestricted power over human "inferiors" can lead to the brutalization of that elite. From their earliest days the sons of the plantation masters grew up in an environment that conspired to prevent them from acquiring the values of moderation, self-restraint, and respect for human life. As infants they were surrounded by slaves instructed to cater to their every whim. As they grew into children, they encountered few checks on their behavior, including their inclinations to boyish sadism. Unlike most children, however, these pampered young lords found themselves in a position of authority over other human beings. That is to say, instead of indulging their puerile sadism by pulling the wings out of insects, they found themselves in a position where they could pull the teeth out of Negroes or torture them with thrashing.[4] When these children grew up to become undisputed lords of the manor, they had even fewer restraints on their base impulses. Adult plantation masters commonly satisfied their taste for violence by watching cocks and male canaries fight to the death, by beating dogs and horses, and by persecuting slaves.[5] The British biologist Charles Darwin was so revolted by the combination of wicked tempers, lust for violence, and groveling servility he found in Brazil that he vowed never to set foot in a slave country again.

> Near Rio de Janeiro I lived opposite to an old lady who kept screws to crush the fingers of her female slaves. I have stayed in a house where a young household mulatto daily and hourly was reviled, beaten, and persecuted enough to break the spirit of the lowest animal. I have seen a little boy, six or seven years old, struck thrice with a horsewhip (before I could interfere) on his naked head for having handed me a glass of water not quite clean. . . . I have seen at Rio Janeiro a powerful negro afraid to ward off a blow directed as he thought, at his face.[6]

The depraving influence of untempered authority upon the elites of colonial Latin America was reinforced by the cultural and racial gulfs that existed between the lords and their inferiors. To be sure, in medieval Europe education and privilege rendered the chasms between classes so wide that the nobles could scarcely regard the lower orders as the same form of humanity as themselves.[7] In the Iberian colonies this class perception was not essentially different; it was simply compounded by racial contrasts and even vaster cultural distances. There, the debate among the elites was not whether Negroes and Indians were fundamentally different kinds of human beings but whether they should be classified as human beings at all. Only after long and acrimonious discussion did the Holy Christian Fathers decide that Indians possessed souls, and their piety only went far enough to grant them the status of legal minors.[8] Negroes were denied even this honor until later times. Furthermore, the Church's official conclusions were not necessarily shared by the laity. Slaveholders in Brazil, for example, sincerely believed that the dark underlings who surrounded them were not fully human but were "a link in the chain of animated beings between ourselves and the various species of brute animals."[9] Likewise, in the Andes Mountains the elite often looked upon the Indians of their region as a subhuman species and commonly referred to them as the "animal closest to man."[10] The basic point here is that attitudes are very often influenced by social structure, and any society that provides its elite with practically unrestricted power over a racially and culturally distant labor force whose very humanity is up for argument is more likely to have intensely exploitative social relations than a society with a more favorable historical legacy.

Even more directly related to the question of economic underdevelopment were the attitudes of Latin America's elites toward work. These social elites were swayed by an ethic that may justly be called "conspicious indolence." Instead of admiring the ideal of work, they were actively hostile to it and made every effort to avoid the appearance of engaging in useful labor.

The roots of this prejudice against work can be traced to the aristocratic ideals of Iberian society. People who claimed aristocratic status in that hierarchically ordered society were intent on demonstrating they were different from and superior to members of the lower classes. To avoid being associated with common people, they were careful to avoid any task that might have been carried out by common people. As a consequence, the aristocrats were hard pressed to find any form of truly productive activity that they did not consider beneath their dignity.

This same attitude toward work, of course, greatly influenced the Iberians who settled in the American colonies. These Iberian immigrants aspired not only to make a fortune in the New World but to acquire a sizable group of serfs or slaves that they could use to free themselves from the acute indignity of having to earn their living by their own labor. No matter how humble the origins of these immigrants or how accomplished their manual skills, they were gripped with the ambition of putting behind their undistinguished pasts and becoming noble landlords, grandly independent of the base concerns of the inferior classes. The historian Leslie Byrd Simpson wrote of the frantic struggles of aspiring aristocrats in Mexico who were possessed by this mentality:

> A Spanish immigrant might be a farrier, a carpenter, or an *arriero*. No matter. By hard work and frugality, or by any means, he would acquire a piece of land. He had taken the first step toward nobility.

If he could accumulate enough to save his children from useful and humiliating work, he was well along the way, even though his children despised him for an uncouth *gachupin* (Spaniard). Succeeding generations became progressively more emancipated, until, if the estate could stand the strain, the family emerged as a useless colony of parasites. This was only possible, of course, because there existed a servile class to support them.[11]

This need to escape productive labor did not mean that the New World elites were adverse to all strenuous effort. In fact, they expended considerable energy to avoid any sign of effort—at least the kind of effort that suggested the status of those obliged to subsist by their own labor. Gilberto Freyre describes the extremes to which these practices grew among the lords of the Brazilian plantations:

Every white in the Big House had two left hands, every Negro two right hands. The master's hands served only for telling the beads of Our Lady's rosary, for playing cards, for taking snuff from snuff boxes, or *corriboques*, and for playing with the breasts of young Negro and mulatto girls, the pretty slaves of his harem. . . .

It was the slaves who literally became their masters' feet, running errands for their owners and carrying them about in hammock or palanquin. They also became their masters' hands—at least, their right hands; for they it was who dressed them, drew on their trousers and their boots for them, bathed and brushed them, and hunted over their persons for fleas. There is a tradition to the effect that one Pernambucan planter even employed the Negro's hand for the most intimate details of his toilet.[12]

Conspicuous indolence was only one method the Latin American elites used to demonstrate their noble independence from productive labor. Conspicuous consumption was another. By consuming and displaying worldly goods in an ostentatious manner, members of the wealthy classes could flaunt not only their wealth but also their freedom from the vile pursuits of the lower orders. People caught up in this mentality competed with one another in gorgeous displays of elegance. One Argentinean aristocrat, for example, made his mark on society by changing into eight magnificent sets of attire a day and spending the day on parade.[13] When the elites were preening and promenading in this fashion, they were doing more than indulging in hedonistic pleasure; they were making calculated bids, employing the devices of conspicuous consumption, to elevate their social prestige.

Because the social elites of Iberian America avidly clung to values that discouraged modernization, the economic advancement of the entire society would have been served better had these elites been isolated and prevented from influencing the rest of the population. Human beings, however, especially those in hierarchically ordered societies, have long shown an inclination to imitate their social superiors.[14] Lower-status men and women in Latin America frequently demonstrated this by their inept attempts to ape the fads and fashions of the upper classes.[15] Far more serious, however, was their willingness, even eagerness, to adopt the attitudes and emulate the behavior patterns of their "betters," including those that resulted in the exploitation of human beings under their control.

A particularly graphic example of this could be seen in the behavior of a group of lower-status individuals called *mestizos*. Mestizos were the illegitimate and often forsaken offspring of Europeans and Indians.[16] A well-known historian on this subject, Magnus Mörner, described the contempt of whites for mestizos "as good as boundless."[17] In compensation, mestizo contempt for the lowly Indian was, if anything, even more pronounced. Disdained by the members of the highest social stratum and disdainful of those of the lower, mestizos suffered the severe identity problem of those in the middle who do not know who they are; and they attempted to deal with this strain by not only imitating but *exaggerating* the worst abusive characteristics of the social superiors who spurned them. Despite this or because of it, mestizos were often hired to manage the labor forces on mining and agricultural properties. Once ensconced in these positions of authority, they were given to asserting their superiority by terrorizing the people under their power. De Ulloa frequently observed mounted mestizos yanking Indians to work sites with the hair of these poor wretches tied to the horses' tails.[18] On the argicultural estates, mestizo overseers, who could deal out punishments at their own discretion, were often regarded as far more vehement and tyrannical than the manor lords.[19]

In addition to the values and attitudes that coarsened the quality of social interrelationships, individuals of lesser status in Latin American culture were profoundly influenced by the aristocratic attitude toward work. Notions that certain types of toil, particularly manual toil, were beneath them were acquired even by lowly servants, who devised amongst themselves their own hierarchical order of position and privilege. In Brazil, for example, white servants sent on a shopping errand would characteristically insist on being provided a Negro to carry the package home, even if the burden was something as trivial as a ball of yarn.[20]

People with middle-class status were especially swayed by this prestige ethic. Even those in difficult economic circumstances looked with utter disgust upon almost all forms of socially useful labor. An American traveler in nineteenth-century Brazil made these observations about the strength of this attitude:

> Brazilians shrink with something allied to horror from manual
> employment. . . . Dr. C ____, an old resident, says that the young

men will starve rather than become mechanics. He, some years ago, advised a poor widow who had two boys (one 14, the other 16) to put them to trades. She rose, left the room, and never after spoke to him, although he had attended her family professionally for years without charge.[21]

The gravely offended widow's response suggests that the abhorrence to manual labor in Brazil stemmed not from slothfulness but from a concept of personal honor that unfortunately eliminated from consideration almost all possibilities of genuinely productive endeavor. Those concerned with raising or maintaining status defined such status in part by their own occupation or that of their family members. So meticulous could they be in shunning any sign of manual labor that they even tried to avoid carrying packages in public. An English resident in Brazil was once startled to observe that his houseguest refused to carry home his own overnight bag and instead sent a slave from four miles away to do the task for him. An aversion to physical exertion? The luggage consisted of a toothbrush and a comb.[22]

THE AMERICAN LEGACY

The investigation of the historical point of departure of one culture is only complete when compared to the experience of another. In this case the attention should be shifted from the relatively poor countries in Iberia and Latin America to the more affluent ones in Western Europe and North America. The comparison makes for a study in sharp contrasts.

We have previously observed that as developments on the Iberian Peninsula were strengthening the values and prestige of the aristocratic class among the Spanish and Portuguese, some peoples living in northwest Europe were beginning to emerge from their feudal backgrounds and prepare the way for more complex and productive economies. The people mainly responsible for organizing this expansion of economic activity have generally been called the "middle class," an amorphous group belonging neither to the class of nobles nor to the class of serfs but situated somewhere in between the two feudal poles. When the "Commercial Revolution" fused with certain scientific, technological, and organizational advances and gave way to something scholars have labeled the "Industrial Revolution," the attitudes and outlooks of this middle class[23] became dominant throughout Europe, supplanting the mentalities more characteristic of aristocratic and peasant cultures.

As with other trading peoples throughout history, the European middle classes tended to develop values and moral codes that were suitable to their profession of carrying on commerce. For example, they placed a high value on the kinds of productive activities they themselves were engaged in and were inclined to judge individuals on the basis of their success at these concrete endeavors rather than on their privileged station or noble birth. They possessed a keen sense of legal honesty in business dealings because smooth commercial relationships depended in good measure upon the mutual confidence underlying mercantile transactions. They preached the virtue of honoring business agreements and contracts, knowing well that a businessman's reputation for integrity was one of his invisible assets. They held that punctuality and reliability were important when making appointments and attending meetings for they knew that lost time was lost money. They praised the virtue of frugality because they understood the value of an ample stock of investment capital. They cultivated the ingenious technique of compromise, useful when self-reliant individuals needed to come together to cooperate in common ventures.

The commercially minded of Western Europe even went so far as to modify Christianity, reshaping it into a religion that sanctified their way of life. Many of them eagerly embraced the stern revisionist doctrine of Calvinism, which ignored the horsehair garments of the ascetic, ridiculed the precious silks of the aristocrat, and dressed its own adherents in drab, cheerless, black cloth. Grave and austere Calvinism denounced the life of leisure, the lovemaking, the pleasure seeking, of frivolous aristocrats and instead substituted the somber ideal of work for its own sake, measured success in life in terms of material prosperity, and described the practice of business as an especially effective means of getting to heaven.

In general, early middle-class morals and values stressed the pious, disciplined, early-to-bed, early-to-rise life oriented toward investment, production, and an ever-increasing standard of living. They were almost a studied reaction against aristocratic values; and so for whatever defects they might be criticized, they were certainly not aristocratic defects, which had the effect of discouraging economic progress. In fact, as they had developed by the eve of the Industrial Revolution, middle-class beliefs, mores, and customs were ideally suited for that revolution, the most recent and most spectacular phase of a prolonged process of modernization in Europe.

While this society of commercially minded people was evolving in Europe, some of the hardiest bearers of middle-class values left their homelands and settled in the non-Iberian parts of the New World, particularly in those areas of what is today the northern United States. Many of these immigrants fled to America to escape persecution and were understandably antiaristocratic in their politics and values.[24] It was partly because of their antiaristocratic disposition that the sturdy yeomanry of America possessed a highly positive attitude toward work and manual labor.[25] De Tocqueville, when traveling in America, never ceased to be startled by the enormous release of energy he found everywhere about him. Sights common enough especially in the more backward parts of Europe, the soporific lethargy of reluctant serf laborers, the cultivated indolence of their aristocratic masters, seemed foreign to the experience of Americans. De Tocqueville discovered the most extreme version of this in the western-frontier state of Ohio, and at one point he marveled, "There is not a *single*, absolutely not a *single* man of leisure. . . . Everyone has his work, to which he devotes himself ardently."[26]

Despite some aristocratic pretenses that could be found in its older cities, the young republic of America was the area of the Western world where the emerging middle-class way of life reached its fullest development. It was America, in fact, that produced Benjamin Franklin and through him the most celebrated written expressions of early middle-class values. By the time the eighteenth century drew to a close, Franklin's almanac of immortal maxims (for example, Time is Money) and his autobiography of a "self-made man" had sold millions of copies around the world in scores of languages.[27]

The Europeans who settled in America often found life hard in their adopted country, but it would have been difficult for a deity to design an environment more propitious for the growth of their particular values and institutions. Even had these immigrants wished to be the masters of a servile mass of humanity, conditions in the northern areas of America dictated against it. Unlike the situation in Latin America, where millions of Indians lived in dense, complex, agrarian-based civilizations, the primitive natives of America were utterly unfit for agricultural labor or any other form of economic exploitation; furthermore, they were few in number and collectively weak, and they could be pushed off into the dark forests without the extensive warfare that might have brutalized the new arrivals. Nor were the northern settlers tempted to import masses of Negroes, for most of the settlers lacked the capital for such an expensive investment and their farmlands were not suitable for the kinds of luxury export crops that would have made a slave system economically viable.

In sum, the pioneers who sought their fortunes in the American wilds had to work in order to survive, and nowhere within the European cultural orbit was there a people more willing to do so. If the land was sometimes difficult to farm, it was always plentiful. There was no predatory class of aristocrats with the power to divide it into expansive estates. Virtually all in early America could aspire to their own plot, and relying on their own persistent labor, reap the necessities, if not the luxuries, of life.

These observations on the formation of American values must, of course, be limited to the northern part of the country. South of the Potomac the climate was mild, the land perfect for cotton and tobacco, and the area attracted many scions of the English aristocracy who possessed both the funds and the disposition to import slaves. Eventually the northern United States with its greater population, dynamism, wealth, and military power prevailed over the South and set the moral tone for the entire nation. But as the British sociologist Stanislav Andreski has properly concluded, had the South succeeded in separating itself from the Union, it would probably have been dragged down by its cultural heritage to the level of its Latin American neighbors.[28]

Notwithstanding this rather large exception, the British outposts in America were blessed with subtantial advantages over their Iberian counterparts. At the time of the discovery of the New World, Western Europe was undergoing changes within itself that were to prove monumental. Through the modernization-developmental perspective, American civilization inherited the most "progressive" elements of this evolving European culture. It was in a relative sense born free, free of aristocratic privilege and prejudice or, in the fighting words of the Chilian writer Francisco Bilbao, free of the "sickly castes of Europe . . . [of] their habits of servility and their worldly manners," free of "eighteen centuries of slavery and decadence."[29] During the nineteenth century, Latin American intellectuals frequently took up their pens, faced north, and with Bilbao exclaimed, "Everything has favored you. You are the sons of the first men of modern Europe."[30]

History, like life itself, is unfair; Bilbao and others were only recognizing this when they pointed out how history had so obviously unfolded to the advantage of the peoples who settled in North America.

THE CHARACTER OF MODERNIZATION-IMPEDING VALUES

When discussing the relationship between cultural values and economic development, it is essential not only to identify the values that impede modernization but also to examine their character. One vital aspect of their character that should be considered is the strength of their grip upon human beings. Specialists who study economic underdevelopment often underestimate the resistance of values and customs to change, and some even write as if old habits can be discarded with scarcely more effort than it takes to cast away old shoes once their lack of usefulness becomes apparent. Many of these analysts have proposed a plan of action that seeks to use the "revolution of rising expectations," that is to say, the longing of the poor for a higher standard of living, as a means of inducing the poor to discard values that hold back their economic advancement. The logic behind this plan, a logic which has launched massive educational efforts and precipitated a blizzard of "community development" projects such as those conducted by the U.S. Peace Corps, is that people can be persuaded to alter accustomed ways of doing things once they see that these changes are in their own self-interest. Implicit within this point of view is the assumption that reasonable, calculated self-interest is more powerful than the counterforce of custom. The fact is, however, that the roots of modernization-impeding customs often extend to far greater depths than many hopeful scholars and politicians would dare imagine. They extend to a level where they receive their strength and nourishment from the most formidable self-interest of them all, a human being's sense of personal dignity and self-esteem.

The connection between one's customary social conduct and one's innermost feelings of self-esteem might best be understood by investigating the notion of *positive identity*. In contemporary psychology the behavior of an individual human being is often analyzed in terms of the individual's search for *identity*, his yearning to answer the question, "Who am I?" If, however, we apply this useful notion of identity to the subject matter of this chapter, we must extend it to include the idea that an individual is interested not only in what he is, in self-definition, but in what it is about himself that he can be proud of. An essential part of an individual's search for identity is his hunger for a feeling of personal dignity, the ability to accept himself for whatever he perceives himself to be.[31]

An individual's sense of self-esteem is, in turn, strongly influenced by the social esteem bestowed upon him by his fellow human beings. This relationship exists because it is obviously easier to think well of himself if those surrounding him do so. Responding to a force sociologists call peer-group pressure, people tend to conform to what others expect of them in order to secure their respect and acquire a psychological benefit known as social prestige. The problem for modernization arises when individuals, for the sake of social prestige, conform to dominant prestige patterns that, in addition to conferring status, result in social behavior that retards economic development. Specific examples of how efforts to maintain social esteem (and ultimately personal self-esteem) can lead to modernization-impeding behavior will be brought out later in some detail.

A discussion of the values and customs in Latin America requires, first of all, an inquiry into the more general question of Latin American *national character*.[32] National character, it should be kept in mind, is a concept that deals with important but relative differences in the collective personalities of peoples; while human characteristics are universal in that they are present in all nationalities to one degree or another, what defines national character is the relative emphasis of these traits among each people. One of the most significant ways in which the national character of Latin Americans and Americans is different is the manner in which each people tends to view human relationships within its society. As might be expected from their respective historical traditions, Latin Americans show a far stronger tendency to view human relationships in terms of hierarchy than do their more egalitarian minded American counterparts.[33]

We have seen that while the Iberian settlers in the New World readily accepted the aristocratic bias toward a natural superior-inferior ordering of human beings in society, the British settlers were moved by an antiaristocratic bias which prompted them to stress the basic equality of all human beings. Since human beings are similar and dissimilar in innumerable ways, a legitimate case can be made for both perspectives—how different (and unequal) human beings are as well as for how alike (and equal) they are. Obviously, the more culturally similar and homogeneous a people really are, the more likely the psychology of equality will be able to take root among them.

The English men and women who colonized America were not only well disposed to the idea of equality, but because of the conditions they encountered on their new continent, they were able to develop a relatively homogeneous society that encouraged both the preservation of their egalitarian intellectual ideals and the firm rooting of egalitarian emotional reflexes. Indeed, almost everything about early America fostered the idea and psychology of equality. While a well-born, wealthy, and cultured elite certainly did exist, the other extreme—a downtrodden, degraded general population—was nowhere to be seen. There were no beggars in the land, no cringing, submissive serfs bowing before their overlords in the countryside, no turbulent, ungovernable mobs in the cities. The American masses* were assured economic independence by the abundance of land; in Jefferson's time over 90 percent of them were simple villagers and agriculturalists working in their own trades or on their own farms.[34] Nor were the broad masses bereft of political power or culture. Because of democratic institutions, they acquired considerable political power; and owing to an excellent public education system, the great majority (over 90 percent by 1840) could read and write.[35] An auspicious confluence of conditions, then, produced in early America a prosperous, literate, politically influential, and relatively homogeneous population whose members were not obliged to feel servile to the elites

---

*These comments, of course, apply only to white Americans.

which did exist. The absence of forsaken, impoverished masses within the country reduced the cultural distance between classes and prevented the secretion of strong emotions of superiority and inferiority that would have killed the incipient egalitarianism its settlers brought to its shores.

The impulse to perceive human beings as essentially alike and equal has gone through various phases in American history, but relative to Latin American culture, it has always been, and continues to be, the prevailing reflex. After the Civil War, when Americans started to industrialize in earnest and millions of bewildered, intimidated, illiterate European peasants began to pour into American cities, the emotional roots of egalitarian attitudes were threatened. Outside of the large cities, however, the basic egalitarianism remained unchallenged, and as America's industrial progress gradually created a broad, affluent middle class of blue- and white-collar workers whose economic and cultural opportunities made it possible for them to regard themselves as not radically different from even the wealthiest of American citizens.

In Latin America the contrasts were remarkable. To begin with, the Iberian Americans were subdivided and controlled by conquerers who made no pretense to a fondness for egalitarian notions. Futhermore, the idea of a natural, profound dissimilarity and inequality among people blended in well with the panorama of Latin American society where the elites were exalted and the masses demeaned. Vast differences in wealth, power, status, culture, and race separated human beings into a hierarchy where mestizos were regarded by those above them as contemptible offspring of illegitimate unions; and Indians and Negroes, as missing links between themselves and the animal kingdom. When egalitarian ideals finally arrived in Latin America, mainly through the influence of the French Revolution, they were eagerly seized upon and excitedly discussed by participants of certain intellectual circles who found them alluring and avant-garde; but so alien to the emotional experience of Latin Americans was the notion of the essential sameness and equality of human beings that the ideal had no real effect. It simply appeared and hovered above Latin American life like a bright but faraway star.

Owing to their particular historical heritage and social experience, contemporary Latin Americans tend to view human relations very differently than North Americans. Latin Americans are inclined to look upon human beings as obviously dissimilar, unquestionably unequal, and as a consequence, as holding different hierarchical positions in society. In visual terms, this would be akin to viewing the human beings of a society standing on a stairway with the lowest on the bottom and the highest at the top. Americans, in contrast, because of their egalitarian background, are inclined to see themselves as all standing on the same level as if distributed over a plain. Among both peoples there is ranking according to higher or lower status, but with Americans this ranking is strongly counteracted by an attitudinal disposition the historian Dennis Brogan has called "equality of estimation."[36] Using the device of equality of estimation, Americans are able to reason that since people are "essentially alike" and "essentially equal," those with more social status are "essentially" no better than those with less. Viewing human relationships from this perspective, one can accept and even openly admire the accomplishments of others and their consequent rise to a status higher than one's own and at the same time continue to feel essentially equal—still entitled to respect and self-esteem. The hierarchical outlook, on the other hand, tends to etch into the emotional reflexes of people a far closer association between their relative position on the status stairway, the respect others afford them, and their own sense of self-esteem, with the result that if a recognized equal rises in status, the sense of equality (and self-esteem) of those left behind may be threatened.

To better understand the shifting of status in Latin American society, it would be helpful to focus more closely on the actual movement up and down the social-status stairway and then identify the factors that determine position upon it. To begin with, the stairway should be visualized as extremely long, with an almost uncountable number of small steps that imperceptibly yet steadily change color from deepest black at the bottom to shades of grey around the middle to purest white at the top. Upon those steps, which signify relative ranking in status, the participants in a hierarchical value system place each other.* From a distance Latin Americans can clearly recognize distinct classes in the black, grey, and white areas, but even closer they can scarcely discern the differences in color from one small step to the next; so while they agree there is a class line between, for example, the upper lower class and the lower middle class, they rarely agree on the precise place to draw it. When advancing or declining in status, it is possible for participants in this hierarchical social gamesmanship to move by just one or two steps or to take so many that they find themselves without question in an entirely different class category.

Ascending and descending, then, is the essence of the game. The question is, by what means does it take place? As is the case in any society, there are certain factors, or *status determinants*, that cause

---

*There are, of course, Americans with a strong hierarchical orientation and Latin Americans with only weak tendencies of this kind, but here the concern is with the overall strength of the hierarchical orientation in each culture.[37]

people in Latin America to have more or less social prestige. The most important of these status determinants in Latin American culture are wealth, power, race,* occupation, and education. Less important and more subject to debate as to their precise value are considerations such as location and type of residence, method of transportation, social associates, quality and style of clothing, and mastery of decorum and manners.[39]

It is possible to point out the most important factors in Latin American culture that influence status; however, one of the characteristics of the hierarchically ordered society is that virtually any object, however small, or any action, however obscure, can in some way carry a status connotation. Thus, Latin Americans are prone to watch for the most minute details that may carry a message of an increase or decrease in status, such as a daily change of cufflinks, the habit of using a briefcase, a slight fraying at the collar, or the purchase of one's lunch from a street vendor instead of in a restaurant.

An even more significant characteristic of this kind of society is the increased *importance* of status to people's sense of self-esteem. All societies, of course, in some way rank people according to status; but the prestige patterns in an egalitarian society allow a person with little status to feel "essentially equal" to those who have much status. In hierarchical societies this notion of all human beings being essentially equal is lacking, and so it is psychologically much more difficult to separate one's status from one's personal sense of self-esteem. Status or social prestige under these circumstances becomes very important because people need a positive opinion of their own self-worth (see p. 18).

The status implications of race in Latin America are quite complex and deserve some explanation. Latin Americans use many different kinds of categories to identify one another by race ranging from pure Caucasian at one end to various types of mixed-bloods in the middle to pure Negro or Indian at the other; and Latin Americans of all categories ascribe the highest status to pure Caucasians, lesser status to mixed-bloods, and the lowest status to pure Negroes and Indians.[38] Although Latin Americans are generally highly conscious of and preoccupied with racial differences, they are not racist in the strict sense of the term because they do not condemn a person to inferior social status simply on the basis of race as true racists would do. To be more precise, Latin Americans with Negro or Indian racial characteristics can rise quite high in status—even higher than than those with pure Caucasian characteristics —provided they acquire the *other* status determinants such as wealth, power and education. A common saying in Latin America is "Money whitens," which means that money has the effect of partially or even totally canceling out a low-status genetic start in life.

To even the casual observer from an egalitarian culture, the increased importance of status symbols in Latin America is apparent. To cite only one example, almost all societies around the world confer upon people extra social status for earning a university degree; but in Latin America the status advantage of these titles, or *títulos*, is so great that people pursue them whether or not they offer any economic or educational benefit. This is the major reason why Latin American countries are overrun with lawyers for whom there is no work. It is also the reason why many Latin American universities have long functioned as what Latin Americans sometimes call doctor factories, graduating an endless supply of titled personages, including medical doctors and engineers with only a theoretical, nonutilitarian knowledge of their respective fields. Another sign of the special importance of these títulos is that those who have them display them (that is, *Dr.* for Ph.D.'s and physicians, *Ing.* for engineer, *Lic.* for lawyer, *Arq.* for architect, and so forth) at every opportunity—on nameplates above doorbells, after signatures in letters, on namecards and personalized stationary. Lest anyone overlook these scattered reminders, polite conversation calls for formally addressing holders of títulos with the appropriate appelation, "Doctor," "Engineer," "Lawyer," or "Architect," preceding the name. Such titles wield enough social prestige that even a head of state might not be willing to give up his occupational title for the new one of "President." When, for example, the Peruvian architect Fernando Belaúnde Terry assumed the presidency of his country, he was always introduced in ceremonial occasions as "Architect Fernando Belaúnde Terry, President of the Republic."

Hierarchical prestige patterns are an important aspect of Latin American culture to consider because they foster greater combativeness and discord in human relations than would otherwise be the case had more egalitarian prestige patterns prevailed; and harmonious social relations are a vital factor in the modernization process. This does not mean that people with hierarchical outlooks cannot modernize. The Japanese have a strongly hierarchical view of human relationships yet have developed compensating values that have eliminated any problem a hierarchical ordering of society might cause in their economic development. Without such compensating values, however, hierarchical prestige patterns tend to reduce the level of cooperation between individuals, which, of course, severely inhibits modernization.

The connection between a society's prestige patterns and the degree of social harmony it is likely to experience lies in the way those patterns induce individuals to regard people who experience success in some endeavor and increase their status. The prestige patterns of an egalitarian culture render it reasonably easy for individuals to watch their peers advance in status and still offer them genuine congratulations. Indeed, if the self-esteem of a person left lower on the status ladder were shaken by another's good fortune, this could easily be interpreted as a sign of peevish immaturity. On the other hand, the successful individual is aware of social pressure against his gloating and seeing himself as "better" than someone with less status. In an egalitarian culture, the two individuals are still the same and equal in essential respects and need not regard each other with pride on one side or envy on the other.

To the participants in a culture with a hierarchical emphasis, it is simply harder for that reasoning to become meaningful at their emotional depths because, as mentioned above, for those participants there exists a far closer relationship between the social prestige their culture affords them and their sense of self-esteem. The hierarchical prestige system inclines those within it to feel threatened by the "rise" of one of their peers, since moving up the status stairway implies being superior to or better than those remaining at a lower level. To recapture their positions of "equality," the "inferiors" may strive to "rise" as well or failing that, may feel pressured to pull the "superior" back down to their own level, a practice known in Spanish and Portuguese as "deprestiging" (causing another person to lose prestige) [desprestigiar].[40]

Individuals caught up in the prestige patterns of a hierarchical society have in their interpersonal relationships two basic choices before them: they may actively and forcefully strive to increase their status over others, or they may simply hold back and carefully guard against others doing this to them. The two alternatives involved in this social gamesmanship bring out in the participants two fundamental styles of social conduct. Some are notable for their aggressive pursuit of status. The Peruvian anthropologist Carlos Delgado has called these character types arribistas (loosely, unbridled upward strivers).[41] The successful among them are widely known in Latin America as vivos, individuals "alive" to every opportunity for self-advantage. Their counterparts in style might be referred to here as "defenders," for they assume mainly "defensive" stances meant only to prevent "aggressive" arribistas or vivos from achieving their aims.

Defensive or aggressive social behavior can characterize communities of individuals as well. Groups of people with a relatively more defensive emphasis to their social conduct are most commonly found in the hamlets, villages, and smaller towns of rural Latin America. To gain some insight into the customs and mores of these defender communities, it would be helpful to view them as social organisms, analogous in some respects to the human organisms that comprise them. Similar to the evolution of the human body, human communities develop over time protective social instincts that manifest themselves in the mores and customs of the people. The pattern of social reflexes found in Latin American defender communities seems to be shaped to contain potentially aggressive striving for status that would otherwise be brought out by hierarchical prestige concerns. Prevailing customs and mutual expectations apply pressure on community members to confine themselves to defensive, that is, alert but nonaggressive, postures, where each waits and watches for another's attempt to "prestige" himself (increase his social prestige) while avoiding such behavior himself.

These defender communities might also be thought of as social systems with defenses against any upsetting of the existing distribution of social prestige. Such defenses are most effective in discouraging the temptation to assume overtly authoritarian airs and the inclination to physically abuse others for the sake of demonstrating power and raising status. Inhabitants are accustomed to react with stern measures against such conduct, rendering it difficult for violators to sell their products, establish credit, or hire needed labor. An anthropological team from one village reported that the habitual aggressors there were "simply beaten, imprisoned, or even killed."[42]

Another well-known practice that conspires against changes in the status equilibrium (and in some villages keeps everybody at approximately the same level of poverty) is the "beggar thy neighbor" ethic which prevents individuals from raising themselves over others by accumulating savings. When community inhabitants take note that one of their own has an increased store of wealth, they apply social pressure on the individual to lavish it all on a community religious activity such as the purchase of candles for the Church, a new cloak for the Virgin, fireworks for a holiday, or even an entire float for a parade resplendent with hundreds of candles and waxen images adorned in elaborate costumes.[43]

Individuals suspected of being too aggressive in the pursuit of status can also be checked by more surreptitious leveling mechanisms. At times this retaliation may take the form of a sudden physical assault, but far more common are the spreading of malicious gossip behind the backs of the supposed transgressors, the secret vandalizing of their property, or the marshaling against them of the mysterious forces of witchcraft and black magic. The fear of black magic can be a powerful restraining influence upon the status aspirations of a superstitious people because, quite simply, they believe in it and are quick to attribute any ill fortune that passes their way to the evil sorcery of some unknown enemy.[44] In a classic study of a community dominated by defender personalities, the Colombian sociologists Gerado and Alicia Reichel-Dolmatoff observed:

> Every individual lives in constant fear of the magical aggression of others, and the general social atmosphere in the village is one of mutual suspicion, of latent danger, and hidden hostility, which pervade every aspect of life. The most immediate reason for magical aggression is envy. Anything that might be interpreted as a personal advantage over others is envied: good health, economic assets, good physical appearance, popularity, an harmonious family life, a new dress. All these and other aspects imply prestige and, with it, power and authority over others. Aggressive magic is, therefore, intended to prevent or to destroy this power and to act as a leveling force. As a system of social control, Black Magic is of tremendous importance, because it governs all interpersonal relationships.[45]

The practices that restrict status mobility within a defender community also have the effect of habituating its inhabitants to a lifestyle of uniformity and conformity. For example, instead of the urban value of conspicuous consumption, the cautious defenders are obedient to the ethic of inconspicuous consumption. This mentality evinces itself when women who walk the streets with their purchases are at pains to conceal them from the invidious glances of others or when people are careful not to discuss what they had for dinner the previous night lest someone interpret this as an attempt to boast and gain status.[46] George M. Foster, an anthropologist who conducted extensive research in the Mexican village of Tzintzuntzan, observed that the windows of houses facing the streets were usually closed with shutters; he later discovered that the homeowners were afraid not only of thieves but also of inquisitive peepers who might see and covet something inside the house and spread their envy by gossip throughout the village.[47]

The same reasons that cause individuals to avoid revealing differences in the consumption of material goods incline them to be very conformist in dress, speech, and manner. Their approved ways of visiting and greeting one another are formal and inflexible. If the rule upon arriving at a party is to shake everybody's hand, then everybody's hand must be shaken no matter how many there are or how long the task requires. To be different exposes the individual to two avenues of attack: if the individual does something wrong, or envy, which may lead to indirect reprisal if the deviation from custom might possibly suggest an attempt to increase status. Consequently, interpersonal behavior among these rural defenders appears careful and controlled, almost wooden, and elaborately formal and polite. To the Reichel-Dolmatoffs, "The principal feature of overt behavior is the extreme control the individual exercises over all his actions and works," behavior they describe as "suppressed, stylized, and stereotyped . . . devoid of all spontaneity and warmth."[48]

In some respects these stiff social exercises are not unlike the rigidly defined and rigidly applied codes of protocol that have been drawn up to facilitate relations between wary and watchful nation-states. By scrupulously adhering to prescribed defensive deportment, individuals can communicate their intention of not disturbing the social equilibrium by "prestiging" themselves over others. In his Mexican case study, George M. Foster describes this outlook:

> The ideal Tzintzuntzeño spends his life walking a psychological tightrope, on which a single misstep, to right or left, will spell disaster. On the one side lie the everpresent dangers of gossip, criticism, character assassination, and perhaps witchcraft and physical attack. Too much ambition, to much aggressive action, too much improvement in one's way of living, or even no reason at all, will invoke them. But on the other side lie the even more frightening dangers that threaten the person who is not able to defend himself, who is not sufficiently macho to avoid being a target of others, who falls behind his rightful place in the order of things. The only safety lies in holding to a straight and very narrow path.[49]

The safest path on which to tred is, however, still very slippery and treacherous. Even when behavior is guarded, cautious, and "correct," a cloud of suspicion and fear continues to hang heavy over interpersonal relationships. "All human motivations," write the Reichel-Dolmatoffs, "are believed to be essentially suspicious . . . [and] every individual expects the worst from his fellow men."[50] Such expectations burden interpersonal relationships with apprehension, mistrust, and emotional anxiety.[51] People retreat behind their personal armor, carefully weighing the words of others, noting their gestures, and distrusting even their faces of impassivity. Ever vigilant, they are apt to use the term *defend* to describe their perception of their role in a world populated by capricious and untrustworthy human beings. When asked, "How are you doing?" they might respond, "Well, I'm defending myself" (*Pues, me defiendo*).[52] Oscar Lewis, in a major anthropological study of a small rural Mexican village, renders this picture with discerning detail:

> Although living side by side, Tepoztecans communicate little of their innermost thoughts, aspirations, fears, likes and dislikes and, for the most part, remain strangers to one another . . . There is a readiness to view people as potentially dangerous, and the most characteristic initial reaction to others is suspicion and distrust . . . In Tepoztlán the motives of everyone are suspected. . . . Lack of trust is not only present among non-relatives but also exists within families and affects the relations of husbands and wives, parents and children, and brothers and sisters. . . . Children are scolded for giving things to their friends or for being trusting and generous in lending articles to persons outside the family. Children or others who expect sympathy and help are called fools and are derided. It

is attitudes such as these which daily reinforces the Tepoztecan's
harsh view of life and throws him upon his own resources. . . .

Friendships, as defined in terms of mutual trust, loyalty, aid,
and affection directed toward one individual, are few in Tepoztlán,
and are avoided rather than sought. . . . Cases of lifelong
friendships are rare. . . . Friends are viewed by adults as potential
enemies, as a source of trouble, and a waste of time.[53]

Little effort is required to imagine the severe emotional strain
such patterns of interpersonal relationships impose upon the isolated,
distrustful individuals who comprise defender communities. Behind
the expressionless visages worn by the men, behind the downcast eyes
of the women and children, an enormous tension builds up that rarely
erupts outside the family circle. But the internal emotional cost is
high. An American doctor who worked for ten years in the highlands of
Peru was astonished at what he initially discovered among the
inhabitants of those seemingly placid, slow-paced, sun-drenched
mountain villages:

The one thing we never dreamed we'd need in the mountains was
tranquilizers. Soon after we arrived, we were sending for them in
quantity. What they suffer from is what we call agitated
depression, insomnia at night, sleepiness during the day, burning of
the hands and feet, headaches, dizziness, butterflies in the
stomach.[54]

From a description of the defender personality and the kind of
community where this characteristic social behavior is more
successfully enforced, we pass to a discussion of the arribistas or vivos
and the environment where they are most likely to flourish. The
arribistas can be distinguished from the defenders in the way they
react to the pressures of the hierarchical prestige system. They share,
to be sure, many of the behavioral and attitudinal characteristics of
the defenders. When they are merely seeking to maintain their status
position, they are controlled, rigid, extremely suspicious of the
motivations of those around them, and most alarmed at the prospect
of another's rise in status. They differ from the defenders mainly in
that instead of seeking only to defend the present status balance, they
are far more ready to hustle aggressively for status and position over
others.

The people in areas where arribistas are prevalent appear quite
different from those in defender communities. They are far less
reserved, withdrawn, constricted, and somber—for more open,
assertive, and uninhibited in expressing their emotions, which may
range from utter joyousness to dark despair.[55] They are also more
sociable and ready to undertake friendships, although underlying

these relationships is a frequently voiced uncertainty as to how far "friends" can be trusted.

People with more pronounced arribista characteristics can be found in divers social settings both rural and urban, but they are most likely to be found in urbanized environments. So evident is this that the word *urbanidad* (urbanity) is used in some parts of Latin America to approvingly describe that agile vivo quality of artfully sidestepping blows and dealing them out in return.

The reasons why an urban situation is likely to induce arribista behavior are not difficult to understand. To begin with, urban centers have historically been the meeting ground for the pushers, the drivers, the hustlers, those with high expectations and soaring ambitions whether legitimate or otherwise. Futhermore, because of their size and impersonality, cities tend to offer greater scope of action to the aggressively ambitious than do small towns, where everybody knows everybody else's business. Persons who depart from the norms of a modestly sized community have to face that community the next day and the next. But the anonymity of urban areas often shields individuals from the consequences of their own social behavior, and this, multiplied many times over, tends to raise the overall level of aggressiveness within urban culture.

Reinforcing these influences upon urban populations is the fact that cities are places where the gleaming symbols of inequality are most in evidence and where rich and poor commingle within each other's view. This situation inevitably plants ideas in the minds of some men and nurtures ambition, often intemperate ambition, in their hearts.

And just as Latin American cities can be dazzling in their look of oppulence, they can also be shocking in their tales of poverty. Urban poverty in Latin America is qualitatively different from rural poverty because the poor in cities suffer from a harsher form of economic insecurity. While the poor in rural areas will usually have a plot of land to farm when times are hard, the poor in cities may have absolutely nothing to fall back on if they lose their jobs. Needless to say, this kind of insecurity can quickly escalate into desperation, and desperate men are difficult to control.

The problem of social aggressiveness brought out by an urban environment is compounded by the fact that since World War II Latin America has urbanized so quickly that today well over a third of Latin Americans live in population centers of 20,000 or more.[56] The urban character of contemporary Latin American culture is also accentuated by the tendency of most urban Latin Americans to congregate in the largest cities. For example, in 1970 population centers of over a quarter million inhabitants supported 76 percent of all urban Argentineans,

69 percent of urban Brazilians, and over 60 percent of urban Mexicans, Chilians, Peruvians, and Venezuelans.[57] And as spectacular as the spread of urbanization has been in the past, present demographic trends indicate that it will be even more dramatic in the future. *Conservative* estimates from the United Nations predict that by the year 2,000, Mexico City will be the largest urban center in the world, with an astonishing 31.6 million inhabitants. Close behind will be São Paulo with 26 million, followed by Rio de Janeiro with 19.4 million, Buenos Aires with 14 million, and Bogotá with 9.5 million.[58]

Social aggressiveness in Latin American urban centers is also aggravated by the special character of urbanization in Latin America. Unlike the case of the cities in the pioneer industrial countries (where the living conditions of the poor were bad enough) the number of people living in Latin American cities is growing far more rapidly than the productive capacity needed to support them. There are several reasons for this, but certainly very important are the facts that Latin America has the highest birthrate of any major area in the world and that improved public health systems have in recent decades been able to cut the death rate drastically in both the urban and rural areas. The consequent burden on Latin American cities has been incredible, for they have had to absorb not only their own proliferating numbers but also the surplus population that the countryside can no longer support. The result of all this had been that life in the impoverished sections of the continent's cities is disintegrating into a confused rush of competitive turmoil both for the poor unfortunates born within them and for the new arrivals from the rural areas who appear with little more than the ragged shirts on their backs, bewildered wives, and hungry children.

Thus, for a number of reasons—the desperate lives so many urban dwellers are forced to lead, the constant reminders of the wealth necessary for high status, the diminishing of social controls on overtly belligerent behavior—the arribista potential of the hierarchical personality has in Latin American cities been released from its cage. Because this type of social conduct is growing increasingly important in Latin American culture, it would be helpful to examine it in some detail.

The typical behavior of the arribistas will vary considerably depending upon the individuals with whom they are dealing. To be more precise, the arribistas view their fellow human beings as either above, below or at approximately the same social level as themselves; and they typically treat superiors differently than inferiors or equals. To begin this discussion, then, we might first start by studying the nature of the arribistas' superior-inferior relationships.

The number of superior-inferior relationships in Latin American culture are many and their character varied. A classical example is, perhaps, the position of the estate lord over his serfs, but others include the position of the high-level functionary over his subordinates, the bureaucrat over ingratiating supplicants, the police officer over intimidated citizens. Depending upon the situation, a superior-inferior relationship within the hierarchical prestige system inclines one side toward paternalistic conceit, haughtiness, or towering arrogance and the other toward servility that may range in degree from the very subtle to the manifestly abject.

The lordly pretensions of superiors and the self-abasing gestures of inferiors tend to be most extreme where the differences between human beings are most extreme. They are especially blatant in the Indian regions of Latin America where the *indio bruto* (brute Indian) is still regarded by his betters as the "beast closest to man"—an attitude not much improved since colonial times. For example, a survey conducted in Paraguay in the 1970s showed that 86 percent of the whites and mestizos interviewed were openly willing to describe Indians as "inferiors" and 77 percent, to classify them as forms of life on the same level as "animals."[59] Along with such attitudes from the past, many practices from the past are still common today. Those beings of an order higher than the Indians, the mestizos (discussed on p. 13), continue to exact cherished social prerogatives from unprotesting human inferiors. The Andean Indian, when addressing the mestizo, customarily holds his hat in hand and respectfully lowers his eyes. Upon meeting a *mestizo* on a narrow pathway or sidewalk, the Indian unhesitatingly gives way and allows the superior presence to pass. When walking "together," the mestizo leads and the Indian trails behind. If enough seats are not available at a community function, the mestizos take all there are. When an Indian is invited to eat at a mestizo's home (usually due to some special godfather-protector arrangement), the humble guest will most likely sit on the ground in the patio while the gracious host dines inside at the table.[60]

One of the ways an arribista superior can aggressively strive for status is to demonstrate the power and authority he has over an inferior by actually using that power. This prestige consideration can easily tempt holders of power to misuse power, which at its worst can lead to extremely oppressive and thoroughly violent human confrontations. The extent to which this can brutalize relations between superiors and inferiors is demonstrated in a small episode of Colombian national life that took place during the 1960s. The incident began innocuously enough when a group of mestizos invited some Indians to eat at a ranch located on the Colombian prairie. As the Indians were eating their food, the mestizos emerged from the ranch house with guns, machetes, hatchets, and clubs and slaughtered at least sixteen of them, including women and children. Such atrocities are not uncommon to the area, but by some quirk this particular case found its way to trial. The defendants freely admitted their part in the massacre; nonetheless they were found *not guilty*. How could anyone, pleaded the defense, born and raised in that part of the country be expected to consider that eradication of an "animal closest to man" was any more serious than the slaughter of any other brute creature of the lower orders? The jury retired, deliberated, and finally accepted the argument.[61]

Of course, most relationshiips between superiors and inferiors in Latin America do not end in blood-stained prairies. By far the most prevalent exchange between them is not violence but flattery. The amount of flattery found within the hierarchical social systems in Latin America is so overwhelming that the Venezuelan writer Pedro María Morante was moved to declare flattery the most distinguishing national characteristic of his countrymen.[62] Flattery figures importantly into status-seeking behavior because arribistas who are truly skilled and alive (vivos) can rise in prestige both by extracting flattery from inferiors or by ingratiating themselves with superiors.

The technique of influencing superiors through flattery is one of the most crucial in the vivo's arsenal. A basic vivo strategy is to attach himself to, and win the favor of, a superior who is able to protect him against aggressors and open up avenues of ascending to power and authority. Since superiors generally thrive on demostrations of servility, one way for ambitious underlings to enlist their aid is to play upon their vanity with flattery.

The technique of flattery, of course, is not unique to Latin American culture, but its practice is so pronounced that it is an indispensable method of advancement in most fields of endeavor, far outdistancing other considerations such as merit or seniority. Pedro María Morante explains:

> An opportune felicitation not only has the negative value of avoiding a visit to jail; it also has positive value: it helps to obtain a good job, . . . Merit is valueless: to burn the midnight oil studying law, to master medical science or mathematics, all these are less effective than to know how to flatter. Those who know their own worth and have too much self respect to prostrate themselves, find that the roads which lead to success are thronged with incompetents climbing to success under official protection. And the incompetents who have already arrived on top establish a reign of ineptitude over ability, of *viveza* [a word that refers to the quality of being *vivo*] over probity . . . . This is the humiliating triumpth of mediocrity![63]

The flattery enjoyed by superiors, what Carlos Delgado refers to as the "genuflexive adulation,"[64] may seem like the consummate reward for someone who has risen to the top. However, the practice of genuflexive adulation brings to a superior its own special tribulations. The sycophants who bow before the superior are sometimes motivated not just by an instinct for survival but by a passion for advancement; and so if it suits their purpose, they may turn upon the object of their flattery. The constant chorus of complaints about the *falta de confianza* (lack of trust) one repeatedly hears in Latin America is nowhere more insistent than among those elevated individuals who hold the envied postitions of status and authority. A superior, then, is confronted with two choices: He can surround himself with stupid, incapable men who are "safe" because of their own ineptitude. Or he can gather about him quicker, shrewder subordinates, more useful for carrying out his directives but dangerous should they ever discover a faster route to their own advancement through their leader's destruction.

As might be expected, most daily human contact and interpersonal exchange that occurs in Latin America does not take place among individuals obviously higher and lower than one another but among individuals of approximately equal social position. In these situations, participants in the hierarchical prestige system are keenly aware that the rules of the game still allow for fluctuations in status, usually in small increments. Since one individual may cause the "deprestiging" of another, the most aggressive arribista types often settle into protective positions where their movements, like those of their defender counterparts, appear controlled, careful, and conformist. Even in these defensive stances, however, all participants are fully aware of the danger that hangs heavy in the air: that others, or indeed they themselves, might be tempted to switch subtly and suddenly to the offensive in an attempt to alter the status equilibrium by making someone else lose face. The anthropologist Eric Wolf depicts this tense scenario as follows:

> As men expect hostility and aggression from others, so they must rise to defend themselves with hostility and aggression. They advance upon each other, ever circumspect, ever ready to defend themselves, ever willing to take advantage of the chink in their opponent's armor.[65]

Even in situations where all participants are striving to confine themselves to safe, defensive maneuvers, the atmosphere is so highly charged with distrust that imagined slights can have exactly the same consequences as deliberate offenses. Samuel Ramos explains how the essentially conservative protective attitude of simply being prepared to expect the worst from others can sometimes induce a person to attack when only defense was intended:

> A trait intimately connected with distrust is susceptibility. The distrustful type is fearful of everything and lives vigilantly on the

defensive. He is suspicious of all gestures, movements, and words. He interprets everything as an offense. In this attitude the Mexican goes to unbelievable extremes. His perception has clearly become abnormal. Because of his extreme touchiness, the Mexican quarrels constantly; he no longer awaits attack but steps forward in order to defend. These pathological reactions often lead him to excesses, even to the point of committing needless crimes.[66]

In isolating the factor of extreme mutual distrust, Ramos points out an important mechanism behind the proverbial "Latin touchiness." A leading Colombian academic has labeled it "irascible sensitiveness."[67] People more often refer to it as plain old Latin "hot blood." But whatever the name, Latin Americans and foreign observers alike have long marveled at this hypersensitive sense of Latin "pride" or "honor" that can suddenly and inexplicably erupt into uncontrollable and violent tempers.

The ways in which antagonists can lock together in combat are numerous in choice, varied in the skills they require, and usually verbal in nature. The most obvious of these verbal techniques is the unrestrained full-fanged assault. The objective of this method is basically straightforward—attack, gore, and mortally wound. The combatants here feel no social pressure to tone down their language, to rely on understatement, or to appear sober, gray, and moderate. Flamboyant rhetoric will fly between them until both fall back in exhaustion. To outsiders this kind of exchange is most evident in the ·political arena, where those on the opposite side of the aisle are not worthy opponents, adversaries, or even enemies, but traitors to anything that is scared—the Fatherland, the Mother of God, the Cause of Humanity.

A far more demanding and common form of verbal aggression is calumnious gossip behind a rival's back. The forked tongue can curl and sting in a hundred different ways. It can weave a fabric of falsities, lies, and half-truths in order to diminish the influence and erode the prestige of an enemy. It can also combine flattery with slander by vilifying the competitor of someone whose favors are sought. Ramos describes the techniques relying on envenomed words as nothing less than psychologically savage. The Mexican, he charges, "is ingenious in detracting from others to point of annihilating them. He practices slander with the cruelty of a cannibal."[68]

Even more skill is required in indirect verbal dueling when an aggressor stands face to face with an opponent and knifes him without the dupe ever realizing it. As every vivo knows, the appropriate weapon here is a phrase that can carry a double meaning. For example, a seemingly innocent but cleverly turned remark using the word *leche* (milk) can have buried within it a reference to sperm and can be used to insinuate the lack of courage, or worse still, the lack of masculinity of the person under attack. One of the most artful forms of the veiled verbal thrust is to stab a victim with a statement that appears to flatter him but actually contains a hidden insult subtle enough for the victim not to notice but obvious enough so that others will.[69]

Normally the techniques of verbal aggression are countered in nonviolent ways, but a predilection to use these methods of baiting human beings might well be compared to the unnerving habit of striking matches in a room crammed with gunpowder. Particularly in those areas with pronounced traditions of physical violence, the perpetrator who constantly plays with fire might well set off an explosion in the form of a sanguinary reprisal. Writing from Colombia, which has the highest homicide rate in the world, the sociologist Orlando Fals-Borda makes these observations about the readiness of the villagers he studied to restitution of "honor" by blood:

> His [the peasant's] sense of honor and personal pride seems to be always at high pitch, and minor events or mere words and jokes can be taken as threats. He is patient and calm, but when these threats, large or small, goad him into action, he is blind and fanatical, often cruel. . . . Petty incidents generate brawls. For instance, a fierce *machete* fight started in one of the hamlet stores simply because one peasant corrected another in the pronounciation of the word *gafas* [glasses].[70]

Thus far in this discussion, the primary focus has been on social behavior among men. However, in Latin America about half the population happens to be women, and this brings us to a whole new vital theme in Latin American interpersonal relations—*machismo*. One of the images that Latin America projects to the Western world is a society rife with exploitation, usually thought of in terms of economic exploitation. But if we were to specifically search for the form of exploitation that inflicted the most severe emotional punishment upon the greatest number of people on a daily, hourly basis, in many regions of Latin America we would need look no further than the practices of machismo.

Any discussion of the Latin American *macho* complex should begin by pointing out that as with other types of exploitation, the virulence of aggression against woman varies substantially from area to area. The condition tends to be at its worst in the more backward, nonhomogeneous parts of Latin America. While plainly evident in defender communities, it becomes aggravated as more lower-income families get caught up in the chaos of urbanization. Furthermore, within any area or social situation there are those who do not respond or respond only to a limited degree to the social pressures that result in macho conduct.

The impulse to macho behavior is tightly bound up in the male's attempt to realize social prestige, status, and self-esteem. The exertion of power brings status, and machismo urges power seekers, who wish to conquer and subdue all in their path, to view woman as vulnerable creatures to be mastered both sexually and physically. If machismo seems to center on women, this is an illusion. It is a game of status played exclusively by males; women participate only as pawns in the elaborate movements to win prestige. In the words of the Mexican psychologist Aniceto Aramoni, "The woman is a trophy in an arena disputed by men . . . like a toy in a shop window [that] can be selected and relinquished without any participation on her part. . . . Among *machos* . . . the woman is a prize in a competitive struggle; as a person, she matters little."[71] As with all traits of national character, machismo must be seen in relative terms. Machismo "objectifies" a woman in the sense that she is used by males as an object to achieve status among males. The extremes to which this "objectification" is commonly carried out in Latin America is what has made machismo around the world one of the most widely known features of Latin American culture.

The macho complex has been described as a "limitless sexual deficit."[72] One of the distinctive characteristics of machismo is that men are encouraged, teased, pushed, and bullied into prodigious sexual acrobatics with a wide variety of women. About this prestige ethic, Gerado and Alicia Reichel-Dolmatoff write:

> While women look to marriage, free union, or concubinage almost exclusively for economic security, men try above all to prove their virility and to procreate as many children as possible, for economic and prestige reasons. A man will state with pride how many children he has fathered in marriage, how many with concubines, and how many "on the street" (*en la calle*), i.e., during occasional relations which might have lasted for only a few moments. To procreate children is felt to be the only outlet, the only definite proof of masculinity.[73]

Even when a man is satisfied with a monogamous relationship or with no relationship at all, he is pressured by his peers into maintaining his status by at least the appearance of sexual prowess. Men, desperate for reassurance and acceptance, flatter, beg, cajole, and even beat woman into seduction. Their mistresses and illegitimate children are not fleeting rumors to be hidden at all costs but are flaunted before all and held aloft with pride. Western women in Latin America sometimes learn about machismo by falling into the arms of a macho and afterward discovering that every embrace, every kiss, every sensitive touch is known and savored by the snickering males of her lover's acquaintance.

Once the master has thoroughly subjugated, used, and secreted all usefulness from a conquest, he is not reluctant to leave her cold and emotionally (if not physically) bruised, for this is regarded as a sign of the strength and vigor of the male overlord. Machismo is at its worst when a man refuses to relinquish his rights over a former conquest even after casting her aside but rather feels the need to continue to exert his control. María Elvira Bermúdez writes of the Mexican macho:

> After he has ceased to be interested in a woman, he still demands eternal fidelity and objects to anybody taking the place which he has voluntarily abandoned. Any woman on whom he ever deigned to cast his eyes must cherish his memory unsullied or take the risk of injury or even death.[74]

As might be expected, the ethic of machismo has an enormous negative impact on the quality of marital relationships in Latin American culture. To begin with, macho practices put serious economic strain on family life. Macho pastimes such as wining and waltzing lovers displaying and supporting mistresses, are frequently costly prestige activities which families of modest or moderate means can ill afford. These economic considerations, of course, are especially important to the wives of the poor who even with caring and responsible husbands would hardly have enough to properly nourish their children. Inevitably, it is upon the backs of the urban poor that the economic consequences of machismo fall most heavily.

Another attitudinal feature of machismo that has an exceptionally disruptive impact upon marital relationships is macho jealousy. The conquest and seduction of women, we have seen, is one means by which jousting males vie with each other for prestige. But the supply of women must come from somewhere, and if a seduced woman happens to be part of another man's private store of goods, the loss of status for the cuckold will leave him burning with anger and shame. Macho jealousy under these circumstances can approach a torrent. The most effective action a fearful male can take to prevent the unthinkable is to build a fence around this woman and restrict her activities outside the home. The extent of these protective measures varies widely in Latin America according to the region and class. But even in the most economically advanced areas of Latin America among the most sophisticated people, the male characteristically is very suspicious of nonsexual friendships between men and women and often concludes that they are impossible.[75]

Among the poorer classes, especially those of the less "Europeanized" areas, routine male jealousy swells to such proportions that it would be classified as pathological in Western European or North American society. Upon marriage, husbands strap their spouses with bonds that allow astonishingly little freedom of movement. Men commonly force their wives to completely sever all social contacts they had before marriage, not just with male acquaintances, but also with girlfriends whom the husbands regard as potential liaisons between their wives and covetous lovers. To cite an example, an anthropologist who studied a Texas Mexican-American town for two years, could find in all that time only two cases of married women who regularly visited other women to whom they were not related.[76] Oscar Lewis, in his study of the Mexican village of Tepotzlán, made these observations:

> Tepoztecan men are, for the most part, suspicious and distrustful of their wives and believe that they are capable of being unfaithful to them at the first opportunity. Men are unanimous in the belief that women must be kept under strict surveillance and control. The adulterous activities of men reinforce this attitude toward women. ... To insure his wife's loyalty, the husband seeks to isolate her from outsiders. ...
>
> Wives are generally forbidden to have female friends, and most women discontinue all friendships at the time of marriage. Husbands view such friends as potential arrangers or go-betweens for the wife and lover. Men frequently drop their own friends after marriage or do not encourage them to visit for fear that some intimacy might develop between the wife and the friend. The majority of husbands are suspicious of any activities which take the wife away from home. During the first few years of marriage, most wives are not permitted to leave the house unaccompanied. In cases where young couples live alone, the wife will prefer to ask a neighbor or a relative to make purchases for her, rather than risk her husband's anger or the gossip of others by going to the market alone. Although some young wives now go out alone, they are considered suspect by others.
>
> When a woman leaves the house, she is expected to return in the shortest possible time; any delay on her part may earn her a sound scolding or beating. Gossiping with other women is discouraged and sometimes punished. ...
>
> The suspiciousness and jealousy of some husbands is extreme. There are cases of wife-beating merely because the husband saw a man standing at the street corner near the house and suspected him of being his wife's lover. If a wife's work is not done by the time the husband comes home, or if the children and animals look neglected, he may suspect her of having spent time with a lover. In one case, a husband noticed that the family cat ate ravenously at night as though she had not been fed all day, and he accused his wife of having been out with someone. If a wife is unusually careful about her appearance before going out, or if she is reluctant to have sexual intercourse, her husband's suspicions may be aroused.[77]

As intimated in this passage, another destructive influence in marital relationships is the readiness of the Latin American macho to resort to physical violence against his wife. This practice, of course, is by no means universal, but it is so common that the subject appears again and again in everyday conversation and in social research conducted by both foreigners and Latin Americans.[78] A disheartening sign is that the problem seems to be aggravated by poverty in urban environments; and, as we have seen, the city poor are a cultural group rapidly expanding rather than diminishing in numbers. The identifiable immediate reasons for wife beatings are many and may stem from nothing more than a desire on the part of the macho to demonstrate authority and control over his spouse. As George Foster discovered among the subjects of his research, "Many [husbands] believe a wife, however good, must be beaten from time to time, simply so she will not lose sight of a God decreed familial hierarchy."[79]

It should hardly be surprising to learn that the effect of macho behavior is to encourage an adversary relationship between man and woman, husbands and wives. María Bermúdez writes that in her country the woman is taught from early adolescence to regard the man "as her enemy," that "her mother, aunts and teachers are continuously admonishing her to live in constant vigilance against his unworthy tricks," and that "if she gives him the slightest opportunity, he will deceive and humiliate her."[80] Likewise, Oscar Lewis reports that "self pity and a sense of martyrdom are common among married women," that "women readily express hostility toward men and often characterize all men as 'bad,'" and that many female interviewees would "break down and cry when telling their life stories."[81]

For men as well as for women, the cost of machismo is high. With their conjugal relationships of mutal support weakened if not destroyed by macho conduct, María Bermúdez describes the male victims as cast into "suffering isolation" (soledad padecida).[82] Instead of finding their marital relationship a refuge where they can safely empty their souls and rediscover their confidence and morale, they find that their compelling urge to be macho poisons the air within their home and makes it an extension of the battlefield outside. The final ironic cruelty of machismo is that it invades the last possible sanctuary of males, who sorely need a secure harbor in which to renew themselves in their struggles with the world outside.

The heavy price that the Latin American male must pay for macho behavior can be full appreciated only by looking at the kind of world that the macho must face—alone. It is a world replete with suspicion, hostility, and distrust, where an individual must constantly be on guard to defend his status position. It is also a world ravaged by exploitation, where an individual must constantly be on guard to defend his means of livelihood. It is a world, according to one particularly qualified observer, where "the choice is only to skin or be skinned."[83]

Obviously, these are conditions which vary in intensity according to the circumstances, and not surprisingly, they definitely worsen in situations where *arribista* or *vivo* aggressiveness is less controlled.

The rules of survival in the world of the *vivo* are approximately the same as those that have governed people anywhere; the rewards are high and alluring, the competition rife and ruthless, and the contestants clever and determined. According to the rules, rewards go not to the most deserving, the most needy, or the most productive but to the most powerful and the relatives and favorites of the most powerful. The powerful are those who master the manipulative skills of slander and flattery, who know how to curry the favor of the correct people, who are adept and flexible enough to choose the right side and to switch sides at opportune moments.

Certainly similar rules played with equal seriousness prevail in some pockets of Western society, but what distinguishes Latin American culture is that there exists little refuge for someone who tires of the incessantly competitive strife. One of the classic features of a parasitic, exploitative society is that the individual who desires only to live quietly, peacefully, and modestly from the fruits of his own hard work and honest labor, has available to him very few corners in which to hide. If he produces wealth, exploiters and social parasites are there to take part of it from him. If he holds some petty position, like a minor niche in an institutional bureaucracy, he has to defend it strenuously as if it were a great treasure from assailants who employ unscrupulous tricks. And if he isn't busy defending his livelihood, he is defending his *dignidad* (honor) from attacks, real or imagined, launched by those who might gain from his humiliation. The little fellow, then, who wishes nothing more than to be left alone, must also force himself to learn and refine the delicate arts of *defendar*—of cultivating the favor of the right protector, of choosing the most useful allies, of damaging the reputations of potential enemies by gossipy half-truths and outright slander.

The pervasive exploitation and the "skin-or-be-skinned" ethos of Latin American society have become tragically aggravated within the expanding subculture of urban poor, whose desperate economic situation has stimulated predacity and whose special vulnerabililty has caused this predacity to have greater impact on their lives. Whether the districts they dig themselves into are called *villas miserias* as in Argentina, *barriadas* as in Peru, *favelas* as in Brazil, or *tugurios* as in Columbia, the problem is growing and it is alarming. The actual visual panorama of these concentrations of poor people's shelter varies considerably from conditions that appear tolerable to those that have so shaken visitors I have guided that they were unable to walk on. What is most frightening, however, is not the actual economic standard of living in these settlements but the worsening condition of social relationships as more and more surplus humanity pours into the urban grinder.

We had previously observed that the particular characteristics of the urbanization process in Latin America are not conducive to the formation of human communities that meet the inhabitants' needs for order, justice, and material support. Productive capacity in urban areas has failed to keep up with the accelerating population growth, inevitably raising the social temperature. This has not led to the revolutionary upheaval in the cities that so many critics predicted in the 1960s but rather has resulted in urban multitudes whose members have turned upon one another. The people compete for whatever there is to compete for; their ambitions are aroused by the glittering display of consumer goods so lavishly enjoyed by the wealthy, and their susceptible imaginations are stimulated by the visual and audio media which pour out endless messages about the happiness and prestige that material items can bring. The heightened awareness of a better life nearby, the heavy dosage of consumerist propaganda, the persistent insecurity, and the unrelenting struggle for survival have all acted to increase the combativeness of social relations, which is precisely the same direction encouraged by prevailing hierarchical prestige patterns. Within this boiling cauldron, it is the vivo who is best fit to outlast the rest and to emerge triumphant.

But the social behavior of the vivo is also the cause as well as the effect of these conditions. Unrestrained by effective social control and bereft of social consciousness, Latin American vivos have turned the continent's belts of urban poverty into bear pits of strife and exploitation. Combatants unsheath long knives and go at one another, selecting those who appear most vulnerable and weak. Children learn at an early age that there are no ethical canons or lofty commandments in this arena. They understand that the rule of law and codes of morality are but dictums carved into marble slabs far above and far removed from the real life on the streets below. They see innumerable conflicts between people where the outcome is not determined by a delicate balancing of right and wrong but by a confrontation of power, pure power. They learn that those who wish to succeed or simply to keep from being trampled upon had better grab for power as best they can.

The need for power in this kind of society makes poverty in Latin America an especially difficult burden to bear. It may seem obvious to state that one of the special problems of the Latin American urban poor is that they lack money, but in these conditions money is more than money—it is power. The poor in Latin America need money not only to maintain an adequate standard of living but also to acquire power either to ward off or to insulate themselves from the effects of an exploitative social environment. To make this point even more explicit, the urban poor in Latin America actually require more money to achieve a tolerable existence than would be the case were they living in a well-ordered, nonexploitative culture where they did not feel threatened and harassed at every turn.

To get a sense of the kind of life led by the poor in Latin America's large urban centers, it would be best to listen to someone who actually lives in this type of environment. Roberto, a youth singled out from the multitudes of Mexico City, describes an existence that with variations and elaborations can be heard with remorseless repetition in urban areas all over contemporary Latin America:

> The law of the strongest operates here. No one helps the ones who fall; on the contrary, if they can injure them more, they will. If one is drowning, they push him under. And if one is winning out, they pull him down. I am not an intelligent person but at my work I always come out on top—I earned more than my fellow workers. When they noticed it, they got me into trouble with the boss and pushed me out. And there is always someone who tells who robbed, who killed, who said what, or who is going bad.
>
> Could it be for the lack of education? There are so many people who cannot even sign their names! They talk about constitutionalism—it is a pretty resounding word, but I don't even know what it means. For me we live by violence, homicide, theft, assault. We live quickly and must be constantly on guard.[84]

In this passage Roberto focuses on the sense of desperate competition that is felt by the people within the realm of his experience. To gain some awareness of the parallel moods of fear and distrust that accompany this way of life, the reader might imagine being guided through one of the more graphic of these urban settlements. We choose evening as a time to visit the area, for it is darkness that makes the fear in the people most obvious. We have been warned by the inhabitants of the settlement that crime is rampant; and we note that they seem to believe their tales, for only a few of them venture out to disturb the night. Indeed, as these figures pass us by, they appear to be nervously glancing about. Occasionally a drunk staggers along, too poor to rob of anything but his life.

There is an overwhelming presence that dominates the scene before us, and it is not silence but living, howling creatures from the canine world. Virtually everyone has a dog—for protection, of course. As we slip through the darkness along the roads and paths, we stir up a crescendo of violent wailing. Many of these dogs are inside the homes but hundreds more are running wild and loose, and as we approach, they charge at us from every direction. The first thing we, as outsiders from a more affluent culture, notice is that the dogs of these poor are the most miserable-looking, stunted, and mangy mongrels we have ever had occasion to behold. A reminder that poverty is ugliness flashes through our minds—but no time for such musings—the second thing we notice is the fangs. These wretched creatures are the lowest form of life upon which aggression can be taken out. They are kicked around by their masters and brutalized by gangs of children who are themselves brutalized. These dogs are vicious. Pick up a rock and the beasts halt, throw it and they attack; raise the arm as if to hurl another and again they stop short, loudly barking and growling. Fortunately, most of these creatures appear to be as cowardly as they are ugly; they prefer to sneak in from behind for a stealthy snap at the heel. But be careful. How many of these terrors are rabid? On quick nip and jaws that broke the skin will disappear into the night.

At last we reach our destination, a small dwelling of brick, straw, and wood. Knock. No answer. What madman walks the night? We knock again, shouting our identities. The door slowly cracks open, then opens all the way. We have arrived—but, one hopes, not without a certain empathy for the insecurity and fear that pursues these people into their very dreams.

One of the most alarming features of the compounds that entrap the urban poor is the pronounced disintegration of the family as a viable institution. Despite problems caused by male egocentrism, the family unit in Latin America has traditionally been strong and cohesive in the sense of providing mutual protection for its members. And little wonder. Confronted with a threatening and hostile world, the family has always been the most logical social group where human beings could band together in self-defense. Further fortifying family solidarity have been other factors such as tradition, common economic strivings, and the prospect of inheritance.[85]

In today's Latin America, however, the disorienting effects of impoverished urban living are tearing apart the traditional family structure among the urban lower classes. Men who feel economically and emotionally insecure attempt to find release in the hallowed vices of women, gambling, and drinking. The quantities of alcohol swallowed is nothing short of stupendous, a constant concern for Latin American reformers. Walking through one of these areas on a Sunday afternoon, one can see drunks, it seems, everywhere—staggering, urinating, shouting profanities. Men who indulge in these vices, of course, must cut deeply into family finances to do so, and this creates a constant source of friction between husbands and wives. Husbands often react to the economic pressures burdening them by running away and leaving their wives and children to their fates.[86] One researcher, to cite an example, discovered that in the low-income sections of Panama City only one child in five or six was living with both parents.[87] Abandoned mothers often try to enter into some form of consensual union with a man in order to secure economic relief. A prevalent pattern is for a man to stay with his woman until she is pregnant and desert her while she is swollen and unattractive.

And what happens to all the children? Some families, of course, resist dissolution no matter what the pressures. But all too commonly, children are not brought up with firm, consistent discipline. Physical punishment is frequent, chaotic, and largely unrelated to the child's behavior. The most outrageous brutality is widespread—like the seven-year-old Colombian boy who was castrated by his mother's lover, or the infant Venezuelan girl in Caracas whose tongue was cut out by her enraged father.[88] One practice is to sell small girls as domestic servants, a kind of permanent bondage where they receive no pay, just scraps off the table and used clothing. Often the men of the household will force them into sexual intercourse soon after purberty, and then these unwanted children produce more unwanted children.

Finally we arrive at the most extreme condition of human debasement. Latin American cities are spawning throngs of homeless, brutalized children, some no more than four or five, who have fled their violent hovels to make their own way on the streets. Their numbers appear to be large and are growing larger; authorities throw around figures like 60,000 in Chile, 200,000 in Venezuela, 700,000 in Mexico.[89] Nobody knows for sure.

How do they survive? Well, those who do survive sleep upon sheets of cardboard on balconies, thresholds, trash heaps—anywhere that the police will not pursue them. They obtain money to spend by selling newspapers or flowers, or by shining shoes—but mostly they live by thievery. Even before they are tall enough to pick pockets or swift enough to yank watches off wrists, they steal anything that can be pried loose. They steal windshield wipers and sell them back to the owner the next day. They steal license plates and sell them to those who want to avoid the license tax. In most Latin American cities, there is virtually nothing too petty to steal.

For these children life is a daily ordeal of survival. Their days are dominated by one word—food. Those who find it have to fight off other street urchins to keep it. They learn to resort to violence at an early age, and they use violence not just to defend themselves but to satisfy their baser impulses. In Bogotá some of these children have ended their brief lives as charred remains, because during the night boyish sadists had set fire to the newspaper upon which they slept.[90]

The street children not only have themselves to fear but virtually everyone else as well. The police chase them. Their more fortunate countrymen hate them—and it must be admitted that they have their reasons. The natures of these street imps are as wild and uncivil as the profanity in their mouths. The situation casts us into the completely impossible position of having to criticize children to whom we can scarcely assign culpability. But in truth many of them are growing into the kind of social misfits who will make up the future urban rabble of Latin America. When one remembers that it was a clamoring mob considerably smaller than the estimated 150,000 abandoned children in Buenos Aires that saved the sliding career of Juan Perón in 1944, the potential political impact, all the way to the highest affairs of state, of these deformed, socially conscienceless human beings is something to be pondered.

Just as there are conditions that encourage the development of vivo personality traits, there are conditions that discourage it. We have seen that, in general, conditions today in Latin America favor the growth of this form of social comportment. But there are many Latin Americans who do not conform, or conform only imperfectly, to the dominant behavior patterns. A quick look at some of these exceptions may deepen understanding of the norm.

Observations about national or collective character in Latin America (see Note 32) must first of all be qualified along geographical lines. The more homogenous populations of Southern Brazil, Costa Rica, Argentina, and Chile, with their smaller racial differences and less severe traditions of violence, do not have the same tolerance for the more abusive manifestations of status seeking. The social behavior of these peoples is also influenced by their higher level of economic prosperity. The substantial middle-class populations of these areas have less need to be socially aggressive than people who constantly suffer from economic insecurity.

People who have come to be relatively free of psychological as well as economic stress make up another group able to remove themselves from prevailing prestige patterns. This is particularly true of individuals who are content with their present level of wealth and status and therefore are relieved of the burden of envy and desire to "rise" higher. Often the male individuals of this type are good family men, refusing the status enticements that would encourage them to be macho; while in many ways they relinquish accepted devices to "prestige" themselves, they are better able to resist the prestige ethos of the outside world because their warmer family relationships offer them emotional shelter.

Another category of people that shows particular resistance to engaging in combative social relations is the elderly, and the reasons are not difficult to surmise. These scarred veterans of life's vicissitudes stand at the end of their road; from this sobering perspective, they are in an ideal position to gain the insight that ultimately it matters little whether they go up or down the status stairway. The more pronounced calmness and detachment that researchers have observed in older people[91] often allows the elderly to view the rewards of social combat with skepticism and to willingly abandon the battlefield to younger and more ambitious men.

A considerably different group, which is in a better position than most to be less preoccupied with status rising, is the uppermost stratum of the upper class. These people usually have every determinant of status in their favor, including wealth, race, power, education, and employment. They need not feel insecure about their status or be obsessed with climbing to the top when they and everybody else agree they are already there. A great many high-status people, of course, are not like this, but the basic point is that those who find themselves securely at the summit of society find it easier to refrain from aggressively pursuing status than those who passionately want to climb still higher.

One further group located at quite the opposite end of the status scale from the upper class has, in its own fashion, also shown considerable independence from gladiatorial prestige behavior. This group might be best described as a subculture made up of *closed Indian communities*.[92] Again the key element seems to be the ability of the people within this subculture to derive emotionally satisfying alternatives to the dominant prestige patterns that induce socially disruptive conduct. To adequately discuss the closed Indian community would require a chapter in itself; but very briefly, these communities of Indians have succeeded in doing just what the name implies, in "closing" or shutting themselves off from the influences of the surrounding society. Depending for their livelihood upon subsistence agriculture, they are economically self-sufficient and scarcely participate in the national cash economy. More importantly, they do not participate in the value ethos of the dominant culture. Instead, they live within their own, substantially different moral environment, distinguished by deities and religious rites that center around their agricultural way of life. These are the spiritual conceptions that suffuse their mental universe with meaning, filling it to the point where they have no desires for, or even comprehension of, an existence beyond the one they are living. They seem as impenetrable as rocks and impervious to modernization efforts made on their behalf; but no one should pity them because their religion and low, realistic expectations afford them a psychological and emotional contentment that escapes the classes to whom they are subservient.[93] Some care, however, must be taken not to overromanticize these villagers. Within their culture exists plenty of social pressure and tension that pushes them to conform to group norms. However, the individuals of these communities, even while submitting before social compulsion, receive something vital in return. These closed Indian communities are the human associations in Latin America nearest to the "corporate village" or "dignified poor" notions that have sometimes been thrown about carelessly by undisciplined intellectuals.

The distinctive culture of these villagers is, unfortunately, today everywhere retreating before the encroachments of the outside world, so those who still live immersed in this special value ethos are numerically not greatly significant. For reasons too elaborate to detail here, the inhabitants of closed Indian communities are "opening" their mental defenses and are beginning to be influenced by the prestige patterns of the surrounding culture.[94] As they do this, the insulation protecting their positive identity and sense of self-esteem begins to wear thin and the lower-status members of these communities begin to accept the alien notion that they are not just distinct but inferior. At this point they are psychologically lost, and those who were once exceptions to the prevailing value system are no longer exceptions.

THE PUBLIC VIRTUES

A discussion of the inharmonious social relationships that afflict Latin Americans is important to a study of modernization because these relationships have an enormous influence on the level of public virtue among Latin Americans. Modernization is a manifestly collective enterprise that requires a great deal of cooperation among the people of a society; and if Latin Americans have trouble cooperating among themselves, then this will inevitably have a negative impact on their economic development. We can see this even with the ethic of machismo. If, for example, a macho is in the habit of acting selfishly and tyranically toward his wife and family, then it is quite likely that he will carry over his egocentric spirit into the other areas of his life such as his business or political activities that have a direct bearing on economic development.

Perhaps the most basic of the public virtues is cooperation, which might be narrowly defined as the ability of people to work together in matters of common self-interest. There are few who would contend that this public virtue, relative to what exists in modernized societies, has evolved to a high state in Latin American culture. It is said, in fact, that one of the rare things that Latin Americans can agree upon is that they cannot agree upon anything. Latin Americans have another oft-repeated line, *Cada cabeza es un mundo* (Every head is a world unto itself), that captures the lack of cooperative spirit they commonly perceive among themselves.

The poverty of cooperative spirit in Latin America has no class boundaries, but it is among the poor that the lack of cooperation and its debilitating effects on economic advancement can be illustrated most graphically. As a community developer living and working among the urban poor, I found myself struck by the following observation: the more primitive and less complex the living conditions of the people, the easier it is to devise simple, practical ways of improving their living standards with projects requiring a small per capita outlay of capital, a modest contribution of labor, and a minimal amount of cooperation. Take, for instance, the following example, which is indicative of how uncomplicated and obvious numerous self-help projects can be. Many of Latin America's worst shantytown communities are dug into inhospitable hillsides that surround or lay within city perimeters. In one such area where I worked, the walking lanes that people had to use to go up the hill were very steep and constantly wet and slippery from the waste water thrown out the front doors of nearby huts. As if this were not enough, the paths were littered with chunks of soggy garbage that beckoned unwary passersby to slip and skin their knees. The climb up these passageways was exhausting even for a young man; yet day after day I witnessed tired old women hauling forty pounds of drinking water up these formidable inclines. Why, reason demanded, did not the people living alongside these paths come together, sacrifice a little beer money and spare time, and construct some concrete steps? Even earthen steps, requiring no contribution of funds at all, would have been a great improvement.

As every foreign community developer knows, this idea may have a cultural bias, and solutions should emerge from the community itself. The next step, then, is to talk to people and probe for "felt needs," common problems crying out for solution. To a remarkable degree I, and others in similar situations, discovered considerable uniformity of opinion among the shantytown inhabitants about what their problems were. In the community where I worked, most people, without any knowledge of what was on my own mind, presented the same basic list of needed community projects, in pretty much the same order of priority, with many of the same solutions: self-help, cooperation, and voluntary contributions of money, time, and labor.

As far as the stairway idea was concerned, there was no cultural bias in it. As one might expect, these people constantly complained about wearing themselves out just to climb to their homes every day. A stairway would have taken one or two Sundays or holidays to build, and yet the people of this community had endured, and shared, the problem for years. What was holding them back from eliminating this aggravation in their lives? The solution was already planted in their minds, and they experienced the "felt need" in their tired feet. The money obstacle was minimal or nonexistent, and the labor requirement trifling in comparison with the energy expended climbing stairless inclines. This left but one element wanting—the spirit of cooperation. This problem of a *falta de cooperación* (lack of cooperation) is, in fact, a lament heard among the urban poor—as well as Latin Americans of other classes—with endless repetition.

From what has previously been said of Latin American culture, the causes behind this lack of cooperation are not difficult to see. Latin

Americans are separated by numerous cultural factors that render mutual assistance difficult. Individuals who habitually regard one another with hostility, suspicion, and distrust are not likely to work well together no matter what their common interests. Individuals who are concerned with "defending" themselves are disinclined to become involved in community projects and tend to pass their days in social isolation.

Prestige considerations are another powerful factor that frequently hamper cooperative behavior. Logically speaking, when people discover they have certain needs in common that can be met only with cooperative behavior, it should be relatively easy for them to work together and help one another satisfy those needs. In the Latin American context, however, hierarchical prestige patterns create emotional self-interests in people that can prevent them from focusing on their material self-interests. For example, individuals who participate in a community meeting must agree upon a common course of action, but to do this they must usually accept a proposal from one of the assembly members. The problem is that this might increase the prestige of the person who made the proposal. In an atmosphere highly charged with prestige concerns, it is very possible that individuals will vote against a sound proposal simply because they want to prevent one of their own from gaining in status, or perhaps because some want their own alternative plan accepted for the sake of status. Thus, owing to a complex tangle of prestige considerations more immediately important than their material self-interest, participants at these kinds of meetings often end up vociferously denouncing a well-conceived self-help project and thereby contribute to their own condition of stagnating poverty.

Because the prestige considerations of a topic under discussion are often more important than the topic itself, Latin Americans have been known for taking a dramatically different stance on an issue they argued passionately for a short time before.[95] I have witnessed this in a community development context when an individual would lay out to me in the privacy of his own home an idea for community improvement and then shortly afterward firmly oppose it in a public meeting only because he felt threatened by the person who first voiced the proposal before the assembly. Likewise, I have seen collective gatherings erupt into a crescendo of angry denunciations when every one of the participants had expressed to me individually and privately essentially the same outline of community problems, needs, and solutions. Interesting to note is that most of the people included among their main problems the inability of community members to agree on common plans of action.

Because the poverty of cooperative spirit is a widespread social problem in Latin America, it manifests itself in many ways. Perhaps the example that Westerners most often use to illustrate this problem is the frequent and unashamed breaking of queues. An almost daily example of queue breaking could be found at a certain bus stop I often used one block off a main avenue of downtown Lima. Every evening of every working day, commuters would form a long line on the sidewalk awaiting the arrival of minibuses to carry them home. When a vehical approached, stopped, and opened its doors, the once-solid phalanx of people would crack and thirty to forty men, women, and children would rush for the opening—shoving, squeezing, and wedging their way in. A handful of the fittest would emerge triumphant and the vanquished would slowly fall back into the neat line—only to charge again at the arrival of the next minibus. The inability of people to engage in a rudimentary form of cooperation such as standing in line is not significant in itself but is simply symptomatic of the countless failings of cooperation that take place on a daily basis in Latin America and that do much to hold back the continent's social and economic development.

The problem of lack of cooperation is closely related to a larger cultural dilemma that exists in Latin America: namely, that many of the prevailing values and prestige patterns are not compatible with the kind of orderly, nonexploitative society most Latin Americans would like to live in. The behavior of individuals within a society is most effectively regulated by shared values and a shared consensus on how social prestige is to be allocated. Ideally, prestige patterns should be so structured that individuals who contribute to the common good are rewarded with social esteem and those who harm it are punished by a loss of social prestige. In Latin American society, this is not the case. So long as an individual is successful in his quest for wealth, power, or some other form of personal advantage, he is likely to increase his social prestige even if his actions are damaging to the society around him.

The prestige patterns which dominate Latin American culture have encouraged the proliferation of asocial misfits who are contemptuous of law and oblivious to the harm they inflict upon society. As we have previously seen, the successful among these are called vivos and the skills they display are referred to as viveza. In the words of Carlos Delgado, vivos recognize "no moral limitations in social combat. . . . Every instrument is permissable and every means is licit. The very crudeness of competitive action is justified by its results: 'to rise,' 'to arrive,' to enjoy prestige and power"[96] Despite this, vivos are widely, if privately, applauded by other Latin Americans. Success and success alone is what determines whether they are awarded social prestige.

A society that is afflicted by prestige patterns that bestow status upon the successful regardless of the social consequences of their actions is deprived of its principal weapon in controlling the predatory behavior of the individuals within itself. Such a society is inevitably characterized by social behavior that has sometimes been described as anarchic individualism. In Latin America this behavior is commonly referred to as *individualismo*. Whatever the name one wishes to apply, the people within this type of society appear not as cooperating entities but as individuals or factions furiously working against one another to the detriment of their own common good.

To amplify this notion of socially harmful prestige patterns, it would be helpful to contrast the Latin American situation with that of the United States. American society has historically been far more successful in exerting social control over its citizens by withdrawing or granting social prestige according to the degree of harm done, or contributions rendered, to society. The custom of public philanthropy can be used as an indicator of the way prestige patterns can work to the benefit of the society at large. In the typical year 1975, U.S. citizens donated 54 *billion* dollars in money and volunteer services to as many as six million public service organizations.[97] Up to about a sixth of this can be explained by the income tax advantages involved.[98] Most of the remainder was probably due to the social pressure people feel to make charitable contributions and the prestige they receive when they willingly comply.

An even more relevant example of prestige patterns working to regulate society is provided by Japanese culture because the Japanese, like the Latin Americans, are prone to view human relations hierarchically. In Japan, this has not resulted in the kind of anarchic individualism that characterizes Latin American society because of the presence of strong social control, the development of which will be discussed in Chapter 6. Briefly, the values and prestige patterns of Japanese culture oblige those who seek social respectability to direct their energies into socially beneficial activities. Anarchic individualists, even successful ones like the Latin American vivos, would never be honored in Japanese society.

In conclusion, then, a society does not have to eliminate individual self-interest in order to "control" its members adequately but only to regulate the pursuit of individual profit so that it is beneficial, or at least not harmful, to the society at large. The best means a society has for doing this are cultural prestige patterns which keep individuals in line by threatening them with a loss of respect and esteem. If, however, a society quickly allocates social prestige simply on the basis of individual self-gain, it will have nothing with which to pressure its members into socially constructive endeavors.

The detrimental effects of inadequate social control upon economic modernization can hardly be overstated, and it is to the particular details of this problem that we must now direct our attention.

3
"Loose Sand"

Economic leadership is perhaps the most important, and easily the most overlooked, contributing factor to the development of modern, productive economies. Economic modernization, like any other complex form of cooperative social activity, requires initiators and prime movers. Because of this, in dealing with the problem of national poverty in Latin America, a useful starting point is to examine the quality of economic leadership in that society.

In the pioneer countries that first edged down the road to modernization, the chief organizers of economic activity were businessmen commonly referred to as "entrepreneurs." In countries that industrialized later, the men who took upon themselves the chief responsibility for fostering economic development were state officials. In order to investigate the prospects for modernization in Latin America, therefore, we must look closely at what history has shown to be the two most likely modernization elites: entrepreneurs, who carry out their activities as private citizens or public officials, who perform economic tasks in the name of the entire society. First, the entrepreneurs.[1]

PRIVATELY LED MODERNIZATION

Perhaps the single, most outstanding feature of entrepreneurship in Latin America has been the enormous importance of the foreigner, or more specifically, the foreign investor and foreign immigrant. In some parts of the continent, members of the native landed elite did become involved in certain areas of entrepreneurial activity such as cash crops, insurance, importing, and banking. By and large, however, foreigners have supplied the real entrepreneurial drive in Latin America, particularly in the risky manufacturing enterprises. A statistical and historical picture of this social phenomenon will appear in later pages, but for now our concern is why more Latin American entrepreneurs did not appear upon the scene.

A first step in answering this question would be to point out that the relatively few Latin American entrepreneurs who did exist usually came from the small social elite. This indicates that something seemed to have prevented the members of the middle and lower classes from becoming economic leaders. For example, in the São Paulo of 1930, not a single native Latin American manufacturer could trace his origins to the middle or lower classes, a situation very different from the developmental experience of more industrialized countries.[2] Obviously, if the middle and lower classes, the greatest potential source of entrepreneurs, were not producing them, then entrepreneurs would be in short supply in the society as a whole. Our original question, then, might be rephrased to ask why so few economic initiators, organizers, and risk takers emerged from the masses.

One popular explanation for this is that Latin American elites have always constructed insuperable barriers to social mobility in order to frustrate the strugglers below who aspired to better their economic and social positions. If such difficult obstacles really existed, however, then first-generation immigrants should have been even less prepared than native Latin Americans to overcome them, for the new arrivals from Europe were not only poor and illiterate but deficient in the knowledge of local languages and customs.[3] Nonetheless, these immigrants were very successful in advancing themselves through economic enterprise. For example, one study carried out in 1956 found that the rate of social mobility in the immigrant city of São Paulo was greater than in Kansas City, a representative urban center in the legendary land of the self-made man.[4] The explanation why native Latin Americans did not experience similar success has to be other than the claim that the opportunities were not there.

Another widespread notion as to why more entrepreneurial talent has not come forth from the Latin American masses might be called the "lazy bones" theory. This theory holds that most Latin Americans cannot better themselves because they are generally shiftless, no-good, improvident, and lazy. This view is not heard in public often and is certainly not the fashion among intellectuals and officials; yet it repeatedly creeps up in off-the-cuff remarks and casual conversations. While the lazy bones idea seems to be sanctioned by the prevailing folk wisdom, its validity has been seriously questioned by careful academic research that has found the Latin Americans under study to be thrifty, frugal, and hard-working.[5] Why the discrepancy? Just how did the lazy bones notion come about in the first place?

To answer this it would be helpful to specify the kinds of values, or "economic virtues" that characterize entrepreneurs. Entrepreneurs, of course, need to be diligent, persistent, and frugal; but even more important is their overall *orientation* toward work. A peasant cannot be considered an investment-minded entrepreneur if, through strenuous effort, he assiduously accumulates gold coins only to bury them under the floor of his thatch hut. Genuine entrepreneurs aim for an ever greater return on their invested labor and capital; and if their enterprise efficiently increases the production of needed goods and services, it can be said that they have contributed to their country's economic development.

Western economists commonly assume that entrepreneurial types exist in all cultures in sufficient numbers. They describe the human family as economic animals (with entrepreneurs as a special capital-investing subgenus) and talk of people as acting "rationally" when in lieu of chasing prey or migrating to fresher pastures, they are earnestly pursuing the largest reward for their labor and capital. The whole elaborate edifice constructed by these theory builders rests upon the assumption that human beings are naturally inclined to desire more economic benefits. The beauty of their assumption is that it is universally true. Its difficulty is that it is more universally true in some cultures than in others. In Western culture, where this school of thought originated, the dominant prestige patterns are more conducive to "rational" economic behavior in general and to entrepreneurial behavior in particular, than are those of Latin American culture.

The only effective means of illustrating this is to treat in some detail the results of relevant anthropological and sociological research, beginning with the meticulously recorded observations of the Reichel-Dolmatoffs. The two Colombian investigators described certain work-related behavior traits that have often caused onlookers to conclude that Latin Americans are lazy: "Although there are always opportunities for earning money," they wrote, "very few people in the village take full advantage of them."[6] However, in contrast to observers who are content with surface explanations, the Reichel-Dolmatoffs perceived that the forces underlying the seeming lack of interest in economic self-betterment were not the time-honored vices of sloth, indifference, and lethargy but concerns over the prestige implications of work. These prestige concerns pushed the village inhabitants toward a routine of social behavior that was incompatible with good entrepreneurship, that is, incompatible not necessarily with the diligent performance of work but with the diligent performance of work oriented toward profitable investment and increased productivity. In the Reichel-Dolmatoff's words,

> Every day there arise . . . opportunities for earning a living beyond the narrow limits of mere subsistence, either by wage labor, domestic service repair jobs, or transportation service or by the

home manufacture of salable goods. But those who might profit by such work are often more than reluctant to accept what might be to them an unpleasant and even dangerous position.

There are two principal reasons for this attitude. In the first place, the prospective worker feels himself in an inferior position as soon as he agrees to work for someone else. His self-esteem (amor propio) is affected, and he feels humiliated and slighted because by working for others he admits publicly his needy situation (su situación de necesidad). To be in need is humiliating. A self-respecting person who wants to be respected by others takes pride in saying, "I have no need" (no tengo la necesidad). In the second place, to work for more than subsistence or a given maintenance level is almost always interpreted as social ambitiousness, and the individual is thus exposed to the envy of others who might try to curb this ambition by gossip or magic. It is, therefore, not only the employer-employee relationship that is avoided as far as possible, but even independent work for one's own benefit, because it is likely to produce a notable surplus.

All this, of course, does not mean that hired labor, or labor of any other kind, is nonexistent or that all people live on a mere subsistence level. Physical necessity and prestige factors are powerful incentives to work, but the scope and intensity of this work are severely limited by the considerations mentioned above. The continuity and range of the effort made in making a living or in exploiting to the fullest all potential resources, do not depend so much upon the individual's intentions, ambitions, or capacities but rather upon this recognition of certain limits which his society imposes upon him. Every individual has to know just how far he can go in his efforts; just how much prestige he can afford to lose in one sphere if he is to acquire it in another. Each man must judge for himself how much of his labor effort will be accepted as adequate and normal by society and how much might be interpreted as aggressive behavior and ambitiousness unbecoming his particular class-status. What the casual observer would simply call laziness, inertia, or lack of responsibility must then be viewed rather as evidence of a very fine social balance which has to be maintained by a conscious effort to restrict one's personal ambitions and potential resources. People do not shirk labor; they have developed their own patterns of work according to their own particular socioeconomic structure, their value system, and the physiological conditions inherent in the climate and their health status. . . . It seems that the nagging insistence with which members of one culture call those of others "lazy" is partly due to incomprehension of this highly complex balance.[7]

The Reichel-Dolmatoffs, then, attributed to a distinctive prestige system and not to the vice of laziness the difficulty Colombian villagers experienced in forming the kinds of mutually advantageous work agreements that in Western culture would have been fairly easy to arrange. In the passage quoted above, they have highlighted two specific prestige considerations, the first of which should sound very familiar: Typically, the villager was very sensitive to the possible effect the acceptance of an inferior employee function might have on his social position. And since this sensitivity did not disappear after the job began, it not only influenced how determinedly he looked for work but how efficiently he carried out the work. The degree to which this status concern could limit the work efforts of even an individual in substantial economic need is revealed in the following passage:

> In all labor relations absolute equality of "dignity" and "respect" is called for, and it must always be understood that by agreeing to work for another person no position of inferiority is implied. . . . The first difficulty arises as soon as the employer begins to look for laborers. Very rarely, practically never, can a person be approached directly and asked to work for a certain time and wages. This would be embarrassing for both parties and most humiliating for the one who is offered the work. The latter is likely to refuse, to feel offended, or even to answer haughtily, "I myself am looking for hired help." Such arrangements, therefore, must be made through an intermediary, a relative, a friend, or a compadre who, with the necessary diplomacy and caution, suggests that the one accept the work and conditions offered by the other. . . . Once the work has been explained in detail, it is common that the laborer asks for some time to "think it over." This is done even though a man may be in urgent need of cash or may have already decided to accept the work, because in this way he can show that he is not pressed and in no way eager to work for others. Days or even weeks may pass before the employer is notified of the final decision, and meanwhile the laborer, in his daily conversations, makes occasional sly allusions to his popularity as a hard worker, his willingness to "help out others who are pressed for workers," or his reluctance to accept the work, he being a busy man himself. In this manner the laborer affirms his independent position and rationalizes the humiliating aspect of the work.
>
> These attitudes continue when the employer and employee finally meet face to face. It is the laborer who speaks now in a loud, angry, and demanding voice, who criticizes and disobeys, who complains constantly about the work, the food, and the wages. The employer, on the other hand, speaking in a low and casual tone, is as polite as possible and tries to persuade the laborer to perform his work in a certain way. Apparently simple tasks become now problematic: the felling of a tree, the mending of a fence, the harvest of an acre of coffee. The laborer's standard reply is that "it can't be done" (no se puede), and he will produce a great many reasons why the work is impracticable under the given circumstances: because it is too late or too soon; because the wood or the burro or the tools are useless; because it is a loss of time and

effort; and so forth. However, meanwhile the work proceeds. If it does not turn out to the entire satisfaction of the employer, the laborer certainly will not accept the blame for it, but will put it upon a great many other circumstances. All this is, of course, a standard pattern of behavior, well known to the employer who has to accept it if he wants the work done at all.[8]

The situation described by the Reichel-Dolmatoffs (which can be found in many areas of rural Latin America)[9] illustrates how a person's work life can become thoroughly entangled in prestige calculations. In such circumstances, the person is not likely to respond as rationally to economic incentives as are people regulated by prestige patterns more conducive to modernization. This, in turn, has an understandably inhibiting effect on the growth of entrepreneurship. When a people's value system hinders their desire to maximize their return on their time and labor, it is highly improbable that many effective entrepreneurs will emerge from their ranks.

Even more discouraging to the development of entrepreneurship is another point brought out by the Reichel-Dolmatoffs. In the passages quoted they refer to an extremely important cultural feature, in evidence all over Latin America as well as within Latin American communities in the United States, which shall be identified in this essay as the *envy reflex*.

The envy reflex is a cultural problem that deters entrepreneurs from performing one of their most useful social roles. The process of economic development requires that people save capital and use it to increase the output of goods and services. The envy reflex discourages the maturation of entrepreneurial individuals who are willing to take the lead in this vital enterprise.

The envy reflex in Latin American culture owes much of its strength to the prevailing hierarchical view of human ordering. As described earlier, if an individual grows in wealth and rises in social prestige, he is readily seen by others as threatening, as becoming "better" than they are. Consequently, a person who patiently piles up a capital surplus, even if this surplus is intended for investment, is apt to be negatively viewed by his peers as "aggressive" and "socially ambitious" (pp. 54–55).

The envy reflex can be very intimidating to an individual who might otherwise attempt to improve his fortune through entrepreneurship. A potential entrepreneur can hear all about him remarks, stories, and conversations similar to those recorded by an anthropologist in the Mexican-American town of Mesquito:

Neighbors are against one, it is asserted, and one's good fortune only excites their envy and hostility. Those emotions are expressed by such recurrent statements as: "People don't want to see you get ahead, that's the way of *la raza*." [Mexican-Americans] Another frequently heard comment maintains that "Individiousness is all around one; you can't improve your lot without *la gente* working against you." Also, "I don't know what it is about *la raza* but you can't work together with anyone." These and other familiar citations from the everyday conversation of Mexican-Americans in Mesquito describe the qualities which they, themselves, attribute to social relations.[10]

In Frontera, another Mexican-American community, a person with entrepreneurial ambitions would run up against the same discouraging social attitudes. The anthropologist Octavio Ignacio Romano writes:

> *Envidia* or envy constitutes a major problem for the local citizens, for it is generally considered a dominant characteristic of *la raza*, or the race, as people of Mexican ancestry commonly call themselves. The acquisition of readily desirable goods, or a declaration of ambitions to better one's station in life, are believed to be certain ways in which to elicit *envidia* among neighbors. . . . "We can't lift our head (better ourselves) without the neighbors becoming envious and the gossip begins. Right away they say we are pretentious." . . . The Frontera males assert that the first to react with envy and to attempt to make a person fail is a neighbor or another person who is also of Mexican ancestry. Thus, it is said, "One's own people will always seek a way to make a successful man fail because they are envious."[11]

And in case a general familiarity with the prevailing social prejudice is not warning enough, the potential entrepreneur is also likely to hear about the specific hazards of rising too far above others. Oscar Lewis wrote about the following kinds of retaliation against successful people in the Mexican village of Tepotzlán:

> Successful persons are popular targets of criticism, envy, and malicious gossip. A new calf or cow may come home with a deep slash from someone's machete. Some unknown enemy may stone another's dogs or drive away his chickens or pigs.[12]

Another research study tells of similar pressure brought to bear upon two brothers who were "pretentious" enough to want to succeed in business:

> Two brothers who enlarged their cantina into a small night club were boycotted by their former friends. Several times the screens on the windows were slashed and the window frames broken. One

night a truck "accidentally" rammed the wall of the establishment and the large crack had to be repaired at considerable expense. "We are doing a good business but our customers are strangers, not friends," one of the brothers said.[13]

While actual acts of retaliation can be significant, it is the ever-present threat of retaliation, the pervasive fear of the envy reflex, that does the most harm to the growth of entrepreneurship. This fear can be seen at work in the case history of Prudencio, a capable, conscientious Mexican-American who was employed in a retail store owned by an American. Prudencio's qualities were so obvious that the proprietor took a personal interest in him and his future success. The account continues:

> When the owner moved to another section of the country, he offered to sell the store and its stock to Prudencio, urging the latter to buy the enterprise. Prudencio remembers that his hesitancy was such that he rejected the plan, but the Anglo [Caucasian Americans of non-Latin origin] continued his encouragement. Finally, the owner of the store offered the business at a very low sum, to be paid in very reasonable monthly payments; he went so far as to act as Prudencio's cosigner when he borrowed the money from the bank. (Throughout his recollections of the business deal Prudencio attributed to himself a passive role, and to his Anglo patron the active role.)
>
> Several years later Prudencio accepted an additional position with another Anglo as a drive and delivery man on an ice route, depending on his wife to manage the store. Sometime later the Anglo owner made plans to move elsewhere and offered the small business to Prudencio. Once again Prudencio refused to expand his commercial interests. The Anglo, however, insisted that if he left the business to anyone, it would be Prudencio. He offered the delivery truck to Prudencio on the following terms: if the purchaser could not pay for the vehicle during the first six months, the Anglo would present it to him as a gift. Prudencio agreed to the deal and says proudly that he paid for the delivery truck in the first five months.
>
> Prudencio attributed his timidity and passivity in those business negotiations to the knowledge that, "Your own race doesn't like to see you get ahead." He says there is much invidiousness in Mexiquito, and people have come up to him on the street to tell him that his businesses would be failures within three months. Furthermore, he recalls that before he became an independent businessman, he was on very good terms with the other workers at the produce shed. When he took over the store and later, the delivery route, the men acted as if they didn't know him.[14]

Although the case history of Prudencio ended satisfactorily, it serves to illustrate how in normal circumstances the envy reflex and the fear of *envidia* can work to discourage the spirit of entrepreneurship. People who would like to advance themselves by becoming entrepreneurs often find that the enormous social pressure exerted upon them by their neighbors and friends renders the sacrifices not worth the rewards. If, therefore, a Latin American modernizing elite wishes to conjure up the spirit of entrepreneurship among the broad masses and to multiply the number of capital accumulators, risktakers, and organizers of economic activity within the society, then it must do more than offer ordinary Western-style incentives such as tax breaks or low-interest loans. It must also confront the extremely stubborn cultural problem of envidia, or the envy reflex.[15]

The emphasis placed here upon values like the envy reflex does not mean that other factors such as poverty, illiteracy, exploitation, bureaucratic corruption, union intransigence, and so forth, do not also discourage the growth of entrepreneurial spirit. It must be noted, however, that these other factors were obstacles to the European immigrants as well. That many immigrants overcame them shows that they could be overcome; and the fact that relatively many more immigrants overcame them than did native Latin Americans is an indication that problems relating to Latin American cultural values are what have been really decisive in holding back entrepreneurship in that society.

Another way of examining the critical link between cultural values and economic leadership is to take up the question of entrepreneurial quality in Latin America. The first thing that must be recognized is that entrepreneurial quality is relative—that is to say, some cultures produce better entrepreneurs than others just as surely as some cultures produce better writers, inventors, scientists, soldiers, sculptors, and soccer players. In earlier decades American businessmen were undoubtably the crown champions of entrepreneurship, and today the Japanese probably deserve that title. Latin American entrepreneurs, in general, have shown themselves to be far less effective as economic leaders than their counterparts in more industrialized countries. The concern here, however, is not with ranking but with how Latin American cultural values have held back the development of economic leadership in that society.

An inquiry of this type is greatly aided by existing academic research. Since the days of Adam Smith, economists have recognized the vital importance of capable entrepreneurship to economic development. In recent decades researchers influenced by this tradition have turned their attention to Third World countries and have compiled a considerable body of literature examining the relationship between values and entrepreneurial capacity.[16]

One study along these lines was done in the early 1960s by William Foote Whyte, a leading professor of industrial relations. While working in Peru, Whyte observed in interpersonal relations social behavior that appeared to be caused by a relative lack of mutual trust among Peruvians. To bring this attitude to the surface, Whyte administered a specially designed questionnaire to U.S. and Peruvian students and indeed found a significant (Whyte used the term "enormous") difference between the amount of trust shown by the American and Peruvian respondants.[17]

Assuming this relatively low level of trust to be prevalent throughout Peruvian culture, Whyte tackled the question of what effect this would have upon the conduct of directors and managers in Peruvian industry. The professor believed that the cultural problem of a deficiency of trust was preventing Peruvian industry from adopting needed managerial reforms. This is a matter of considerable consequence because advances in managerial efficiency are as least as important to economic development as are advances in technology.[18] However, Third World countries like Peru cannot simply import the latest management techniques from industrialized countries if their particular values are not compatible with those techniques. Whyte pointed out that overcentralization of authority was a definite problem in Peruvian industry. He also recognized that Peruvian industrial leaders would not copy the decentralization methods their American counterparts found so successful so long as they did not trust their subordinates enough to delegate authority. Whyte went on to explain that even if industrial leaders were willing to experiment with the new approaches, lower-echelon managers, because of their mutual distrust, would not be able to work effectively together. These managers would then be forced to go to their superiors to resolve their differences—the very superiors who delegated the authority to them in the first place.[19]

Another inefficient managerial practice encouraged by the general climate of distrust is nepotism. Latin American entrepreneurs frequently hire relatives to run their business operations rather than seek out the most competent and trained workers from the general population.[20] The reason they do this is far more compelling than a simple benign interest in the prosperity of relatives. These businessmen feel engulfed in a world populated by untrustworthy human beings and so naturally place great emphasis on finding subordinates who will not betray them. And who else are more likely to be loyal and obedient than the members of their own families, tied to them by blood and marriage? Capable individuals who do not share these basic human bonds with the chief decision makers are either not admitted into the firms or are left holding the less responsible positions within them.

Of course, many Latin American businesses are too large to be managed entirely by family members, and here outsiders are able to advance to important posts. But even in these situations the fundamental spirit is still the same: aspirants for promotion are expected to exhibit the preeminent virtue and those who are selected are referred to as *hombres de confianza*, men of unquestioned loyalty. The fact that loyalty is valued over ability tends to bring to the top individuals who are best at demonstrating loyalty rather than those who are best at increasing productive efficiency. Francisco Matarazzo, Brazil's leading entrepreneur a generation ago, selected managers who were so unreserved in their exhibitions of obedience that when they took leave of Matarazzo's office, they bowed deeply and walked backward toward the door.[21] A far more typical as well as harmful way that subordinates characteristically demonstrate unswerving obedience is to perform as yes-men for their superior, never to criticize their superior's decision even if they feel it is wrong.[22]

Aside from influencing entrepreneurs to choose poor managers, cultural values incline them to make other types of business decisions that impede maximum production and growth. For example, Thomas Cochran, an economist who made a detailed study of the attitudes and habits of Puerto Rican businessmen, could not find a single instance of a voluntary merger between firms despite the obvious economic need of many to do so.[23] Cochran attributed this remarkable discovery to the "unyielding individualism" of the heads of Puerto Rican firms. "Men with moderately successful businesses," Cochran explained, "do not want to become but one of several executives in a large company."[24]

There are basically two reasons behind the unyielding individualism to which Cochran refers. The first is that businessmen who have difficulty trusting one another are apprehensive about sharing power. The second is the explanation suggested by Cochran: Latin American businessmen are swayed by hierarchical prestige concerns, and it is usually more attractive to remain the top executive in a smaller firm than to accept a lesser position with a larger company.

The same basic dislike of sharing authority with others is a vital force behind an often-noted phenomenon of the Latin American business world—the underdevelopment of the stock market. An illustration of this can be seen in a Brazilian survey of business leaders carried out in the early 1960s that revealed that 93 percent of the businessmen interviewed had not so much as thought about selling stocks in their companies.[25] The sale of stock, of course, would have meant the relinquishing of at least some potential control to the investors who held the portfolios. The inevitable result was that with the exception of a few businesses that might have been able to generate sufficient funds from their own profits, Brazilian companies were severely limited in their ability to invest for future growth and expansion. Little wonder, then, that an enormous country like Brazil could at that time boast of no more than 380 enterprises employing over 500 workers, less than .5 percent of all existing firms.[26] Significantly, half of these larger companies were concentrated in the single city of São Paulo,[27] where heavy European immigration has served to make the value patterns in that area the least Latin American and the most modern of any part of Brazil.

Another attitudinal problem of Latin American entrepreneurs is their rather frank and open aversion to taking risks.[28] An adventuresome willingness to take economic risks, of course, has long been recognized as a vital element of good entrepreneurship. It is important to consider, therefore, the cultural factors that stimulate or inhibit the business urge to gamble on innovation and growth. In Western society prevailing prestige patterns motivate entrepreneurs to continue to build and to grow long after the point where an increase in income is able to increase their standard of living.[29] But in Latin American society prestige patterns tend to deter entrepreneurs once they have achieved a moderate level of success. Latin American entrepreneurs realize that the expansion of a business enterprise almost always entails a substantial risk of failure and bankruptcy and that bankruptcy would cost them dearly not only in income but in social prestige. In the highly status-conscious Latin American culture, the possibility of a sharp drop in social position is a very alarming prospect. Latin American entrepreneurs calculate quite correctly that in expanding their businesses they would lose far more status through failure than they would gain through success. This influences many smaller businessmen to avoid the risk of pushing their companies toward a larger and more productive stage of growth.

Owing in large measure to the various cultural problems outlined above, Latin American entrepreneurs tend to organize businesses that are undersized, stuffy, and sorrowfully lacking in innovative spirit. They are famous for the high markups they foist upon the consumer and do not seem too excited by ideas that might improve their situation, like the revolutionary notion of increasing profits by reducing prices and augmenting output. For example, when Sears, Roebuck established their first store in Rio de Janeiro, the American managers discovered that many of their suppliers refused to enlarge their production even with a guaranteed buyer. One clothespin manufacturer, in a remarkable piece of inverted economic behavior, demanded a higher unit price for 10,000 dozen clothespins than he did for 1,000 dozen.[30]

The relative lack of venturesome entrepreneurial spirit in the Latin American business world has the effect of not only reducing productive investment but deflecting it away from the areas most critical to the human needs of underdeveloped societies. Too many investors, for example, prefer to sink their capital into urban land and luxury real estate, which are considered less risky than basic manufactures and agriculture.[31] They also are very shy of long-term investments that would extend their risk over prolonged periods of time.[32] The uncertain political and economic conditions that prevail in many parts of Latin America, of course, have something to do with this. But causes related to values alone are sufficient to have made the scarcity of venture capital a problem even in a country like Mexico, where political stability, a strong currency, and a probusiness government dominated the scene for many years.[33]

Another, somewhat different value problem that influences the quality of entrepreneurship is the relative lack of prestige Latin American society bestows upon people who engage in business. This is an important consideration because prestige is often a more powerful incentive than money. A society that officially embraces the goal of economic modernization should richly reward with social prestige those people who take the lead in organizing economic enterprises. Unfortunately for the cause of Latin American modernization, the amount of prestige that Latin American society affords its businessmen is rather stingy compared to what is given in more industrialized cultures.

To find the reason for this we have only to look at Latin American history, and once again we see Latin America as a victim of its own historical heritage. During colonial times social prejudice against vile, unaristocratic business occupations was very strong. If, for example, a student wanted to enter the prestigious University of San Gregorio, he first had to establish by a detailed legal process his "purity of blood" and to prove that none of his ancestors had ever debased the family lineage by engaging in trade.[34] Prejudices of this sort have considerably softened over the centuries, but the legacy of the past still shows its unmistakable imprint on Latin American values. An indication of this is found in the previously mentioned cross-cultural survey of William F. Whyte (pp. 60–61), which revealed that while a high percentage of American students hoped someday to become businessmen, only 4 percent of their Peruvian counterparts expressed such a preference. As with adolescents anywhere, the Peruvian students tended to aspire to the most socially prestigious kinds of employment, which in their minds were the titled professions—law, medicine, engineering, and the military.[35]

The relative lack of prestige given to people who engage in business discourages quality entrepreneurship in the obvious way of deterring talented individuals from becoming entrepreneurs. In far less obvious fashion, it also discourages quality entrepreneurship by causing the entrepreneurs who do exist to develop poor work habits.

An important example of this can be seen in the attitude of Latin American businessmen toward manual labor. Because businessmen derive so little prestige from their occupations, they are sensitive about their status positions and try to avoid manual labor, which they fear will lower their status even more. The problem with this attitude is that by refusing to do manual labor they diminish their effectiveness as business organizers and managers. It is the responsibility of managers to locate and repair the small hitches that can hold up an entire production process, to design more efficient assembly lines, and to motivate workers by resolving their grievances and devising incentives. All these skills require the kind of knowledge and understanding that is best learned from first-hand experience on the factory floor. In the early factories of nineteenth-century America men called shirt-sleeve entrepreneurs used to work all day doing many of the same jobs as their sweaty employees.[36] Even in the larger, complex companies of contemporary America, engineers, executives, and managers commonly dirty their hands helping to set up assembly lines and to work out problems on them. But because Latin Americans in comparable occupational roles are concerned about their status positions, they are reluctant to engage in these same manual tasks. United States subsidiaries in Latin America have found much difficulty in persuading prospective Latin American managers to spend time on assembly lines even during their training periods.[37] Latin American firms encounter similar problems. One Colombian industrialist, for example, complained to a researcher that he had just lost eight out of ten new college graduates he had hired because they felt that their work demeaned them.[38] Given attitudes such as these, there is little wonder why a survey of leading Colombian entrepreneurs found that not one of them in their entire occupational histories had ever undergone the potentially valuable experience of working at a manual job.[39]

If Latin American businessmen are anxious to avoid situations that will lower their status, it is understandable that they might also look for ways to raise it. Despite the fact that businessmen receive little prestige from their occupations, they can rise very high on the social-status scale by other means. The most obvious and potent tool available to them to raise their prestige is their wealth. In order to use this tool effectively, however, they must display their wealth by lavish consumption and spending. In other words, if they wish to enjoy the prestige of the Latin American social elites, they must participate in the same game played by those elites—conspicuous consumption.

The ethic of conspicuous consumption has a very negative effect on the quality of entrepreneurship in Latin America. It causes Latin American business leaders to spend so much on present consumption that they do not allocate enough capital for productive investment. An example of this can be seen in figures from the early sixties comparing the consumption-investment patterns of Chile and Great Britain. While Chilean owners of income-producing property consumed 64 percent of their income, saved 21 percent, and paid 15 percent in taxes, their British counterparts consumed 30.5 percent, saved 27.4 percent, and paid 30.5 percent in taxes. If the Chilean rich had had the resolve to pull in their belts and consume only to the same extent as the British, the investment rate of their country could have been doubled.[40]

The vast inequality of wealth in Latin America is often justified by a superficial comparison with Western societies during their early phases of modernization. It is said that this lopsided concentration of capital is necessary to achieve the astounding rates of investment that marked the bustling days of the early industrial revolution. A differing value system, however, renders what was workable in one culture unworkable in another. Despite some flamboyant displays of conspicuous consumption in the pioneer industrial countries, Western culture was permeated by the influence of the Protestant ethic, which induced most economic leaders to save and invest a large portion of their capital.[41] Latin American culture, in contrast, has no comparable restraining values, and Latin American business leaders spend too much of their incomes on consumer goods and services and too little on capital investments. The social behavior of Latin American capitalists, in short, is not the same as that of the majority of European capitalists, whose constructive investment-mindedness and useful social function was well described by the economist John Maynard Keynes:

> Europe was so organized socially and economically as to secure the maximum accumulation of capital. . . . The new rich of the nineteenth century were not brought up to large expenditures, and preferred the power which investment gave them to the pleasures of immediate consumption. In fact, it was precisely the inequality of the distribution of wealth which made possible those vast accumulations of fixed wealth and of capital improvements which distinguished that age from all others. Herein lay, in fact, the main justification of the Capitalist System. If the rich had spent their new wealth on their own enjoyments, the world would long ago have found such a regime intolerable. But like bees they saved and accumulated, not less to the advantage of the whole community because they themselves held narrower ends in prospect.[42]

In addition to conspicious consumption, Latin American entrepreneurs frequently engage in another practice designed to win them social prestige—conspicuous idleness. While the custom of conspicuous consumption wastes the capital resources of entrepreneurial leaders, the custom of conspicuous idleness wastes their time and talent. Conspicuous idleness is a practice that attempts to demonstrate glorious independence from the need to have to work for a living. As with conspicuous consumption, it has its roots in the Latin American heritage of aristocratic values where the proudest and most prestigious individuals were those unfettered by the base economic concerns of the servile multitudes. Modern conditions, of course, have modified this value, but even today a leading scholar on the subject of business behavior in Latin America can assert, "The prevailing attitude toward profit in Latin America remains affected by the desire to get rich quick and then perhaps to retire early and to live happily—that is, idly—ever after."[43]

While an early retirement after an impressive climb to success might not always be possible, a kind of semiretirement might well be. Often executives who reach the top in their companies do not regard their promotions as an opportunity for more responsibility and achievement. Rather, they regard them as an opportunity to push the dead weight of work onto the shoulders of subordinates. The Argentinean Tomás Fillol writes of this prevalent managerial attitude in his own country:

> The Argentine thinks of advancing himself in order that he may pass the burden of petty work to others; to many people, success means reaching a point in the organization where they no longer have to work or where they can come and go as they please.[44]

In their attempts to compensate for the relatively low prestige of their occupations, Latin American entrepreneurs are also noted for getting involved in nonbusiness activities that will increase their social standing. This has the effect, of course, of reducing the time they can spend improving and expanding their business operations. An example of this can be seen in the life of Torcurato Di Tella, one of Argentina's leading entrepreneurs. During his career Di Tella built up one of the largest industrial empires in Latin America and, by the standards of his culture, was a man unusually engrossed in his business ventures. Yet Di Tella took considerable time away from his career as an industrialist to become a landlord overseeing vast, rolling acres; a belated student laboring for a university degree; and finally an associate professor teaching courses at an institute for higher learning.[45] Di Tella, of course, substantially raised his social status by acquiring these new identities; but because he felt the need to pursue them, the underdeveloped Argentinean economy lost a considerable amount of the time and energy of one of its most creative entrepreneurs.

The importance of cultural factors that weaken entrepreneurial dedication might be better appreciated by looking at the kind of commitment to work characteristic of entrepreneurial elites in the successfully modernized countries. In general, entrepreneurial elites in the West and in Japan have demonstrated considerable dedication to their productive tasks. During the early decades of the industrial revolution, business leaders were often devoted to their work to the point of extreme self-sacrifice. One of these pioneer entrepreneurs, for example, used to punish himself regularly with 20-hour workdays; another used to spend four sleepless nights a week sitting over and tending boiling cauldrens of factory brew as if caring for sick children; another tenaciously fought diabetes for the last eight years of his life and was advising his subordinates even on his deathbed; still another found that his injured leg reduced the time he could devote to supervising his factory, so rather than suffer this, he ordered the troublesome thing cut off.[46] Entrepreneurs who own and run their own businesses today may not exhibit the near-fanaticism of the early pioneers, but they still typically labor 80 to 100 hours a week. Businessmen who do not own but simply manage corporations for stockholders also demonstrate tremendous dedication to their jobs, and they expect their workload to increase rather than decrease as they rise through promotions. For example, a survey of top corporation executives in the United States showed that on the average they devoted 60 hours per week to their jobs plus found the time to contribute 5 hours per week to some form of community service.[47]

The lives led by the managers and entrepreneurs in the successfully modernized countries reveal the kind of dedication that is often required to build up an efficient business and to keep it running smoothly. Of all the human attributes that make a person a good manager, none is more important than a tenacious, unflagging determination to overcome recurring problems and constantly improve production methods. When, as happens in Latin American society, prevailing values and prestige patterns weaken this steady dedication to economic tasks, they inevitably reduce the caliber of management and entrepreneurship as well.

The shortage of top-quality entrepreneurs in Latin America is as obvious as the problem of poverty itself. The late American industrialist Henry J. Kaiser was fond of expressing the essence of the entrepreneur's vocation with this favorite motto: Find a need and fill it. In Latin America it is obvious that there are many economic needs, and it is just as obvious that not enough people are finding and filling them.

To anyone with an eye for such matters, Latin America abounds in ways for entrepreneurs to make money for themselves (and provide employment for workers) by satisfying clearly visible economic wants. A team of economists from the International Bank for Reconstruction and Development once visited Cuba in the early 1950s and after careful study drew up a long list of such opportunities. Example: 11 million kilos of raw tomatoes were exported annually and 6 million kilos returned to Cuba in various forms such as tomato sauce, paste, and ketchup. Why didn't someone take advantage of this economic need?

Example: Meat industry byproducts were not processed in Cuba but had to be imported; yet large quantities of scraps from Cuban tanneries, perfectly suitable for industrial use, were either exported for processing elsewhere or simply thrown away and wasted. Example: Most Cuban tanneries imported the tannin used in their industrial process while vast quantities of mangrove tannin grew wild in Cuba's swamps just begging to be exploited.[48]

The reasons behind the sluggish development of the Latin American economies do go beyond the cultural factors which inhibit the growth of sufficient numbers of talented economic leaders. However, there can be no doubt that progress has been held back by the fact that many opportunities to find and fill economic needs have just stood there, like so many orphans, because no one was around to adopt them and develop their promise. This was, in fact, the principal reason why the European immigrants in Latin America were much more economically successful in relation to the native population than were those immigrants who piled off the ships in New York. The immigrants in Latin America were unchallenged by the same vigorous competition in business affairs that their counterparts encountered in North America. They were also unencumbered by the same value impediments that held back native Latin Americans. Thus the immigrants who disembarked on Latin American shores were able to seize the neglected opportunities they saw everywhere about them and to use them as vehicles of economic prosperity and social mobility.

GOVERNMENT-LED MODERNIZATION

The weak spirit of entrepreneurship in Latin American culture has made it difficult for Latin Americans to follow the Western model of modernization, where economic development was left mainly in the hands of private businessmen. Latin Americans have, however, come up with an alternative source of economic leadership—the government. Given the scarcity of economic leadership in the private sector, this is an idea born from necessity. The question here is whether this idea is viable. Can state officials by concentrating economic power in their own hands provide more effective economic leadership than private entrepreneurs?

The notion that government officials, not businessmen, should be the prime movers behind economic modernization has a strong appeal to many people. This appeal is based in the idea that while private economic elites are commited first and foremost to self-gain, state economic elites are responsible for the public "good," which in this case is economic modernization. It follows, therefore, that since government officials plan their economic activities to *directly* encourage modernization, they are more likely to reach this objective than owners of private enterprises, who are chiefly concerned with the far more narrow end of profit.

This line of reasoning draws its strength from the notion of how governments are supposed to function; it would obviously be considerably weakened if in fact governments failed to carry out their social responsibilities. Government elites are certainly capable of action in the public interest but are just as capable of using their power in their own self-interest to the detriment of the public good. Any discussion, then, as to the feasibility of government-led modernization must first consider the kinds of government elites likely to come to power in the various countries of Latin America.

The quality of political leadership in today's Latin America is unfortunately still very much influenced by the heritage of the past, where government leaders have generally used their power as a means of securing personal benefits. For well over a century after independence, most Latin American countries were ruled by dictatorial warlords (*caudillos*) who fought their way to power with rifle, machete, and barbarian vigor and whose interest in government was hardly in public service but in raiding the public till. Other countries in Latin America were dominated by constitutional governments manipulated by oligarchies, which were less oppressive in many respects than personal dictatorships but were still riddled with the vices of nepotism, bribery, and thievery.[49]

Perhaps the best indicator of the effect of this ignominious legacy upon contemporary Latin American governments is seen in the continuing widespread practice of misappropriating public funds. It is in this area that high officials most clearly reveal their attitude that public office is an opportunity for personal gain.

The degree of corruption among Latin American government elites varies in different countries, periods, and administrations, but overall there can be no doubt that by Western standards the extent of this public vice is enormous.[50] While a few Latin American presidents have been paragons of deliberate, scrupulous honesty, most have accumulated a fortune while in office. The amounts involved in some of these heists are large enough to numb the imagination. According to the most reliable figures available, the Cuban chief of state Fulgencio Batista piled up 50 million dollars during his first term of office and 200 million more during his second exhibition of public service. Estimates of President Juan Perón's pillaging of the Argentinean national treasury run as high as 700 million. When the military finally sent Perón hurriedly packing in 1955, a police search of one of his mansions uncovered 20 million dollars in loose cash lying around the house. In Mexico, where it is said that not a single general of the Mexican Revolution could stand up to a 50,000-peso broadside, estimates of the ammunition aimed at President Miguel Alemán range between 500 and 800 million dollars. Ironically, the all-time champion looter appears to have been the leader of one of the smallest and poorest countries, Generalissimo Rafael Trujillo of the Dominican Republic. After a modest beginning as a post office clerk and army private, this "Benefactor of the Fatherland" (as he liked to call himself) owned personally or through his extended family virtually every sizable factory, estate, firm, and bank on the island. When suddenly cut down by assassins' bullets in 1961, the Benefactor died a billionaire.[51]

The inescapable conclusion from such figures is that not only did these powerful public figures steal but they stole without pity. What can one individual possibly do with 50 million—100 million—400 million—700 million? This is simply incomprehensible corruption, and the problem is aggravated by the fact that due to the instability of Latin American politics, such characters are often quickly replaced by a new gang of gluttonous thieves hungry for the same rich banquet that comes with the discharge of public duty.

Corruption of this magnitude by government elites is a clear example of a phenomenon called *social parasitism*. Social parasitism can be broadly defined as a practice by which some members or groups of society take a far larger share of the collective wealth than they contribute toward its production.[52] Social parasitism exists in varying degrees in all societies, but the same disease at the same stage of maturation is far more harmful to people in poor countries than to people in rich ones. The reason for this is obvious: the majority of people who live in underdeveloped countries subsist precariously between poverty and destitution and posses little or no surplus they can afford to lose to parasitic exploiters.

As spectacular as the thievery by government elites can be, the attitude underlying this practice is even more harmful, for it is the cynical attitude toward public service that encourages government elites to accommodate the considerably more destructive parasitic practices of other groups. Corrrupt government leaders are, needless to say, anxious to hold onto their political positions and their opportunities for illicit gain. Because of this they were disposed to give in to the parasitic demands of "mass" interest groups which were made up of large numbers of people and which, owing to their enormous size, were capable of inflicting substantial damage upon society.

Only in the last few decades have interest groups made up of large numbers of people come to participate in Latin American political life. During the nineteenth century, jousting for political power was restricted to relatively small contending factions, a few caudillo "armies," a number of political parties, the urban middle class, and occasionally an enraged urban mob. The vast bulk of the people, mainly rural agriculturalists, generally ignored the whole affair and aspired only to be left alone as much as possible. The whole system depended upon the overall apathy of the masses, the traditional docility of the peasants, the rural isolation of the majority, and the small size of the cities.

During the course of the twentieth century, the Latin American masses came alive. This change took place not suddenly but gradually, and the process continues even to this day. The appearance of ever larger groups of contestants in the arena of Latin American power struggles has been the single most significant development in Latin American politics in this century.

The social forces working to bring about this dramatic transformation were global in scope. By the final quarter of the nineteenth century, the economies of the far-removed regions of the world were being woven together by Westen nation-states into a historically unprecedented, interdependent economic system. Latin America, with empty lands and natural resources to offer, was also being drawn into this tightening network of trade and communication. Immigrants entered the continent in vast numbers; foreign invesment increased in geometric leaps; economies grew, cities grew, and population, especially in the urban centers, exploded. The enormous social changes that overtook Latin America in the twentieth century produced multitudes of people anxious to join an ever-widening circle of politicized activists. The two interest groups that figured most prominently in this process were the urban middle class and urban labor. We will examine each in turn.

There are many Western observers of Latin American society who look upon the growth and political emergence of the Latin American middle classes with great favor. It is close to an article of faith among them that a large middle class is the necessary foundation for a prosperous and stable society. They view, therefore, the expansion of the Latin American middle class as a sign pointing to a bright horizon of economic progress and political maturity.

These observers, of course, place such high hopes on the Latin American middle class owing to the important economic contributions that middle-class people have made in their own countries. They fall into difficulty, however, when they assume that the notion "middle class" can be cleanly transferred from their own culture to Latin America. The reality is that the two superficially similar social groups commonly referred to as "middle class" in their respective societies are quite apart in their range of values, their capacity for productive endeavor, their extent of prosperity, and their state of political contentment.

One factor that has encouraged this misplaced hope on the middle classes of Latin America is that certain parallels do indeed exist between them and the middle classes of the economically advanced Western states. Among their numbers are some of the more productive members of society: technicians, engineers, businessmen, and managers. The greater part of the Latin American middle class, however, is made up of superfluous white-collar workers, most of whom are loaded onto the government bureaucracies.[53]

To understand the difference between the middle class in Latin America and the industrialized West, it is important to understand how middle-class status is determined in those two societies. Middle-class status in the West is based mainly on income and standard of living. In Latin America, however, it is based on a far more complex series of factors such as family, profession, education, and dress. A Latin American, in other words, could be almost penniless and still enjoy middle-class status provided he possessed some of the other factors that elevated status. Conversely, he could have a very good income and not be considered middle class if he earned that income from manual employment, which is associated with the lower class. As a result of this, people who aspire to a middle-class status identity have a powerful incentive to shun manual labor and to seek out white-collar employment. The difficulty is that there are not enough productive white-collar jobs to satisfy the enormous demand for "dignified" employment, so people apply heavy pressure on the government to provide nonproductive white-collar positions.

The stupendous wastefulness of bureaucratic employment has long been a problem in Latin America, as is well documented by succeeding generations of foreign visitors. The nineteenth-century traveler Henry Koster, for example, could hardly suppress his amazement when he wrote of the government bureaucracy in Brazil:

> The number of civil and military officers is enormous; inspectors innumerable, colonels without end, devoid of any object to inspect, without any regiment to command.[54]

Thomas Ewbank, who visited Brazil several decades later, expressed similar astonishment:

> The government is beset by applicants for every species of office by which a few hundred milreis can be got. Every department is full to overflowing. Broods of embryo diplomatists seek initiation in the various grades of *attachés*. Swarms solicit commissions in the army —in allusion to which, it is said the officers will in time outnumber the men. The Church is next besought for the means of genteelly soaring above the lower orders, but she has shaved more heads than she can shelter.[55]

A look at the kinds of jobs Latin Americans hold suggests the seriousness of the bureaucratic problem in contemporary Latin America. Statistical data reveal that the proportion of people employed in white-collar administrative functions in Latin America approaches, and in some countries equals, the proportion employed in the most advanced industrialized states.[56] This is striking because the pattern in developed countries has been for this kind of employment to increase apace with factory productivity, so that fewer workers produce more basic material goods as others are freed to provide less essential administrative services. Latin America, in other words, supports a percentage of administrative personnel considerably in excess of what the presently industrialized countries required at a similar level of development. Bring into this calculation the widely held view that much of the governmental administrative staffing in modernized countries is unproductive, then the Latin American economy appears heavily burdened by an extraordinary number of functionless functionaries.

People living in Latin America need neither a knowledge of history nor an awareness of the relevant statistics to acquire a strong sense of the advanced state of bureaucratic parasitism in that society. Virtually all foreign residents, merely through their own personal experiences, will swear that the affliction has gone beyond anything known in the industrialized states; and their opinion is readily shared by Latin Americans with some familiarity with Western countries. Not surprisingly, the outward signs of bureaucratic parasitism are most obvious within the government ministries. A simple walk through many of them, interrupted by a few random conversations, is enough to impart an impression of severe overcongestion of personnel and under utilization of labor. Huge areas of office space are filled with desks so closely packed together that it is, at times, a difficult task to maneuver through them. Still, there may not be enough desks for all, and many workers simply stand and chat amiably or meander about. Some of them will freely talk about the bureaucrats who do not even have to appear at work, those who are so well connected that they have no contacts with their ministries beyond the paychecks they receive through the mail. Another version of the no-show bureaucrat, one hears, is the fellow who walks into the office in the morning, places his hat on the rack, and returns to pick it up again in the afternoon. Other state employees do pass the day working—but at other jobs. A survey taken in Uruguay revealed that 8 percent of government employees there were working at second jobs during the same hours they were supposed to be working for the state.[57] Still other government toilers who do not care for outside employment can be seen in the bars and cafes surrounding the government buildings; and with little or no prompting, they will flash their employment credentials and boast about what they are getting away with.

Bureaucratic parasitism wastes to a shocking degree the two principal factors that increase production—labor and capital. We see in these underdeveloped lands a vast number of economic tasks that should be carried out in order to provide for basic human needs. At the same time we see countless hands avoiding productive labor and innumerable overstaffed bureaucracies consuming capital that could be devoted to productive investment.

These observations confirm that, again, it is not so much the scarcity of capital resources that keeps nations impoverished but how those resources are used. A scarcity of capital is admittedly a real problem Latin American countries have to overcome. But an abundant supply of capital is in itself not only insufficient to modernize an economy but is even likely to worsen the underlying social malaise that weakens productive capacity. History has demonstrated this time and time again when world demand for a certain raw material suddenly surges upward and the country producing it is soon awash with investable funds. It happened with guano in Peru, nitrates in Chile, rubber, diamonds, and gold in Brazil, and it is happening today with oil in Venezuela and Ecuador. The money pours in and inevitably excites ambition—the kind of ambition that is shaped by modernization-impeding values. More people than ever begin to raise their expectations and demand "honorable employment," that is to say, freedom from manual labor. The government, hearing these appeals from the people attempts to satisfy as many as possible by hiring large numbers of applicants at low salaries. And when the bonanza ends, which it always does, the strained productive capacity of the country has to carry an additional load of those who will not stoop to "vile employment."

This is hardly the breed of middle class that has made the industrialized nations stable and prosperous. The majority of those who make up the Latin American middle class do not comprise a solidly affluent sector of society because they contribute so little to production. Nor do they form the unshakable support of a stable government. They are, in fact, prone to bite the hand that feeds them because it doesn't feed them enough. A British sociologist remarks, "Penurious, embittered, and clamorous, the Latin American middle classes . . . do not contribute enough to production, but stake large claims to consumption, which they expect to be satisfied by some political slight of hand."[58]

And the government elites, why do they cave in to a clamor that is so obviously contrary to the best interests of the economy? The most obvious answer is that these elites are motivated by the crassest political opportunism. When high political figures are willing to bleed the nation with their own corruption, it is probable that they will not be too concerned with the social costs of placating the parasitic sector of the middle class when this will enhance their political positions. Aside from weak resistance at the top, there is also the strong pressure from below. The rank and file of the parasitic middle class are a sizable and strategically located group of demanders, and in an age of mass participation in politics even tough dictators must pay them heed. Politicians who depend upon votes to win office are even more vulnerable. Vote-seeking candidates to public positions need supporters to help them actively carry out their campaigns, and their supporters normally expect patronage jobs in return. It would be difficult to deny these partisan followers the anticipated rewards of their labor, for their voting muscle alone can be considerable. For example, in Colombia a political scientist worked with the relevant statistics to estimate the number of votes these intensely involved political activists could reasonably be expected to muster from themselves, family, and friends; and his calculations produced a figure one-third of the potential electorate and equal to the total number of actual voters![59]

The governing elites in Latin America have responded to middle-class demands with such a crazy patchwork of concessions that the policies would make sense only if the politicians were deliberately designing the system to self-destruct. The loudest noise the leaders hear is for more and more white-collar jobs; so by intentionally keeping the salaries low, they load onto government organizations the heaviest bureaucratic cargo possible. Often they have to create entirely new "auxiliary" departments beside the old in order to accommodate the spillover. Government officialdom keeps expanding as if propelled by some invisible law.

Rather than speed up the delivery of public services, the sheer numbers of superfluous nonworkers actually slow it down, which adds to the inefficiency of the proverbially lethargic Latin American bureaucracies. In order to give everyone something to do, routine tasks are splintered and parceled out to the crowds of employees. The results are especially blatant to Westerners residing in Latin America, who are often bewildered by the number of stamps they have to procure, the offices they have to visit, and the stairways they have to climb in order to take care of the simplest matters.

Another policy that lowers the efficiency of the bureaucracy while raising the public's level of frustration is the payment of niggardly salaries to government workers. This practice encourages, indeed almost obliges, an underground network of petty bureaucratic corruption that has become a pervasive and demoralizing aspect of Latin American life.

Legislation dealing with the retirement of public workers is still another feature of these state-employee systems that exacts a high social cost. A useful indicator of the responsibility (or opportunism) of governing elites is whether they have designed a pension program their respective economies can afford. The temptation for political leaders is, of course, to tranquilize demanding state bureaucrats with promises of generous pensions. This not only placates the workers for the moment but shifts the problem of living up to these commitments to future leaders. A review of the pension legislation in Latin America reveals that political elites in most countries have already been moved by a monumental though intemperate love of humanity. Or what is more likely, they have already discovered the political advantages of such a maneuver and consequently have written extremely liberal retirement plans into the lawbooks. In Argentina, state employees can retire with full pension at 50 years of age, in Chile even younger. The most damaging case of abundant magnanimity is found in Uruguay, where members of the military who have put in 15 years of service can retire as early as 32. Uruguayan women with children can claim a partial pension with only ten years of service. The legislation in Uruguay has had its predictable effects: in 1972, to cite one example, 350,000 pensioners had to be supported by a working population of less than a million.[60]

There is no advanced, highly productive society in the world that can afford such plans; and it is, of course, utterly senseless that underdeveloped countries should have them. When political elites shrink before the clamor of middle-class public employees, they grant themselves temporary relief. But certainly in the long run their policies induce greater instability into the political system. More non-producers rush in to fill the places of those who are granted early pensions. A few of the retired may find useful employment that is not beneath their dignity; but most have nothing to do but sit in their cafes with other idle men, lean over their coffees and cinzanos, and grumble about the damned politicians.

If the middle class is the hope of some observers concerned with the future of Latin America, those who work with their hands and who for convenience are often called labor, are the hope of others. Like the middle class, labor also has enlarged its size and influence in recent decades and inflicted its measure of social parasitism upon Latin American societies. To raise this issue may also raise the eyebrows of more than a few readers; for the popular image of the laboring masses in Latin America is that they are regularly trampled and spat upon and therefore seem hardly in a position to wrest more than their just share of economic rewards from the society at large. It is not labor in general, however, that is socially parasitic; it is only a privileged segment of it, a segment that is commonly referred to as an "aristocracy of labor."

An inquiry into this labor aristocracy is best initiated by stressing the basic problem that laboring people have always had in Latin

America, namely, that overall the standard of living of the laboring masses has been low and that this has been the result of too little production rather than too much exploitation. A comparison with the economic conditions of American workers whose real earnings during the nineteenth century were the highest in the world, illuminates this point. In the United States, the initiators of economic activities were far more numerous than their counterparts in Latin America; and the very extensiveness of their economic activities created a demand for labor, rendered it relatively scarce, and drove up its price. In contrast, Latin American developers and owners of economic enterprises were relatively few in number, found labor relatively overabundant, and therefore did not have to compete with one another for workers by raising wages. Unassisted by natural market conditions, the workers in Latin America could hope to increase their purchasing power only by unionizing and reducing the vast inequality of incomes between themselves and the wealthy elite that owned the income-producing property. Latin American governments at the time, however, almost reflexively sided with employers over employees on the issue of redistributive justice. But even if the workers had succeeded in their unionization struggles, enlarging their share of a very limited productive output would have improved their lot only marginally.

An aristocracy of favored worker unions began to emerge from the laboring ranks during the early decades of the twentieth century. The Latin American labor movement contributed significantly to the increasing trend toward participation of mass interest groups in national politics. The process was given considerable impetus by certain ambitious political leaders like Vargas of Brazil and Perón of Argentina. These leaders recognized the great potential of strategically located labor unions and championed the workers' cause in order to strengthen their hands as they played political poker. For example Vargas during the first ten years of his administration, from 1931 to 1941, signed into law over 160 pieces of legislation which directly and significantly benefited labor.[61] Over the years labor unions have also learned to appreciate what flexing their muscles can accomplish. They have been greatly helped by the instability of Latin American politics and the tenuous grasp that many political leaders have on power. Often heads of state, anxious to maintain themselves in office for as long as possible, have found it expedient to accede to the demands (no matter how unreasonable) of labor interest groups rather than risk strikes and violence on the streets. This has been especially true of civilian chief executives who were constantly menaced by the threat of a military coup should they appear unable to control surging mobs of protesting workers. It has been pointed out that under these circumstances, union strikes and violence are best understood, not as the last desperate recourse of a frustrated proletariat, but as a specific institutionalized tactic aimed not at factory owners but at government leaders possessing the authority to force management to come to a settlement.[62]

As a consequence of union pressure upon political elites, most Latin American countries have become (on paper) among the most advanced social welfare states in the world. Politicians have written into heavy lawbooks a veritable blizzard of benefits such as minimum wages, maximum hours, automatic salary increases, profit-sharing plans, vacations, paid sick leaves, overtime compensation, religious and national holidays, savings funds, housing allowances, medical services for workers and their families, scholarships, accident insurance, severance pay, retirement pay, and death payments. It is said in Latin America that prounion legislation should not be weighed by the kilo but by the ton.[63]

The most obvious comment about the politicians of poor countries who grandiloquently pledge the social benefits of rich countries is that they cannot deliver what they promise. If, for example, Cuban primary school teachers had received what was guaranteed them under the 1940 constitution (a monthly minimum wage equal to one-millionth part of the national budget), they would have been the best-paid primary school teachers in the world.[64] By and large, the only workers able to receive promised benefits and ample salaries are those who belong to labor organizations powerful enough to force government leaders to grant them what they want. The result of this is that in Latin America certain organized groups of proletarians are far better provided for than the rest of the working class. Chilean copper miners, for example, earn three and a half times the averge worker's salary;[65] Venezuelan oil workers, who make up less than 3 percent of the labor force, take home nearly half the total wages paid in the country;[66] Mexican petroleum workers value their employment so much that their jobs have become virtually hereditary sinecures passed on from father to son.[67]

The main problem with the favored members of the labor aristocracy in Latin America is not so much their higher incomes and greater privileges (which may be expected if they work in captial-intensive enterprises) as the destructive way they wield their power. Their power lies in their strategic location, almost always in the cities and often in the vital extractive industries. And unless their power is curbed by superior power, they are usually ready to use it regardless of the harm they inflict upon the larger society. Although privileged and sometimes pampered in their salaries and perquisites, they are the first to desert their jobs, which are so crucial to the health of the nation, and parade in the streets with more demands. Furthermore, even as they make ever larger claims upon consumption, they commonly insist on an array of rights that lead to less production. Prominant among these union "rights" are "featherbedding" schemes, immunity from dismissal (*inamovilidad*), and veto power over technological change—rights which have the effect of diminishing work discipline and discouraging attempts to raise productivity. Comparable union practices are, of course, found in industrialized countries; but if harmful there, they are utterly devastating to underdeveloped societies, which are economically weak social organisms that can sustain less parasitism.

Just how far labor unions are willing to carry their fight for socially irresponsible advantage and just how cynical and opportunistic political authorities can be in allowing them to do so is illustrated by the case of urban labor in prerevolutionary Cuba. In 1951 the International Bank for Reconstruction and Development (IBRD) published an exhaustive study of the labor situation in Cuba. It is well worth discussing this report in some detail because only through such specifics can the reader unfamiliar with Latin American conditions fully appreciate the parasitic and exploitative potential of a powerful labor aristocracy.

A good beginning would be to examine the pay and productivity of the unionized Cuban dockworkers. The Cuban dockworkers made up only 1 or 2 percent of the total working population, but they were in an excellent position to strangle the Cuban economy because the country had to import so many of its vital commodities. In prerevolutionary Cuba, the longshoremen's union insisted on the right to set workers' rates; and because the union monopolists were backed up by the government, employers were forced to comply. In wielding this authority, the unions showed little restraint. For example, the dockworkers in this underdeveloped country received 40 to 50 dollars per eight-hour day for handling sugar, 64 dollars per day for loading cordage. For unloading butter and sausage they earned 74 dollars per day, for guava jelly 111 dollars, for matches 135 dollars. These wages, it should be kept in mind, were in 1950 purchasing power and doubled when union members worked overtime and holidays.[68] Since the per capita income of Cubans at that time was about 500 dollars a year,[69] the gulf between the earnings of ordinary Cuban workers and those of the labor aristocrats was immense indeed.

The remarkably high salaries of the Cuban longshoremen could only have been justified by large advances in productivity. Yet during the period when the longshoremen's wages and benefits were soaring, productivity not only did not increase but declined, and not only declined but declined precipitously. Shipping companies estimated that between 1940 and 1950, overall efficiency dropped by 50 percent. Where in the late 1930s a gang of stevedores could unload and reload 2,000 to 3,000 pounds of cargo in 19 hours, by 1950 the same job required several regular working days plus a large number of overtime hours at double wages. Caught between the pressures of higher wages and higher inefficiency, dock prices were squeezed upward. To place an automobile aboard a vessel in Havana cost $18.47 on regular time or $36.95 on overtime. The same job in Miami cast $2.00 with no extra charge for overtime. To load phosphate rock on a ship in the United States cost $0.35 a ton, to unload it in Cuba cost $2.82 per ton. So onerous were the charges levied by the unions that importers were sometimes forced to abandon their shipment on the docks, for by the time the union members had finished handling their merchandise, the owners could no longer afford to claim it.[70]

The sorry spectacle of productivity falling victim to shortsighted group self-interest was a familiar occurrence not only within the longshoremen's union but within urban unions throughout prerevolutionary Cuba. The union practices that did the most to cripple efficiency were deliberate overstaffing, resistance to technological change, and refusal to allow management to dismiss parasitic workers.* Unions were able to implement these practices only because government stood by their side in contempt of the larger interests of the nation. An appreciation of the self-centered recklessness with which organized labor wielded its power can best be acquired by reading lengthy passages from the IBRD study:

> Cuban industrial development has been greatly retarded by labor's resistance to new machinery, modern methods, or virtually anything that will increase the efficiency of production. There is hardly an industry in Cuba that has not been affected by this, and to some it has been positively disastrous.
>
> Cuban cigar makers have successfully opposed the introduction of machinery which would replace the laborious hand rolling. As a result, with rising wages, the costs of production have increased to the point where the once famous Cuban cigars have virtually disappeared from many of their old export markets. Some important textile mills have actually been forced out of business, and others have been saved only through government intervention. Some sugar mills are unable to take full advantage of new mechanical developments for loading, unloading, and handling sugar-bags. . . .
>
> When improved methods or machinery are introduced into a factory with permission of the workers, it is generally under the stipulation that the same number of workers be employed as were used under the older, inefficient method. The workers also commonly

---

*In the Cuba of this time, a Roman Catholic culture where divorce was almost unheard of, there was a saying that it was easier to divorce a wife than to fire a worker.

see to it that the new equipment turns out no more products than the old.

As an illustration, a Cuban tire factory possessed several tire-building machines, one of which is of a new design and allows the operator to turn out twice as many tires as the older machines without the expenditure of any more time or effort on the part of the worker. In practice, however, it is found that the new machine is making exactly the same number of tires as the older ones do.

Other examples are numerous. Candy-wrapping machines in Habana are operating at the lowest possible speed. In one cordage mill equipment turns out 60% of its rated capacity of output. A large soap company bought a mechanical feeder designed to serve two machines at once, then was forced to install one such feeder on each separate machine instead so that two attendants would be required.

Cuban noodles are sold in little twists that are coiled by hand. One manufacturer bought a modern unit which not only made the noodles but delivered them already twisted. His workers protested, and the machine was repeatedly sabotaged until he agreed to operate it with the twisting mechanism removed. . . .

Where a new machine is to be introduced, workers are not satisfied with the mere retention of employees who might otherwise be displaced, and their transfer to other useful work in the factory. They have generally insisted that the displaced workers be retained in the same department, even if there is nothing for them to do there but to watch the machine and draw their pay. If there is other work that they might do, the *sindicatos* have required that the employer hire additional laborers for it. . . .

One railroad estimates that 40% of its payroll is for work not performed. Before the Government came to the assistance of a textile mill to prevent it closing its plant, it had nearly a thousand extra employees. . . .

It has been judged that gentry cranes at Matanzas and Habana do work which would otherwise require four winch operators; therefore in each case four men are paid, although only one operates the crane. This sort of thing, together with the difficulty of discharging a worker for any reason, has brought about the "featherbedding" of a great number of workers throughout Cuban industry. . . .

Most employers and independent observers believe that much of labor's entire attitude is based on its virtual immunity from discharge. . . . From an examination of the law itself, it would appear that an employer has ample recourse to dismissal in cases of unsatisfactory workers. . . . In practice, however, employers maintain that the situation is quite different. . . . One employer stated that he had made 60 appearances before the labor courts without a single favorable decision.

In a period of six years, another company was said to have filed 200 applications for permission to discharge workers for cause and did not succeed once.

It is difficult to describe the extent of this alleged one-sided interpretation of the law and its practical effect on business without the use of concrete examples. A few actual cases, reliably reported to the Mission as by no means unusual, will illustrate a situation which may tax the credulity of the reader:

Case 1: Several workers in Company B entered the factory at night and committed acts of vandalism and sabotage on the production machinery. They were caught, tried, convicted and sentenced to a penal institution. At the same time, of course, they were discharged by their employer and the discharge was upheld by the labor court.

Two years later, these workers—now freed—appealed the decision of the labor court and won. The employer was forced to reinstate the men in their original jobs and to pay them full wages for the elapsed time, including the time spent in prison.

Case 2: A worker in Company C developed a reputation for defiance and "soldiering," and was warned repeatedly. One day he was found sleeping on the job. Numerous witnesses were available, and to provide incontrovertible evidence, photographs were made.

The usual discharge proceedings were instigated. The worker did not deny his identity in the photographs. The labor court ruled, however, that while the evidence showed the man to have been reclining, it did not prove beyond all possible doubt that he had been asleep. Therefore, since it was considered that the full charge against him had not been proved, the case was dismissed and the employer was ordered to retain the worker.

Case 3: A maker of textile fabrics discovered that a certain employee had been systematically stealing quantities of cloth for several months. Knowing the difficulties of discharging a worker, the employer set up a rather elaborate watch on the man in order to catch him in the act and to secure the required evidence.

It was found that his method was to take the cloth to the washroom, wrap it around his body under his clothing, and walk out of the plant gate with it at closing time.

When the thief's pattern of operations and timing had been fully established by repeated secret observations, the stage was set to trap him. On a day when he was known to be carrying stolen cloth, he was met at the plant gate by a delegation of police, labor and management representatives, photographers and other witnesses. He was searched and his loot removed in front of cameras to insure his conviction for theft, which would be necessary in order to discharge him legally.

He pleaded guilty, claiming that it was his first offense, and there seemed to be little doubt of the outcome. But the court, taking into account the fact that his conviction would give the employer grounds for his discharge, ignored his admission of guilt and dismissed the case.

Case 4: The law requires that the employer must begin discharge proceedings by notifying the employee of his dismissal in writing. The courts have required that the employer present this notification, countersigned by the employee, as evidence that the employer has complied with the regulations.

Factory Manager E, who claims that his case is not unusual, tried to follow this procedure but found the worker unwilling to acknowledge receipt of the notification. After 15 days of such attempts the nonplussed manager consulted the labor office for assistance. But there he was told that they could not consider his request for help because he had not yet shown that he had notified the employee properly. The employee is still on the payroll.[71]

Working-class and middle-class parasitism have been emphasized here because the role of union rank-and-filers and low-level government officials in fostering social parasitism is usually overlooked. Part of the reason for this inattention is that whenever the members of these interest groups come together in large numbers to lodge their protests, they easily appear as the masses; and most observers are used to thinking in terms of the Latin American masses as the exploited, not the exploiters.

To bring this out does nothing to change the fact that the more traditional targets of social critics—small, wealthy, elite groups—are also highly vulnerable to charges of social parasitism. Agricultural landlords (*latifundistas*), for example, have long been notorious for wallowing in luxury in the capital cities of Latin America and Europe and making no contribution at all to the production of their estates. Likewise, major businessmen have often been rightly criticized for pressing their governments for sky-high tariff barriers that have allowed them to foist monopolistic prices upon captive consumers. Businessmen have also used these tariffs to eliminate foreign competitors who would have put pressure on them to increase productive efficiency.[72]

The rise of mass interest groups in Latin America has had much to do with the extraordinary inflations that have ravaged that continent. Inflation is, broadly speaking, the result of too much paper money in relation to the available supply of goods and services. The first way these groups have encouraged inflation is by adopting parasitic practices that have diverted labor and capital away from productive uses. This has reduced the potential supply of goods and services and effectively diminished the purchasing power of the currency.

Far more important, however, has been the pressure these interest groups have put on the government to expand the money supply. Inflation was never a serious problem in Latin America until the twentieth century, when interest groups representing large numbers of people began to participate in the political system and make demands upon it. Latin American governments, contrary to their widespread image, were often very sensitive to these pressures and attempted to mute the cries of the politicized sectors of the masses by providing more jobs, services, and privileges. The problem was that the political elites possessed very little control over these mass interest groups and were not able to inject discipline into their ranks and spur them on to greater productive efforts. Increased production, of course, could have generated increased tax revenues to pay for the increased government payrolls and social services. As it was, political leaders regularly spent more than they brought in and made up the deficit by the simple expedient of printing more money.[73] Inflation was the inevitable consequence.

Uruguay, which has had one of the more inflation-prone economies in Latin America, offers an example of how far these events could develop. By 1960 the government there was providing employment, mostly parasitic employment, to over one-third the labor force. Forty-eight percent of Uruguayan state employees worked a "government week" of 29 hours or less, while an additional 20 percent managed a 36-hour week. All state workers enjoyed the privilege of virtually ironclad job security as well as the right to retire at 55, 50, or even earlier. Discipline, diligence, and productivity were absent from this system. In 1972, 19 out of 22 government corporations were losing money despite the high prices they were charging. The state-run Uruguayan airline had the distinction of being the most inefficient in the world when judged on an employee-per-airline basis. (Between 1958 and 1966 the number of operational aircraft fell from nine to six, yet the number of workers on the payroll rose from 700 to 1,000.) Obviously, with so many consumers making increasing demands upon very limited production, inflation was a serious problem in Uruguayan life. In the 15 years between 1955 and 1970, the country underwent an inflation of *9,000 percent*. The Uruguayan inflation was a harrowing experience and was a major factor in the end of democratic government in that country.[74]

Perhaps the most grievous case to date of inflation brought on mainly by demagogic populism, took place in Argentina after the triumphant return to power in 1973 of Juan Perón and his wife Isabelita. Perón's followers eagerly greeted the restoration of their leader with outstretched hands, palms up. Perón could only attempt to live up to his populist reputation as a Great Provider in one way—by running his money presses to the melting point. In two years, Perón's presses printed so many notes that they equaled the total nominal value of all bills issued in Argentina since the early nineteenth century. The results horrified Argentinean economists, who pointed out that it was cheaper to paper walls with the national currency than with wallpaper.

Wallpaper hangers agreed, claiming they could do their jobs less expensively with 100 peso notes than they could with their conventional covering.[75] By the time a highly predictable military coup ended the Perón administration, inflation was raging at an annual rate of 4,000 to 6,000 percent.[76]

Inflation and the social parasitism that feeds it are not only social evils but evils that point an accusing finger at Latin American governments and cast into doubt their capacity for economic leadership. We have previously seen that many students of modernization seek to place the major responsibility for economic leadership on government elites. But if such a modernization strategy is to be effective, these elites must be willing to conduct a drive against the social parasitism that is holding back development. The record shows, however, that the guardians of the common interest in Latin America have usually allowed, and even encouraged, the growth of parasitic self-interests. Again and again, the Latin American political system has yielded the same kind of political leaders, those who have been misguided into thinking that the parasitic privileges they extend are in the national interest; those who have been intimidated by the strength of the special interests; or those who have been motivated by the same base opportunism that has directed their pilfering fingers into the public till. The conclusion is, therefore, that before theoreticians of economic development can place too much hope in the ability of political elites to become the modernizing elites of Latin America, they must first face the issue—forthrightly and honestly—of the quality of those who lead.

THE REFORMERS

Most Latin Americans would have no trouble agreeing with the contention that the caliber of political leadership is a serious problem in their respective countries. Rarely do they demonstrate more earnest passion than when denouncing politics in general and politicians in particular. However, Latin Americans, particularly the politically minded among them, also commonly express the hope that a changing of the guard on the political front will usher in a bright new era on the economic front. To examine the widespread belief that the dilemma of unsatisfactory economic development can be solved by placing the "right" men in office, we shall next evaluate the prospects of successful modernization when the political elites are made up of the best men possible—leaders who are honest, sincere, and above all, determinedly bent on economic reform.

Leaders with these kinds of personal qualities can conceivably be either democratic rulers or dictators. It is necessary, then, to look at both types of modernizing elites and how they might be helped or hindered by the structure of the governments they head.

The special problems faced by democratic modernizing elites are readily apparent. The executive branch of any democracy can function effectively only if there exists a relatively high degree of voluntary cooperation between itself and the other sectors of government and society. When, as is the case in Latin America, democratic leaders are confronted by the single overwhelming national task of accelerated economic growth, the willingness of those under them to cooperate must be especially strong. But instead of the spirit of cooperation being more developed in Latin American culture, it is, like the economy, underdeveloped.

Latin Americans have always been a difficult people to rule—and this has been particularly true for modernizing leaders who have to share political authority and respect democratic rights. Opposition parties in the legislature, like those challenging Eduardo Frei of Chile and Fernando Belaúnde of Peru during the 1960s, have often used their power for extremely partisan ends, blocking or holding up reformist legislation or bleeding it to death with amendments. Political enemies have taken advantage of the traditional freedoms of press, speech, and assembly to revile their nation's leaders, to picture them as without a single redeeming virtue, and to bark at every movement they make. Large sectors of the uneducated masses, cynical of government in general and suspicious of any specific government programs, have frequently offered stubborn resistance to well-intentioned government initiatives.

Another difficulty encountered by democratic modernizing elites is that they commonly find themselves in a weak position to fight social parasitism. Even to arrive in power they need votes, and to get those votes they require energetic party activists who characteristically expect something in return—usually government employment—as a reward for their vital support (see pp. 75–76). And, as discussed earlier, democratic leaders often feel the hot breath of the military upon their shoulders. Civilian politicians know full well that if a protesting interest group decides to express its discontent with violence on the streets, the army may feel obliged to dispose of it in the name of restoring order (see pp. 78–79).

Even in those countries where democratic leaders feel somewhat protected by a military tradition of nonintervention in politics, the most dedicated reformers are still forced to tolerate another serious variety of parasitism not yet discussed—military parasitism. Along with latifundista (landlord) parasitism, this manner of wasting investment resources has probably received the most attention from commentators on Latin American development. And little wonder. Every year the military establishments of most Latin American countries relentlessly consume 20 to 30 percent of the national budgets.[77]

Despite the vast sums spent on arms, it is difficult to imagine what the armies, navies, and air forces in Latin America are supposed to be used for. The armies are too numerous to be needed in maintaining internal peace; yet they are too small to resist the invasion of a world power from outside the continent. The expensive and prestigious arms systems avidly sought by military leaders are of no use in quelling civilian strife; nor are they effective in competing with great powers. It seems there is little these Latin American militaries can do except fight among themselves. This has, however, happened only occasionally in the past and is such a remote possibility at present that it hardly justifies a massive drain on the national resources. Further reducing the prospect of intracontinental war is the fact that if one nation brazenly attacks another, the remaining countries of the Western hemisphere have committed themselves by the Rio Pact of 1947 to taking action against the aggressor. Participation in an armed response is not obligatory; but since the United States could stop this kind of invasion with little difficulty, and since it has a vital stake in stability south of the border, the possibility that it could be persuaded to abide by a majority decision to send troops to the battlefield must be seriously considered by any potential belligerent.

Latin American military establishments are, perhaps, even better known for their wastefulness than for their uselessness. It has been suggested that officers deliberately keep the size of the armies artificially large in order to create more highly paid positions for themselves.[78] Despite this tactic, however, the ratio of bemedaled officers to ordinary soldiers is still far out of proportion to what it is in other military organizations. In the early sixties, for example, the Argentinean defense establishment had less than one-fifteenth the fighting men than that of the United States, yet it supported as many generals.[79] The fringe benefits enjoyed by these officers also tax the nation dearly. Latin American officers reside in well-furnished accommodations, work in handsome offices, socialize in gilded clubs; and after they have served 15 or 20 years, they have the privilege of retiring at full pension. There are even instances where military officers have had their gambling debts paid off by the government.[80] In Latin America, no price is too high to pay to the defenders of the fatherland.

The detrimental effects of an overblown military establishment on economic development are so obvious they need little comment. A military with an appetite for soldiers gobbles up manpower that could be engaged in more productive endeavors. A military with a fondness for advanced weapons systems purchases the kind of machinery that cannot be put to productive use. And not only are supersonic jets unsuited for plowing farmlands, but for every one of these costly contraptions imported into the fatherland, thousands of tractors remain outside.

Some of the problems encountered by democratic modernizing elites suggest the advantages enjoyed by development-minded dictators.

In Latin America these dictators are usually military men who rise to power on the crest of a military coup. The main advantage of military dictators is their ability to impose a higher degree of social unity than is possible under their democratic counterparts. Their monopoly of political power allows them to frame reformist legislation without worrying whether their cherished plans will be killed or emasculated by recalcitrant parliamentarians. Their monopoly of brute power enables them to silence critics who, in their view, are hiding behind democratic liberties while propagandizing "lies" and opposing needed reforms. Their muscle also enables them to be more resistant than democratic civilians to the threats and shrill demands of parasitic interest groups.

The added leverage possessed by a dictatorial modernizing elite does not mean, however, that it does not have formidable obstacles to overcome. The first problem of a military dictator is that usually he is leader not of the military but only of a dominant faction within it. Military establishments in Latin America are rarely as united in thinking and sentiment as external appearances might suggest; rather they are split by diverse interests, philosophies, ambitions, and personal rivalries. For a general to win and retain the backing of the military in his claim to national leadership, he has to play games similar to those of despised democratic politicians, involving himself in deals, maneuvers, and compromises. One of the most serious compromises he usually has to make is to military parasitism. Although he may have more control over this than a democratic ruler has, a military leader must normally indulge to a considerable degree the wants of the officers below him for more perquisities, troops, and wasteful arms expenditures.

A good way to illustrate this point is to look at the record of Juan Velasco Alvarado, a Peruvian general who ruled his country between 1968 and 1975 after grabbing power through a military coup. Velasco succeeded in capturing the attention of the world media by claiming to be a "revolutionary" military leader and by backing up his inflammatory rhetoric with decisive attacks on what he regarded as the "privileged" sectors of society—foreign investors, domestic capitalists, landowners, and other elites unlovingly referred to as imperialists and oligarchs. But as revolutionary and reform-minded as Velasco liked to think of himself, he not only did nothing to curb the military parasitism of his country but substantially aggravated the problem. Velasco did this by greatly expanding the size of the Peruvian army even though it was already too large before he came to power. He then set out to make the army the best-equipped striking force in the Andean region by purchasing from various countries around the world a fleet of helicopters, 200 tanks, 2 dozen jets, 3 destroyers, several submarines, 1 cruiser, and piles of artillery.[81]

There is no way of knowing whether General of the Revolution Velasco shared his fellow officers' enthusiasm for expensive weapons systems or merely indulged their weaknesses in order to purchase their loyalty. What is certain is that not even a leader from the ranks of the military can make too much progress against the parasitism of his brethren-in-arms. The simple fact is that a military reformer's colleagues are in a position to throw the weight of foreign-made tanks against him should he try to divert a portion of the military budget into economically useful projects.

While a military dictator may not be able to do too much about the parasitism of the armed forces, once he has solidified their support, he has in his grasp the power to curb the excesses of other parasitic groups. However, limits of brute power must also be recognized. A military strongman can make an enduring impression upon intractable interest groups by a determined show of cold steel; but if he miscalculates and causes too much blood to flow in the streets, the ghosts of the martyrs will rise from the gutters and urge the survivors on. Furthermore, brute power is useful only for pulverizing pressure groups and reducing their consumption demands; it is not effective in stirring people to maximize their productive efforts. For a modernizing dictator to make the greatest headway against social parasitism, he must master not only the technique of eliminating opposition but also the far more difficult art of conquering hearts and minds.

Aside from very real restrictions on their capacity to reduce social parasitism, the effective power of modernizing dictators is also limited by the difficulties they encounter in implementing reformist legislation. In theory, of course, a dictator's authority is very impressive because he does not have to worry about opposition parties and can pass into law just about any reform plan he desires. But after the dictator formally signs the new laws, what does he do with the legislation in his hand? He can pass decrees by himself but he cannot, by himself, put them into effect. For *implementation* he must send all orders to the state bureaucracies. We must now examine these government burearucracies and judge their fitness for carrying out the commands of a modernizing elite.

If a modernizing leader could select the quality he would most want for his organization of bureaucrats, he would probably choose efficiency—the ability to execute his orders with vigor and effectiveness. Organizations are most efficient when the workers within them are both competent and motivated, and therefore organizations are most likely to be efficient when they hire workers who have demonstrated high performance. One predicament organizations must deal with is that performance—specifically, the quantity and quality of output—is in many jobs very difficult to measure. Partly because government employees commonly perform the kind of work where incompetents are difficult to identify and weed out, and partly because of other reasons, government institutions around the world have acquired a deserved reputation for being among the least efficient of large bureaucratic organizations. In Latin America this universal human problem is severely aggravated by the fact that merit as judged by performance is not even the starting point for the hiring of state employees. Instead, the chief standards in Latin American bureaucracies are political loyalty and personal connections.[82]

Inside the government bureaucracies the standards for determining promotion are basically the same as those that govern the selection of employees. A system such as this discourages workers from channeling their energies into performing their jobs well. Instead, it rewards those who best master the art of bureaucratic infighting such as assessing the power of factions and choosing the right side, cultivating allies and superiors with flattery, and stinging enemies with indirect criticism or outright slander. Well-suited to the natural tendencies of hierarchical values, this kind of bureaucratic system encourages employees to busy themselves with hatching intrigues and counterintrigues, conceiving powerplays, and nursing grievances. Somewhere in the midst of these Byzantine manueverings, the simple straightforward idea of doing a good job is lost.

The problem of inefficiency in state bureaucracies is rendered even more serious by the fact that few outside pressures exist to force these organizations to switch their focus to merit and performance. Business bureaucracies, we have seen, suffer from some of the same ailments as their government counterparts (see pp. 60–62). However, in many cases businesses, especially those which compete in overseas markets, have to hire genuine talent, or at least train family favorites to do their job well, just to be able to compete in the marketplace. Nothing comparable to market discipline troubles state bureaucracies. Government is not only a monopoly but it is a monopoly that can legally oblige its consumers (that is, the taxpayers) to buy the "services" it provides. As a result of this difference in external constraints, it is possible to find within the same culture a business bureaucracy staffed by highly motivated people alongside a government bureaucracy that functions as a storehouse for deadwood.

Owing, then, to a number of converging causes—the monopolistic nature of state services, the difficulty of measuring performance in many public jobs, the influence of Latin American hierarchical values, the political power of state employees, and the weakness and opportunism of political elites—government bureaucracies in Latin America are case studies in human organizational inefficiency.

Since inefficiency is a universally familiar phenomenon and the term itself is very relative, a feeling for the sheer magnitude of this problem in Latin American state bureaucracies is not easy to convey.

Perhaps the best method would be to follow the painful progress of an American professor as he attempted to perform a seemingly simple task—retrieve a package from a Chilean post office. It is important to keep in mind that the following report does not caricature a Latin American bureaucracy but accurately describes one, and that the incident itself, as the professor takes care to explain,[83] is by no means unusual:

> November 28, 1956, postman brings notice that parcel being held in post office customs. Plastic airplane costing $2.69 involved. On December 3, recipient of notice goes to post office, battles crowd, fills out form, is told to come back on December 27. Protestations based on fact that Christmas normally comes on 25th useless. December 27, at 3:00 p.m., when post office supposed to open for afternoon session, supplicant appears. Necessary clerk strolls in from lunch at 3:37. Half hour later clerk grumpily releases information that papers not where they should be, but upstairs. Up to third floor to clerk No. 2. Not there. Downstairs. Again to clerk No. 1, snarled reply. Back upstairs to clerk No. 3. Latter pleads ignorance, says clerk No. 1 wrong. Downstairs to manager No. 1, who scolds clerk No. 1, who finds documents. Upstairs again to pay .25 fee, then downstairs again to pay duties of $6.00. Then waits until package is disgorged from storage room. Three-quarters of an hour later, no package, no visible interest among clerks in finding it, palms sweaty, heart pounding. Back to manager No. 1, who invites torturee into storage room to find package, now officially proclaimed lost. Joins troop of six persons looking, finds package, in correct bin, wearing correct number, in exposed position. Leaves 5:45 P.M., exacts vengeance on Chilean drivers all the way home.[84]

As much as foreigners undergoing such treatment deserve a fair measure of sympathy, it is the Latin Americans who have to bear the real brunt of government bureaucratic inefficiency. For example, an Argentinean who wishes to do nothing more than register a used car has to handle a mound of paperwork over an inch thick and endure an arduous bureaucratic process that costs him literally hundreds of working hours.[85] And there are times when the costs of inefficiency run even higher. In Jamaica a sick man once requested a state-run hospital to have a blood sample taken and analyzed. The staff lost the sample. On three more occasions the man gave blood and on three more occasions the staff lost the sample. The Jamaican finally gave up—resigned to suffer his illness without assistance.[86]

Further weakening the efficiency of Latin American government bureaucracies is another infirmity at least as serious as incompetence and indifference—bureaucratic corruption. Corruption is an affliction that takes its toll in virtually any kind of society. What distinguishes corruption in Latin America is its pervasiveness and intensity. The problem, of course, is not uniform throughout the continent: the extent and severity of corruption varies according to the country, the period, the institution, and the individual under discussion. The Chilean police corps, for example, is remarkable in that it is not regarded by the local citizenry as a gang of uniformed bandits; yet Chilean customs offices are overcrowded with thieving rascals. And no matter how mired in corruption a particualr bureaucratic agency may be, there are always those stubbornly principled persons who refuse to drop their buckets into somebody else's well. Generally speaking, however, corruption is a way of life in all levels of Latin American government bureaucracy and is practiced by most of those who are able to manuever themselves into positions of leverage.

Corruption is of great concern to modernizing elites for a number of reasons. First of all, it is another form of social parasitism: it channels money into the wrong hands, that is to say, unproductive hands. It also frustrates the efforts of economic leaders, either government or private, who are genuinely attempting to organize productive enterprises. Those faceless, venal government bureaucrats will deliberately hold a businessman's paperwork, misfile his forms, or send him halfway across town to the wrong office until he gets the idea that he has to bribe to secure his legitimate wants. Goods he has shipped, mailed, or imported might either be stolen or "misplaced"—like the 18,000-dollar, 2,000-pound Chyrsler water purifier that was "lost" as soon as it entered the customs building in the Lima docks.[87] Such trifles have a way of remaining permanently "lost" or resurfacing badly damaged unless suitable renumeration is forthcoming. And the victim cannot simply wave his money in the air, ask how much, and get the dirty business over with. He has to waste a great deal of time laboring over complicated negotiations filled with hints, innuendos, and verbal circumlocutions without the unsavory subject of bribery ever being directly mentioned. A whole service profession has grown up around the practice of corruption—shadowy figures who have special knowledge of the middle ground between briber and bribed and, for a high fee, can greatly facilitate communications.

Bureaucratic corruption, like other causes of organizational inefficiency, is constantly vexing to the dedicated modernizing leader because it makes him feel like a captain at the helm of a rudderless ship. The broad grey bureaucratic mass below him simply doesn't respond to his direction. He may have a heart swollen with good intentions and a desk full of reformist decrees, but he just can't find the people to put them into effect.

American readers may have some sense of what it is like to depend upon corrupt state bureaucracies through their long involvement with a dissolute government in Vietnam. When Americans began to pour into Vietnam to bolster that government's anticommunist war, the number of Vietnamese millionaires with Swiss bank accounts seemed to grow proportionally. Consumer goods from the United States, bound for military commissaries, mysteriously wound up for sale on the streets. There were even horror stories of American arms and ammunition being peddled to the Viet Cong. Everything, huge amounts of money, equipment, arms and supplies, was given to that government; yet it never acquired the strength to succeed in its most elementary objective—survival.

Although attracting far less press coverage, this sort of abuse of American foreign aid has been going on for years in Latin American countries. Perhaps the most heartbreaking incidents of foreign aid corruption take place in disaster relief programs. Periodically a natural calamity like an earthquake or a flood will strike some Latin American country, and oftentimes foreign countries will rush in transports laden with relief supplies. Despite the fact that tampering with this aid amounts to mass starvation and misery, much of it regularly disappears on arrival at the stricken country. In the aftermath of an earthquake in Chile, the United States sent 120 million dollars to help rehouse the dislocated. A year and a half later, only 3,000 out of 40,000 homeless had seen any benefits from the massive infusion of funds.[88] Similarly, five years after a terrible earthquake had destroyed the Peruvian town of Yungay and 100 million dollars had been sent to assist the reconstruction, the beginnings of a new town had hardly begun.[89] Where did the money go? One reporter covering a natural disaster in Honduras caught a glimpse of an answer: in broad view he witnessed Honduran soldiers driving Red Cross workers away from planes loaded with relief supplies so that they could run off with the goods themselves.[90]

The problems experienced by American foreign aid officials are minor compared to those of Latin American political leaders. These leaders find that the corrupt bureaucrats under them can diminish or even neutralize the effectiveness of the programs they are trying to implement. For example, in Panama an attempt to raise the inheritance tax on the rich was thwarted by low-level government appraisers who eagerly took bribes in exchange for low appraisals on estates.[91] In Mexico a government fund to provide cheap credit for small farmers was quickly depleted by the lootings of strategically placed officials.[92] In a number of countries subsidized housing built for the poor has provided housing for the well-to-do instead because families with money were able to bribe their way in.[93] Still another interesting case took place in Peru when the political leadership attempted to meet a critical rice shortage by importing huge quantities of the grain to sell to the poor at below-market rates. Somewhere along the distribution process 220,000 sacks simply "disappeared." The "hiding" place was discovered sometime later—a government warehouse. Virtually everyone involved in the handling of the rice had conspired to keep it off the market, drive up the price, and then sell it at inflated value.[94] What can a modernizing leader do when his entire bureaucratic staff, from the petty to the powerful, are involved in such a fraud?

Lower-level bureaucrats can also frustrate the intentions of modernization elites by abusing their power and exploiting the very people they are supposed to be serving. The abuse of bureaucratic power is, of course, common in every society, but such behavior is especially likely to occur among government bureaucrats who are motivated by hierarchical prestige concerns; for the hierarchical prestige system inclines those holding power to raise their status or demonstrate their position of superiority by exerting their power over others (see p. 31). The Mexican psychologist Francisco Gonzalez Pineda has shed some light on the emotional life of the petty bureaucratic tyrant in his country by singling out a "public servant" representative of many others and by following him through a typical working day:

> In the office he [a government inspector] treats his superior with feigned respect although he considers him ill-natured, demanding, inept and dishonest . . . although he hates him and whispers behind his back; but as it is not to his advantage that his superior realize this, he behaves in an obliging, even servile manner. . . .
>
> It is when he arrives at the inspection site that he encounters his daily moment of glory. . . . Because now the Mexican inspector feels sure of himself, important, powerful. Within himself he feels the same emotions as he does when playing dice, only in the game he is now going to play he will be a sure winner and his thrill consists of not yet knowing *how much.*
>
> Yes, this inspector is important, very important, because a thousand times he has proven to himself that when people see him arrive, they begin to act fearful and servile, or they try to flatter him, or they fall into an exasperated emotional state that resembles the impotence felt by a child. He knows that there is no such thing as a person to be inspected who is innocent; they are all guilty. Thus he feels justified in going through the ritual of fining them, then pardoning all or part of the fine in exchange for some "special arrangement."[95]

Gonzalez Pineda's description illuminates the dilemma faced by modernizing leaders: whom to entrust with authority within a society where dominant cultural prestige patterns encourage rather than inhibit bureaucratic abuse of authority. Again it must be emphasized that the severity of the problem varies considerably according to the geographic area, the bureaucratic sector, or the individual in question; so, not all Latin American government functionaries who wield power should be identified with the insecure exploiter pictured above.

Obviously, the problem is most pronounced in regions and situations where people are separated by deep cultural and racial chasms. For example, one is immediately alerted to the possible misuse of power when a mestizo bureaucrat has been given authority over an Indian citizen in a district where the *mestizo* has been brought up to regard the *indio bruto* (brute Indian) as the "beast closest to man" and the indio bruto has been taught to approach the mestizo with hat pressed closely to the chest, shoulders stooped, head bowed, and eyes cast humbly to the ground.

The critical importance of effective bureaucratic machinery to a state modernizing elite is suggested by the fact that there has been no historical example of a country depending heavily on the government for economic initiative that has successfully modernized its economy while burdened with a corrupt and inefficient bureaucracy. Even in countries such as England and France, where economic leaders were mainly private individuals, economic growth proceeded only up to a point before serious bureaucratic reform measures were instituted.[96]

Perhaps a more concrete way of making the same point would be to consider the results of a specific reform instituted some years ago by an elite group of modernization-minded planners working within the Colombian Ministry of Education. The reform strategy of these officials was well thought out and consisted of two basic elements. First, the traditional school textbooks were revised so that the new versions emphasized practical subjects useful to the economic development of Colombia. Secondly, the traditional teaching method of rote memorization was prohibited so that teachers were no longer allowed to instruct by having students mindlessly memorize and echo the "knowledge" dictated to them in class. From the Olympian heights of the Ministry of Education, the new texts and pedagogy were sent out to principals and schoolteachers all over the country. Let us now leave the capital city of Bogotá, follow one of those long, winding dusty mountain roads to the rural Colombian town of Aritama, enter the community schoolhouse, and observe, through the eyes of trained researchers, the impact of the mandated educational reforms:

> The modern government texts and the curriculum for rural schools in Colombia are well conceived and well adapted to their purposes, viz., that of imparting a basic education. The strongly emphasize practical matters such as agriculture, reforestation, health, and nutrition. They are well printed and carefully edited in language suited to each grade level. However, the rural teachers use these texts in a very limited way. . . . the teachers select from the official curriculum only those subjects that tend to affirm local values. Thus "citizenship" (cívica), "manners" (urbanidad), the care of dress and shoes, needlework, the making of paper flowers, or the

tying of ribbons are taught, while all tasks connected with agriculture, housekeeping, hygiene, are ignored.... the child is systematically taught the high prestige value of good clothes and of ceremonial behavior, and is made to abhor and to ridicule all manual labor and co-operative effort.... Teachers are very critical of the government program and consider certain subjects quite useless or even offensive. Such government initiatives as reforestation or the establishment of kitchen gardens through rural schools are ridiculed and openly attacked. The teachers say: "It seems that the government thinks we are a bunch of wild Indians, asking us to make our children plant trees and vegetables."

The daily subject matter depends very much on the whimsy of the individual teacher.... Hardly any teacher in Aritama uses the government textbooks, preferring to employ for teaching purposes a number of their own "copybooks." These copybooks have been handed down from one teacher to another, from friends and relatives, such as from aunts and nieces, and contain a more or less complete outline of subject matter arranged as questions and answers. The method of teaching consists of having the children copy, in the course of the year, all the questions and answers and making them memorize both. The teacher reads aloud a question and the children repeat it in unison at the top of their voices for ten, twenty, or fifty times. The answer is read and memorized in the same way, and then some time is spent copying these same questions and answers into individual notebooks, in exactly the same sequence and wording as is found in the teacher's copybook.... As these notebooks have been copied and recopied for years and years, many errors have slipped into the transcriptions, and the children are taught many quite meaningless or contradictory statements, e.g., "Every action which demonstrates religion is uncivil." (*todo acto que demuestre religión es inurbano*).... The following are excerpts from the notebook of one of the teachers. On citizenship (instrucción cívica) it says, for example: "Monarchy is a form of government which does not exist among civilized nations." A sample question in citizenship is "What has man been created for?" The answer: "To live in society." Under natural sciences there are the following problems. Question: "How does the rabbit reproduce itself?" Answer: "Directly." Question: "How does the bee sleep?" Answer: "Standing." Question: "What are the fins of a fish for?" Answer: "To descend, ascend, or maintain itself in a vertical position." There are many dozens of similar questions and answers on cows and pigs and sheep, taught day by day to the second-graders. During the same term Colombian history (*historia patria*) is taught. Sample questions are: "What kind of people inhabited America before Columbus?" Answer: "A people which had no knowledge of commodities." Question: "How did Bolívar die?" Answer: "Naked, as he was born." ...

The teachers themselves in their ignorance and lack of perception contribute to this confusion.... When lecturing on the economic geography of northern Colombia, the same teacher mentioned among the natural resources the existence of orchids (which are of no commercial value) but did not mention petroleum, coffee, or sugar cane. She also pointed out the importance of the pearl trade, although this was discontinued many years ago. When speaking of the economic importance of roads, she said that it was high time a motor road was built between two certain lowland towns, in spite of the fact that such a road has existed for the last twenty years and that she herself had often traveled on it. All this confusion arose only because she was using a copybook which had been written *before* the road had been built, *before* coffee became a major cash crop, and *before* the pearl trade had declined. . . .

To examine a child the teacher recites a question and adds the first two or three words of the answer, thereupon the child continues; a moment before the child finishes the answer, the teacher asks a new question followed by the first words of its answer, and so a monotonous stimulous response chant is set into operation. There is no need for the child to think, the only requirement being a certain ability at rote memory. If a question is phrased in an unaccustomed manner, the child is totally unable to answer; by the same token, should a child try to phrase an answer in original words, he would be reprimanded for doing so.[97]

This is hardly the description of an educational system that has undergone sweeping modernization reforms. Nowhere do we see the reforms issued in Bogotá working to improve education in this rural school. Nor do we feel the proverbial winds of revolution that were supposed to blow away the choking dust of archaic tradition.

The teachers were the obvious reason why the reforms did not work. The problem was that the teachers were brought up to believe in values that were very different from the modernization values implicit in the reforms. For them secondary education was not an opportunity to engage in productive employment but a means of escaping "vile employment." For them knowledge was not a utilitarian tool used to harness the forces of nature but a prestige ornament used to raise status within the local community. For them digging away at a garden plot in order to augment economic well-being was not a reasonable activity but a humiliating exercise; it was manual labor fit only for inferior beings of lesser status like "wild" Indians.

Little wonder, then, that the teachers did not embrace the new ideas sent down by the modernizing elite. And since the teachers were not willing to change, nothing could be done to make them do so. Their jobs were secured by political patronage or personal connections, not by how they taught their classes; and this system was too rooted in self-interests to be easily amended. And even if their employment depended upon their teaching methods, who would police the classrooms—more lower-level bureaucrats with the same upbringing and cultural values?

The failed educational reform in Colombia, illustrates the burden that inefficient bureaucracies place upon modernizing elites. Whether the power these elites wield is constitutionally curtailed or theoretically absolute, they are plagued by the same basic frustration—an inability to institute sufficient social changes. Dictators, of course, have certain advantages over their democratic counterparts. They, at least, can pass into law unadulterated reform legislation and possibly silence overt opposition to it. A good number of them, it seems, can make the trains run on time and sweep the beggars off the streets. But there is only so much a dictator can accomplish with the point of a bayonet, otherwise most of Latin America, indeed, most of the Third World, would be modernized. It is thus not too surprising that so many Latin American government leaders have arrived in office with the cry of reform on their lips only to fail miserably in their promises. To be sure, a large number have been simple opportunists and hypocrites. Yet others, devoted to superior moral standards, have no doubt discovered that once having won power, they did not have the power to carry through essential reforms. To a major extent their problem has been the sadly inadequate bureaucratic machines at their disposal. Because these truculent apparatuses have balked at responding to directions, those on top who operate the levers and buttons have been robbed of a good measure of their power and, consequently, of their ability to institute reforms.

A reformer bent on rapid development can confront a corrupt and debilitated bureaucracy in essentially only one way: he can replace it or at least replace key parts of it with reliable individuals who will support his policies. But how many trusted followers can the average political leader expect to find in this land where corruption is a way of life and where falta de confianza (lack of trust) is a constant preoccupation? He may, of course, tap personal sources—family members, amigos de confianza (trusted friends), a core of like-minded colonels or generals—but at the outside these will provide only enough solid backers to staff the top levels of government.

In order to make his bureaucratic organizations responsive to his direction, a modernizing leader needs battalions, not platoons—a vast army of assiduous, disciplined followers who are willing to carry out his plans and reforms as if they were their own. For example, a leader would require thousands of teachers and principals just to fill the educational bureaucracy with people who are sympathetic to his particular educationl objectives. Just how many faithful enthusiasts a modernizer needs to overhaul the bureaucratic machinery successfully will vary according to the population of the country; but generally it can be said that at the very least he requires enough willing supporters to staff the lower-level supervisory positions of the bureaucracy so that every worker will be within easy reach of a sturdy loyalist determined that the developmental reforms be carried out to the letter.

In the writings of Latin American reformers we can indeed see this very dream forming itself into words—a dream that visualizes the modernizing leader as a kind of general at the head of a whole army of steadfast soldiers who share with him common beliefs, hopes, passions, and ideals, and who, at his command, fan out across the country, mingle with the masses, and implement the enlightened reforms that aim for a brighter tomorrow.

THE CONGLOMERATION

Latin American modernizing leaders dream of vitalizing their bureaucracies, not simply because of the kinds of bureaucracies they head, but far more importantly, because of the nature of the societies they govern. Unlike the rulers of the countries that first underwent modernization, Latin American political leaders have never governed populations already well endowed with the values and cohesiveness necessary for modern economic deveopment. When Latin American reformers, therefore, aspire to turn their bureaucratic organizations into effective instruments of power, they view this not as an end in itself but as a means of transforming masses that, seen through their modernization perspective, are not the stuff of which viable nation-states are made.

It was perhaps Sun Yat-sen, the founder of modern China, who best expressed the deep grief of an ardent modernization leader in the Third World. The Chinese leader looked out over the human hordes he governed, despaired over their woeful lack of social discipline and in a rich, concise metaphor, described them as "loose sand." To know what it is like to rule over "loose sand," pick up a handful of the stuff. Watch as it dribbles through your fingers. It lacks cohesiveness. What you have in your grasp is a marvelous raw material—but you cannot do anything with it. Without substantial reprocessing, you cannot *build* with it. It was the torment of Sun Yat-sen that he held in his hand the millions upon millions of loose individuals that made up his country, yet heaped together, were nothing more than a formless jumble of self-interests. If he relaxed his grip in democratic fashion, he had even less control over them. If he tightened his grip, no matter how hard he squeezed he could not hold them together to form a disciplined nation-state—that is to say, a *people* capable of cooperating amongst themselves and of realizing great collective tasks.

Like the prerevolutionary Chinese, the Latin American peoples as they exist today are a raw material generally unsuitable for the designs of ambitious developmental elites. Through the modernization point of view, these masses are seriously deficient in the kinds of social mores and the degree of national consensus necessary to achieve an acceptable level of long-term economic development. Also through this point of view, these masses cannot properly be called communities of people at all. The term *conglomeration* describes them better. The Argentinean writer H. A. Murena captures the spirit of this in the following passage:

> There is no community in Argentina. We do not form a body, though we may form a conglomeration. We behave as if each one were unique and as if each one were alone with the unfortunate consequences which result when that is the situation. The hand functions independently of the head, the mouth independently of the stomach, and so forth. I am thinking of one of the most enduring realities of any community. In a real community there have to be groups that struggle for different goals; from that struggle comes movement, the life itself of a community. But these groups understand that they form part of a whole in order for the movement not to result in chaos or anarchy. . . . In place of this kind of community life, Argentina has rancorous, factious chaos, periodically illuminated by coups d' etat. Argentina is not an organism of which all feel themselves a part. Each organ believes itself the whole and functions as if it were more important than the whole. Is there any more succinct definition of sickness? Who is to blame? No one. Everyone.[98]

The people of a society inevitably appear as a chaotic conglomeration whenever they routinely conduct themselves as if the well-being of society has nothing to do with their own individual well-being. Another way of expressing this is that the masses appear as a conglomeration when, lacking acquired habits of civic virtue, they are not accustomed to cooperating well together. As discussed in a previous section (see pp. 47–51), the level of civic virtue in a society should be viewed less in terms of morality than in the structure of prestige patterns. The real core of the problem of public spirit in Latin American culture is that the dominant prestige patterns do not sufficiently regulate social behavior to enhance the common good; that is to say, social responsibility is not sufficiently rewarded with social esteem nor is conduct that harms the larger society sufficiently punished.

As a result of the prestige patterns prevailing within the conglomeration, individuals do not feel pressured by the expectations of their fellows to channel their energies into socially useful activities. Indeed, much of their energy is spent holding each other back. People engaged in productive enterprises find they are often discouraged by their peers from rising even if their work obviously contributes to the collective well-being and would easily earn social approval in modernized cultures. However, vivos, who manage to rise while wreaking social havoc, are widely admired on the basis of their success alone.

In a similar vein, groups of individuals organized to promote their own subnational interests do not feel restrained from pushing their demands too far by the threat of an outraged public. Rather, the public expects that by their very nature these interest groups will strive to gain advantage for themselves and to protect their members in a dangerous and hostile world by squeezing everything they can from everybody else. Restraint and moderation in the name of the public good are seen as weaknesses that will be exploited by tougher competitors. Even the government is assumed to be guided by the principle of unbridled self-interest, though it is the one institution of society formally set up to guard the common interest. When enough members of society organize themselves into powerful, broad-based interest groups, the tendency is for the masses to demand more than the economy produces. Inflation begins to be a serious problem that often wipes out the gains of the mass interest groups, which prompts them to complete the vicious circle with a whole new set of demands, threats, and violent demonstrations. The whole society seems swept up in a "rancorous, factious chaos." It appears as not a community of people but a conglomeration of contending individualities and interests.

Life within a conglomeration has its own special character, which is useful to touch upon in order to give the reader a sense of the frustrations of having to cope daily with this kind of social disorganization. One of the most notable experiences of living within a conglomeration is the need to constantly contend with the effects of ineffiency. The problem of inefficiency in Latin American society is widespread and chronic and is the fuel that fires much conversation, humor, and satire among natives and foreigners alike. It seems that when people are not angrily denouncing it, they are trying to relieve its effects through escapist displays of humor or envenomed displays of cutting wit. Western businessmen working in Latin America are in an especially good position to offer cross-national comparisons, and the conclusion at which they almost inevitably arrive is this: when they can get necessary tasks done at all in Latin America, they have to spend double, triple, quadruple, the time on them than they would on similar business back home.

A related but less obvious feature of a conglomeration is the particular outlook or attitude toward life that people are inclined to adopt as a result of the trials of living within a conglomeration: people think of life in general as unorderly, uncertain and unpredictable, and consequently fraught with potential peril. Human beings and human institutions are seen as too undependable to be trusted. People tend to feel there is little they can rely upon and, especially outside their own personal circle, few they can count upon. From the depths of their emotions they frequently encounter that sinking, helpless feeling that because large portions of their lives interlace with the undependable and uncertain society around them, there is much about their lives that is beyond their capacity to control.

Such attitudes are characteristic of people living within the conglomeration because the undependability of their fellow human beings and the uncertainty of events are experiences they must repeatedly endure. A few examples of simple, commonplace uncertainties suggest the depth and gravity of the problem. If a man orders a shirt dry cleaned, he may not be certain it won't come back stiff as cardboard. If he makes a business appointment for a specific time, he may not be certain when his opposite number will show up, or for that matter, whether he will show up at all. If he mails a letter or package, he may not be certain it will arrive at its destination. (Postal workers do not respect the sanctity of the mails; they open and pilfer packages and when bored, open and read letters.) If the man decides instead to communicate by telephone, he may not be certain of getting a line, or if he gets a line, of connecting with the right party. If he chooses to take a bus or train, he may be reasonably certain that the transport will arrive late, but he does not know by how much or when the transport does arrive, whether his reservations will be honored. Nor can this individual insulate himself from the uncertainties of the world outside by driving his own car. Huge chuckholes at the busiest intersections, which yawn menacingly for months before being repaired, may be strewn between him and his destination. Even more dangerous are the other drivers who travel at breakneck speeds, prefer horns to brakes, recklessly weave through traffic, and rarely carry insurance. (A good percentage don't even have legal license plates.) If his vehicle is hit by one of these speedsters, he may not be certain that the repair shop will not take out some of the well-functioning parts of his car and replace them with nearly worn out ones. Amid the disorderly, unruly life of the conglomeration, problems are apt to suddenly and unexpectedly spring up from almost anywhere. People living within a conglomeration, therefore, must bear up under uncertainty and emotional stress in a wide variety of situations—situations that if repeated in stable, well-managed communities would create little anxiety.

This latter observation leads us to the final feature of life within a conglomeration to be discussed here, one that is of particular interest to scholars and to propagandists alike—exploitation. Latin America is commonly regarded by people within and without its borders as a continent rife with exploitation. When the familiar ideological image is invoked—of oligarchies grinding the masses under their heels—what is normally suggested, implicitly or explicitly, is that wealthy elites exploit the impoverished masses by means of some form of economic parasitism. This view of exploitation in Latin America is not so much wrong as misleadingly narrow; and because it focuses only on a limited aspect of exploitation, it obscures rather than illuminates the larger problem.

To begin with, the interplay of social forces within the Latin American conglomeration is very complex, and there is no way the economic exploitation can be reduced to a simple model where one small group exploits and extracts all the unearned advantages from all other groups in society. We have seen that a diversity of socially parasitic groups exists in Latin America and that the larger groups can cause great damage to society. This, of course, is true even when the majority of their members, as with the case of the superfluous government bureaucrats, are poorly paid. When examining the problem of exploitation in Latin America, therefore, it must be understood that it is not just sectors of the wealthy classes but sectors of the poor that possess the power, and use the power, to exploit the poor.

The potential of the poor for exploiting the poor is even more clear when we examine the kind of suffering that weighs most heavily upon their lives. Exploitation is a concept that deals with the misery human beings inflict upon others for their own advantage or profit; and unfortunately, the miseries of the poor have too often been articulated in doctrinaire fashion by middle-class intellectuals and have too rarely been seen through the eyes, or felt through the senses, of those at the bottom of society. The most difficult burden the poor of a conglomeration have to carry throughout their days is the debilitating strain of overcharged emotions. The cultural and physical environment in which the poor live doesn't afford them enough relief from their fears, hates, insecurities, frustrations, anger, and envy. They feel they have to be constantly alert to the dangers they sense all around them, even when no dangers are actually there. They must unceasingly preoccupy themselves with what might go wrong, with worries about providing for tomorrow, with people who might take advantage of them, with people who might get ahead of them. The passions they experience are universally human, but they experience them erupting in their bellies and burning in their heads again and again just to get through an ordinary day. At the end of those days lived in suspicion, fear, and insecurity, they are drained, emotionally exhausted. And when their family relationships are torn asunder by macho behavior and their homelife becomes a part of the tension and struggles outside, they have even less chance of discovering the comfort of rest, repose, and renewed confidence.

The poor of a conglomeration are capable of exploiting the poor (in the sense of inflicting emotional grief) in ways the rich never can. This is because the poor are surrounded by the poor while the rich are distant beings with whom they have little contact. It is the people in the immediate radius of their own lives—their husbands, neighbors, friends, acquaintances, passers-by—who have the best opportunity to cause direct injury, provoke anxiety, arouse suspicion, and catalyze defensive passion. Envy, for example, is a terrible burden carried by many in deprived economic circumstances; and while they might envy the rich and the mighty in the class above them, they will never do so with the same intensity they might envy the small success of a neighbor next door. Rage is another powerful emotion that fequently fires their insides, yet their rage is far more likely to be set off by the fancied attempt of an acquaintance to "deprestige" them than by any action perpetrated by a remote social elite. The most useful way of trying to sense the human costs of this type of exploitation is to look at the victims, like those people cited earlier in this chapter to illustrate social interaction—the old and the weak who were knocked about when the bus queue broke into a stampede, the discouraged community inhabitants who could not convince their neighbors to work with them on common projects, the men at the local bar who distrustfully scrutinized each other for veiled verbal slights, the peasant who found his new calf slashed by some envious onlooker, the newlywed wife who was forced by her husband to sever all social contact with her friends. As always, it is by focusing on victims, not on ideology, that the observer of contemporary Latin America can best understand the kinds of happenings that bring about the greater part of the dehumanizing, gut-wrenching, emotionally enervating exploitation in that society.

The implications of this view of exploitation within a conglomeration are enormous for those in Latin America who plot and plan revolution in order to rid their society of the abuse of man by man. It means that when the revolution comes and socially parasitic elites are no longer there to exploit the masses, the battle against exploitation will have just begun.

4
THE NEGATIVE
NATIONAL IDENTITY

Even more important than social conditions themselves to a discussion of revolution in Latin America is the reaction of Latin Americans to those conditions. Latin Americans who react most vigorously against the conditions they see about them are usually quick to identify themselves as Latin American nationalists. It is necessary, then, to take up the question of Latin American nationalism. Who are these nationalists who protest so loudly and why does the spirit of nationalism burn within them?

A first requirement for being nationalistic is, of course, knowing that one belongs to a nation. This awareness of nationality cannot always be taken for granted. In the latter part of the nineteenth century, Peruvian mountain Indians heard rumors of a great war between Peru and Chile (War of the Pacific, 1879–83), but not knowing any better, they could only imagine a struggle between a general named Peru and another general named Chile.[1] Even today, deep in the backwaters of remote Latin American jungles, primitive Indians pass their lives without suspecting that in addition to however they identify themselves by tribe, they are also Brazilians, Peruvians, Venezuelans.

Since a basic awareness of national identity is no longer a matter of consequence in contemporary Latin America, a far more important consideration as to what makes individuals nationalistic is their emotional disposition toward that national identity. We have seen in a previous section (see p. 18) how human beings tend to seek out for themselves a positive identity, that is, to define themselves in such a way that they can accept what they see themselves to be and, as a result, feel self-esteem and personal pride. Nationalists are individuals who, in order to achieve this inner state of self-acceptance and self-esteem, experience an emotional need to feel proud of their national identity. Nationalists have, in other words, an emotional need to feel proud of being members of the particular nation to which they belong. It is important to understand that nationalists cannot control these emotions: like it or not, they feel their own self-worth is dependent upon their evaluation of this nationality.

Nationalist types are best understood not as a single category of people but as people with varying degrees of nationalistic emotion. The more important their national identity is in their personal emotional lives—regardless of whether they feel good about this national identity or not—the more nationalistic they are. Almost all Latin Americans are nationalistic to some extent. However, some Latin Americans feel within themselves an especially compelling need to be proud of their national identity; these are the more passionate nationalists that one finds in Latin America.

The close connection between an individual's sense of self-worth and his feelings about his national identity is difficult for Western Europeans and Americans to understand fully because few of them have had the same experience in their emotional lives. Western Europeans have, in periods of their history, been moved by intense nationalist emotion; but such collective passion has greatly diminished among them since the decade of the thirties and the years of World War II. Americans, isolated in a distant continent with no formidable enemies to speak of, have traditionally had a weaker sense of nationalism than Europeans, and not since World War II have they felt this sentiment very forcefully.

Partly due to this, observers from Western nations generally use the notion "pride in country" as if all peoples everywhere were "proud" of their country in essentially the same proportions. Statements reflecting this assumption are very polite, but they are not necessarily true simply because they are polite. The fact is that the national character of a people can vary as much as the individual character of a person, which means that a people may or may not enjoy a sense of confidence, security, and pride in its national identity. As with individuals who may have positive identities or negative identities, national collectivities of individuals may have what can be termed *positive national identities* or *negative national identities*.

Of course, the official view of all representatives of all nationalities is that their respective peoples are proud of what they are—whatever they are. Officially, all peoples are blessed with positive national identities. Beneath the rhetoric, however, the reality may be quite different, and there are many ways of evaluating and verifying such claims. In this book it is necessary for us to confront frankly the question of whether Latin American nationalists can, as they would like to do, take genuine, self-assured pride in their membership in their national collectivities. The weight of the evidence, which takes up the better part of the following two chapters, responds with a decisive no.

DEPENDENCIA

Latin American nationalists must live with negative national identities because they cannot help but regard the overall accomplishments of the societies to which they belong as unimpressive when compared with the achievements realized by others. This is a complex and lengthy subject, and a discussion of it draws us into one of the most important and explosive issues in contemporary Latin America—*dependencia.*

To those acquainted with Latin American affairs, dependencia is a familiar word. For some time now the term has been tossed about by the educated in Latin America, and in the latter part of the 1960s, it appeared in the United States bouncing through the halls of American academia. Dependencia is a word replete with emotional as well as conceptual implications, and because of this, it only inadequately translates into the English word *dependency.* The routine meaning is clear enough. Dependencia refers to the foreign ownership and control over the productive capacity in Latin America and, less commonly, to the political and cultural influence of these same foreign centers. But dependencia is not just another analytical concept stored in the toolbag of intellectuals but a word that reflects the presence of strong emotional undertows deep below the surface issue.

In order to illuminate the problem of dependencia at these shadowed depths, we might begin by examining the conceptual method of the Australian archaeologist V. Gordon Childe as he investigated essentially the same phenomenon in other societies. Of course, as an archaeologist Childe was interested in civilizations very distant from our own; but by evaluating the usefulness of the conceptual categories he used in the study of these cultures, we can temporarily remove ourselves from the passions of the present age and deal with peoples who for some time now have been free of emotional self-interests to defend.

Childe observed that during the long, slow process of mankind's progress, somewhere around 3,000 B.C. three cultures, Egypt, Mesopotamia, and India, began to show signs of developing remarkably high levels of civilization. Gradually they withdrew from a way of life entirely devoted to food production and moved toward the creation of cities, classes, and specialized professions such as priests, scribes, scientists, artists, technicians, and merchants. Childe called these three societies *primary centers of culture* owing to the fact that they were the developers of advanced forms of civilization. Surrounding the primary centers of culture were less "advanced" peoples; Childe labeled these *secondary centers of culture.* These secondary centers were the borrowers of the ancient world: the Giblites, for example, borrowed from the Egyptians, and the Cappadocians borrowed heavily from the Mesopotamians. Childe employed the term secondary center of culture to identify not simply those civilizations that borrowed (for Egypt, India, and Mesopotamia were borrowing from each other constantly) but those civilizations that borrowed without making any innovations of their own or any significant improvements on what they took from the primary centers. The Egyptians, for instance, continuously improved their writing script over time; but the Giblites preserved the archaic characters adopted from the early Egyptian dynasties and kept them unchanged for over a thousand years.[2]

Different levels of civilizations are as real today as in ancient times. What is known as modern civilization, which has evolved into its recognizable form during the last two hundred years, is the most distinctive that has ever appeared in human history. It is most distinguished by the organization of large numbers of people into nation-states, the growth of nationalism among them; the scientific, industrial, and managerial revolutions; and in some states, the successful functioning of mass-based democracies. The foundations for modernized societies were first laid in various countries located in Western Europe. Britain and her colonies in America, the Low Countries, and France led the way, soon to be followed by other European nations and even later by that strange anomaly, Japan. There has been and continues to be a tremendous cross-fertilization of ideas, inventions, and goods among these societies. Often vaguely referred to as the West (see p. viii), they are the primary centers of culture of the modern world.

In the context of modern world civilization, the Latin American nations can be classified only as secondary centers of culture. The reason for this is offered by Latin American critics themselves, who are frequently heard to berate their peoples for their "absense of creativity" or their "imitative impulse." The Peruvian intellectual Augusto Salizar Bondy, for example, describes his country as a "culture of dependency" (*cultura de la dependencia*) and has voiced this complaint: "To the challenge of the twentieth century we respond merely imitating, without originality, without vigor, without nerve, like children in the contemporary world."[3]

It is obviously necessary to examine why terms such as culture of dependency and secondary center of culture appropriately describe Latin American society. For a society to be classified as a primary center of culture, it must make contributions on the same level as those it has received from other primary centers. Latin America comprises a formidably large area, with resources and population roughly comparable to those of Europe or of the United States; if it were to be a primary center of culture, its achievements would have to be considerable. It is often possible to observe Western liberals leaning over backward and ending up in the most awkward postures in order to arrive at a generous estimation of Latin American contributions to modern world culture;[4] yet the limited number of examples they are able to find suggests the opposite of what they are trying to prove. Admittedly the evaluation of the accomplishments of a modern-day secondary center of culture is a prickly path to tread not just because of the emotional implications involved but also because the subject lends itself only partially to empirical verification. The attempt must be made, however, and with enough caution, one hopes, that it will be judged fairly and free of bias.

The most impressive achievement of modern civilization, the indispensable foundation upon which so many other achievements depend, has been the development of highly productive economies. Latin Americans are well aware that relative to the peoples of modernized societies, they are not leaders but followers, not creators but borrowers, in the arts of efficient production. There are many ways that Latin Americans are reminded of this, as in their constant exposure to the word *underdeveloped* or their continued reading of unfavorable economic statistics. However, perhaps the most enduring impression of their inferiority in economic activities is imparted when they look at the economic life that does take place around them and observe that much of the drive is supplied by a foreign culture.

One of the most important reasons why the mark of the "foreigner" is so deeply imprinted upon the productive output of Latin America is that immigrants and their descendants (who are notoriously slow in losing their "foreign" identities) have gained such prominent positions in the economic enterprises of that continent. The results of statistical research reveal in a systematic way what is very obvious to casual observation: a strong correlation between foreign immigrants and productive enterprises. In the two prosperous Brazilian states of Rio Grande do Sul and Santa Catarina, for example, surveys show that 80 percent of the industrial capacity was developed by people of European origin.[5] Further north in the giant manufacturing center of São Paulo, almost three-quarters of the industries there were found to be headed by immigrants or recent descendants of immigrants.[6] Similarly, research conducted in Argentina disclosed that nearly half the entrepreneurs in the country were immigrants and that a majority of the remaining entrepreneurs had immigrant backgrounds.[7] Latin American countries with proportionally fewer immigrants relative to their total populations show basically the same pattern of vigorous immigrant leadership in economic activities. At no time in the demographic history of Chile has the percentage of foreign born in that country been over 4 percent, yet a 1963 survey of the largest industrial establishments in Santiago revealed that 76 percent of the heads were immigrants or the children of immigrants.[8] Again, in Colombia, a country of negligible immigration, a 1960s study of the National Association of Industrialists found that 41 percent of the business leaders in Bogotá were foreign born.[9] Still another survey carried out in Panama in 1940 discovered that 45 percent of the men actively engaged in manufacturing and commerce were foreigners.[10] More investigations in Venezuela uncovered the fact that immigrants started a third of the new enterprises begun in the country during the 1950s.[11]

Research in other parts of Latin America tells a similar story of the disproportionate influence of people with non-Latin American backgrounds in the economic life of their adopted countries.[12] The fundamental reason behind this has already been made clear: despite their obvious initial disadvantages, immigrants in Latin America encountered only weak competition from the native population in the production of goods and services; and so, essentially by default, they were able to take the lead in many different areas of business endeavor (see pp. 52–69).

The prominent role of the immigrant in the saga of Latin American business leadership could hardly stand in greater contrast to the immigrant experience in the United States. In North America the ragged foreigners found the natives both highly motivated and well prepared to engage in business affairs and therefore were hard pressed to overcome their handicaps of language, culture, illiteracy, and lack of connections. While the new arrivals in North America could make a living, they were not able to grab the reins of business leadership because these were already tightly clenched in the grasp of the native-born. To illustrate, in 1870 86 percent of the business leaders in America were from "old" families that could trace their origins back to colonial times. Only 10 percent were foreign-born or children of the foreign-born.[13]

The distinct aura of foreignness that pervades the productive life of Latin America is also greatly enhanced by the towering presence of foreign businesses and foreign imports on the continent. Particularly in the large urban areas, Latin Americans are continuously bombarded with sensory evidence of two realities: the prolific productivity of foreign civilization and their own economic dependency upon that civilization. All a Latin American has to do is look down the street and observe the milling throng of four-wheeled chariots which display a profusion of *gringo* (foreign) names: Plymouth, Chrysler, Oldsmobile, Cadillac, Ford, Toyota, Volkswagen, Büssing, Mercedes, Fiat, and an occasional stunning Rolls Royce or Bentley. Above, streaking across the sky, the Latin American may view the flying vehicles of mechanical civilization. To many in these backward lands, the airplane symbolizes the soaring ambition and endless potential of modern man. Yet all bear the seal (DC-8, DC-10, 727, 747, TriStar) of a particular kind of man—the *gringo*. Back down on earth, the gaze of the Latin American encounters numerous other reminders of foreign culture such as stores full of foreign products and foreign stores (Sears, Roebuck, Woolworth's, Colonel Sanders Kentucky Fried Chicken) full of foreign products. The most obvious visual evidence of gringo wares, however, is not inside the stores but outside on the streets. Huge signs, massive billboards, and glowing neon lights overpower the skyline and advertise an array of company names that might make a foreigner wonder whether he has ever left home: General Motors, B. F. Goodrich, Goodyear, Firestone, Du Pont, General Electric, Xerox, Nikon, Viceroy, Winston, Cinzano, Fanta, Pepsi-Cola, Coca-Cola. Surrounded on every side by foreign goods, the well-to-do Latin American is likely to wash himself, deodorize himself, perfume himself, feed himself, transport himself, and entertain himself with foreign imports or the domestically manufactured products of foreign companies. This, combined with the fact that many of the "native" manufactures of his acquaintance are produced by transplanted foreigners, is enough to make his awareness of the dependency of Latin American economic life upon foreign culture a strong one indeed.

One of the more striking manifestations of dependencia, not just in economic activities but in other areas of Latin American life as well, is the widespread practice of relying on foreign advisors. Latin American military establishments are an especially outstanding example of this, if only because they so often describe themselves as quintessentially "national" institutions. Latin American military officers have long been impressed with Western military power and have often exhibited something akin to reverence for Western authorities of war. Consequently, they have imported these authorities in great numbers hoping that the foreigners would not just teach tactics but instill in their troops Western-style discipline and esprit de corps. First to start this tradition in Latin America were the Chileans when in 1885 they brought over a troop of German officers to toughen their forces. Other Latin American militaries were not to be outdone. Soon foreign military missions were popping up all over the continent—Germans in Argentina and Uruguay, French in Brazil and Peru, Italians in Ecuador and Bolivia, and British in just about everybody's navy. Since World War II Americans have taken over as the major advisors.[14] Perhaps the best-known demonstration of Latin American military dependencia in the postwar era took place after 1959 when Fidel Castro proved the effectiveness of guerrilla jungle warfare. The U.S. army responded to this challenge by dispatching special troops to Panama to train them how to fight and survive in tropical forests; and soon American youths raised on the prairie farms, city streets, and suburban patios of North America were in the jungles of Latin America teaching Latin American soldiers how to fight and survive in their own backyards.[15]

Outside the military, Latin Americans engage foreign advisors and proselytizers in an extraordinary variety of other pursuits. Latin Americans bring in foreigners to build dams, factories, and hospitals. They recruit foreigners to run agricultural estates and to manage factories. They reach abroad for "experts" to draw up national plans, revamp national budgets, restructure state bureaucracies, and even to write legislation.[16] Everywhere foreigners are seen filling missionary posts (at least half the priests in Latin America are foreigners[17]), leading charity crusades, catalyzing community development projects, advising labor leaders how to fight capitalism, advising police forces how to fight communism.

The phenomenon of dependencia in Latin American life is perhaps most evident when considering the enormous imbalance of exchange between Latin American and foreign culture. Such an imbalance exists because Latin America is a secondary center of culture, that is to say, a culture that is a borrower rather than a creator of the significant advances of modern civilization. Latin Americans implicitly recognize this state of affairs when they rely so heavily on the help of foreign advisors, whom they view as representatives of a culture where all the spectacular advances of modern life seem to be happening. Western scholars who study and write about the high points of modern civilization implicitly recognize it when they do not discuss the subject of Latin American contributions, presumably because they believe there is nothing to discuss.[18]

The most certain evidence of the lack of eminent achievement originating in Latin America is found in those fields of human endeavor most closely related to economic development where the notion of achievement is measurable to some extent. In these particular disciplines, even the most sympathetic observer would be hard pressed to think of anything of world consequence coming out of Latin America—any great scientific discovery, any undiscovered principle in physics, chemistry, or mathematics; any technological breakthrough; any pioneering feat of engineering; any important invention; any eventful innovation in management techniques. The United States, which shares with Latin America a similar historical lifespan and a roughly comparable profile of natural and human resources, has produced over one hundred Nobel Prize winning scientists. Latin America has produced two, both Argentineans (the most "European" country of Latin America) and both sons of French immigrants. Again the foreign factor.

An evaluation of the accomplishments of Latin Americans in the social sciences, because they are "softer" disciplines than the natural sciences, must necessarily rely more on value judgments. But from the standpoint of the test of time, there has been no Latin American social scientist with the stature of a Weber in sociology, a Marshall in economics, a Freud in psychology, or a De Tocqueville in political science. Today Latin American universities are importing on a large scale the latest social science fashions from Western centers of learning. They are, in fact, importing many of the worst along with the latest, an indication of the propensity of Latin Americans to absorb much of what is bad about Western culture as well as much of what is good.

A discussion of "high culture," specifically philosophy and the arts, requires the most subjective judgments of all, and here we can only depend upon the admittedly nebulous reckoning of "generally accepted world opinion." It is in the area of high culture that Latin America makes its best bid to a claim of excellence. In literature Latin Americans have received six Nobel Prizes, and other writers are highly regarded. In painting, the Mexican mural artists Rivera, Orozco, and Siqueiros are of unquestioned world stature, but the school has declined since their deaths. In symphony music one Latin American composer, Heitor Villa-Lobos, ranks as an undisputed world figure. The list cannot go far beyond that point. There has been no school of philosophy nor any great philosopher emerging from Latin America. There have been no renowned schools of classical ballet, of opera, or of sculpture. Thus in Latin America's contribution to the arts, we definitely see that intangible something critics call "excellence," but the excellence is found only in scattered pockets. It can fairly be said that the continent has never had a reputation as a cultural mecca. In fact, the tradition in Latin America has long been for its aspiring artists to voyage to Europe and to remain there as expatriates.

Another area of Latin American life where *dependencia* is very evident might be called "popular culture" because this is the culture that reaches not just educated elites but large masses of people. The popular culture in Latin America that is directly imported from abroad or obviously inspired by foreign models is transmitted to the masses by the powerful printed media and the even more powerful electronic media. To appreciate, then, the impact of imported foreign culture upon the masses, it is important to see just how thoroughly permeated with foreignness the media in Latin America has become.

Foreign influence in the printed media available in Latin America is first noticeable in the great number of foreign magazines that are widely distributed throughout the continent. Newsstands in major cities do a brisk business in foreign language journals like *Time, Newsweek, Playboy, and Reader's Digest.* Other magazines like *Vogue, Better Homes and Gardens, House Beautiful, Good Housekeeping,* and *National Geographic* find their way into the homes of the more sophisticated. The only empirical study available in this area revealed that out of 200 elite families surveyed in Puerto Rico, 198 had American publications in their homes and 173 had four or more.[19]

There are available in Latin American news stores not only many foreign publications but also many imitations of foreign publications. *Time* and *Life* formats are especially prevalent. A magazine called *Desfile (Parade)* is a faithful copy of the American magazine *Parade* right down to the use of its name, its cover design, its size, its grade of paper, its layout of articles, and even its delivery system (sandwiched in between the Sunday newspapers).

The actual content of the Latin American printed media likewise displays a heavy foreign influence. The Mexican anthropologist Julio de la Fuente, for example, analyzed the newspapers in his country and concluded that "fifty percent of the total number of pages in the newspaper indicate the dependence of both the newspaper and the readers on U.S. civilization."[20] For information about the outside world, Latin Americans generally look at the globe through the lenses of United Press International, Associated Press, and Reuters. For amusement they laugh at comic strip characters almost exclusively from abroad—creations like Donald Duck, Dennis the Menace, Peanuts, B.C., and Wizard of Id (Mago de Id). For enlightenment, counseling, and titillation they are frequently able to turn to political, advice, and gossip columns from the United States. In addition to the articles, the cartoons, the formats of the publications, and indeed, the machinery that prints the material, much of the news in the printed media also originates in foreign countries. Latin Americans are constantly reading stories of every description about the fashions, ideas, movements, lifestyles, and people in the United States and Western Europe. Particularly prominent on the pages they scan are feature articles and gossipy blurbs about the Beautiful People and *bombas sexy* of America and Europe. Brigitte Bardot, Angie Dickinson, Raquel Welsh, Ann-Margret, Glenda Jackson, Liza Minnelli, are examples of typical bombas.

The advertisements that support the printed media also serve to emphasize the foreignness saturating Latin American culture. The amount of advertising dedicated to the selling of foreign goods is enormous. The fact that in 1965 every one of the top dozen advertisers in Brazil was a foreign company gives some idea as to the persuading power these foreign corporations can muster.[21] Day after day all over the continent, millions of Latin Americans turn billions of pages and observe uncountable gringo footprints upon their culture. Continuously passing before their eyes are names such as Xerox, Omega, Fiat, Chivas Regal, Lufthansa, Israeli Aircraft Industries, Sheraton, Boeing, First National Bank of Chicago, Massey-Ferguson, Shaeffer, Pentax, Ballantine's, Bayer, Mercedez-Benz, Rothman's of London, Old Spice, Pall Mall, First National City Bank Travelers Checks, John Deere, Volkswagen, Pracktica, Black and Decker, Westinghouse, Sears, General Motors—the list is endless. The impression of foreignness is further strengthened by the fact that the people who market foreign products often do not even bother to translate the brand names into Spanish or Portuguese; thus, when Latin Americans see advertisements for cosmetics ("Touch and Glow," "Bright and Clear") or for motor oil ("Atlantic Super Premium Motor Oil," "Shell Super Motor Oil," "Mobiloil Special"), they find English terms seeping into their daily vocabularies. Native Latin American companies sometimes contribute to these obligatory English lessons by christening their products with English names. (They feel this gives their products an extra touch of class.) It is for this reason that the Brazilians who cannot afford imported cigarettes because of the high tariffs smoke domestic brands called "Hollywoods" ("King Size"), "Sheltons," "Charms," "Hiltons" (with "magnifilter"), and "Ministers" ("Super Kings"). Consciousness of foreignness is also reinforced by foreign-created advertisements that are used to sell foreign merchandise. Polaroid, for example, advertises its cameras to Latin Americans using the same suggestive pictures it presents to Americans—happy, all-American parents snapping shots of their happy, all-American children. In similar fashion, Johnson and Johnson sells its BandAid to Latin Americans with the help of a little blond boy with an adhesive bandage on his finger—a tot as cute as he can be but hardly representative of a cute Latin American child.

Those who live by the pen are normally much attracted to the idea that their pen is mightier than someone else's sword. If this is true, then the electronic visual medium is mightier than both. Television and cinema are the two basic types of electronic visual media; and in Latin America both beam out with an impact unmatched by the printed media, the steady, unmistakable message of dependencia.

Of these two mediums, television is the newer and the less far reaching, but is also one that is becoming more and more available to the masses. It is, perhaps, in low-income areas that the sheer power of television is most easily appreciated. I have seen poor families purchase a television set before they buy a refrigerator, a decent stove, or the materials that would allow them to finish their half-constructed living quarters. When a set arrives on the block, it causes a general commotion. Young and old (but especially the young) crowd into the lucky household every evening, pay a small fee, and sit wide eyed before the screen.

And once the set is turned on and their faces are transfixed on its glowing images, what do they see? Largely materials created and produced by foreigners.[22] Latin American television swamps its viewers with old foreign films and old foreign serials like "Hawaii-Five-O," "Police Woman," "Mission Impossible," "Mannix," "Bonanza," "Lassie," "Along Came Bronson." Even domestically produced television programs can have a decidedly foreign flavor, like the imitations of "American Bandstand" that feature Latin American teens bouncing about to foreign music. When programs are interrupted by advertisements, often the audience is exposed to more advertising of foreign products. Sometimes the ads are the same as those used in the United States, so Latin American TV watchers gaze at American actors pushing American wares while incongruously speaking dubbed-in Spanish.

Television, piped into people's living rooms, bedrooms, and kitchens, is potentially the most powerful of the electronic visual media. However, since television has not yet come into its own in Latin America, cinema remains the more influential of the two and accordingly deserves its proper share of comment.

In Latin America movies are regarded as a basic commodity of life, and as with other basic commodities such as bread, milk, and rice, the prices of tickets are controlled by the government and kept well within the reach of the common person. Many films can be seen for just a few cents—scratchy oldies-but-goodies shown in large, smoke-filled auditoriums to viewers who sit shoulder to shoulder on rude wooden benches and who are willing to tolerate the projection breaking down half a dozen times a night. Movie films in Latin America are not only cheap but also widely available. For example, on any given day in Lima, approximately 300 movies may be spinning through the reels in the city's theaters; this is considerably more than the number showing in the comparably sized metropolitan area of Philadelphia.[23]

The overwhelming majority of the films daily screened in Latin America are imported from the United States and Europe. Domestically produced movies in most Latin American countries are few and far between. Only Brazil, Mexico, and Argentina have sizable native film industries. And even in a country like Brazil, anywhere from ten to twenty foreign movies are imported for every one made at home.[24]

If the preponderance of foreign films is surprising, then their influence, especially on the pliable imaginations of the young, can be astonishing. Little Latin American boys play cowboys and Indians—instead of *conquistadores* and Indians or something else more derivative from their own culture. Young Latin American girls swoon more over foreign box office lovers than they do over local stallions. And young men model themselves after the same celluloid heroes. To cite an example, some years ago the Clark Gable film *It Happened One Night* was shown in Argentina: in one unforgettable scene Gable took off his shirt and the audience viewers could suddenly behold—the man was wearing no undershirt! The sale of undershirts in the country plunged sharply downward. Buenos Aires underwear merchants were so distressed at what Gable's bare chest had done to their business they called the head of the movie company in Hollywood and begged him to stop all showings.[25]

One example of a particularly extravagant manifestation of dependencia in Latin American society was the appearance of a Latin American version of Western "hippie" youth culture. The postindustrial notions that became popular among the first generation of Western youths brought up in an era of mass affluence quickly penetrated underdeveloped Latin American society and won many enthusiastic converts among the children of the wealthier classes. Running about in the heads of these youths were half-digested ideas and values that seemed more than a little out of place in countries unable to supply their basic needs in goods and services—the antiwork ethic; the antibusiness ethic; the contempt for rules, boundaries and self-restraint; the concern for enjoying-it-now; the ardent interest in aesthetic creativity; the fascination with the self and with the soulful inner experience. In the exploration of the self, of course, their journey to inner space was helped along by the same mind-distorting drugs favored by their counterparts abroad.

For outward symbols broadcasting inner values, these Latin American youths again looked to their models in the West. Their style of dress, therefore, appeared much the same, ranging from studied casual to studied shabby. They could be seen passing their considerable leisure time striding the fashionable streets of major cities lined with smart shops and boutiques, munching hamburgers and ice cream cones, displaying their tight pants with sewn-on patches, their T-shirts with sayings such as "I Just Got Laid" (in English) and, needless to say, their long gorgeous manes of gleaming hair. The music they listened to was mostly foreign rock, and many of them didn't have a single record in their collections by an artist from their own land. Along with all the other fads, these youthful Latin Americans even imported Woodstocks into their countries. The first rock festival they attended in Chile was the scene of deafening acid rock vibrations, the sweet scent of marijuana wafting through the air,[26] and eight missing girls at the end. One held in Mexico was even more authentic: 200,000 young bodies overwhelmed a small town outside the capital, caused massive traffic jams, and quickly exhausted the available food supplies; entertainment consisted of 12 heavy rock bands, nude frolicking in a nearby lake, and a plenteous supply of drugs; drownings and other accidents took five lives.

As might well be imagined, a complete treatment of the topic of dependencia in Latin American society would require a volume in itself. We have laid enough of a foundation, however, to move into the next important question—whether this subject is worth discussing at all.

This is a point worth considering. After all, in this modern age societies of people influence each other to an unprecedented degree, one hopes exchanging the best features of their respective cultures. What could be the problem with Latin America absorbing from abroad everything it found good and useful? A problem does exist, however, and it lies in the word *exchange*. Latin America is deeply influenced by the massive imports it daily digests from foreign countries while its own influence on the culture and economy of these exporting countries is, at best, only marginal. This imbalance of exchange, in other words, clearly marks Latin America as a secondary center of culture. The fact that Latin America is a secondary center of culture would not be of the slightest importance if Latin Americans themselves did not care. But many Latin Americans do care, and as a general rule, the more nationalistic they are, the more they find themselves concerned.

Possibly the best expression of this nationalist concern has been rendered by the famous Uruguayan intellectual Alberto Zum Felde. Zum Felde, of course, was well aware of the sensitivity of the subject he chose to drag onto the stage of public discussion, for he was doing nothing less than calling upon his countrymen to honestly face and rigorously analyze the fact that they were the Cappadocians and Giblites of the modern age. However, Zum Felde strongly believed that the problem of a people "unable to create its own forms of culture" could only be solved by dealing with it.[27] It was precisely because he was an ardent nationalist dedicated to finding answers that he challenged his fellow Latin Americans to "descend to the plain of hard facts" and to confront the dilemma of dependencia.[28]

The fact that Zum Felde was probing essentially the same phenomenon that V. Gordon Childe had studied made his analysis of his own living culture similar to Childe's description of the secondary centers of culture of the ancient world:

> As in the domain of Biology, there are in the domain of human history parasites of cultures. Our Latin American culture consists of one of these parasitical forms. We have lived and still continue to live absolutely at the expense of European production, like the plants and animals that cling to larger organisms, and from whose vitality they sustain themselves ....
>
> There is no doubt that what we call "our culture" today is an imported product, ready made, arranged, labeled, ready for consumption, that arrives on board of transportation vessels. To even speak of "our culture" is strictly speaking not conceptually or linguistically possible, because what we can rightfully call *ours* is only that which is a product and expression of ourselves.[29]

The acute embarrassment suffered by the zealous Latin American nationalist over dependencia stems not simply from the imbalance of cultural exchange but from a particular difficulty that normally arises when one society tries to adopt the culture of another. The problem is that the process of cultural transference is not at all easy, and when a secondary center of culture attempts to copy desired features of a primary center, the imitation is likely to be imperfect—even inept. V. Gordon Childe explains this as it took place among societies in ancient times:

> But in the process of diffusion culture was degraded. People who have learned a new technique are apt to apply it clumsily; proficiency requires generations of practice and of discipline. . . . There thus arise different grades of civilization, varying degrees of approximation to the standards set by the primary centers.[30]

Not surprisingly, Zum Felde discovered the same tendency toward unsuccessful imitation manifesting itself in Latin American society:

> The parasitical type of culture complies with the form and the letter of the culture, not its living spirit; as such it is superficial and artificial [superficial y postiza], a false culture [falsa cultura]. . . .
> Culture in most of our America exists in a state of falsity; it is the appearance of culture and not the reality, of seeming and not being; the culture here is on loan and has not really taken root.[31]

What distresses a Latin American nationalist like Zum Felde, therefore, is that not only do his people need to imitate but as is usually the case with people from secondary centers of culture, their imitations are poor and often laughable reflections of the original. On the one hand, the nationalist sees his countrymen failing in their attempts to imitate those aspects of foreign culture he would like to see adopted, for instance, when their compatriots import expensive foreign technologies and then for any number of reasons are forced to abandon them for scrap. On the other hand, he sees his countrymen, swayed by the prestige of foreign labels, imitate aspects of foreign culture he deems inappropriate for his nation, for instance, the Latin American hippies who in their bumbling attempts to mimic the youthful offspring of affluent societies appear awkward, inauthentic, and more than a little absurd.

The emotional dilemma of the Latin American nationalist is further aggravated by the fact that it is not just he and his fellow nationalists who recognize the deficiencies of Latin American imitations but also foreigners from those very countries whose culture is admired and eagerly imitated. For example, no Brazilian whose heart is swollen with nationalist sentiment is likely to be indifferent to the following observations of a French writer and visitor to his country:

In all disciplines such as philosophy, mathematics, literature, science, and theology, everything must be drawn from English, French, Italian, and German works. In fact, Brazil has as yet not produced anything noteworthy in these subjects. The Brazilians have not yet outgrown the state of translations and adaptations. . . .

One could review most aspects of Brazilian civilization and in almost all would discover an inexplicable deficiency, an imperfect imitation, a sign that this does not evolve from the spirit of the people, spontaneously from the land. And from this analysis would follow, I believe, the impression which slowly grows upon the visitor as his stay in the country lengthens, that all European civilization and culture transplanted here have but weak and shallow roots.[32]

Writing about the same time as this Frenchman was a prominent Brazilian nationalist leader whose words reveal the kind of sensitivity Latin American nationalists characteristically feel toward foreign opinion of this sort:

The attitude of the old [European] countries with regard to us has always been a profound disdain to the point where the educated people there ignore our very existence. We have been treated like poor relatives from the rural backlands who stand open mouthed [embasbacados] at the marvels enjoyed by our city kin. We have been looked at with the same irony as one regards ridiculous imitators, the plagiarizers and falsifiers of authentic objects.[33]

In the last analysis, however, the real heart of the problem of dependencia for the Latin American nationalist is not that foreigners recognize it but that he recognizes it. Even if the foreigner hides his unfavorable opinions behind a tightlipped smile or camouflages them under a suffocating liberalism, the Latin American nationalist cannot escape the emotional turbulence that dependencia creates for him, for he cannot escape the same basic issue that Alberto Zum Felde thrust into the light of open scrutiny: "They [the Europeans] treat us as inferiors; and we cannot deny that they have their reasons. What they think of us is what in reality we really are: consumers of their industrial products and their culture."[34] The undeniable reality of dependencia obliges the Latin American nationalist to feel ashamed of his nationality when as a nationalist he longs to feel proud. And because his collective nationalist identity is such an integral part of his emotional makeup, he feels part of any deficiency he sees in his people no matter how positively he may regard the success of his personal life. The Latin American nationalist finds himself the captive of a national inferiority complex—a phenomenon to which we must now turn our attention.

THE NATIONAL INFERIORITY COMPLEX

The expression "inferiority complex" is commonly used today by people both within and without the field of psychology. For this reason it is essential from the start to emphasize that the term *national inferiority complex* has a meaning quite distinct from the usual understanding of an individual's personal inferiority complex. To state that a Latin American nationalist has a national inferiority complex does not mean that he feels inferior to foreigners from primary centers of culture. A Latin American *may* feel inferior to these foreigners, but he may also be completely free from such emotions and still have to bear the strain of a national inferiority complex. The elements necessary in the idea of a national inferiority complex are first, that a Latin American be a nationalist, that is to say, that at least a part of his sense of self-esteem be dependent upon his evaluation of his nationality; and secondly, that this evaluation be a negative one. In other words, a Latin American with a national inferiority complex does not necessarily suffer from what he perceives himself to be but from what he perceives his people to be. In addition, there is nothing a nationalist can do about the fact that he cannot feel indifferent to how he regards his countrymen. He is, so to speak, a prisoner of his nationalist group identity and the emotions that beset him from within.

For obvious reasons the national inferiority complex is a subject that appears far more frequently in the private conversations of Latin Americans than in their statements destined for public consumption. The issue does, however, have a way of poking its way to the surface in speeches and in published materials, if only for a moment before it disappears.

Political leaders are understandably the most reluctant to bring up this problem but on occasion will mention it in their public discourses. Juan Perón, for example, maintained that the "Latin race" was afflicted with an "inferiority complex" because it found itself on the second level of humanity."[35] Rafael Trujillo, after a rather crude and rambling interpretation of Dominican Republic history, concluded, "And so it was that the country found itself in a collective state of what psychologists call an inferiority complex."[36] Salvador Allende of Chile exhorted his people to overcome this complex, or more specifically, to "vindicate Latin American culture without feeling ourselves inferior."[37]

Not surprisingly, Latin American social critics have been inclined to address this delicate topic with greater vigor. The most famous of these has been a Mexican psychologist by the name of Samuel Ramos. Ramos straightforwardly declared, "It is my thesis that some expressions of Mexican character are ways of compensating for an unconscious sense of inferiority,"[38] and he spent the better part of a long career elaborating on that basic statement. The notion of inferiority has turned up in the words of other Latin American writers as well, although not with the same copious detail that Ramos lavished upon the idea. A fellow Mexican, Leopoldo Zea, admitted to something he called "our absurd inferiority complex" in order to denounce it.[39] The Chilean Tancredo Pinochet flatly affirmed, "We lack confidence in ourselves. We have an invincible inferiority complex."[40] The Brazilian scholar Helio Jaguaribe observed, "A consciousness of the limitations of the country and the frustrations caused by them, aggravated by comparisons with the fully developed countries, generates an inferiority complex that sterilizes the national sentiment and tends toward cosmopolitan ideals."[41]

The national inferiority complex is a common point of conversation among foreign travelers and residents in Latin America, and so the theme naturally finds its way into the writings of foreigners as well. For example, an American academic doing research in the Dominican Republic commented, "Among Dominicans, there has traditionally been a kind of national inferiority complex, a sense of fatalism and despair, the belief that the country and its people would always be condemned to poverty, chaos, foreign domination, instability and backwardness."[42] Another U.S. professor wrote of this same "pervasive inferiority complex" he sensed among Spanish Americans, "They are haunted by fear that truth may inhere in the common Yankee contention that they are inferior in economic and political affairs and in the Spanish assumption that they are spiritually retarded."[43] And the unofficial dean of American Latin Americanists a generation ago, Clarence H. Haring, wrote from his wide experience, "The inferiority complex is a fact easily observed in Latin Americans and requires little comment."[44]

Haring's statement basically sums up the intellectual labor that has been done on the concept of the national inferiority complex. With the exception of its treatment in Ramos's work, which is too flawed to be of much value,[45] the idea has never been fashioned into an analytical tool and used to explain certain kinds of social behavior. Instead, the national inferiority complex has been looked upon only as a descriptive category and simply mentioned as a feature of Latin American life. There are basically two reasons for this: First, the topic is a somewhat touchy one that neither Latin Americans nor foreigners like to play with. More importantly, once the national inferiority complex has been discovered and identified, it has not occurred to observers that anything else should be done with it.

But the national inferiority complex is too important a phenomenon for students of Latin American affairs to simply dig up, ponder for a short while, and then rebury; for it is the national inferiority complex that causes Latin Americans to have a negative national identity (see pp. 106–7), which in turn deeply influences the character of Latin American nationalism. What this means, of course, is that an understanding of the national inferiority complex is essential to an understanding of nationalist behavior in Latin American society.

The subject of the national inferiority complex appears and reappears in conversations and writings about Latin Americans because evidence of it is found everywhere in the swirl of daily living upon that continent. One way for the foreigner, or gringo, in Latin America to appreciate this is to simply melt into the ebb and flow of everyday life there and observe how Latin Americans characteristically relate to someone from a primary center of culture.

To the average American whose interest in Latin America may be limited and whose impressions of the continent may be largely shaped by news reports, Latin America may seem like quite an unfriendly place for gringos. Mostly due to extensive media coverage, the story of anti-Americanism south of the border is well known north of the border. Most Americans are acquainted with those ill-fated journeys of prominent politicians who periodically set out for Latin America on "good-will" tours and "fact-finding" missions. Vice-President Nixon became enbroiled in the most famous of these episodes in 1958 when the only thing that kept him from being physically mauled by an aroused Venezualan mob was the bulletproof shielding of his limousine. The Rockefeller mission was greeted with a similar spirit by violent crowds of protesting demonstrators and spectacular bombings and burnings of American property. Robert F. Kennedy's trip to Chile yielded him an expertly aimed glob of spit in the eye in addition to whatever "facts" he might have been looking for. Nor are leading American politicians the only targets of Latin American anti-Americanism. Ranking American embassy officials and important American businessmen have been harrassed, abducted, abused, and, at times, slain in cold blood. As a consequence, Americans in these positions have not always felt secure in some countries of Latin America. One American ambassador to Argentina felt obliged to sleep in an explosion-proof, steel-lined bedroom, drive about in a bulletproof limousine, and recruit a 250-man private army whose sole duty was to keep him alive.[46] A visiting delegation of American businessmen conducted their business in that same country surrounded by a whole platoon of heavily armed guards, some of whom toted flame throwers and wore double rows of hand grenades around their waists.[47] One often-repeated example of anti-Americanism in Latin America took place in 1922 when a Cuban newspaper suddenly appeared on the streets one day with this eye-catching headline: "Hatred of North Americans Will

Be the Religion of Cubans." The text which followed was hardly more reassuring: "The day will have to arrive when we will consider it our most sacred duty of our life to walk along the street and eliminate the first American we encounter."[48] With incidents such as these so widely reported in the United States, there is little wonder why many Americans might entertain some doubts about the hospitality offered to gringos in those countries to the south.

Anti-Americanism, however, is only the highly visible, highly deceiving media image of how Americans are likely to be received in Latin America. Prominent Americans are the targets of Latin American anger because they represent American power—both political and economic power—against which Latin Americans feel they have some cause for complaint. However, most Americans in Latin America, like most Americans in the United States, are too ordinary to represent American power and so are looked upon only as representatives of American culture. The attitude of Latin Americans toward American power ranges from admiration to fear to hate, while their attitude toward American culture is generally one of awe and admiration. By representing this broader idea of a great American culture and not the more narrow one of great but of often bitterly resented American power, ordinary Americans in Latin America not only can avoid being the targets of politicized hostility but, quite the contrary, can enjoy the privilege of considerable unearned social esteem.

This phenomenon is most obvious among those Americans who make only enough money to place them in what would be by Latin American standards the lower middle class and therefore are in no position to gain social status on the basis of high incomes. There are quite a few of these Americans of modest means throughout the continent—teachers who teach just enough to get by, travelers who never seem to move on, community development workers who labor for love or adventure but for little money, students in search of knowledge, artists in pursuit of inspiration, a few who are best described as lost souls, and many others with varied stories to tell. Some of these are well educated, which raises their social prestige, and most possess Caucasion racial features, which does the same. But what foreigners from the "advanced" primary centers of culture can find is that they are invested with a kind of automatic social prestige that in terms of social status elevates them above Latin Americans with similar qualifications of income, education, and race. Particularly when they begin to sense the added *importance* of status in Latin American culture, ordinary Americans living in that society are less likely to encounter anti-American discrimination than experience a strange feeling that they are getting something for nothing.

Of course, the experience of the gringo, whether American or European, in Latin America depends very much upon the gringo. As many have proven time and again, it is easy for a foreigner to limit his contacts with the culture and learn next to nothing about it. But if a gringo learns the language and is open and accessible enough to allow the drift of events to carry him to many corners of Latin American life, he will begin to understand his position within the prestige system. If properly disposed, a gringo will be readily approached by all sorts of Latin Americans, be asked many questions, become engaged in interminable conversations, and quite possibly be offered drinks, meals, a place to stay, or even a fiesta the following evening. One nearly penniless Frenchman of my acquaintance gorged himself on fine Argentinean steaks, potatoes, custard, and wine the entire breadth of the pampa. This goes beyond traditional Latin American hospitality, the kind of hospitality Latin Americans normally extend to each other. Its cause is a fascination with the foreigner, with the gringo who was born and raised in a primary center of culture.

Again, with the right attitude the social life of the gringo in Latin America should be more than he can handle. At the beaches where in some countries the bathers seem to segregate themselves automatically according to class and color, the gringo can easily mingle with the social elite. Often rumors of evening parties will drift through the air, but these social gatherings are selective: Latin Americans who appear at the door are screened very carefully but gringos are always welcome; they have status enough. At these affairs Latin Americans seem flattered when they notice that a gringo has taken the time to learn Spanish or Portuguese; and they sometimes reveal hurt or anger when he has not. Others will appear almost shocked with pleasure if he demonstrates a smattering of knowledge about the politics, culture, or history of the country.

Still other signs suggest a tacit concession of status to the foreigner in Latin America. The gringo may experience the freedom of transgressing social barriers that obstruct ordinary Latin Americans. For example, if casually or even sloppily dressed, a gringo may find he can penetrate posh hotels, exclusive clubs, and other elegant spots of the privileged where a similarly attired Latin American would scarcely make it up the steps. By the same social magic, he may notice a little extra bowing and scraping at cafes and restaurants. Some gringos have even found landlords who prefer to lease their apartments to foreigners whenever possible and have used this leverage to negotiate lower rents.

The social freedom, the little courtesies, the favored treatment—these are the results of the special consideration commonly afforded a foreigner from one of the *países avanzados* (advanced countries). And with some practice a gringo can translate his social advantage into a measure of power. One technique the Peace Corps has used with some effectiveness is to have an American volunteer act as a spokesman for a poor Latin American community in order to enhance the chances of procuring needed services from a lethargic government bureaucracy. A gringo volunteer dressed in dirty Levis, dusty boots, and rumpled shirt with the tail hanging out can often reach the ear of the right government official, whereas an ordinary Latin American could hardly hope to get beyond the information counter. On several occasions I have found myself being smartly escorted past long lines of patient supplicants to a district mayor's office in search of such results. Others have even managed to talk their way into the richly carpeted chambers of cabinet-level officials.

Residing and working in Latin America are not only gringos but *gringas* (Western women), and these foreign females undergo somewhat different experiences because of their sex. Considerably more than gringos, attractive gringas are likely to be lavished with attention to a degree they would not dream about back home. Often this attention is not entirely welcome, for on the streets their presence will commonly elicit from passing males gestures that convey an explicit sexual message—lusty comments, quick, delicate pinches, not so delicate grabs on the posterior. At times when a young blade or group of young blades spot a foreign woman, they will follow behind her for several city blocks. The sight of a gringa walking on a sidewalk has been known to stop cars, set off horns, and reverse the course of motorcycles. Part of this, of course, is due to her sex, but the commotion caused by a foreign-looking female seems to be in excess of that prompted by a Latin woman of superior beauty. Also suggesting that her foreignness adds to the appeal of a gringa in Latin American culture is the fact that many Latin Americans consider marriage to a Western woman highly desirable and prestigeous.

Not surprisingly, Western men and women in Latin America find it very easy to accustom themselves to being the beneficiaries of ego-boosting prestige patterns. This situation, however, may create problems for the very people it appears to favor. Some of those who have left Latin America and returned home have experienced difficulties adjusting to the fact that they were no longer automatically special and were once again just one among many. And for those who remain behind, unearned, undeserved status, like unearned, undeserved wealth, can be a positive hazard to the character. An example of this can be found among certain circles of Americans living in Brazil who are referred to by Brazilian critics as "the little gods." The Brazilians who use the term do not have in mind Americans of the classical colonial mold who sit around segregated bars, drink gin and tonics, look suspiciously at the lettuce in their sandwiches, and ceaselessly complain about the lazy and unreliable "natives." On the contrary, the little gods usually mix well in Brazilian social life, speak the language, and have a few or more than a few Brazilian acquaintances. On the surface everything seems placid enough, yet there is an aura of confidence about the "little gods," really an air of smugness of those who are sure of their status. To some sensitive Brazilians, the little gods seem enveloped in a mood of haughty self-satisfaction even while overtly friendly, loquacious, and charming.

Foreigners enjoy easy status in Latin American society because they are associated with the modern world's primary centers of culture. Latin Americans can acquire status by associating themselves with these same países avanzados. Since Latin Americans are not foreigners, they accomplish this by other means such as tracing their family geneology to foreign countries, engaging in foreign travel, earning degrees from foreign schools, mastering foreign languages, assimilating foreign culture, keeping abreast of foreign trends and fashions, and consuming foreign goods.

For Latin Americans, the single most effective way of associating themselves with foreign culture is to look foreign, that is, to be favored with the right (Caucasian) racial characteristics. This brings up once again the subject of earlier discussion that pointed out the well-developed sensitivity of Latin Americans to differences in racial characteristics and their reflexive habit of translating facial features, hair "quality," and varying degrees of skin pigmentation into levels of status (see p. 22). The more Northern European–looking a Latin American is, that is to say, the more likely it appears that this forebearers originated in the most successful European countries, the richer is his reward in prestige. Since women depend more upon physical appearance for their social prestige than do men, a Northern European look is especially advantageous to them. It is for this reason that the dreamgirls featured in Latin American magazines, televisions, and movies usually conform to Caucasian standards of beauty no matter what the racial composition of the country. Mexican movies are a good example of this because their number is quite large and they are made to entertain a mainly mestizo population. Mexican movies feature leading starlets who are almost always very European in appearance and are frequently smashing blond Caucasians. This means, of course, that the cinema queens who activate the fantasy life of Mexican men hardly resemble typical Mexicans at all.

Needless to say, Latin Americans with fairly recent European origins have strong incentives to maintain their image of foreignness. Before World War II many immigrants and their progeny, especially those with Northern European backgrounds, strove desperately to preserve a rigidly separate national identity and acted as if they were intent on reconstructing a piece of Europe on Latin American soil. The tendency today is for the descendants of immigrants to regard themselves as Latin Americans but "distinct" Latin Americans with lineages that stretch back to Europe. Those whose progenitors were

Northern Europeans are most emphatic about this—for instance, the *angloargentinos* (English-Argentineans) who have for generations carried on their visibly different life style within Argentinean society. Italian visitors to Latin America, who in Italy are used to a steady diet of stories about Germans, the Swiss, and Swedes treating their countrymen working abroad as inferiors, are pleasantly surprised to find that in Latin America the descendants of Italians glory in their Italian ancestry, owing to the social advantage it affords them.[49]

Aside from stressing family geneology, there are other ways in which Latin Americans can, in varying degrees, associate themselves with the highly admired primary centers of culture. Some of these methods demand money and others call for diligent effort; whatever the requirements involved, Latin Americans who can afford it are very much given to the sport.

One way that Latin Americans can associate themselves with the primary centers of culture is to learn one or more of the languages spoken in those centers. These languages are not only widely studied in Latin America but commonly studied with devotion. French was the rage before World War II; English is dominant now, with German and even Italian being quite popular. While there are obvious practical benefits involved in learning foreign languages, it is the prestige, not the monetary reward, that accounts for the kind of attention expended on such study. A former American ambassador to Argentina noted that elite families in that country took their French so seriously that sometimes they taught their children that prestigious language before they allowed them to learn their native Spanish.[50] A French traveler of the 1930s observed this same fascination with the French language among Brazilians, and he added that he frequently ran across Brazilians who spoke French better than many Frenchmen.[51] I have found this degree of linguistic perfection not uncommon even among English-speaking Latin Americans of middle and lower middle class origin who had never stepped outside the city, much less the country, of their birth.

Latin Americans can also identify with the West by learning as much about its literature, music, cinema, personalities, customs, fashions, and latest trends as they can. Generally speaking, the more knowledge they can display of Western culture, the more prestige they will gain. Latin Americans acquire this knowledge primarily from the media, which, as we have seen, is full of news and stories from and about the West. Latin Americans also learn much about the West through their educational systems. They learn, in fact, more about American and European peoples in their schools than they do about peoples who share the same continent or even the same borders. The best way for Latin Americans to acquire knowledge of Western countries is to spend some time traveling or residing in them. This fact, far more than the superior education, is the reason why Latin American elites prefer to send their sons and daughters to foreign universities, even for degrees in liberal arts.

Still another common technique that Latin Americans use to identify with the advanced countries is to surround themselves with Western goods. Latin Americans tend to assume automatically that foreign goods are higher-quality goods. However, even when domestic products are cheaper and of comparable quality, Latin Americans will often prefer imports because of the prestige that displaying these foreign items will bring. This social attitude is quickly demonstrated by following a Latin American conspicuous consumer guiding visitors around his house for a detailed lecture. Here, earthly goods are pointed out and acclaimed not only for their intrinsic merit but also for their point of origin: appliances from America, furniture from Italy, suits from Britain, windows from Spain, and that scotch in your hand —from Scotland. Nor am I the only person to be honored with such tours. The American historian Leslie Byrd Simpson once described what he saw in a Mexican home crammed full with the artifacts of prestige:

> It was a museum piece of velvet draperies, chandeliers, spindly chairs, artificial flowers, and stuffed birds. "Isn't it beautiful!" she [the proud owner] exclaimed. They don't build houses like this anymore. *There is nothing Mexican in it!*[52]

Owing to the strength and prevalence of the prejudice against domestically made goods, Latin American manufacturers have had to resort to some uncanny tricks to work their way around it. The less forthright have simply imported foreign containers and stuffed locally made products into them.[53] The more honest have tried labeling their products with a foreign name, hoping somehow that this will endow them with a little class. Latin American merchants have also employed a version of the latter technique by giving their shops foreign names like Larry, Jenny, Daisy, or Kent, even though inside they do not offer a single imported item for sale.[54]

Apart from the enormous amount of attention paid to Western culture and the status significance of anything associated with it, Latin Americans reveal their lack of confidence in themselves and their national inferiority complex by their extreme sensitivity over Western attitudes toward their society. The problem is not so much that Westerners think ill of Latin America but that they hardly think of Latin America at all. What this neglect implies to Latin American nationalists is that Westerners do not pay attention to Latin American culture because they see little within it that is worth paying attention to. Latin Americans, of course, receive constant reassurances from Western politicians about the "equality" of peoples; but while Latin Americans insist on such statements, they cannot help but recognize that they have the flavor and consistency of a bland liberal mush spooned out with (usually) unintentional condescension. The reason for this is that Latin Americans know as well as everybody else that peoples, like individuals, are not equal in the sense of being the same in every particular; and they are haunted by the idea, which is substantiated by the disinterest of those they admire so much, that their differences and inequalities (such as their underdeveloped economies) might reasonably be construed as marks of inferiority.[55]

As if bothered by the fact that the primary centers of culture do not reciprocate respect and esteem, one senses among Latin Americans a real hunger for international recognition, a yearning to produce renowned individuals and realize outstanding accomplishments that the rest of the world will look at and admire. This attitude is seen in the excitement caused by small achievers in Latin America who, after scoring some modest successes abroad, find their deeds received with delight back home and their persons elevated to the status of national heroes or heroines. A recurring illustration of this is the treatment lavished upon Latin American beauty queens. Latin American women are without question greatly accomplished in the art of femininity; and because of this, the most striking among them have frequently walked off the stage of premier international beauty contests wearing the crown. When this happens, the queen returns home to full-blown headlines, mammoth parades through the capital, receptions with the president, and toasts and honors without end. Another example: In 1968 a young Peruvian lad (who was a student at the University of Michigan and a member of the swimming team) won the U.S. intercollegiate 200-meter relay. Peru's leading newspapers welcomed the event with front page photographs, exuberant articles and biographies—in short, far more coverage than a small-town American newspaper would have given one of its favorite sons for the same achievement.[56] Heroic status of a similar nature is given to Latin Americans who play major league baseball in the United States, to soccer players who do well in international competition, and to athletes who return home victorious from the Olympics.[57]

If success in these sports events can be important, then so can failure; and nowhere are Latin Americans more emphatically reminded of failure than in the flag-waving, anthem-playing Olympic Games. When the news of these games fills the sports pages every four years, Latin Americans read about the triumphs of other peoples, not of their own young athletes. Between 1896, when the modern summer Olympics began, and 1968, all the Latin American countries combined had won only 23 gold medals, 11 of which were captured by Argentina during that country's better years. Latin America was considerably outdistanced by the United States, which during the same period won 545 gold medals, and was also surpassed by countries with far smaller populations, like Denmark with 28 gold medals, Switzerland with 37, the Netherlands with 38, and Finland with 80.[58] Whether this is important or not depends entirely upon the attitude of Latin Americans; and Latin American nationalists tend to regard Olympic success as Western European nationalists did during the 1936 games in Berlin—as a sign of the national vigor of a people and their ability to achieve excellence. In 1968, when the games were hosted in Mexico, Mexicans were frequently heard in private conversations dejectedly describing themselves and their fellow Latin Americans as a "weak race."[59] The subsequent emergence of Cuba as a repectable sports power was a direct nationalist reaction against this sense of humiliation, and at present it is as much a part of the spirit of revolution in Cuba as the organized effort to eliminate the humiliation of economic underdevelopment.

In addition to these signs of a nationalist craving for international recognition, Latin Americans are prone to reveal their sensitivity to foreign opinion in much more direct fashion. At times this takes the form of protests over the way the foreign media depict Latin America. For example, on one occasion an Ecuadorian ambassador lodged a strenuous objection to an article in an American magazine that referred to his country as "tiny and poverty-ridden." The ambassador made it clear he preferred the description "relatively small and underdeveloped."[60] The ambassador's neighbors in Peru went one step further when faced with a similarly offending article in the American business magazine *Fortune*. This particular article took note that "the annual budget of Peru is slightly less than that of General Motors." The statement was not only accurate but effective as a way of conveying to American readers the relative smallness of the Peruvian economy. Peruvian leaders, however, were so insulted that their sovereign state should be compared to a U.S. company that they banned the magazine from the country.[61] That the high-level government officials of a country should react in such a fashion to a mere article in an American magazine is, to say the least, remarkable.

This same sort of sensitivity or hypersensitivity is also evident in the interpersonal exchanges between Latin Americans and gringos. Gringos in Latin America are continually being asked what they think of the country they are visiting. If, however, they wish to express negative criticisms, they can freely do so only after they have established mutually understood relationships of equality with the Latin Americans who are listening. Otherwise, the foreigners' unfavorable appraisals, even if they are widely shared by Latin Americans, will likely be seen as a confirmation of a sense of superiority that Latin

Americans readily imagine gringos to have. Latin Americans, in fact, are so sensitive to subtle signs of superiority that they can sometimes detect them when they don't exist. Even observers very sympathetic to Latin American viewpoints admit that it is difficult for gringos, no matter how they might try, to allay all such feelings of suspicion.[62]

The importance of the opinion foreigners hold toward Latin American society tends to rise in proportion to the importance of the foreigner. In the late 1950s, a well-known North American arrived in Peru and was, of course, inevitably asked by reporters about his impressions of the country. One of the questions the interviewers directed at him was, "Do all the people of the United States think that Peruvians wear feathers and ride llamas?" The American answered diplomatically and assured them that very few of his countrymen held such conceptions. The following day the results of the interview appeared in the Lima press under the headline "Not All Americans Believe Peruvians Wear Feathers And Ride Llamas."[63]

The distinguished foreign visitor must tread with extreme care in Latin America, for if he or she allows some indiscreet remark to slip, the repercussions can sometimes endure beyond a lifetime. In 1912 a famous French actress briefly visited Latin America and upon her return to France was asked by a reporter what she thought of the people there. Actresses are media figures, not bound by the conventions of diplomacy, and they often feel pressured to think up cute remarks for public consumption. She responded, "They are Indians who wear coats." Apparently this rather limp attempt at humor by a flighty French actress found its way back to Latin America and darted "across the Continent from mouth to mouth."[64] Over half a century later when everyone connected with the affair had long departed, a sensitive Cuban writer was still smarting. Angrily recounting the incident, he proceeded to fling it at the U.S. State Department: "Sometimes we Latin Americans feel that the State Department of the United States simply looks upon us as Indians, uneducated Indians without the coat."[65]

THE SUPERIORITY COMPLEX

An important reason why Latin Americans are sensitive to feelings of superiority on the part of foreigners is that very often foreigners really do harbor such sentiments. The emotional reflex of superiority is, in fact, the logical counterpart of the national inferiority complex because the same social conditions that have produced the one have also produced the other.

As with the inferiority complex, evidence of the superiority complex can be found in various places. It most clearly appears in the published writings of foreigners who made their observations before World War II. The reason for this is not that the conditions which have created these sentiments have changed drastically but that the prevailing Western conventions of public "respectability" have. Before the war writers who were considered "respectable" were allowed much more than is the case today to hold the beliefs that a hierarchy of civilizations existed in the world and theirs, at least in some respects, was unquestionably superior to Latin American civilization. The kinds of statements made by these authors reveal much about the attitudes of both the authors and their readers. For example, one respectable American journalist at the turn of the century was well within the bounds of public propriety when he made this matter-of-fact observation about what he saw in Brazil: "The native Brazilian regards the foreigner who comes to his shores as a very superior being and, comparatively speaking, this appreciation is apt to be correct."[66] Comments that would sound rasping and even "racist" by contemporary standards were quite acceptable to the audiences of the American writer Wallace Thompson even though he described Mexican society as a "bottomless pit of age-old degeneracy of mind and emotion."[67] Differing standards of public propriety are equally evident in more kindly treatments of Mexican society, as in Harry L. Foster's *A Gringo in Mañana-Land:* "When one travels through Mexico, one is amazed to discover that the Mexicans do not appear a cutthroat lot."[68] A ready and gracious acceptance of their own society's incontrovertible superiority over the Latin American was also possible for Western scholarly figures: Charles Darwin's experiences in Latin America led that eminent biologist to describe Argentina as a "savage nation" and Brazilian society as scarred by "moral debasement."[69] In the early twentieth century a sociologist from the University of Wisconsin could stand before his colleagues and, without running the risk of discrediting himself, call Mexico a "sick society" because the people lacked the "moral character and social institutions of the descendants of the Puritans."[70]

As a general rule the published writings of foreign observers of this era show very little praise for Latin American society venturing beyond the trivial or the romantic. Sometimes their tone betrays exasperated anger and hostility but more often pity and condescending amusement. Again and again appear terms and expressions such as the following: "inordinate pride," "duplicity," "high threshold for sustaining pain," "apathy," "lethargy," "inertia," "lack of initiative," "inalterable indolence," "natural laziness," "ignorance," "complete absense of responsibility," "disposition to talk rather than to act," "disposition to make money by intrigues rather than by legitimate business."[71]

These generations of commentators were also much given to a particular brand of paternalistic sympathy that treated Latin Americans kindly and firmly, as one would children who required guidance. The following passages written by American authors discussing the Cuban people are typical expressions of these paternalistic sentiments:

> The creoles of Cuba are neither angels nor brutes; they are, it is true, a long-suffering and somewhat indolent people, lacking in a great degree the stern qualities of the Anglo-Saxon and the Anglo-Norman races, but nevertheless intelligent, if wanting culture, and not without those noble aspirations for independence and freedom destitute of which they would cease to be men, justly forfeiting all claim to our sympathy and consideration.[72]

> In their present experiment to realize their aspirations, there should be stretched out to the Cubans not the strong hand, but the helping hand of the United States. . . . Cuba will be benefited by the presence and the example of many Americans who will settle on the Island.[73]

When it came to expressing their feelings of superiority, however, foreigners in Latin America spoke far more strongly through their actions than their published writings. Many of these foreigners did not respect the culture of the country they were living in and therefore did everything they could to preserve their own national identity. The main method they used to achieve this was to band together in foreign enclaves, or *colonies*, surrounded by the country rather than living in it. In general, the more backward the area of Latin America, the more pronounced were the sentiments of superiority and inferiority, and the more complete the isolation of gringos became. In Guatemala, for example, Americans working for the United Fruit Company went so far as to fence in their residential area with barbed wire in order to discourage any unauthorized "natives" from wandering in.[74] Foreigners in other countries did not segregate themselves to this extent, but they did commonly stress their apartness from the natives by living together in their own special neighborhoods, by celebrating their own national holidays while ignoring those of the host country, by flying their own national flags over their homes, by sending their children to their own schools, and by entertaining in their own clubs.[75] Foreigners of British origin were especially keen on preserving every detail of their national culture. They characteristically spent much of their social time in elaborate retreats they built for themselves where they could play rugby, cricket, and billiards, discuss British politics at the bar, and lunch on kidney pie. In the most torpid climates they dressed their servant girls in black cotton dresses with lacy white aprons and had them serve up steaming hot cups of tea with Crosse & Blackwell biscuits at precisely the proper time of day.[76] These habits are still conspicuous enough to cause British visitors I have encountered to claim that nowhere in their experience have they seen British quite so quintessentially British as the British expatriates in Latin America.

World War II serves as a convenient though very rough divide to mark a perceptible change, not so much in the sentiments that foreigners in Latin America feel but in the manner in which they are willing to express them. For a number of reasons, the proclivity to interpret differences among societies in terms of superiority and inferiority is definitely not in fashion in this postcolonial era of Western civilization. When Western visitors and residents in Latin America feel the emotions of superiority, most are much more inclined than was previously the case to be discreet about them outside their circle of intimates, while others have a tendency to feel guilty about the fact that they experience them at all.

Symbolic of the way Western writers on Latin America have responded to the changing definition of acceptable public etiquette has been the terminology they now use to classify impoverished Latin American countries. Old-fashioned terms like "backward" and "uncivilized" (French authors were fond of *l'Amerique sauvage*) have come to be regarded as in bad taste. The expressions now favored are "underdeveloped countries," "LDCs" ("lesser developed countries"), and most favored of all "developing countries" (whether they are developing or not).

These new names have been little source of comfort to the hungry masses of Latin America; but since they are more acceptable to the better-fed classes, they can justifiably be regarded as an improvement over the previous terminology. The difficulty is not in the names themselves but in the fact that the new diplomatic language reflects the disposition of contemporary analysts of underdevelopment to shy away from criticisms that might make them sound like pompous imperialists denigrating the natives. The social critics' squeamishness about this has been instrumental in introducing what the Swedish economist Gunnar Myrdal has identified as a condescending "diplomatic" bias into much of the current literature on underdevelopment.[77] As a result of this bias, tough issues like corruption are avoided or nervously dismissed as unimportant. (Some Western writers, applying an obvious double standard, have condoned government corruption in Third World countries as a form of government taxation.) Understatement of problems is considered more impartial, objective, and scholarly. Pessimistic assessments require bolstering by more evidence than optimistic ones. Worst of all, the question of values and their relationship to underdevelopment is ignored or glossed over because it appears to touch upon the delicate subject of moral behavior. Facilitating the latter deficiency has been the fact that Western economists, who have dominated the study of underdevelopment, are encouraged by their training to focus on the scarcity of capital impediment to economic growth (see pp. 5–7). By doing so they have been able to write entire books on the problem of underdevelopment while avoiding a discussion of modernization-impeding values, which are the most important cause of the problem to begin with.

Unlike foreign social critics, who are under a professional obligation to be as unflinchingly candid as possible in their observations, foreign residents in Latin America have much more freedom to adopt the style of public decorum with which they feel most comfortable. While foreigners who live and work in contemporary Latin America still commonly reveal sentiments of superiority, they also have been influenced by the more diplomatic style of the postwar period. The trend now is to avoid being taken for "ugly Americans" or loudly prideful chauvinists. When they have emphatically negative statements to make about Latin American culture, they are more likely to confine them to the safety of private conversations. They also have shown some adaptability in altering those aspects of their lifestyles that could be interpreted as implicit statements of superiority. Today, they are more inclined to recognize their responsibility for learning the native language, less inclined to segregate themselves from the rest of society, and particularly the younger foreigners in the Europeanized areas of Latin America, more willing to socially mix with Latin Americans on a regular basis.

The changing notions of public propriety among Westerners in Latin America have resulted in a more pronounced conflict between what they think they should do and what they feel like doing; this, in turn, has brought about a shift in the kind of paternalism that Westerners are apt to display. When motivated by old-fashioned paternalism, Westerners tended to think it commendable of themselves to treat many Latin Americans with benevolent sympathy as they would children in need of growth and fatherly advice. Today they are inclined to think it commendable of themselves to treat Latin Americans as equals. There are foreigners who avoid this paternalism by relating to Latin Americans as a group more or less the same as they do to members of their own national group. Many others, however, cannot avoid revealing subtle and not so subtle paternalistic airs. Some of these are paternalist out of expediency—like the smug little gods whose adoption of fashionable egalitarian manners doesn't quite cover their pride and arrogance. Others are paternalistic out of sincerity—like the earnest liberal types who diligently plunge into a social gathering in order to prove to Latin Americans (and to themselves) how equal they are.

The problem with the new paternalism is that many Latin Americans sense it and resent it. Although they see more

Westerners making the effort to be equal, they still recognize it as an effort. What they see is the same internal conflict that the veteran Latin Americanist Frank Tannenbaum perceived when he wrote,

> We treat Latin Americans as a lesser people. We cannot really help ourselves and we cannot conceal our feeling. Latin Americans sense it in every gesture and attitude, even when we are condescendingly egalitarian. That is why the United States is watched with an unhappy sense of inferiority.[78]

THE NEGATIVE NATIONAL IDENTITY

The lack of confidence Latin Americans have in their national identity inevitably means they have what we have previously labeled a negative national identity (see p. 107). Disappointment over their national identity is something that Latin Americans *feel*, and some Latin American nationalists feel it very deeply. At times Latin Americans experience the pain of a negative national identity when they look at their country's history and see that it has not been very successful. Felix Palavacini, for example, a former minister of education in Mexico, contends that Mexican students perceive Mexico's history largely as a story of failure:

> The history of Mexico which is taught in the schools is one which related that disaster after disaster crossed Mexico's path. The students leave school with disillusionment for what has happened to their country and with little optimism toward the future. This leads to the inferiority from which Mexicans suffer and their attitude of false nationalism which is not patriotism.[79]

But this is only the most obvious way that Latin Americans can experience disappointment over their national identities. They can also experience it during the course of their ordinary daily routine when they have to contend with the values and social behavior of the people surrounding them. How values and social behavior can trigger in Latin Americans negative feelings about their national identity is the result of several factors that require some explanation.

Latin America is often described as a land torn by internal conflict, but the most significant conflict of all taking place in that continent is one largely ignored by most observers. It is not a conflict of arms, of parties or of ideologies, but of value systems. The values that are conducive to the process of modernization, that bolster national strength, and that enhance national pride are those that are challenging the status quo. The values that are on the defensive are those that prolong national weakness. The latter values are not only the "traditional" ones normally associated with "feudal" or "semifeudal" societies but also those likely to develop when human beings are uprooted from their village agricultural environments and placed in large urban centers where the old problem of a struggle for survival takes on a substantially new character.

The most important part of the contest in this continental conflict of values is definitely not between believers who espouse fundamentally different ideals. The majority of Latin Americans are basically agreed on the standard nationalist goal of a strong, prosperous, well-respected nation-state as well as on the kinds of values that are most likely to bring about this end. The real battle is between what Latin Americans cognitively judge to be ideal behavior and the kind of behavior they feel caught up in for reasons of either emotional or material self-interest. Latin American vivos, for example, are well aware of the need for cooperation and trust among human beings, but they are afraid of changing their lifestyles for fear of others taking advantage of them once their defenses are lowered. An assembly line engineer will usually accept the idea that he should, when necessary, dirty his hands on the machinery for which he is responsible; but he is not likely to do so because the prestige patterns of his society do not support the idea that manual labor is dignified. No matter how completely the engineer and others around him have accepted the logical argument that manual labor should not be beneath them, they are still emotionally conditioned to react to such activities as humiliating and "deprestiging." Everywhere in Latin America values which discourage modernization are losing the battle for intellectual respectability. They are, however, still firmly grounded in prevailing prestige patterns and vicious circles of individual self-interest. And because these values are so deeply rooted in the emotional and material self-interests of the people, there is nothing, absolutely nothing, in Latin American society more difficult to reform.

Latin Americans have come to think highly of modernization values, not because of their inherent beauty, but because they recognize that such values have assisted the more affluent peoples of the world in achieving their high levels of economic prosperity. Not surprisingly, Latin Americans have also come to make a close association between modernization-encouraging values and the values held by inhabitants of modernized countries. So strong has this association grown in the consciousness of Latin Americans that they sometimes identify a specific modernization-encouraging value by naming it after a foreign nationality. Punctuality, for example, is not a well-developed trait among Latin Americans; consequently, if a Latin American wishes to emphasize that he expects someone else to be on time for say, an appointment at six o'clock, he will sometimes convey this idea by insisting that the other person arrive at six o'clock "American time" (*hora americana*). Mutual trust is another modernization-encouraging value that is weak among Latin Americans; thus, when a Latin American wishes to assure another that he indeed intends to keep his word, he expresses this by referring to his promise as his "English word" (*palabra de inglés*). In a similar spirit, Chileans once loved to refer to themselves as the Englishmen of Latin America because they felt that they were better endowed with modernization-encouraging values than other peoples on the continent. In other periods, Argentinean and Southern Brazilians have been impressed enough with their relative levels of economic virtue to lay claim to the title "Yankees of South America."

Just as Latin Americans are strongly inclined to associate modernization-encouraging values with foreigners, they are strongly inclined to associate modernization-impeding values with themselves. What this has meant is that since Latin Americans have grown more and more dissatisfied with the values that hold back their progress and quality of life, they have also grown more dissatisfied with the values they recognize as characteristic of their own people. This kind of dissatisfaction is widespread and influences the poor and illiterate as well as the better educated. Latin Americans might be heard to curse loudly their "bad Spanish blood" (referring to their heritage of Hispanic values), or to regret sadly that their country was colonized by Iberians and not by the British or French. More frequently, they bitterly attack particular values. The envy reflex, for example, is a habitual target of their anger, and the following remarks are typical of the criticism they vent against it:

> My people cannot stand to see another rise above them. When I rented my own little store, my best friends became jealous. When I painted my house, my neighbors thought I was trying to shame them. And after I purchased my new car, several people stopped speaking to me. Every one tries to pull the one above him down to his own level. If you try to get ahead, you make enemies. If you don't get ahead, you are criticized for laziness or stupidity. My people are hard to live with.[80]

> Thinking of Mexico's system of life, I am very disappointed. It is just that when I was living in the United States, [this man had worked in the U.S. as a *bracero*, a temporary farm worker] I could see that people were glad when a friend got ahead, you know what I mean? "Congratulations, man, it's great that things are going good for you." Everybody would congratulate him if he bought a new car or a house or something. But in Mexico, when a friend of mine, with a lot of sacrifice and hard work and skimping on food, finally managed to buy a new delivery truck, what happened? He parked it in front of his house and when he came out all the paint was scratched off. If that isn't pure envy, what is it?

Instead of trying to raise a person's morale, our motto here is, "If I am a worm, I'm going to make the next fellow feel like a louse." Yes, here you always have to feel you are above. I have felt this way myself, that's why I say it. I guess I'm a Mexican, all right. Even if you live on the bottom level, you have to feel higher up. I've seen it among the trash pickers; there's rank even among thieves. They start arguing, "You so-and-so, all you steal is old shoes. But me, when I rob, I rob good stuff." So the other one says, "You! Turpentine is all you drink. At least, I knock off my 96-proof pure alcohol, which is more than you ever do." That's the way things are here.[81]

Latin Americans also work their resentment of the envy reflex into heavy-hitting parables:

Once, long ago in Mexico, a pastor was tending his sheep while he watched a pot in which he was boiling milk. He noted that the lid rose and fell, and surmised the connection between the movement of the lid and the steam inside. That is how the steam engine was first invented. But the pastor was quickly killed by his neighbors, who were envious of his discovery. Thus, Mexicans will always be poor and ignorant, and Americans will be educated and rich.[82]

One of the Latin American values most passionately despised by Latin Americans—or more specifically, by Latin American women—is machismo. The unhappiness Latin American women feel over macho aggressiveness is reinforced by their becoming increasingly aware that the exploitative practices they suffer at the hands of their men are not so much universal male traits as Latin American male traits.[83] This awareness, as well as the rage that consumes many female victims of machismo in Latin America, is well expressed by a lower-class Mexican girl who had these words for the "famous, cursed, Mexican machismo" of her experience:

I, like an infinite number of other Mexican women, was part of that cruel game, in which the domineering male wins. . . . There is nothing generous, noble, or worthy about it. . . . It is a barbarous act of egotism and advantage, adorned with persuasive words. . . .

How I wanted to pack my things and go far away! I dreamed of going to the border, to California. Perhaps I would marry a *gringo*, who would be more understanding than Mexican men. . . . I could never get along with a dominating, imperious man. I didn't like crushing authority. I didn't want to feel inferior. . . . I couldn't be sweet or submissive enough to please the men here. The *macho* Mexican, in his pride and vanity, considered women inferior and enjoyed humiliating them. Only he is right and only his feelings count. In a discussion, he is not interested in learning the truth, but only in out-talking the others. If a man in a Nash is overtaken by a Chrysler, he will speed to pass it, to show he is superior, after all. A women cannot walk alone, without some virile man asserting his "rights" over her.[84]

All this relates to a discussion of the negative national identity because even Latin Americans who do not normally think about Latin America's position in the world often see about them social behavior they recognize as exploitative, an impediment to modernization, *and* characteristically Latin American. Exposure to such behavior tends to trigger in them negative feelings about being part of, and identified with, a national collectivity where the behavior is especially pronounced. Since they regularly encounter social conduct they hold in low regard, they also regularly experience negative feelings about their national identities. It is in this way that the negative national identity becomes for them a frequent and familiar part of their routine lives.

The significant impact of the negative national identity upon the broader Latin American population is demonstrated by the propensity of ordinary Latin Americans to express repeatedly and emphatically in private conversation their poor opinion of their national culture. In my own experience, I found Latin Americans disposed, almost eager, to bring up this issue, including complete strangers who would approach me in public places and spontaneously launch into lengthy discussions on the subject. While conversations of this sort take many different shapes, the comments made and the feelings conveyed by the Mexicans in Oscar Lewis's anthropological studies are very typical:

> Marta Sánchez, a young woman discussing the United States: I imagine it [the United States] is a country so civilized that even the people are different. Here, if there isn't something in it for a person, no one will do you a favor. Or if someone does, when you least expect it he demands repayment. Here people have too much self-interest. Of course, there are good people, too, but in Mexico one does not progress. We have freedom to do and undo as we please and we don't exactly die of hunger, but it is like being in a stagnant pond—there is no way out, one cannot get ahead. From what I have seen in the movies and newspapers, it is not that way up north.[85]

> Roberto Sánchez, a young man of the same family:
> Mexico is my country, right? And I have a special and profound love for it, especially for the capital. We have a freedom of expression and above all, a freedom to do whatever we please, that I haven't found elsewhere. I have always been able to earn my living better here—you can support yourself by selling squash seeds. But regarding Mexicans, well, I don't know whether it is because I myself have behaved badly, but it seems to me that there is a lack of good will among them.[86]

> Pedro Martínez, an old peasant reminiscing toward the end of his life:
> In a republic like ours, we cannot progress. We are remaining behind. We are ambitious but we cannot do a thing because we are

not organized. That's why we Mexicans are not worth much. The peasants are ignorant and more than a little stupid. And if one gets to know something, right off he tries to exploit the poor, the ones who are at the bottom. . . .

In the United States it must be different. I think there the people are more educated and have a conscience. And where there is education, there is money. They have lots of companies and societies that get together capital and because they know how to behave, it doesn't go to their heads. On the contrary, they progress. There is cooperation there because everyone understands, everyone knows, everyone can speak. There are lots of good heads there and naturally things go well. But not here in Mexico. Here everyone is for himself and takes advantage.[87]

Unquestionably the most important lesson we can learn from the existence of the negative national identity is that it forces Latin Americans to work toward achieving a positive national identity—that is to say, a national identity of which they can be genuinely proud. Contemporary Latin Americans do not feel free to admit openly that they are engaged in this quest but rather use indirect language when talking about it. For example, they often express their search for a positive national identity in terms of a quest for national definition or meaning. In every country in Latin America, politicians and intellectuals claim to be searching for something they call "Brazilianism," (*brasilidade*), "Chileanism" (*chilenidad*), "Peruvianism" (*peruanidad*), or "Venezuelanism" (*venezolanidad*). Sometimes they lengthen these words into phrases and say they are in pursuit of national "realities" or "essences," such as the "Colombian reality" (*realidad colombiana*) or the "Mexican essence" (*esencia mexicana*). On other occasions they ask themselves the familiar identity question but couched in nationalist terminology: "Who am I, this Argentine?" About this the Venezuelan critic Arturo Uslar-Pietri has written:

The first question we should ask ourselves is: "What is the Latin American? What are we?" Never before has a society had, to such a degree, this tragic obsession, which might be called the "ontological anguish" of the Latin American. . . . The Latin American has always, somewhat like Hamlet, pondered his real nature by asking himself, "What am I? White, Negro, Indian, *mestizo*, European, something that partakes of all this, or something distinct?" This deep concern for knowing what we are, what I have called the "anguish of being," has existed since the Conquest.[88]

Mexico's leading social thinkers also appeared to be motivated by the identity quest when they established a prestigious journal formally dedicated to the "discovery and evaluation of the essence of the Mexican" (*descubrir y valorar la esencia del lo mexicano*). One of their number, Leopoldo Zea, has said that while nothing comparable to this "preoccupation with [national] being" exists among Western peoples, it is nonetheless of crucial importance to Mexicans.[89] Another famous Mexican intellectual, Octavio Paz, has described this search for "being" as nothing less than a national "crisis":

> The whole history of Mexico, from the Conquest to the Revolution, can be regarded as a search for our own selves. . . . We have never succeeded in creating a form that would express our individuality. . . . What we desperately need is a concrete solution, one that will give meaning to our presence on earth.[90]

In the following chapter we shall discuss in specific terms how Latin Americans have sought to discover their national reality—that is to say, to realize a positive national identity. This will introduce us to the vital subject of nationalist behavior in Latin America, and we shall see how the concepts of positive and negative national identity are absolutely indispensable to a proper understanding of Latin American nationalism.

5
LATIN AMERICAN NATIONALISM

The negative national identity is such a powerful psychological force in Latin American life that virtually all forms of nationalistic behavior can be seen as an attempt to deal with it. One way that some Latin Americans try to deal with a negative national identity is to deny they have any nationalist identity at all. In place of a nationalist identity, these Latin Americans adopt what may be called a *cosmopolitan antinationalist identity*. Latin Americans who adopt this alternative means of self-definition insist on being evaluated as individuals, not as members of a particular nationality. Through their point of view, every civilized human being should absorb the best features of world civilization; and more importantly, each individual should be judged on how well he accomplishes this, not on whether his society has made significant contributions to that civilization. Latin American antinationalists argue in this fashion because they regard their national culture as inferior and do not wish to feel any more responsibility or shame for its deficiencies than foreigners do. At all costs they want to avoid having their sense of self-esteem depend upon their evaluation of the society in which they happen to be born. The main techniques by which these antinationalists attempt to disassociate themselves from their society is to criticize severely and frequently the negative features of their own culture and, secondly, to learn as much as possible about a culture they do admire, namely Western culture. Obviously, Latin Americans who are in the best position to pursue seriously this kind of identity are wealthy Latin Americans who have the time and money to be educated in Western ways.

Another method Latin Americans use to deal with their negative national identity is that instead of trying to deny their national identity, they attempt to change its character from negative to positive. Latin Americans who prefer this might be referred to as *adoptive nationalists* because they feel that in order for their people to become equal to Western peoples and reap the rewards of a positive national

145

identity, their countrymen will have to imitate and adopt many of the cultural characteristics of Western peoples. Because they believe they must look to the West as a model, adoptive nationalists frequently praise Western culture while harshly criticizing aspects of their own. But the spirit in which they do this is entirely different from that of the cosmopolitan antinationalists: instead of trying to escape their national identity, they are attempting to change their society sufficiently so that their people can take genuine nationalistic pride in who they are.

A third way Latin Americans have of dealing with a negative national identity is simply to say they have a positive national identity. Because these nationalists are reacting against the tendency of many Latin Americans to look up to Western culture and down upon their own, we shall call them *reactive nationalists*. Reactive nationalists are easily identified because they do just the opposite of what adoptive nationalists do—that is to say, they extravagantly praise their own culture and severely condemn the West as spiritually inferior or morally bereft.

Reactive nationalism has come to completely dominate public life* in Latin America today. This has not always been the case for adoptive nationalism reigned supreme in the nineteenth and early twentieth centuries. Because the study of nationalism in Latin America lends itself to historical perspective, we shall begin our inquiry with the emergence of adoptive nationalism in the nineteenth century.

ADOPTIVE NATIONALISM

The origins of adoptive nationalism can be traced to the earliest decades of political independence when the newly freed Latin American countries ended their long colonial isolation and were opening up to foreign cultural influence. It was during this period that Western Europe was arriving at a point where it could influence Latin America and other foreign societies to a profound degree. The reason for this was that European society at that time was developing into the most spectacular civilization history had ever seen. What made this particular civilization so different from those that had preceded it can best be seen in the radically new meaning the Europeans gave to the concept of human progress. Until the rise of modern European civilization, people lived in a world (and could scarcely imagine any other) where human progress was a glacial process that could be measured

---

*In the private conversations of Latin Americans, all three viewpoints, reactive nationalist, adoptive nationalist, and cosmopolitan antinationalist, are frequently heard.

only in millennia. People, in other words, lived in essentially the same manner as their ancestors did hundreds or even thousands of years earlier. The modern era of human history began when Western Europeans discovered ways of dramatically accelerating the pace of human progress so that it could be witnessed within the brief span of an individual's lifetime.

The most obvious feature of the progress taking place in Europe was the incredibly rapid development of its productive capacity. For 10,000 years before the modern European period, human civilization had created comparatively few improvements in production techniques. During this long, technologically stagnant stretch of history, people used only the simplest tools and machines and relied mainly on human or animal muscle to propel them. And because of their technological primitiveness, the masses of humanity throughout the world were poor and stayed poor. It has been estimated that on the eve of the modern age, the average annual per capita income in the world was about one hundred dollars—no more than in the days of Caesar Augustus.[1] Europeans began to break out of this pattern of poverty and low productivity when they started to develop complex power machinery driven by the energy stored in fossil fuels. Eventually European innovations in both technology and management led to a vast social transformation known as the Industrial Revolution. Within a few decades after this upheaval began, Europeans had produced more goods and services than had all previous generations of humanity combined.

The great appeal of this production revolution, of course, was that it promised to make life better for human beings. Slowly, as more and more people gained from the expanding output, the European masses improved their standard of living. The economist Adam Smith boasted that the average English worker was richer than an African chief of "ten thousand naked savages."[2] Since benefits such as nutritious diets, adequate clothing, sound housing, and efficient transportation are regarded by most people as positive goods, it was with some reason that Europeans came to regard their high living standards as an important measure of civilized life.

Besides raising the general level of consumption among the masses, European progress improved European society in other ways. Advances in medicine ensured Europeans longer, healthier lives and increased the chances of survival for their infants. More productive agriculture, the stockpiling of foodstuffs, and better means of transport enabled them to triumph over the age-old scourge of mass famine. Stronger central governments were able to control highway bandits, sea pirates, and marauding private armies more effectively, thus providing their citizens greater security of life and property.

European society in modern times not only became wealthier, healthier, and safer but also less brutal. In order to see this, let us glance at the hangman's rolls for London in 1781. In that year an Englishman by the name of James Smith stole two half-crowns; another, Charles Sheppard, broke into a house; and another, Abraham Pry, stole a bundle of stockings. All three were caught and summarily executed.[3] Had those poor devils been born among the ranks of more modern Englishmen, society would have dealt with them far more humanely. Common folk in Europe, as part of their regular Sunday entertainment, used to flock to the public executions that snuffed out the lives of Smith, Sheppard, and Pry. As European society proceeded into the new era, these barbaric spectacles, along with witch-hunts, torture, and legalized slavery, were eliminated.

In view of the many humanistic advances taking place in Europe, it is ironic that the kind of modern progress that most captivated the imaginations of the other peoples of the world was the development of Western military power. Like the process of modernization itself, awsome Western military might towering above that of all rivals is of fairly recent historical origin. When Queen Elizabeth I of England dealt with the Great Mogul Akbar of India, she treated him as an equal and with genuine respect. Later generations of European leaders wielded much more power than non-European rulers when they had the advantages of iron and steel ships, heavy guns, honest, efficient state bureaucracies, large, unified national communities backing their foreign adventures, and new managerial techniques such as the creation of the public debt that provided their treasuries with seemingly inexhaustible financial resources. The world had never before seen such power, and the cold shadow of its presence alone was enough to spark frantic attempts at modernization by non-Western peoples.

One of the results of the impressive economic, military, and humanistic advances that took place in Europe was that Europeans developed a strong sense of national pride and self-assurance. Stirring up such high spirits was their belief that they as a people were becoming more and more free. Democracy freed them from arbitrary, authoritarian government; science freed them from the psychic torment of superstition; machines freed them from want and the drudgery of hard work; medicine freed them from the plagues and diseases that ravaged the ancients. Whatever the deficiencies of the present (after all, the new era was only beginning), they would be made up for with more progress in the future. The prospects for the unborn generations looked positively brilliant. Those who had any doubts had only to look at the great distance traveled from the recent, dark past.

Another result of their dramatic progress was that Europeans readily concluded that their culture was the highest form of civilization on earth. No non-European people could outproduce them, threaten them, or claim to be more free. Underlying the nationalisms of the most successful European peoples was a calm sense of self-confidence. "God is an Englishman," claimed English nationalists only half in jest. And in total seriousness they declared that to be born an Englishman was to have won first place in the lottery of life.

The nationalism of Western Europeans was, however, not entirely absorbed in self-congratulation. European nationalists took the time not only to evaluate themselves but also to form an opinion about the fate of less fortunate "backward" peoples. In these thoughts they were strongly influenced by Christian and Enlightenment universalist traditions. They professed the belief that all human beings were rational beings and therefore they were basically equal. Less advanced peoples, they predicted, would eventually follow the enlightened path of human progress that the Europeans had discovered and all would become part of the same civilized world community.

Western European nationalism, then, harbored a kind of dual outlook with respect to "backward" peoples. It was confidently ethnocentric in its view of the present yet also very egalitarian in its view of the future. While it held the European way of life to be the standard of civilized behavior for the entire world, at the same time it expressed the conviction that all peoples of the earth were capable of joining the upward march of human advancement. It must be noted, however, that even the generous, universalist side of European nationalism contained the potential for European arrogance, for what would Europeans think if some peoples of the world failed to live up to the challenge of the oncoming new age?

Bringing Europe to America

It was not just Europeans but also Latin Americans who found themselves looking at the accomplishments of emerging modern Europe with rapt astonishment. Many of these Latin Americans began to dream of the same "progress" and "freedom" for their own peoples. They eagerly adopted the European view that the new civilization Europeans were developing was not just European but universal and was, therefore, destined to spread and benefit the other peoples of the world, including Latin Americans.

Because modern civilization was so closely identified with European civilization, the early Latin American advocates of modernization became what we have termed adoptive nationalists. Adoptive nationalists unabashedly maintained that Latin Americans had to learn about and adopt European culture in order to modernize their countries. They further contended that Latin Americans had to become "Europeanized" in order to become "civilized." Juan Bautiste Alberdi, for example, the father of the Argentinean constitution, stated unequivocally, "Everything that has to do with civilization in our land has its origins in Europe . . . . always is Europe the molder of our civilization."[4] Domingo Faustino Sarmiento, another eminent Argentinean of his time and often regarded as Argentina's greatest president, saw the fullest development of modern European ideals in the United States and accordingly exhorted his fellow South Americans to adopt the culture of that country:

> South America has remained backward and is in danger of losing her providential mission to become part of modern civilization. . . . Let us achieve the level of development of the United States. Let us be America, like the sea is the Ocean. Let us be the United States![5]

The first step to reform was criticism. With the promise of modernized culture on the horizon, the adoptive nationalists unhesitatingly condemned the nonmodern culture they saw about them. In the view of these crusaders, the society in which they lived was a "backward and absurd civilization."[6] It was not their style to search for euphemisms such as "developing" and "lesser developed," for in order to get where they felt they were going, they had to decisively reject where they were. Instead, they described their peoples and countries with approximately the same terminology as the Europeans used, summoning up again and again hard-slugging adjectives like "uncivilized," "backward," "retarded," and "barbarian."[7]

The Latin American adoptive nationalists blamed their cultural backwardness on their historical heritage. They wrote with bitterness about the bad hand that history had dealt them and continuously lectured about the need to consciously break away from the regrettable past. They identified many of the negative features of their cultural legacy as Iberian in origin and often lamented that their continent had been colonized by the most medieval and least modern people in Western Europe. The leading Chilean intellectual José Victorino Lastarria, for example, expressed the following basic idea in many different contexts: "The principal cause of our political and social disaster lies in our Spanish heritage, and we cannot remedy these disasters except by reacting frankly, openly and energetically against that civilization."[8] The Latin American reformers had even less sympathy than this for their Indian and African heritages which they regarded as more distant from the culture of modern Europe than the Iberian. With characteristic vigor, they condemned these other cultural influences as "barbarian," "infidel," "pagan," and "savage."[9]

When discussing culture, foremost in the minds of the Latin American reformers were the values, customs, and social behavior of people. It was precisely these factors that were the central focus of their investigations into the backwardness, or underdevelopment, of their countries. Because they had the common sense to recognize that different kinds of people are apt to generate different levels of economic development, their inquiries into the poverty of nations were not clouded by the types of issues that dominate such analysis today (see pp. 3–7). These reformers were very concerned with the study of culture because they realized that for their people to evolve along European lines, they had to rid themselves of many features of their historical heritage, or more specifically, of values and customs that held back the process of modernization.

The two main strategies adoptive nationalists placed their hopes in to reform the values of their people were education and immigration. With regard to education, adoptive nationalists became ardent supporters of building public school systems that would teach modern values to the younger generations. While president of Argentina, Sarmiento worked so hard at improving his country's educational system that he went down in Argentinean history as the "Schoolmaster of the Nation." Sarmiento was particularly impressed by American culture and ordered a copy of Benjamin Franklin's autobiography—that classic expression of middle-class economic virtues—placed in every Argentinean classroom.[10]

For adoptive nationalists, an even more promising means of encouraging the spread of modernization values was the promotion of European immigration. These nationalists saw great potential in immigration for basically two reasons: First, they could see no more straightforward method of importing European values than hauling them over in the form of European settlers.[11] Secondly, they reasoned that the sight of these immigrants leading their disciplines, productive lives and reaping suitable rewards for their efforts would serve as a powerful object lesson to native Latin Americans and encourage them to imitate the work habits of the newcomers. On the latter point the influential Alberdi wrote:

Each European who arrives on our shores brings to us more civilization than many books on philosophy. He does this by bringing his habits which will in time be spread among our people. A lesson is not well understood if it is not personally seen, touched, and felt. A hard working man is the most edifying schoolbook.

Do we not wish to plant and to acclimatize to our soil English liberty, French culture and the durable work habits of the Europeans and North Americans? Let us plant living specimens of these in our soil by bringing to our land the people who have these customs.

Do we not want to prevail in our America the habits of order, of discipline and of industry? Let us fill America with people who

already have these habits well-developed within themselves. They will know how to communicate; alongside the industrious European the industrious American will form. . . .
If we want our countries to become great in a short time, let us bring from the outside the kind of people we want, those already imbued with the proper virtues and already settled in their ways.[12]

The point of view of these early modernizers might be better appreciated if we look through the eyes of Domingo Faustino Sarmiento and contrast certain immigrant colonies in Argentina with some typical native communities:

Pity and shame are aroused when we compare the German or Scottish colonies in the southern part of Buenos Aires with some of the towns in the interior of the Argentine Republic; in the former the cottages are painted, the front yards always neatly kept and adorned with flowers and pretty shrubs: the furniture simple but complete; copper or tin utensils always bright and clean; beds carefully curtained; and the occupants of the dwellings always industriously at work. Some such families have retired to enjoy the convenience of city life with great fortunes earned by their previous labors in milk, cheese, and butter production. The towns inhabited by natives of the country present a picture entirely the reverse. There, filthy children dressed in rags live amidst the packs of dogs; there, men lie on the ground in the most complete idleness; neglect and poverty are everywhere; a table and some baskets are the only furniture in the wretched huts which are remarkable in their overall impression of negligence and barbarism.[13]

It is obvious that from the very beginning Latin Americans looked at immigration in a very different light than did Americans. On the one hand, Americans were interested in European immigrants mainly for what the foreigners could provide their growing nation in brawn and physical labor. Americans also had an idealistic side to their view of immigration, for when they saw those grey immigrant masses huddled on the shores of New York, they often congratulated themselves for doing the unfortunates a favor. The proponents of immigration in Latin America, on the other hand, had quite a different point of view. They tended to look up to rather than down upon the new arrivals, value them for their spiritual as well as physical qualities, and count upon them to assist in the crucial nationalist task of reforming Latin American customs. One Chilean expressed these attitudes in the following fashion:

The great destiny of the nation does not depend so much on the rapid growth of the population as on its homogeneity and moral and intellectual progress. Thus the object of colonization in Chile is not so much to populate the country as to reform its habits and values. . . .

From this starting point, then, the policy of bringing colonists and establishing foreign colonies is proposed above all for the purpose of introducing to Chile better habits and customs.[14]

Other adoptive nationalists commonly described the social function of immigrants in much the same way. Through their point of view, European settlers were "agents of civilization"[15] who would bring about the "moral advancement of the ignorant masses"[16] by "activating" and "shaking our people from their habits of indolence."[17]

Because adoptive nationalists tended to regard values and morals as one and the same, they looked to the European immigrants to reform not only the values but also the morals of their people. When discussing morality they unashamedly described the immigrants as "superior," their own people as "inferior," and constantly spoke of European settlers "regenerating" (*regenerar*), "bettering" (*mejorar*), or "making more moral" (*moralizar*) the Latin American people. For example, one Chilean proponent of immigration, using the ideas and language typical of his day, wrote that "European immigration" was for Chile a "primordial question," that a generous state subsidy of immigration would render a bountiful return in "moral benefits" (*bienes morales*), and would help Chile approach the "marvelous material prosperity of the United States." Continuing on, he added:

> Human societies are educated like individuals: if you want to teach them, to make them more moral [*moralizarlos*], to rid them of their gross, indolent customs, put them in contact with superior men [*hombres superiores*]. Schools and teaching can do much to preserve customs and improve them, but the rapid regeneration of a people requires the presence and example of another more civilized people.[18]

Another enthusiast for immigration, after making the usual bows to the "fabulous material prosperity" of the United States, also saw the solution for Chile's poverty in terms of making Chileans more moral:

> Let us bring to our soil a population both numerous and intellegent, moral and hardworking, and we will have contributed to the betterment of the bad customs [*malos hábitos*] of the great majority of our people.
>
> Full steam ahead with immigration! Because immigration will cause the immorality [*inmoralidad*] and excesses of the people to disappear.[19]

The theme song of the adoptive nationalists was "Bring Europe to America." The adoptive nationalists meant by this that they wanted to teach both modern values and modern productive techniques to Latin Americans. Because they believed that modern culture was synonymous with European culture, they planned to accomplish their aim by exposing Latin Americans to European ways in every manner possible. They sought to reform the values of Latin American youths by using the public school systems and hoped to reach Latin American adults by literally swamping their countries with European immigrants, investments, and advisors.

The strategy of the adoptive nationalists was to Europeanize their countrymen to a sufficient extent so that they too could build up modern and prosperous nation-states. The ultimate objective was to eliminate the feeling of backwardness that Latin Americans had about their own countries and to give them a sense of pride in their national identities. As the years wore on, however, Latin American nationalists had to face up to the fact that the adoptive nationalist programs were not working or, if they were working to some extent, they were not having the intended effect.

The ideas the adoptive nationalists had on using the public educational system to reform the values of Latin Americans were logical enough as far as they went, but they failed to take into consideration the tenacious hold that traditional values had upon the people who did the teaching. The same phenomenon we have seen in more contemporary times in the Colombian educational system (see pp. 96–98) also plagued the adoptive nationalists in the nineteenth century. The adoptive nationalists had to depend upon the teachers to teach modern values, and the teachers found their sense of self-worth threatened by a value system that was radically different from the one with which they grew up.

Some adoptive nationalists strongly felt that massive immigration was the most powerful method they had of reforming the values of Latin Americans. Their expectation was that the European bearers of productionist virtue would eventually assume Latin American national identities and therefore would become Latin Americans with the same economic virtues. The adoptive nationalists also felt that the dramatic economic progress of the immigrants in Latin America would cause native Latin Americans to adopt the values that made the Europeans so economically successful.

The ideas that the adoptive nationalists had about immigration turned out to be deficient on two accounts. The first problem was that most countries in Latin America did not have enough immigrants even to give the plan a try. The second problem was that even though Argentina, Uruguay, and Southern Brazil did attract large numbers of immigrants, the presence of the immigrants in these countries did not have their intended effect. Adoptive nationalists were correct in their prediction that the immigrants would become economically successful;

but the reaction of the immigrants to that success was different from what the adoptive nationalists foresaw. The immigrants and their descendants tended to think of themselves as superior to the native Latin Americans and therefore resisted assimilation. Native Latin Americans, on the other hand, rather than adopting the productionist values of the immigrants, tended to look upon the prosperity of the foreigners in their land as confirmation of their belief that they were not capable of doing what foreigners could do. In other words, the economic success of the immigrants tended to reinforce the negative national identity of Latin Americans rather than eliminate it.

The overall adoptive nationalist strategy of inundating Latin America with European immigrants, investments, and advisors tended to have the same effect. Those areas that attracted large numbers of immigrants and substantial foreign investment experienced rapid economic growth, but in the minds of Latin Americans that growth was associated with foreigners for the simple reason that foreigners were largely responsible for making it happen. To cite an example, by the late nineteenth century Argentina had become one of the world's largest producers of beef and wheat. Yet it was foreigners who were the entrepreneurial leaders of the beef industry and it was British-built railroads and Italian labor that made Argentina into a wheat-exporting nation. The story was much the same throughout the Argentinean economy. In 1895, for example, foreigners made up 25 percent of the Argentinean population, yet they owned 81 percent of Argentina's industry and 74 percent of its commercial businesses.[20]

The net result of this was that by the turn of the century it was obvious that the strategy of the adoptive nationalists was not working. The adoptive nationalists, we recall, were not simply interested in modernization but modernization that gave their people an enhanced sense of national pride. Most countries in Latin America did not have enough immigration or foreign investment to effect economic development substantially; but even in those areas that did, the economic growth was so closely identified with foreigners that it did not result in the kind of positive national identity that the adoptive nationalists were hoping for.

At the same time that Latin Americans were beginning to doubt whether they would ever catch up with the advanced countries in Europe, the United States was adding insult to injury by showing that an excolony of Europe could match the European nations in rapid progress. Latin Americans were both fascinated and chagrined by the example of the "Anglo-Saxon" republic to the north. The Uruguayan writer Alberto Zum Felde captures well the somber mood of nationalistic Latin Americans of the time:

> The contrast between the enormous development of Saxon America and the lamentable backwardness of Latin America, was weighing on

the conscience of South Americans and was the unavoidable theme of all socio-historical inquiries. Already, some time before, the two most eminent sociologists ever produced in these countries, Sarmiento and Alberdi, had proclaimed the historical triumph of the Saxon peoples over the Latins, and the necessity for us, the South Americans, to adopt the values of the United States, rebelling against the old Hispanic vices that we had inherited from colonial times.

The years that followed did nothing but aggravate the crisis. What South Americans saw before them could not, in truth, have been more disconcerting. Here in the South: unpopulated rural areas; dead cities; ignorant and miserable masses; irresponsible governments oscilating between anarchy and despotism due to *caudillismo* and violent overthrows of governments; paralytic industries; bankrupt public finances living entirely by loans from across the Atlantic; oppressive government parasitism and cynical administration mortality; epidemics of rhetoric and disdain for work infecting the university youth as well as the *mestizo* rabble; and, as a consequence of all this, the idea abroad of our incapacity to provide for and govern ourselves that made us appear as countries in need of outside guidance.

There in the North: states densely populated with civilized and educated people; democratic liberty and civic order more solidly rooted than even in Europe; industrial production and financial activity competing with the best in the world; private initiative and self-government showing a positive development of will and character; and in consequence, a country that by virtue of its domestic strength could rank itself among the great powers of the world.

The failure of Latin America seemed to be a patent fact and the causes of this failure to be none other than the Hispanic and Latin character of our peoples.[21]

In the midst of this Latin American crisis of self-doubt, adoptive nationalism itself went into a crisis. Adoptive nationalists, we have seen, freely used the reform technique of severely criticizing the deficiencies of Latin American culture while lavishly praising European or American culture as a model to follow. In the early years adoptive nationalists could afford to be so forthrightly critical of their countrymen because they reasoned that while their people were indeed behind the Europeans and Americans, this was only because these peoples had been particularly favored by history. The expectation of the adoptive nationalists was that with conscious effort, Latin Americans would assimilate the desirable features of modern culture being nurtured abroad and themselves build up modern nation-states. Latin Americans were willing to accept the adoptive nationalist technique of severe public censure of their values so long as they believed that this would lead to reform and progress. The problem for adoptive nationalists came after several decades when it became painfully obvious that Latin America was failing to bring itself abreast of the Western world. In this changing context, the blistering criticisms of the adoptive nationalists seemed less like a catalyst for reform and more like a public admission of inferiority. Slowly Latin Americans grew restless for a new way of looking at their countries and themselves as a people. Under the pressure of these emotional needs, adoptive nationalism gradually faded from the public side of Latin American life, and in its place emerged an alternative form of collective self-definition—reactive nationalism.

REACTIVE NATIONALISM AND THE IDEA OF SPIRITUAL SUPERIORITY

As suggested by its name, reactive nationalism was a revolt against the condemnatory style and analytical method of adoptive nationalism. Latin Americans who turned to reactive nationalism were emotionally hungry for an interpretation of Latin American life that would vigorously praise their own culture and criticize that of the developed countries.

The first major eruption of reactive nationalism in Latin America took place shortly after the Spanish American War when a young Uruguayan intellectual by the name of José Enrique Rodó published a book called *Ariel*. Latin Americans were obviously ready for this work. It quickly became the most influential book ever written by a Latin American. Millions of Latin Americans not only accepted the ideas it contained but enthusiastically embraced them. And for the father of those ideas, Latin Americans could not do enough. During his lifetime, Latin Americans showered Rodó with honors of every description; and upon his death his countrymen declared a national day of mourning, ordered a state funeral that had hitherto been reserved only for presidents, and turned out by the thousands to weep, to grieve, and to console one another on their loss. Rodó was, in truth, more a spiritual than an intellectual leader for Latin Americans. In the reverent phrases of one of his disciples, "He speaks to our souls with more than earthly music . . . a message deep and grave, luminous and revivifying, that seems a psalm of life, a song of hope, a bugle call of victory."[22]

What was there in Rodó's writings that could have caused such a response from Latin Americans? *Ariel*, Rodó's major work, was primarily an essay about what was bad about North American society and good about his own. Its purpose was to build up Latin American nationalist pride by weakening or destroying the propensity of Latin Americans to admire the United States and to consider it a model for their own countries. When reading *Ariel*, one encounters Rodó talking to Latin Americans about familiar problems and preoccupations:

We imitate those in whose superiority and prestige we believe. Because of this we have a vision of a delatinized America (*América deslatinizada*) reformed in the image of the archetype of the North; we accept this vision voluntarily and not because it has been forced upon us by outside compulsion or conquest; it is a vision that floats through the dreams of many concerned about our destiny, inspires at every step solutions to problems, and constantly reveals itself in proposals for innovation and reform. We have our *Northomania (nordomanía)*.[23]

Rodó's anti-American theme is a classic illustration of the power of an idea whose time has come. The United States during this period had become in the Latin American consciousness the most prominent example of a powerful, modernizing country. In this same era Latin Americans, particularly younger Latin Americans, were finding themselves increasingly uneasy over the adoptive nationalist reform technique of publicly holding up countries like the United States as models for Latin Americans because either implicit or explicit in this kind of exhortation was the message that Latin Americans were backward and inferior to other peoples. Rodó, who was a young man in his twenties when he wrote *Ariel*, showed himself very much in tune with the emotional concerns of his generation. When he came forward and demanded that Latin Americans put a stop to their nordomaniá, he opened up the floodgates to a dammed reactive nationalism. In the ensuing deluge, the traditional "Yankeemania" in Latin America was to give way before a new "Yankeephobia."[24]

The key idea that Rodó relied upon to strengthen the confidence of Latin Americans was his notion of spiritual superiority. Rodó plunged into a long discussion of American culture and demonstrated how it just did not measure up to the "spirituality" of the Latin American way of life. Rodó's major criticism of Americans was their lack of high ideals, generous morals, and philosophic and artistic interests. While Rodó conceded that Americans abounded in vigor and vitality, he accused them of directing their energies toward narrowly materialistic and utilitarian ends. In his words, Americans "live for the immediate reality of the present and for this they subordinate all their activities to the egotism of material well-being."[25] Rodó contended that Latin Americans were a far more sensitive people and did not suffer from these faults. Unlike North Americans, they were not so absorbed in economic self-interest that they were incapable of contemplating some lofty principle, some spiritual ideal. Rodó attributed to his fellow Latins a high degree of cultural and moral refinement: in his mind typically Latin American characteristics were "ideality and order in life, noble inspiration in thought, disinterestedness in morals, good taste in art, heroism in action, [and] delicacy in manners."[26]

In presenting his thesis of the spiritual superiority of Latin Americans, Rodó acted like someone who was going to arrive at a desired conclusion no matter how much evidence got in his way. One example of his startling disregard for inconvenient evidence is his peculiar reading of Alexis de Tocqueville. Because Rodó had never been to the United Sates and had no first-hand knowledge of its culture, he chose to lean heavily upon de Tocqueville for his information and his negative opinions about American society. The French writer did believe that the social condition of equality in America tended to suppress interest in speculative and artistic pursuits; yet he compared Americans unfavorably in these endeavors with Western Europeans, not Latin Americans. In general, de Tocqueville held a very positive view about the spiritual qualities of the citizens of the United States: he regarded Americans as the most advanced practitioners of Western democratic ideals in the world and for this reason described them as the most "civilized" people in the world. As for Latin Americans, de Tocqueville scarcely had the interest to mention them except to say they were still "children," as yet quite "uncivilized," and that Mexicans, due to the "depravity of their morals" were destined to lose much of their territory to an expanding America.[27] It seems that Rodó's use of de Tocqueville was, to say the least, selective. He praised de Tocqueville as an ingenious observer of human affairs and yet arrived at a conclusion of spiritual superiority that de Tocqueville himself would have found astonishing in its inaccuracy.

Just as Rodó was not troubled by evidence that went against his notion of spiritual superiority, he was not concerned with providing evidence to support it. Rodó, in other words, only stated his thesis and did not feel obligated to substantiate it. Rodó talked much about the "genius" and "originality" he found in Latin American culture but declined to give specific examples of this genius and originality. Rodó who spoke with effusive wonder about the great civilizations of the ancient and European worlds and maintained their work was being carried on in Latin America,[28] seemed to by saying that the genius or originality to which he was referring was the kind that resulted in significant contributions to this Western tradition. But in a sense Rodó's very writing contradicted what he was claiming even while he was claiming it. Rodó expressed his ideas in a loose, florid style of writing that was very popular in his day and also, following prevailing fashion, delighted in studding his prose with the names (unfootnoted) of the great wise men of all time. Time and time again Rodó recalled ancient philosophers when he thought it beneficial to his discussion; on over seventy occasions, Rodó tapped the wisdom of modern European thinkers; and even from the culturally lifeless United States, Rodó mentioned Emerson and Poe. The reader, however, looks in vain for a Latin American from whom the Urugayan draws his inspiration.

If an inveterate sage-invoker like Rodó did not allude to a single Latin American man of letters who had influenced the content of his essay, it does not speak well for his contention that Latin American society had produced great works of genius and originality.

Paradoxically, the very vagueness of Rodó's presentation on spiritual superiority was an important factor that contributed to its wide appeal. The idea of spiritual superiority is in itself quite abstract and difficult to clarify, and when laid before the reader in sweeping generalities amid clouds of soaring rhetoric bereft of careful definitions and supporting evidence, it becomes difficult to catch hold of conceptually and to actually disprove. Had Rodó tried to be more specific about what he said, he could have been challenged more easily, and this would not have suited his reading audiences. Rodó's statements about a superior Latin American spirituality provided Latin Americans with a positive interpretation of their society, and since these assertions were too vague to be definitely refuted, they were enthusiastically believed in by people who wanted to believe.

Arielismo was the most influential of a number of early twentieth century interpretations of Latin American life that centered around the notion of spiritual superiority. During this period the idea of Latin American spiritual superiority won widespread acceptance and was used to express and to justify an increasingly powerful reactive nationalism. The popularity of the spiritual superiority idea reached its peak in the first quarter of the twentieth century and then declined. The idea is still evident today in Latin America but no longer holds the same sway over the educated populace there.

Through the Latin American nationalist point of view, the major problem with the theory of spiritual superiority was that it was sustained more by the desire to believe than by plausible evidence. Because of this it served the emotional needs of Latin American nationalists only partially. Sensitive nationalists who search for an idea on which to base a positive national identity long for one they can live with without secret, painful reservations. Latin Americans who pronounced their belief in the spiritual superiority of their peoples were faced by other Latin Americans who ridiculed the idea;[29] and the believers had scarcely a scrap of reasonable evidence with which to support their claim and, more importantly, their own self-confidence. The problem for these nationalists only worsened as the twentieth century wore on and it became more and more obvious that the United States, in comparison with Latin America, was not a cultural wasteland. For example, in the late 1930s, the highly respected Chilean critic Tancredo Pinochet sifted through the available evidence (such as the number of Nobel Prize winners produced by each society) and came to the conclusion that quite the opposite was actually the case: "Up to now," he frankly declared to Latin Americans, "the civilization that we have created in Hispanic America compared to the civilization of Anglo-Saxon America is that of a grain of wheat compared to the entire globe."[30]

Owing to the growing problems associated with the theory of spiritual superiority, Latin Americans eventually adopted another more suited to their needs—the theory of imperialism (*imperialismo*). After the second decade of the twentieth century, nationalism in Latin America began to place increasing emphasis on imperialism, especially economic imperialism.[31] Nationalists were able to accept with greater confidence this interpretation of the national "reality" largely for two reasons. First of all, it was unquestionably better grounded in factual evidence than wispy notions of spiritual superiority; and secondly, the credibility and prestige of the economic imperialism idea was enormously enhanced by the success of the Russian Revolution, which produced world leaders who vigorously testified to its validity. Gradually but steadily, the new theory replaced the old one of spiritual superiority as the foundation of Latin American reactive nationalism. Latin American nationalism continued to be preoccupied with, and hostile to, foreigners, but the theoretical content by which it expressed itself changed from the idea that Latin Americans were spiritually superior to foreigners to the idea that they were exploited by foreigners.

REACTIVE NATIONALISM AND THE IDEA OF IMPERIALISM

As was the case with Arielismo and other statements of spiritual superiority, the theory of imperialismo was used by Latin American reactive nationalists to deal with the problem of a negative national identity. As mentioned, one great advantage of the imperialism idea was that while notions of spiritual superiority were little more than intellectual fantasies, the theory of imperialism was supported by some real evidence. To determine to what extent the widespread belief in imperialism has most likely been due to the emotional needs of the believers, or to the inherent reasonableness of the theory, it would be useful to review the theory's arguments and the historical and contemporary data that sustain them.

As befits an idea that stirs both emotional and economic self-interest, the theory of imperialism in Latin America has grown to be a complex issue obscured by much careless rhetoric. From the many accusations of imperialism that Latin Americans hurl at foreigners, the outlines of three general types are discernable: political imperialism, economic imperialism, and cultural imperialism. Foreigners, it is charged, exert undue influence on the political, economic, and cultural lives of Latin Americans. Central to Latin American protests is the idea that foreigners wield great power in Latin American society and use that power to the detriment of Latin Americans. Many Latin Americans push this to the point where they claim that foreigners from advanced nations are primarily responsible for their condition of economic underdevelopment. When discussing the varieties of imperialism, therefore, it is necessary to ask how much power foreigners have held over Latin Americans; when they have been morally guilty in the exercise of this power; and more specifically, whether they must shoulder some or all of the blame for Latin America's economic troubles. And as a final consideration, because Latin Americans contend that imperialism is both a historical and a contemporary phenomenon, it would be helpful to compare the imperialism of the past and present in order to determine if the problem has lessened or worsened with the passage of time.

Political Imperialism

Accusations of political imperialism mostly have to do with foreign governments applying pressure on Latin American governments to achieve certain ends. The most direct and spectacular form of this kind of imperialism is the old-fashioned land grab. The only significant aggression of this sort in Latin American history took place in a conflict between the United States and Mexico, which resulted in Northern Mexico—better known to Americans as the Western United States—being transferred from Mexican to American control.

The moral questions surrounding this nineteenth-century territorial takeover can become very involved. The Mexicans contended they were morally wronged and based their claim on the principle of national sovereignty. But if Mexicans should have kept those lands by the right of having been there before the Americans, what right did they have to displace the Indians who were there even before them? If the Mexicans chose to use the idea of national sovereignty to legitimize their claim, they had to first assume that the Indians had no right to invoke the same principle, and secondly, to assume that Americans could invoke no moral principle that was higher.

The Americans, however, did have a moral principle they considered more compelling than the rule of national sovereignty. The concept of national sovereignty was a Western invention that came into use along with the rise of the modern nation-state. Americans were inclined to feel themselves bound by it only with nations they regarded as, like themselves, "progressive" and "civilized." This attitude derived from the enormous confidence Westerners had in the "advanced" civilization they were developing. Their complete moral self-assurance in their way of life encouraged them to feel that people who were able to exploit lands and resources for human benefit had a right to them because this furthered the upward march of human progress. A sense for how Westerners tended to look upon the wild, untamed expanses populated by less "progressive" peoples can be acquired by listening to a private conversation of a nineteenth-century English traveler in Latin America. The following passage is from a letter he wrote home to his family:

> Here we are on a voyage up the mighty river, nineteen days out of Buenos Ayres, having been able to sail six of those days. What a country! What a river! How wasted! What business have these Spaniards and Portuguese to lay claim to these magnificant lands, which they do not occupy and never will? Here is another revolution in Buenos Ayres. What is to become of these poor children, these Argentines maltreated by their parents of Spain, tortured by one another? Will they eat one another 'til nothing is left but their tails?
>
> Now the first great fact is, that here in South America are numberless thousands of square miles of the most splendid land in the world for the production of every article the soil will yield to man. Here in Brazil, and in the provinces drained by the tributaries of the *La Plata*, is every variety of soil, mountain, valley, plain, and forest, claimed by a race of people who, like dogs in a manger, will not cultivate themselves, and yet claim a right to prevent others from doing so. What a monstrous folly to guarantee by treaties the possession of these lands to these Iberians!
>
> Now one of two things will be done some day: either the industrious masses of Europe will invade these countries and take by force what they require here for their necessities; or these lands must be silently conquered by the slow and sure process of immigration, and the present owners absorbed in the industrious race that will really people the country.[32]

Americans of the Manifest Destiny era were very much a part of this spirit—and so up to a point were the Mexicans. Just as Mexicans felt justified in ignoring the territorial rights of Indians because they considered them uncivilized, Americans ignored the territorial rights of Mexicans using a similar rationale. Americans commonly regarded Mexicans as uncivilized or semicivilized for a number of reasons: their masses were sunk in apathy and degraded by poverty; their elites were exploitative, corrupt, opportunistic, and violent; and their society lagged behind in every area of modern achievement. To allow their northern territories to remain empty (they contained only 1 percent of the Mexican population) and untilled seemed an affront to the very ideal of human progress. In retrospect, it does appear certain that if Americans had not taken control of Northern Mexico, the area would not be yielding its riches and meeting human needs to the extent that it is today.

While the seizure of Northern Mexico by the United States has given rise to moral questions that are infinitely debatable and at bottom irresolvable, the conquest's effect on the contemporary economic situation in Mexico is far more clear. It cannot reasonably be argued the Mexico's loss of its northern domains was a vital factor in the country's present-day condition of economic underdevelopment. Mexico was poor before the conquest and, not surprisingly, remained so afterward. Few Mexicans lived in Northern Mexico at the time of the military confrontation, and the main population to the south showed little inclination or capacity to tap the area's vast economic resources. If Mexico had not lost half its land to the United States, the country today would be twice as large and still very poor, for holding sovereignty over a potentially rich expanse of territory is of little economic value if the potential is not developed.

There remains one further American possession that may be considered in this discussion of territorial imperialism, and that is the tiny sliver of land that surrounds the Panama Canal. The acquisition of territory in Panama by the United States was the result of a more indirect intervention than was the case in Mexico. The American government encouraged a small group of Panamanian adventurers to revolt and declare their isthmus independent from Colombia. The Americans then negotiated a treaty with the new country's leaders who, in effect, ceded to the United States a strip of land across the isthmus in exchange for building a canal. The moral debate here is similar to the one outlined above. On the one hand, the American action was unjustified by the prevailing norms of national sovereignty. On the other hand, the building of the Panama Canal advanced the well-being of many people, and given the especially sordid and chaotic character of Caribbean politics, those who depended upon the vital waterway were certainly grateful that it was controlled by a stable and dependable country. Economically, Colombians did not gain from the loss of their Panamanian territories, but neither did they lose much because the Panamanian swamplands had little value without a canal and Colombians were incapable of building one themselves. Colombia did forfeit a share of the revenues generated by the canal and canal-related commerce, but the ex-Colombians living in Panama definitely benefited from them, as is evidenced by the fact that Panamanians today have the fourth highest per capita income in Latin America.[33]

For the great majority of Latin Americans, the form of political imperialism that threatened them most was not permanent occupations by conquering armies but temporary interventions by relatively small numbers of foreign troops ordered to secure some specific, limited objective. The number of these interventions that have taken place in Latin America is larger than even critics of the practice commonly imagine. The United States, for example, is responsible for as many as a hundred such actions (mostly in the Caribbean area),[34] and this does not include the many times that the American government has used the threat of armed intervention to influence Latin American domestic affairs.

During the long period when this kind of imperialistic activity was very common, Western governments argued that it was their responsibility to ensure for their citizens in other countries the same protection of life and property they enjoyed back home. In the early nineteenth century Western powers usually landed troops in Latin American countries in order to destroy the colonies of pirates that preyed on Western merchantmen. In later years when Western nation-states had put an end to these seafaring barbarians, they continued their policy of military interventions in Latin America whenever they saw their citizens or interests jeopardized in other ways. From the Western point of view, much of Latin America was very violent and disorderly: bandits infested the hills, beggars and thieves plagued the cities, and bands of political revolutionaries, who were often difficult to tell from the gangs of desperados, rose up against their governments at frequent intervals. Mexico alone suffered through over a thousand politically motivated uprisings during its first century of independence,[35] and there is no way of calculating the violence caused by marauding gangs of criminals. Amid this chaotic climate, foreigners as well as natives were exposed to physical abuse, extortion, robbery, and the destruction of their property. Leaders of Latin American governments, who in many countries seized their offices by illegitimate means, were often corrupt, inept, tyranical, and contemptuous of their own laws and, not surprisingly, of Western conventions of international law as well. One common practice of Latin American political leaders was to negotiate loans overseas and then refuse to repay them, or refuse to honor the debt obligations entered into by their predecessors. In most instances when Western governments ordered their troops into action, it was to protect their embassies during insurrections, to protect the lives and property of their citizens during these same political upheavals or during outbreaks of banditry,[36] and to oblige "irresponsible" Latin American governments to pay the debts they had contracted abroad.

The moral arguments justifying the Western policy of armed intervention rested largely upon the assumption that the world was made up of a diversity of peoples, and that some of these peoples lived on a higher level of civilization than others. This point of view is definitely out of fashion in contemporary times, but in its day it was widely held to be self-evident. Once the idea of a hierarchy of civilizations was accepted, it was quite easy for Westerners to think of themselves as parents and teachers and the less civilized as children. The parents recognized they had no right to intervene in each other's affairs, but in the best long-term interests of the "children," they had both the right and the obligation to chastise them when they acted "irresponsibly." This notion of underdeveloped peoples as children found expression in the kind of Western parternalism that was typical of the day. In the famous phrases of the English poet Rudyard Kipling, Westerners had to bear up nobly under a "White Man's Burden" and to give guidance to the peoples in backward lands, who in their present level of maturity were but "half devil and half child." Sometimes, of course, Westerners saw more devil than child and felt more contempt than parental sympathy—like the American political leader Theodore Roosevelt when he once described the Latin Americans of certain countries as "contemptible little Dagoes."[37]

The relationship between the belief in a hierarchy of civilizations and an aggressive interventionist foreign policy can plainly be seen in the life of this same Theodore Roosevelt. When Roosevelt was a young student at Columbia University, he sat at the feet of America's leading political scientist, John W. Burgess, who taught that if a society of human beings did not exercise the responsibilities of civilized peoples, then it could not demand the right of national sovereignty. With regard to completely "barbarian" populations like the American Indians, Burgess contended:

> There is no human right to the status of barbarism. The civilized states have a claim upon the uncivilized populations, as well as a duty towards them, and that claim is that they shall become civilized; and if they cannot accomplish their own civilization, then they must submit to the powers that can do it for them. The civilized state may righteously go still further than the exercise of force in imposing organization.[38]

And as far as the semicivilized peoples of the world were concerned, like some of the Latin American nationalities, Burgess believed that

> Interference in the affairs of populations not wholly barbarian which have made some progress in state organization, but which manifest incapacity to solve the problem of political civilization with any degree of completeness, is a justifiable policy. No one can question that it is in the interest of the world's civilization that law and order and the true liberty consistent therewith shall reign everywhere upon the globe. A permanent inability on the part of any state or semi-state to secure this status is a threat to civilization everywhere. Both for the sake of the half-barbarous state and in the interest of the rest of the world, a state or states, endowed with the capacity for political organization, may righteously assume sovereignty over, and undertake to create state order for, such a politically incompetent population. The civilized states should not, of course, act with undue haste in seizing power, and they should never exercise the power once assumed, for any other purpose than that for which the assumption may be righteously made, viz; for the

civilization of the subjected population; but they are under no obligation to await invitation from those claiming power and government in the inefficient organization, nor from those subject to the same. The civilized states themselves are the best organs which have yet appeared in the history of the world for determining the proper time and occasion for intervening in the affairs of unorganized or insufficiently organized populations, for the execution of their great world duty.[39]

The plausibility of this argument was strengthened by the fact that at the time when Burgess was lecturing and Roosevelt listening, Westerners lived in an age of expansive self-confidence. Never were they so sure that they knew the definition of the word *civilized* nor so certain that their own way of life was superior to that of any other people. Roosevelt absorbed both the ideas and the confidence characteristic of this time and carried these influences with him throughout his political career. Although he became famous for his talk of brandishing a "Big Stick" in one hand while carrying out foreign policy, at least as far as backward nations were concerned, "Big Paddle" would have been a more appropriate term. As vice-president, Roosevelt warned Latin American nations as he would children of the consequences of not acting like responsible adults: "If any South American country misbehaves toward any European country, let the European country spank it."[40] Later when he was president, Roosevelt grew to fear the possibility of a European power invading a Latin American country under the pretext of collecting its debts and then threatening American security interests by remaining there. To guard against this, Roosevelt issued his famous Roosevelt Corollary which proclaimed that the United States alone would act as policeman and debt collector in the Western Hemisphere and would take upon itself the responsibility of safeguarding the investments of civilized nations. The message of the corollary is well known, but the wording itself merits close attention, for it frankly reveals Roosevelt's perception of a world populated by civilized and uncivilized peoples:

Any country whose people conduct themselves well can count upon our hearty friendship. If a nation shows that it knows how to act with reasonable efficiency and decency in social and political matters, if it keeps order and pays its obligations, it need fear no interference from the United States. Chronic wrong-doing, or an impotence which results in a general loosening of the ties of civilized society, may in America, as elsewhere, ultimately require intervention by some civilized nation and in the Western Hemisphere, the adherence of the Monroe Doctrine may force the United States, however reluctantly, in flagrant cases of such wrong-doing or impotence, to the exercise of an international police power. . . . every

nation, whether in America or anywhere else, which desires to
maintain its freedom, its independence, must ultimately realize
that the right of such independence cannot be separated from the
responsibility of making good use of it.[41]

Although Roosevelt's idea of the civilized regions of the earth approximately coincided with the white man's world, his criteria for defining
civilized clearly depended upon the behavior of peoples and not their
race. He openly admired the decidedly non-Caucasian Japanese for
their success in fashioning a modern nation-state and expected them to
assume the role of teacher and disciplinarian among the more backward peoples of the Far East.[42] Nor did Roosevelt rudely heap all Latin
American peoples into the *uncivilized* category, and he specifically ex-
empted the more "advanced" countries of Brazil, Chile, and Argentina
from coverage by his corollary. To the Argentineans, in fact, he paid
the ultimate compliment of the day: "The attitude of the United States
toward the Argentine should be based on exactly the same frank and
matter-of-fact acceptance of equality and mutuality of respect as is im-
plied in our relations with Germany, England, France, Italy, and
Holland."[43]

The idea of different grades of civilization that Roosevelt and
other Western leaders used to sanction their policy of military intervention in Latin America is hardly surprising in light of the fact that
the same point of view was shared by many prominent Latin
Americans. For example, Chile's most influential newspaper, *El Mercurio*, editorialized in 1914, "There is need to keep in mind the distinction between the honest, stable governments on one hand, and those of
the small and improperly called 'republics' of the tropical zone, utterly
incompetent and anarchistic, on the other."[44] The prominent Argentinean writer Alfredo Colmo went one step further when he described
the more volatile Latin American countries as "uncivilized, semi-
barbaric, almost criminal" and fully deserving of the foreign interventions they brought upon themselves.[45]

Apart from the question of moral arguments that Westerners used
to justify interventions in Latin America, it is also important to examine the actual harm these interventions brought upon the people of
the continent. Since Latin Americans have vented most of their anger
at the interventions of Americans (who were responsible for the great
majority of them), the discussion specifically focuses on American
military intrusions in Latin America.

It is fair to say that most of the harm inflicted by American in-
terventions upon Latin Americans was in the nature of wounded pride.
This conclusion is necessitated by the fact that American troops in
Latin America simply did not cause much physical or economic

damage. To begin with, American interventions went beyond the brief landing stage in only a few Caribbean countries. Furhermore, when American forces actually remained for some time in a Latin American nation, they did not behave as plundering, raping armies laying waste the cities and countryside. Although some abuses were committed by individual soldiers, as a whole American troops on these missions were highly disciplined and well controlled by their officers. Nor did American interventions have much of an adverse economic impact on the Latin American countries involved, for the simple reason that the mere presence of self-contained units of American troops in these lands did not have much economic impact at all. The revenues that Americans sometimes collected to pay to Western noteholders cannot be described as a serious loss to the debtor countries because a large portion of those funds would have gone to unconscionably corrupt political leaders who usually stashed their loot in foreign banks. And again because of the leadership factor, it cannot be said that American interventions disrupted the harmonious political life of any Latin American nation because in no instance did these intrusions force the overthrow of a decent and responsible Latin American government.

Whatever little harm Americans caused Latin Americans during their military interventions was often matched by the modest amount of good they accomplished. In most cases when American troops assumed political authority in a particular country or locale, they governed the people under them more efficiently and honestly than did the native officials they replaced. For example, before the rise to power of the Castro revolutionaries, the most effective and incorruptible rulers in Cuban history were the Americans under General Leonard Wood, who occupied and governed the island for several years after the Spanish-American War. Even when the Americans departed from Cuba, they still on occasion exerted their considerable influence over the country (not altruistically but in their own perceived self-interest) to curb the thievery of corrupt Cuban politicians and to force reruns of blatantly dishonest elections.

Nowhere was the benevolent side of American intervention more apparent than in the area of public health, a fact amply demonstrated by the seven-month occupation of Vera Cruz in 1914. When the Americans took over the administration of this Mexican coastal city, they found themselves confronted with sanitation problems of the gravest magnitude. Surrounding the city were huge stagnant pools of water that made ideal breeding holes for malaria-carrying mosquitoes. Heaps of uncollected garbage were piled up on the streets, providing feasting grounds for packs of homeless dogs and thousands of vultures that circled in the sky overhead. So many flies swarmed about the public marketplace that they literally covered every square inch of the meats hanging on display. The chopping blocks of the nearby butchers were caked with old blood, encrusted with dead vermin, and pockmarked with holes in which lived colonies of maggots. In the poorer sections of Vera Cruz, toilets—public and private—were lacking: people relieved themselves on the public ways, adding human wastes to the dog and vulture droppings that littered the streets and sidewalks. The consequences of such sanitary neglect was, of course, devastating to the people of Vera Cruz: Throughout the city malaria, smallpox, meningitis, syphilis, gonorrhea, and dysentery took a savage toll of the population.

The American invaders lost little time in attacking these wretched living conditions. Shortly after taking over the city, 3,000 American soldiers and a host of hired Mexican laborers began a heroic task of building, digging, repairing, fumigating, sweeping, cleaning, and hauling away the accumulated filth of decades. Sixty-one miles of new ditches were dug to drain most of the fetid pools, and 69,000 gallons of crude oil were poured on others. The city jail was cleaned of its vermin and green slime, a job that required the burning of 1,200 pounds of sulfur and several weeks of noisome labor. Throughout the city, long-ignored plumbing repairs were made and water lines put into shape. Within the public marketplace, the quaint old cobblestones were replaced with easy-to-clean concrete, the windows and doors screened, the roof repaired, flytraps installed, and strict sanitation standards enforced. Each day the city garbage was swept, collected, and burned and the streets flushed with fresh seawater. These sanitation measures were so effective that the hordes of black vultures overhead drifted off to parts unknown—presumably to more hospitable cities. The Americans also combated disease by means of a massive immunization program; before they left the city, they inoculated 46,000 Vera Cruzians against the local scourges. In addition, they fought venereal disease by rounding up the city prostitutes, examining them, and, if necessary, sending them off to the hospital.[46]

The American invaders, of course, made these reforms mainly to prevent their army from being leveled by disease, but ordinary Mexicans could do nothing but gain in the process. The Mexican death rate in Vera Cruz dropped 25 percent during the hot summer months when normally it would have risen. In addition to better health standards, the Vera Cruzian population was treated to the spectacle of courts dispensing impartial justice, a post office that efficiently delivered mail, and a custom house where officials could not be bribed and where favorites could not escape paying dues. All these reforms were well within the capacity of Mexican authorities to institute; but since they did not, many citizens of Vera Cruz benefited in some measure when Americans marched in and took over the city. During the seven months of American benevolent despotism, the people of Vera Cruz experienced, in the words of one scholar, "the cleanest, most effective, most honestly and justly governed city in all of Mexican history."[47]

A full evaluation, then, of American interventions in Latin America can be a somewhat complicated question because these imperialistic adventures had positive as well as negative features. Americans managed to do some good during the course of their armed occupations, mainly because the authorities they pushed aside were such a debased lot and the invaders could have done worse only by deliberate effort. As a well-known student of Latin American society once observed, an enlightened North American military or colonial administration was "in every respect better than a government by seasoned extortioners and torturers."[48]

Despite this significant point, that foreign benevolent despots are apt to be more tolerable rulers than local tyrants, it must nevertheless be concluded that on the whole American military interventions had a very negative impact on Latin Americans, or at least on those Latin Americans who belonged to the educated classes. The reason for this has little to do with the actual damage Americans caused during their occupations. In strictly physical terms, American interventions neither did Latin Americans very much harm nor very much good. The psychological harm, however, the hurt pride, was quite another matter. Even Latin Americans whose countries were never invaded felt themselves bristling with anger over North American interventions in distant Latin American nations. What these sensitive Latin Americans resented the most was not the act of violating national sovereignty in itself but the American attitude behind it that regarded Latin Americans as too "uncivilized" and "irresponsible" to have their countries included in the select group of nation-states where the principle of national sovereignty applied. It is for this reason that Mexican historians have displayed more bitterness over the brief American occupation of Vera Cruz than over the permanent American occupation of Northern Mexico: Mexicans can more easily accept the loss of their essentially empty northern territories, which was primarily the result of an American hunger for land, than the attack on Vera Cruz, which was primarily a result of Woodrow Wilson's contempt for Mexican political culture.[49]

The argument Latin Americans have used against the American practice of armed intervention is that it has enabled Americans to have some control over the internal affairs of their countries. There is no question that the readiness of Americans to use military force has in the past caused many Latin American political leaders to pay considerable attention to advice from Washington. But since the protests against imperialism one hears today are mainly directed at what is allegedly occuring in the present, it is necessary to ask whether Americans are still willing to exert their superior military power in order to have a say in the politics, and an impact on the events, that take place in Latin America.

The most obvious difference between past and present—clear to anyone who can count—is that except in the most extreme circumstances, America's "gunboat diplomacy" days are over. In previous times temporary armed interventions were a regular feature of U.S. foreign policy. Between 1890 and 1933, for example, U.S. soldiers landed uninvited upon Latin American shores no less than 48 times. This era began to wane and finally ended in the years between World War I and World War II. American political leaders altered their policy of armed intervention during this period not because they were suddenly struck by moral lightning but because they were confronted with growing German efforts to use Latin American anti-Yankeeism to their own advantage. Since the announcement of the Monroe Doctrine, the paramount objective of U.S. foreign policy in Latin America had been to keep foreign powers away from the continent; and with the appearance of serious German competition for influence in the area, it appeared more realistic to pursue this basic aim by treating Latin American nations as "equal" sovereign states rather than as misbehaving children. During the administration of Franklin Roosevelt, America completed its change in image from that of a scowling Calvinist schoolmaster conspicuously brandishing a Big Stick to that of a smiling Good Neighbor with hands eagerly extended in friendship. Since this time the United States has directly violated the national sovereignty of a Latin American country only twice—by invading the Dominican Republic in 1965 and Grenada in 1983—and both actions were taken to prevent an outside power (the Soviet Union) from establishing another foothold in the Caribbean.

With the renunciation of force as a regular feature of U.S. policy toward Latin America, the ability of the United States to influence the leaders of those nations has vastly diminished. A succinct example of the impotence of the "Colossus of the North" can be seen in a 20-year squabble over fishing rights between the United States and tiny Ecuador. The point of contention was over how many miles from shore a nation could claim the exclusive right to exploit the sea's economic resources. The Americans insisted that 12 miles was the limit. The Ecuadorians, on the other hand, claimed jurisdiction over 200 miles of ocean, and in some places between the Galapagos Islands and Ecuador, 600 miles. Eventually the dispute simmered down when American fishermen successfully lobbied their own government to extend the U.S. claim from 12 to 200 miles. The question here, however, is not which party was correct—both claims were equally arbitrary—but which party could enforce its will upon the other. In this contest the Ecuadorians emerged the unquestioned victors. Between 1955 and 1975, the Ecuadorian government seized approximately 150 American fishing vessels in "Ecuadorian waters" and extracted some 5.6 million dollars from their owners as a condition for their release. In the old days, the American government would have sent in negotiators flanked by U.S. troops to smooth out differences of opinion. How did the officials in today's American State Department react to this situation? With a series of quivering half-measures. The State Department began by asking U.S. fishermen not to pay the Ecuadorians for fishing licenses in order to uphold the principle of the 12-mile limit. In return, whenever American fishermen were forced to pay fines to the Ecuadorians, the U.S. government promised to reimburse the fishermen for their losses. The ultimate providers of funds were, of course, American taxpayers, who were scarcely aware of what was going on. Meanwhile the American government, which in theory represented the interests of American taxpayers, was nevertheless anxious to avoid any impression of bullying little Ecuador and continued to provide that country with millions of dollars in foreign aid. Included in this aid were gifts of U.S. navy gunboats, which, needless to say, the Ecuadorians used to capture more American fishermen and levy more fines.[50] This, to be sure, was a far cry from the days when an imagined insult to the American flag could have sent the Marines rolling in.

A more serious example pointing to the paradoxical weakness of a powerful nation that will not use its power is the ease with which Latin American governments can nationalize American property with little or no compensation. Even Latin American leaders ill disposed to this brand of politics feel pressured to show they are in tune with the prevailing reactive nationalist temper of their countries. Once again the key point here is not the wisdom or morality of such confiscations but the extent to which the U.S. government feels it can use its vast military superiority to protect the property and investments of its citizens. In the first great nationalization in Latin America, the Mexican expropriation of American oil fields in 1938, Mexicans were genuinely worried about a punishing American military response. Latin American leaders today, whether they nationalize for economic, political, or purely ideological reasons, no longer harbor such fears.

The military junta that governed Peru in the late sixties and early seventies is a case in point. During this period a group of Peruvian army chieftains who described themselves as "revolutionaries" saw fit to nationalize millions of dollars worth of American sugar, copper, and petroleum interests. They did so entirely on their own terms and, as added injury, with an attitude of mocking defiance. For example, when the American oil company involved assessed its losses at $100 million and asked for compensation, the Peruvian generals said they would be glad to pay them $30 million just as soon as the oil company paid back $670 million in "excess profits."[51] The reaction of the American government to all this amounted to little more than a symbolic protest. The

Americans slowed down credits to Peru from international agencies and showed their hesitation even over this tepid measure by refusing to cut off these credits completely. More importantly, they did nothing to stop the Peruvian leaders from borrowing all the money they needed from commercial banks in the United States. Thus, the price that the revolutionary military junta paid for its anti-Yankee nationalization policy was a modestly higher interest rate for the money it borrowed in the United States. The present-day U.S. government is simply not prepared to risk the political consequences that might result from a serious defense of American property abroad.

It is, perhaps, safe to put forth two assertions about when the American government would be willing to use armed force to protect its interests in Latin America. American leaders would most likely defend the Panama Canal from a foreign invasion and possibly—and only possibly—from trouble originating in Panama itself. The only other occasion when they might be induced to take military action in Latin America would be to prevent a communist political group from controlling a Latin American government. It was precisely this perceived threat that prompted the U.S. government to break its Good Neighbor pledge and unilaterally order troops into Santo Domingo and, some years later, into Grenada. However, it must be recognized that the willingness of U.S. leaders to use force against communism in Latin America is considerably tempered by fear over how world opinion would perceive an apparent reemergence of old-fashioned gunboat diplomacy. This concern with its world image was what caused the U.S. government to provide only material support for indigenous anticommunist factions in Guatemala (1954) and Cuba (1961), rather than to employ its own far more dependable troops. the Guatemalan undertaking was a success in large measure because the enemy was made up of coffeehouse communists. In Cuba the local climate spawned a far tougher variety of communist which tore the American-backed Cuban exile army to shreds. In the waning hours of this military debacle, the inhibiting factor of world image played yet another hand: President Kennedy, although faced with one of the worst foreign policy disasters in U.S. history, did not dare to admit his mistake and rescue the operation with the direct involvement of U.S. forces.

The tragedy in Vietnam has further reduced U.S. flexibility in using armed force to combat communism. American Leaders have learned that although troops can easily be sent to any underdeveloped country, determined guerilla units can make it politically impossible to keep them there. This concern was largely what enabled the populist Panamanian dictator Omar Torrijos to extract from Americans in 1978 a new treaty promising eventual ownership and control of the Panama Canal.

Another factor restraining the U.S. inclination to strike down communist governments in the Western Hemisphere is that many people who manage American foreign policy are no longer convinced that communism is a monolithic world entity and that any new communist regime in Latin America would necessarily take orders from the Soviet Union, the real object of American apprehensions. Needless to say, if American officials perceive a communist regime in the Western Hemisphere as only repugnant but not really dangerous, they will be far less willing to take the risk of direct military action against it.

American foreign policy officials, of course, have other means of influencing the internal affairs of Latin American countries apart from armed confrontation. When American authorities feel they cannot use their military power, the main weapon left in their arsenal is their financial power. But the strategy of spending money in Latin America in order to obtain some desired objective is limited in its impact and unpredictable—often perverse—in its results. The American attempts to influence the course of Chilean politics during the sixties and early seventies is an example that reveals much about the effectiveness of this kind of leverage.

According to facts now on public record, the U.S. government became deeply involved in the Chilean presidential election of 1964 in order to keep the Marxist candidate, Salvador Allende, from winning office. To accomplish what they hoped to accomplish, the CIA and the State Department dispatched about a hundred special agents to Chile and channeled some 20 million dollars into projects and schemes designed to frustrate Allende's run for power.[52] But all along the U.S. officials had no need to worry or to spend the tax dollars of American citizens. Allende's opponent, Edwardo Frei, turned out to be one of the most popular politicians in Chilean history, won the election by the largest plurality in Chilean history, and would have trounced his Marxist adversary even if the CIA had backed Allende. If, however, the race had been close and the above-mentioned facts had become known during the campaign, the ensuing scandal could have tipped the election in Allende's favor. The Americans, therefore, not only wasted their money in opposing Allende but in different circumstances could conceivably have brought about the very ends they were trying to prevent.

If this is not enough to suggest the limits of American financial power, the sequel to the story might be. During Frei's six-year rule as president of Chile, Americans literally poured money into the country in the hopes of making Chile a "showcase" for liberal democratic reform. So what happened? The Marxist won the next election. American officials then decided that they had to contrive to bring down Allende, and again their weapon was chiefly monetary. Americans proceeded to cut off some sources of international loans, but like the Peruvian revolutionaries in the neighboring country, Allende found alternative creditors and managed to increase Chile's foreign debt 36 percent in three years.[53] At the same time that Americans were attempting to deny Allende money, they were also supplying Allende's domestic enemies with millions of dollars to assist them in their opposition activities. However, if this clandestine aid had ever been discovered (as it was later), the Marxist leader would have used this evidence of American "imperialism" to bolster his weakening political strength. As it turned out, Allende proved to be an economic incompetent who so thoroughly ruined the already troubled Chilean economy that even the disclosure of American meddling in Chilean affairs would not have been enough to prevent his downfall.

The American attempts to combat communism in Chile were only a recent and rather prominent episode in a long history of efforts on the part of U.S. governments to control political events in Latin America. It is possible at this point to step back and put into perspective the entire issue of political imperialism. There can be no doubt that in the past U.S. governments have exercised considerable influence in the internal affairs of some Latin American countries. We have also seen that this political imperialism, although real, did not cause the great majority of Latin Americans much physical or economic harm. Westerners, especially Americans, used to wield great influence in Latin America mainly because they were once willing to use the superior military power at their disposal. This situation, however, has changed drastically in recent decades and today, Latin American leaders have little to lose and much to gain politically from "heroic" displays of anti-Americanism. So long as these regimes remain noncommunist, American governments are not likely to more than verbally protest the mud thrown in their faces. Even the famed American anticommunism has been softened in recent years, and it is by no means certain that the appearance of a new communist government in Latin America will trigger U.S. military intervention. As far as nonmilitary intervention is concerned, the example of Chile reveals the ineffectual and possibly counterproductive results that surreptitious American plotting can produce.

This does not leave Washington very much direct control over the policies of Latin American governments, and certainly less than has been the case in the past. And yet the cries of imperialism in Latin America grow not weaker but stronger every day. Could, perhaps, this be due to the existence of "economic imperialism"?

Economic Imperialism

The charges Latin Americans level at foreigners for alleged economic imperialism are unquestionably very serious. In specific content they range from complaints about the way foreigners treat native workers to the simple fact that outsiders are able to wield economic influence in Latin American countries. By far the most important accusation, however, is that foreign economic influence is the major cause of Latin American economic underdevelopment. In the blunt words of Cuban-Argentinean theoretician Che Guevara, "Ever since capitalist monoplies took over the world, they have kept the greater part of humanity in poverty, dividing the spoils among the most powerful countries. The standard of living of those countries is founded upon the misery of ours."[54] Variations of Guevara's position are widely held by educated Latin Americans, even Latin Americans who think of themselves as "moderates." It is very important, then, to take up the question of who must be considered primarily responsible for Latin American underdevelopment—Latin Americans, or as Latin American spokesmen so frequently contend, foreigners from the modernized areas of the world.

When Latin Americans get down to actual detail about what they mean by economic imperialism, usually they bring up the issue of foreign investments and their harmful effects on the Latin American economies. One of the major Latin American criticisms concerning foreign investment is that foreigners have concentrated their capital and expertise in "primary" industries such as mining, oil drilling, and agriculture, rather than in manufacturing. Latin Americans argue that this has led to a world economic "system" where the "terms-of-trade" have been unfavorable and have caused them to languish in poverty decade after decade. Latin Americans claim that because foreigners have been able to control the prices of their goods while Latin Americans have not, foreigners have been able to sell to Latin Americans manufactured products at relatively high prices while buying raw materials from Latin Americans at relatively low prices. An important element, then, of Latin American theories concerning unfavorable terms-of-trade has been the criticism that foreigners have made investments in Latin America better suited to their own economic needs than to those of Latin Americans.

One problem with these terms-of-trade arguments is that they shift attention away from the people with the main responsibility for the modernization of the Latin American economies—the Latin Americans themselves. If Latin Americans wanted to build up the manufacturing capacity of their countries, it is neither reasonable nor realistic to expect that foreigners should have done it for them. During the nineteenth century and for a good part of the twentieth, Westerners were preoccupied with developing their own economies. They had little incentive for investing in manufacturing industries outside the Western world, for it was in their own lands that they found the lucrative markets, the developed transportation and communication systems, and the reserves of skilled, well-disciplined labor with wage rates not so high as to make non-Western labor attractive. Their only need for Latin America at this time was for food and raw materials, and so naturally they placed the bulk of their Latin American investments in agricultural, mining, and petroleum enterprises. To have sunk money into manufacturing industries would have been nothing less than foreign aid in an era when it was commonly assumed that nations were responsible for their own welfare.

What could Latin Americans have done under these circumstances? Basically, Latin Americans who desired domestic industry had only one viable option open to them, and that was to do what the Japanese were doing and to build their own factories. To accomplish this they needed to purchase Western technology and expertise, which, of course, required Western capital. The Japanese managed to acquire an initial store of capital by creating a silkworm industry and exporting silk to the West. Latin Americans were in an even more advantageous position to solve the problem of modernization capital because many of them lived in countries with large deposits of raw materials. Westerners contributed to the potential solution in two ways: first, they created the "market," or demand, for the natural resources that for centuries had been of no use to people living on the Latin American continent; and secondly, Western companies were willing to supply the technology and knowledge necessary to extract, refine, and sell the raw materials and to pay Latin Americans a percentage of the earned profits. Far from condemning Latin Americans to economic dependence on primary products, Western investments in extractive enterprises were an opportunity for Latin Americans to accumulate capital and to take the first steps forward toward the nationalist goal of mature industrialization.

The problem with the capital that the Latin Americans earned from the investments of foreigners in their countries was that it was only a tool they could have used to achieve modernization. But for capital to contribute to economic development, it has to be used productively, and capital is most likely to be employed in this fashion by peoples imbued with modernization-encouraging values and attitudes. Capital in the hands of peoples deficient in economic virtue not only is likely to be used unproductively but also tends to have the effect of worsening prevailing values that hold back modernization.

Examples of the detrimental effects of capital are quite common in the Latin American experience. The origins of this debilitating tradition can be traced as far back as sixteenth-century Spain, when that country began to reel under the impact of gold bullion streaming in from the New World. This easy wealth afforded the Spanish the luxury of supporting an exceptionally large population of soldiers, crusaders, chevaliers, dons, hidalgos, high aristocrats, priests, missionaries, theologians, archbishops, ascetics, friars, mystics, and other social types decidedly uninterested in productive enterprise. As a result, commercial, agricultural, and manufacturing activity stagnated; the gold seeped into the hands of more industrious peoples of Europe to pay for the goods the Spanish had to import; and Spain, to this very day, has never fully recovered. Latin American countries in more recent times have also suffered from influxes of easy money from abroad. Throughout the republican era, Latin American economies staggered through a series of booms and busts caused by fluctuating Western demand for raw materials. The first of these great export bonanzas took place in Peru during the mid–nineteenth century with the discovery of huge mountains of dried dung (*guano*) that Westerners found useful as a source of nitrogen. Unquestionably the most valuable excrement in economic history, this bird dung provided the Peruvian government with so much tax revenue that it was able to abolish all other taxes in the country.[55] Instead of channeling this precious pool of capital into productive investments, however, Peruvians directed much of it into the expansion of bureaucratic employment, the construction of prestige projects and luxury housing, and the importation of luxury goods. When the boom finally ended, as all booms eventually do, Peru was left with a larger class of social parasites than ever before and with very little additional productive capacity to support it. The best example in the twentieth century of this phenomenon at work can be seen in Venezuela, where rich deposits of "black gold" have proven to be more of a curse than a blessing. It is scarcely possible to imagine a more effortless source of wealth than Venezuela's petroleum. The oil was discovered by foreigners, extracted by foreigners, refined by foreigners, marketed by foreigners, and burned by foreigners. In return for this privilege, foreigners paid Venezuelans substantial sums of money that could have been used to initiate self-sustaining, long-term economic growth. But instead of stimulating economic development, petrodollars have stimulated traditonal Venezuelan economic vices. The revenues from oil, which have risen steadily over the decades, have served to strengthen the proclivity of Venezuelans to demand from their government parasitic employment, economically sterile subsidies, and other entitlements rather than to produce wealth themselves. Venezuelans have found it easier to import the goods they need than to start their own industries; the industries they have started have remained anemic, providing workers with few jobs and consumers with low-quality goods at high prices. Agriculture has been even more of a disaster. Several decades ago Venezuelans were able to produce enough food both to feed themselves and to export, but by the mid-1970s they had to import half the food they required from abroad. Particularly embarrassing to many Venezuelans has been the fact that they have come to depend heavily upon Americans for traditionally Venezuelan food staples like their favorite black beans and the corn they use to make their tortillalike national bread.[56] The tragic spectacle of abundant capital weakening the productive capacity of the Venezuelan people has obliged Juan Pablo Pérez Alfonso, the former Venezuelan oil minister and founder of OPEC, to look with dismay upon the results of his country's export-induced wealth:

> I may be the father of OPEC, but now sometimes I feel like renouncing my offspring. The income from oil has discouraged us from trying to do with less and arriving at solutions through hard work. This is why we have a line of ships at our harbors, loaded with goods; we think we can solve our problems by buying outside.[57]

Whatever one thinks of the effects of oil revenues on Venezuelan economic life, there can be no doubt that from a strictly balance-of-payments perspective, foreign petroleum investments in Venezuela have provided Venezuelans with a great deal of purchasing power. Certainly no one today would care to maintain that the peoples of oil-exporting countries are suffering from unfavorable terms-of-trade. Between 1955 and 1975, the price of petroleum exports rose five times faster than the price of manufactured goods.[58] If foreign investments in petroleum (which for many years were the largest form of foreign investment in Latin America[59]) cannot be criticized for furnishing Latin Americans with products that perform poorly in international markets, what about foreign investments in other primary products?

It appears that contrary to the popular view of Third World spokesmen, the prices of commodity goods have generally during the last quarter century held their own against the prices of industrial goods from the West. The most convincing evidence of this is found in a study intended by its Third World sponsors to prove quite the opposite. Because Third World leaders and intellectuals have long assumed that their countries were being victimized by the international economic system as it is presently constituted, they have proposed a new system with new rules where the prices of primary products would be linked to those of manufactured goods and would automatically rise with them. In order to present a detailed outline of this proposal, representatives of underdeveloped countries at the United Nations commissioned a team of economists to investigate the relative price movements of primary and manufactured products. The economists, however, did not discover what they were supposed to but instead found that over the long run the prices of raw materials have generally risen as much as the prices of manufactured goods.[60] Since the team of economists was specifically set up to help poor countries and was made up of economists largely from communist and Third

World countries, there is little chance of bias in their findings. The problem is not with the statistics refuting the deteriorating terms-of-trade theory but with the theory itself: it is simply an inadequate means of explaining the underdevelopment of Third World countries.

One further weakness of the terms-of-trade argument that might be considered is that an important feature of it—the complaint over the lack of Western manufacturing investments—has grown increasingly less relevant in recent years. Owing to changing market conditions, most notably to the availability of far cheaper labor in Latin America than in the United States or Europe, Western corporations have often been quite eager to establish branches of their manufacturing concerns in Latin American countries. In fact, because of these shifting market forces, Latin American governments have found they not only can attract manufacturing investments from industrialized countries but can drive some very hard bargains as well. Many governments, for example, have negotiated agreements that give them majority ownership of the foreign enterprise; and still others have demanded—and won—the right to complete ownership after a few years of operation.[61]

An even more common charge hurled against Western corporations in Latin America is that of "excess profits." The allegation that the Latin American economies have greatly suffered from the unfair profits carried away by foreign companies is more difficult to evaluate than the declining-terms-of-trade accusation. To begin with, some judgment must be made as to what constitutes an excessive profit. The average rate-of-return for businesses in the United States is around 11 percent, so presumably the profits in Latin America should be higher in order to induce American companies to invest there. How much higher depends on many factors, including the economic and political risks prospective investors perceive in any given Latin American country. Another problem in examining the accusation of excess profits is that Latin Americans contend much of the profit is hidden from view by means of various accounting devices. But since Latin American critics are the last to have access to the company records that reveal "hidden" profits, oftentimes the figures they throw around are unsubstantiated and are believed only because people want to believe them and because the numbers have gained credibility through the process of repetition. However, despite the difficulties involved in evaluating the question of excess profits, it is nevertheless safe to say that the profits of foreign corporations in Latin America have sometimes been exceptionally high. It is reliably known, for example, that in 1954 U.S. corporations had five times the capital invested in Canada than in Venezuela, yet the profits they took out of Venezuela were greater.[62]

Although the topic of foreign profit rates is widely discussed and hotly debated in Latin America, about the most significant statement that can be made concerning it is that, through the point of view of modernization, the issue itself is not very important. The reason for this is that the profits of foreign companies, whether they have been excessive or not, have not had much to do with Latin American underdevelopment. In fact, foreign investment that earned an unjustifiably high return was more advantageous to Latin Americans than no foreign investment at all because the technology and knowledge of foreigners enabled Latin Americans to convert their natural resources (which were doing them no good underground) into potential modernization capital. Furthermore, even if the earnings of foreign investors in Latin America were excessively lucrative, the fact remains that the revenues from the primary product industries foreigners did so much to develop have traditionally provided Latin American governments with the bulk of their foreign exchange. In 1960, for example, Venezuela received 97 percent of its foreign exchange from exports of oil and iron; Chile, 76 percent from copper and nitrates; Panama, 72 percent from bananas and cacao; Ecuador, 75 percent from bananas and coffee; and Bolivia, 71 percent from tin and lead.[63] The problem has been that Latin American society has not produced the modernizing elites needed to direct these funds into projects that stimulate long-term economic growth. Once again we return to that basic point that it is not the amount of money that is critical to modernization but how it is spent. Because the users of capital in Latin America regularly wasted it through needless consumption, parasitism, and mismanagement, more capital in their hands as a result of a larger share of foreign profits would not have significantly influenced the pace of Latin American modernization.

Another important aspect of the debate over excess profits is that foreign companies in recent times have unquestionably lost much of their ability to wrest lopsided investment agreements from Latin American governments. Due to more favorable market conditions and the political advantages Latin Americans have learned they can gain from reactive nationalist postures, Latin American governments have steadily become much tougher in their dealings with foreign corporations. When, for example, petroleum companies from the United States first negotiated for drilling rights in Venezuela shortly after World War I, they bargained from a strong position and were able to extract from the Venezuelan government a contract to pay as little as 7 to 10 percent of their profits in taxes. The increasing importance of Venezuelan oil over the decades enabled the Venezuelan government gradually to increase its share: by the 1960s, the government was taking 60 to 70 percent of the profits, and just before nationalization in 1976 it was walloping the foreign oil companies with an effective tax rate of over 90 percent.[64] It is, of course, the duty of Latin American leaders to negotiate the best possible contract for their countries, but there is also risk in overly defending the national interest. Today the most likely failing of Latin American governments is not that they will be too compliant in their dealings with foreign corporations but so uncompromising that they will discourage needed investment from abroad. This has already happened in Argentina, where petroleum legislation has deterred foreign oil companies from exploring for more reserves, and in Ecuador, where escalating government demands for more money have driven several oil concerns out of the country.[65]

The example of Venezuela also points to another kind of danger. During the 1950s the Venezuelan dictator Perez Jimenez actually reduced the Venezuelan tax rate on petroleum and obviously settled for less than the oil companies would have been willing to pay.[66] Because of situations like this, critics have charged that foreign companies "dominate" some Latin American governments and therefore are able to win better concessions in the negotiation process than they should have. Even the largest foreign corporations do not wield enough power to remove governments not to their liking,[67] and so in order to influence state officials, they must resort mainly to the weapon of bribery. The subject of corporation bribery became something of a national scandal in the United States in 1975 when the American Congress and media suddenly "uncovered" what American businessmen in Latin America have been doing more or less openly ever since they invested their first dollars there. In light of the pervasive corruption within Latin American governmental bureaucracies, it is hardly surprising that foreign businessmen have long engaged in the practice of bribery and continue to do so to this very day. While some foreigners adapt themselves to this way of conducting business with little hesitation, the more reluctant eventually discover they really do not have much alternative. Representatives of large corporations find themselves approached by Latin Americans who describe themselves as "facilitators" and offer to guide the foreigners through the bewildering maze of government bureaucracy. Usually these middlemen are well connected and can frustrate the best efforts of a businessman who refuses to cooperate with them. In Bolivia the use of such agents is obligatory by law, and while foreigners sometimes hide behind their intermediaries and profess ignorance of how the agents execute their tasks, the plain fact is that they know they have to deal "under the table" or not deal at all. There is no question but that the widespread corruption in Latin America can make it easier for a foreign corporation to obtain special treatment from Latin American public officials. This does not necessarily mean that foreigners can dominate Latin American governments through bribery because bribery is a two-edged sword. There is no reason why corrupt Latin American political leaders and bureaucrats would not try to exploit foreign companies, which are both wealthy and vulnerable, just as they do other sectors of society. A company, therefore, might find itself having to bribe officials just to obtain its legitimate rights. The practice of bribery, then, is more complicated than first perceived. It can work both for and against the foreigners, leaving difficult to resolve the question of just who is dominating whom. The real blame for corporate bribery lies most fundamentally with the prevailing attitudes in Latin American culture that tolerate corruption as a way of life, for these are the invisible underlying forces that encourage, and even obligate, the continuation of this social vice.

The causal relationship that Latin Americans insist exists between Western economic imperialism and Latin American underdevelopment has much to do with the money they see leaving Latin America in the form of profits from investments and interest on loans. They observe a steady flow of cash streaming abroad to already wealthy countries, look back with horror at the poverty of their own lands, and make the connection. While such an idea can be emotionally appealing, intellectually it is simplistic. If foreign investments bring inevitable economic ruin to dependent countries, then Australia and Canada, which have absorbed the greatest amount of foreign investment per capita in the world, would be the poorest countries in the world. Nor can it be said that foreign loans are, in themselves, harmful to the economic health of recipient nations. Many critics of economic imperialism have cited as proof of foreign exploitation the enormous debt being amassed by underdeveloped nations; Brazil, which has an exceptionally high ratio of foreign debt to gross national product (over 20 percent),[68] is one of their favorite examples. But foreign loans, like direct foreign investments, do not necessarily drain wealth but can create wealth provided they are used properly. The United States for the larger part of its history went literally over its head in debt in order to build the canals, roads, bridges, and factories it needed. To America, borrowed money was one of the vital fuels that powered its economic expansion. Loans from abroad were, therefore, a boon and not a burden despite the fact that the United States during the nineteenth century had to service twice as much debt (totaling 40 percent of its gross national product) as Brazil does today.[69]

The weakness of the economic imperialism argument is, perhaps, best seen when reduced to its central variable—which turns out to be capital. This procedure reveals it to be little more than a pugnacious version of the scarcity-of-capital theory of underdevelopment, the main difference being that it delights in blaming the capital shortage on developed countries. As noted in a previous section, (see pp. 5–7), the problem with the scarcity-of-capital approach is that capital is not what analysts should be focusing on, for how much capital is invested is far less important than how capital is invested, and this ultimately depends upon the values and customs of the people who use it.

Again it is oil-rich, capital-rich Venezuela that illustrates the truth of this most vividly. Owing to a combination of nature's beneficence and foreign investment, no country in Latin America has had over the decades a greater relative abundance of investment capital. And because of this advantage, no country in Latin America has squandered more opportunity for economic advancement. Although Venezuela boasts the highest per capita income in Latin America, this is a false indicator of the nation's true level of modernization. Venezuela's gift of oil has served to exacerbate its heritage of modernization-impeding values, and today the country is even more dependent on its petroleum lifeline than in the 1930s when politicians first coined the slogan "*Sembrar el petróleo*" ("Invest the Petroleum Revenues"). When the oil wells run dry or when petroleum is replaced by a less expensive source of energy, Venezuela will almost certainly end up economically bedridden. And just as predictable as Venezuela's shattered economic health is that deep from within the infirmary will be heard the outraged cries of "economic imperialism," louder and more insistent than ever.

Cultural Imperialism

It should be evident from this discussion of political and economic imperialism that although Western governments and corporations can be faulted in their dealings with Latin Americans, there is no conceivable way they can be held responsible for the major problems confronting contemporary Latin American society. Because the idea of imperialism can hardly owe its widespread appeal among Latin Americans to the strength of its arguments, its popularity must be explained by other factors. Ideas that sway large masses of people are often accepted less on their logical merits and more on how well they serve people's needs and self-interests. The most obvious Latin American self-interest the theory of imperialism caters to is economic: if Latin Americans and other Third World peoples can lead Westerners to believe they are indeed the cause of the poverty outside their own land, then the underdeveloped nations stand a better chance of realizing their demands for a global redistribution of wealth. However, even more important to the appeal of the imperialism idea is that it also serves the emotional self-interest of Latin Americans, who are understandably very partial to a theory that blames the misfortune of their underdevelopment on someone other than themselves.

The propensity of Latin Americans to unjustifiably hold foreigners responsible for Latin American problems is particularly obvious in the third form of imperialism that Latin Americans protest—cultural imperialism. Cultural imperialism has been defined by the Peruvian nationalist writer Victor Raúl Haya de la Torre as a condition of servitude where Latin Americans exhibit a "fascination for Europe and a

disdain for everything that is our own."[70] Latin American reactive nationalists feel that foreigners are somehow responsible for how Latin
Americans regard their own and foreign culture. They accusingly
maintain that foreigners deliberately try to impose an invisible state of
"mental colonialism" upon the Latin American peoples, and that
foreigners intend cultural imperialism to work with the other forms of
imperialism toward a complete domination of Latin American life. As
Fidel Castro somberly admonished his countrymen, "We must not
forget that the imperialists didn't base their domination on economic
and political weapons alone but very much also on spiritual weapons,
the weapons of thought and culture."[71]

A widespread belief in the danger of cultural imperialism is indicated by the great hue and cry often heard to take political action
against this foreign menace. Latin Americans concerned with cultural
imperialism argue that their struggle to rid their country of foreign
political and economic influence is in itself not enough because Latin
Americans cannot be truly free until they have achieved "mental
emancipation" (emancipación mental) as well. A publication of a
theater group in Chile expressed this idea of complete liberation in the
following manner:

> The bank is being taken over by the state—a fine achievement for
> our Government. We will nationalize the natural resources. Ex-
> cellent! It deserves the support of all Chileans. But if they do not na-
> tionalize, at the same time, our customs, our spirit, our culture, all
> the rest will be useless; we will never be able to liberate ourselves
> from the subtle and hidden wires with which imperialism is ac-
> customed to choke and exploit our people. We should begin with
> the head, with the motor of human beings, in order to achieve a
> real, a genuine Chileanization.[72]

But if Latin Americans wish to "nationalize" their "spirit," their
"customs," and their "culture" in addition to their foreign-owned
economic assets, what measures can they take to do this? In specific
terms, how can they go about replacing "mental colonization" with
"mental emancipation"? When the Argentinean journalist Ricardo Rojo
journeyed to Cuba in the early 1960s, he noticed one way the Cubans
were combating cultural imperialism: Rojo, a heavy smoker, was
struck by the curious detail that all Cuban brands of cigarettes had
Spanish names; in fact, to Rojo it seemed that everywhere he looked
—at billboards, neon signs, commercial establishments, television,
and movies—King English had fallen from grace.[73] Other countries in
Latin America have also adopted measures to weaken the impact of
"cultural imperialism." Mexico, for example, has passed a law that
will force all foreign companies to use a Spanish name for their products: this means that the Pepsi-Cola Company in Mexico will have

to change the name of its brew to something like Mexicola and that the Ford Motor Company will have to identify its automobile with a name (Aztecmóvil?) that sounds authentically Mexican.[74] Mexican legislators have also considered a law, aimed at "freeing Mexican youth from musical colonialism," that would require radio stations in the country to play Mexican music 90 percent of the time.[75] Juan Perón of Argentina took similar steps toward "mental emancipation" by decreeing that two-thirds of the country's radio plays had to be Argentinean and by heavily taxing the showing of foreign films.[76] Brazil, in a slightly different approach toward curbing the influence of foreign films, required during the mid-1970s that all owners of movie theaters show at least 84 Brazilian films a year.[77] Chile under Salvador Allende also promulgated nationalization-of-culture measures, including one that ordered Chilean radio stations to devote 40 percent of their air time, spread out evenly over the entire day, to music interpreted by Chileans (25 percent) and to Chilean folklore (15 percent).[78] In response to the "Chileanization" of Chilean radio initiative, one reactive nationalist rendered this typical comment: "The Chileanization of radio programs comes at a moment of absolute cultural exhaustion. I sincerely believe that Chileans will turn their eyes once again to Chile and stop thinking, singing, and dancing in English."[79]

Unlike the arguments of political and economic imperialism that, while vastly overdrawn, are at least moored in some bedrock of truth, the criticisms of cultural imperialism are scarcely more than airy flights of the imagination. If cultural imperialism is regarded as a serious issue by Latin American reactive nationalists, then it is cultural imperialism that most clearly reveals their impulse to convert their concern with dependencia into a hail of condemnations against Western peoples. When reactive nationalists in Chile decided in the early 1970s to "Chileanize" the air waves, a radio station owner ventured the question as to whether it was really appropriate to regard Bach and Beethoven as "imperialists."[80] It is just as improbable that Western leaders use the hit tunes of Frank Sinatra or the thumping rhythms of Western rock bands as "spiritual weapons" in order to "choke," "exploit," and "dominate" hapless Latin Americans. The hard reality is that cultural depencencia exists in Latin American society, not because of a foreign conspiracy, but because Latin Americans want far more of what is produced and created in the West than Westerners want from Latin America. From the beginning of their history as independent peoples, Latin Americans have interpreted this imbalance of exchange as a national weakness, and at one time concerned nationalists publicly reacted to the problem by unmerciful doses of self-criticism and stirring exhortations to do better; later they were more inclined to respond with strident declarations of spiritual superiority; today they are more likely to invent exaggerated stories of foreign exploitation.

Over the decades of the twentieth century, the myth of imperialist exploitation has grown up in Latin American society to proportions that are truly extraordinary. Foreigners wielding stupendous powers are widely thought to be tirelessly scheming to carry out imperialistic designs. A few years ago when Ecuadorians of a small city saw a large number of dead fish floating down a river, many concluded that "imperialists" were responsible for the strange event. On another occasion Brazilians in Rio de Janeiro showed themselves willing, even eager, to believe a rumor that the CIA had made the beaches in northeastern Brazil radioactive. Bolivians and Paraguayans are frequently heard to claim that foreigners were the real cause of the devastating war they waged with each other in the 1930s. Intelligent university students will look you straight in the eye and inform you that the CIA has an agent planted in every classroom in Latin America. The filmmaker Fernando Solanas flatly accuses the CIA of controlling all, yes *all*, the printed and electronic media on the continent. One particularly imaginative revolutionary discovered a way of blaming imperialism for earthquakes and hurricanes.[81] Leading Latin American political figures, although normally more sober than revolutionary extremists, nevertheless sometimes seriously contend that the greatest problem facing their countries is "imperialism." And prominent intellectuals and social critics, probing the causes of national poverty, often write as if nothing else mattered except the malevolent hand of the foreigner.[82]

If there is any lesson Westerners should learn from the protest of reactive nationalists against imperialism, it is that anti-Western feeling in Latin America can be extreme, very emotional, and there is little Westerners can do to reduce it by simply changing their policy toward the Latin Americans. Even substantial changes in their foreign policy such as refusing to recognize dictatorships, increasing foreign aid to 1 percent of the gross national product, or agreeing to index the prices of raw materials with manufactured goods will not, in themselves, quell the fires of anti-Westernism among Latin American reactive nationalists; for the most fundamental cause of Latin American enmity is the vast disparity between the "advanced" and the underdeveloped nation-states and the negative national identity that this situation forces upon Latin American nationalists. In the final analysis, the West is hated, not so much for what it does, but for what it is.

If the negative national identity is the fundamental cause of anti-imperialist hatred and anti-Westernism in Latin America, then it is theoretically possible for Westerners to improve the situation by helping Latin Americans develop and by so doing, helping them overcome their negative national identity. The truth is, however, that the capacity of Westerners to promote social and economic development in Latin America (or, for that matter in any nonmodern culture) is circumscribed by conditions beyond their control. They can make available to Latin Americans capital, machinery, and technical, scientific, and managerial knowledge, but the crucial question is what Latin Americans themselves do with these tools. But if Westerners feel frustrated over their lack of ability to substantially reduce anti-Westernism in Latin America, they can take some consolation in the knowledge that short of launching a destructive military attack, neither do they have the ability to do much harm in Latin America. The theory of imperialism notwithstanding, the causes of the major social problems afflicting Latin Americans are almost exclusively Latin American.

THE QUEST FOR A POSITIVE NATIONAL IDENTITY

Because the realization of a positive national identity is the paramount challenge confronting Latin American nationalists, we next examine some of the ways they have attempted to do this and see how successful they have been. The greatest problem for Latin Americans in this endeavor has been that they can achieve their objective in only one way and that way is very difficult: if a lack of notable collective accomplishment has caused the negative national identity, then solid accomplishment is essential to bring about an identity that is more positive. Latin Americans will take genuine pride in their national identity, and they will find a solution to their nationalist dilemma, only when they as a people excel in some of the multifold activities of man so that they as well as others abroad regard their country as a successful nation-state. This, unfortunately, is one of those incontrovertible realities of life that can be obscured but not altered by wishful thinking or liberal sentimentalism.

The Problem of Racial Self-Acceptance

As pointed out in a previous section (see pp. 143–44), there has been no shortage of writers in Latin America who, by means of elaborate "interpretations of the national reality" and "discoveries of the national soul," have attempted to demonstrate to Latin Americans why they should feel proud of their national identities. One of the more prominent, and for outsiders confusing, characteristics of these thinkers has been their frequent preoccupation with the racial character of their peoples. Arturo Uslar-Pietri's question, "What am I? White, Negro, Indian, mestizo, European, something that partakes of all of this, or something distinct?" is quite typical of Latin American identity seekers. One reason for this sensitivity to race is that while few Latin Americans are properly racists in the sense that they believe in the genetic inferiority of certain peoples, many do hold the opinion that nonwhite peoples are in many ways inferior to whites because of cultural differences. Another factor that looms even larger in the Latin American preoccupation with race is that for centuries Latin Americans have been emotionally conditioned by their particular historical experience to reflexively associate non-Caucasian peoples with low status and backwardness. This kind of social conditioning began in the colonial era when non-Caucasians were crowded into the less prestigious classes of society and it was reinforced in modern times when Latin Americans began to regard the culture of white Europeans as the most advanced form of civilization in the world. Because of this heritage of prestige assumptions favoring whites, many nationalist writers whose foremost aim was to instill in their people a feeling of pride in their national identity have also felt compelled to instill in their non-Caucasian countrymen a feeling of pride in their racial identity—to assure them that although they may be Indian, mestizo, or Negro, they were still as capable as Caucasian peoples of building a great nation-state.

The importance of race in the question of positive national identity might first be examined in Argentina, where the people had a national racial identity very much to their liking. Argentineans, in fact, took what can be described only as inflamed nationalist pride in the "whiteness" of their population. In Argentinean society, this kind of pro-Caucasian sentiment was open, obvious, and displayed with absolutely no sense of embarrassment. The authors of the 1895 Census volumes for example, were not reluctant to drop their normally neutral, dry-as-dust reporting style when they presented the evidence showing how a "new and beautiful white race" *(nueva y hermosa raza blanca)* was rapidly becoming dominant in the country.[83] Apparently this lack of neutrality was carried even further by the authorities in charge of the 1920 Census, who deliberately altered the population statistics in order to make Argentina appear "whiter" than it actually was.[84]. Argentineans, of course, not only flaunted their racial pride among themselves but made other Latin Americans keenly aware of it by their annoying habit of invidiously comparing their degree of national "whiteness" with that of other countries in order to strengthen their claim as the leading nation on the continent. Argentineans, for example, took impish pleasure in referring to Chile as a land of mestizos, knowing full well that Chileans also liked to think of themselves as basically a "white" people. Likewise, Argentineans often dismissed Brazil with its large colored population as a nation of "tropicals" and "monkeys" and boasted that it was Argentina that actually had the largest population in terms of the number of people who contributed to national greatness.[85] Some Argentineans even dared to hope that the foremost nation in Latin America would be recognized by Europeans as part of the white man's world and accepted as a member of the inner circle of advanced nation-states. One such optimistic spirit was the famous Argentinean sociologist José Ingenieros, who in 1915 was sufficiently impressed with his country's "new Euro-Argentinean race" to confidently predict:

> There are unmistakable judgements we may make regarding this development of a white Argentinean race—rapidly growing in the past ten years and destined to produce even greater social changes in the next twenty years—that soon this development will permit us to erase the stigma of inferiority with which Europeans have always marked South Americans.[86]

If Argentinean nationalists were trumpeting the "whiteness" of their nation with this much exultation, the feelings of nationalists in countries with mainly non-Caucasian populations might well be imagined. It was not just Argentinean boasting that disturbed these other Latin American nationalists but the fact that Argentina's relatively advanced state of modernization seemed to confirm the widespread idea that a connection existed between a country's "whiteness" and its capacity for civilized progress. In truth, nationalists from other Latin American countries, particularly during the nineteenth and early twentieth centuries, often openly despaired about what to do about the non-Caucasian sectors of their population. When they looked, for example, at their Indian countrymen, what they saw was not an industrious and responsibile citizenry but a sullen, primitive, superstitious, and lethargic people who seemed singularly unadaptable to the demands of modern civilization. The town fathers of the Bolivian city of Oruro once showed their embarrassment over the Indian culture of their country by ordering all the Indians in their jurisdiction to discard their traditional attire and to clothe themselves in the "modern dress of civilized peoples."[87] The Mexican dictator Porfirio Diaz demonstrated a similar sense of shame when he ordered that no Indians be hired at Mexican hotels hosting delegations to a Panamerican conference, lest the distinguished visitors get the idea that Mexico was an Indian country.[88] Diaz's attempt to hide his nation's Indian racial identity is especially curious in light of the fact that he himself was squat, dark-skinned, and heavily Indian featured.

To Latin American nationalists, the most frustrating aspect of their concern over the racial composition of their population was that there was not much they could do about it. This feeling was especially acute toward the end of the nineteenth century when it had become quite clear that, Latin American countries with the exception of Argentina and Uruguay, were not going to attract enough white

European immigrants to alter their racial identities substantially. Nationalists began to grow increasingly aware that in their attempts to discover a satisfactory pride in their national identity, they were going to have to deal with the reality that a large part of their population was non-Caucasian. One of the most influential proselytizers of the new nationalist message was José Vasconcelos, an early twentieth century intellectual and at one time minister of education in Mexico:

> The truth is whether we like it or not, the mestizo is the dominant element of the Latin American continent. . . . Let us adopt, then, the valiant resolution to not argue more about the amount of white blood that makes up our nationality (which is not very much) and confess ourselves mestizos and Indians. . . . Let us frankly place ourselves in the ranks of the colored peoples . . . . it is better to be a colored people with our own distinct culture than a pseudowhite people that lives off the spiritual production of the real whites.[89]

The kind of racial self-acceptance that Vasconcelos urged upon his fellow Latin Americans became an important part of the reactive nationalist movement in Latin American society. Reactive nationalists in search of new definitions of nationalist self-esteem instigated a number of intellectual insurrections that appropriately came to be known as the "nativist revolts." The nativist revolts were in essence a series of reinterpretations of the various Latin American "national realities" that were frank rebellions against the prevailing attitudes toward non-Caucasian groups. The nativist reactive nationalists lectured to their countrymen on why they should accept their nation's racial identity not only without embarrassment but also with a great sense of pride. Although these frequently white interpreters commonly displayed meager knowledge of the cultures they were discussing, they nevertheless claimed to have found in their country's Indian, Negro, or multiracial heritage lofty spiritual qualities that the "materialistic" West was sadly lacking. In addition to "discovering" some form of spiritual uniqueness or superiority, often these intellectuals would uncover a spiritual mission for their people and explain how they were destined to pass on their ennobling qualities to the other peoples, or "races," of the world. By such theoretical techniques, the nativist reactive nationalists attempted to provide their countrymen with ways of looking at themselves as a people that fostered pride and not frustration.

The ideas of José Vasconcelos were typical of this nativist new wave. Vasconcelos plunged into a classic nationalist search for the inner meaning of Mexican civilization and after much study and reflection announced that he had found it in a metaphysical notion he called the "cosmic race." The cosmic race was, in reality, not a race but a culture of exceptional human beings that Vasconcelos foresaw would emerge sometime in the future. The embryonic form of this cosmic race, however, existed in the present and this was none other than the Latin American mestizo "race," that same group of mixed-bloods that throughout Latin American history had been maligned as bastardized and inferior. Vasconcelos maintained that he had discovered a portentous development unfolding in Mexican and Latin American culture that previous generations of nationalists had been too blind to see. It was his observation that Latin American society was functioning as a kind of giant crucible where all the races of the world were fusing together, and by so doing were creating the types of spiritual qualities that allowed the different races to live side by side in the same community. Vasconcelos regarded this as greatly significant because he believed that the races of the earth could not remain rigidly segregated forever and would eventually have to learn to accommodate one another; and since Latin Americans were far ahead of the rest of humanity in this blending process, Vasconcelos claimed that his people had the enormous responsibility of showing other peoples how to undergo a similar evolution. This Latin American mission, declared Vasconcelos, was absolutely essential for the further development of human civilization. It was, in his words, the "only hope of the world."[90] What Vasconcelos tried to show through this reasoning was that acceptance of the essentially mestizo racial identity of Latin American society was not just something Latin Americans should do because they could not avoid it but was actually something of which they could be proud, for in the vision of this Mexican intellectual, the Latin American mestizos were a people chosen by destiny for a great world mission: they were nothing less than the vanguard of the future cosmic race and the best hope for the triumph of world civilization.[91]

The ideas of the nativist reactive nationalists in Latin America often had a decisive impact on the political and social life of their countries. Nowhere was this more true than in Mexico, where nationalists stressed their pride in their non-Caucasian racial identity by glorifying their nation's Indian heritage. While Porfirio Diaz ashamedly tried to hide his country's Indian character, his successors pridefully displayed it to the world. All over the country Mexican reactive nationalists angrily tore down the statues of Spanish conquistadores and replaced them with bronze Indians cast in heroic postures—almost as if twentieth-century Mexicans could avenge the sixteenth century defeat of the Aztecs. The same nativist spirit drove Mexicans literally to dig into their pre-Colombian past by spending a larger portion of their national revenue on archeology than any other nation in the world.[92] What Mexicans were digging for was more than scientific knowledge; they were digging for evidence of the great achievements of their non-Caucasian ancestors. In a larger sense, they were searching for their national soul, for a positive interpretation of their national existence. The kind of frenzied nationalist emotion that was involved in these projects is suggested by the events that took place in the aftermath of the supposed discovery of the bones of Cuauhtémoc, the last Aztec ruler to fight against the Spaniards. The spark that set off the whole affair was the discovery of the bones of Hernán Cortés, the Spanish conquerer of the Aztecs. The historian Leslie Byrd Simpson describes what followed:

> Justice demanded that something be done to balance the account. An enthusiastic Cortés hater, Dr. Eulalia Guzmán by name, went to Europe and dug in the archives, and came up with an unconvincing portrait of Cortés, showing him to have been an undersized, bow-legged, chinless, and thoroughly repulsive cretin—attributes which somehow escaped contemporary observers. The effect of her discovery failing to be as shattering as circumstances demanded, Dr. Guzmán, to no one's astonishment, found the bones of Cuauhtémoc reposing in a secret grave in the village of Ixcateopan, Guerrero, brought thither by his faithful and mourning people through a thousand kilometers of wilderness. A bronze plaque identified the grave beyond a doubt, and a signed statement written by Father Toribio de Motolinía really clinched the matter. Reputable archaeologists, anthropologists, and historians pointed out the patent absurdities in the documentation, demonstrated that the plaque was a clumsy fake, and showed that the bones were a jumble of odds and ends from several skeletons, with a female cranium—besides which, the Aztecs always cremated their noble dead. No matter. The bones of Cuauhtémoc *had* to be found, and anyone daring to doubt their authenticity was a traitor! That irrepressible cynic, Diego Rivera, said that, regardless of the evidence, the bones must be those of the hero and that it was the patriotic duty of all good Mexicans to believe in them. The Party decreed a "Cuauhtémoc Week," and a huge demonstration was staged before his monument in the Paseo de la Reforma in Mexico City. Another myth had been added to the arsenal of the Revolution. Cuauhtémoc, who was certainly a stout fellow, but who was bitterly hated by most Mexicans as the leader of the hated Aztecs, has thus become a symbol of democratic resistance to the oppressor, and a pair of grim soldiers with loaded rifles guard his grave against desecration.[93]

While the furor over Cuauhtémoc's bones has subsided in Mexico, the struggle for a positive national identity has not. Mexican intellectuals, of course, have produced numerous interpretations of the "national reality" which have provided Mexicans with many reasons why they should experience the emotional warmth of nationalist pride. But such ideas can create a truly self-assured national identity only if they are realistic, and they can be realistic only if they are based on real and not imaginary achievements. A theory such as that of José Vasconcelos, where Mexicans are asked to think of themselves as a part of an evolving "cosmic race" destined to save human civilization, is difficult to believe with any degree of confidence even for those who would like to believe. The idea of *indianismo*, or "Indianism," that the Mexican government has done so much to foster is likewise a very weak foundation on which to build a positive national identity. Mexicans might conceivably take genuine pride in their Indian identity if Mexican Indians were a highly successful and respected people. But Indians in Mexico are the most backward, illiterate, impoverished, and exploited minority in the country—are certainly not a subculture with which whites and mestizos are anxious to identify. More modern Mexicans, in fact, commonly disdain their country's Indian population, which puts them in the cuirous position of honoring Indians made of bronze while despising those made of flesh. Nor is it very conceivable that recalling the glories of Mexico's pre-Colombian Indians can be much help to Mexico's problem of national self-esteem. While contemporary Mexicans might take some satisfaction in the thought that their remote Stone Age ancestors were once the most highly developed civilization on the continent, what really matters is the position of their country in the world today. The attempt of Mexican intellectuals and politicians to use race as an integral feature of national pride was exposed in all its absurdity by the famous Mexican artist José Clemente Orozco. Orozco complained to his countrymen, "We are continuously classifying ourselves as Indians, Creoles, and mestizos, thinking only of the mixture of bloods, as if we were describing race horses."[94] He likewise thought it remarkable that Mexicans were still denouncing the deeds of Cortés as if the battles had not taken place centuries ago but in the previous year. Most important of all, Orozco believed that despite all the emotional and intellectual energy poured into the question of racial identity, Mexicans continued to be "people suffering from amnesia . . . we do not yet know who we are."[95]

Great Power Ambition

Latin Americans are faced with the fact that the only solid foundation for a positive national identity is real achievement. This achievement can take many forms but perhaps the most dramatic kind of national achievement is to become what is known as a "great power"—that is to say, to build up enough military and economic power to be able to substantially influence the affairs of other nations. In this century only Argentina and Brazil have had reasonable hopes of attaining great power status and so our discussion of this kind of ambition will focus on these two countries.

Argentina was able to entertain hopes of great power status because owing to the vitalizing impact of immigration and foreign investments, it became the leading economic power in Latin America. During the late nineteenth and early twentieth centuries, Argentina developed the strongest export markets, built the best communications and transport network, and established the most diversified industry of any country in Latin America. Argentina's economic success, in fact, was so considerable that by the 1920s the country had become the sixth wealthiest in the world as measured on a per capita basis.

Despite this economic success, however, Argentina still retained many of the characteristics of an underdeveloped country. For example, one of the biggest problems Argentina faced was that the development was concentrated around the capital of Buenos Aires while the interior of the country remained backward and poor. Millions of diligent immigrants did fan out across the countryside to work the farms, but unlike the case in the United States, the government was not in a position to give the farmers ownership of their own land. The reason for this was that landlords, not the government, owned most of the good land in Argentina, and they were able to block any attempt at land reform. As a consequence, the immigrants became tenant-sharecroppers instead of owners and therefore lacked any incentive to build up the infrastructure of the countryside such as permanent houses, barns, fences, roads, and other lasting economic improvements. Because of this situation, Argentina lost a golden opportunity to harness the full potential of millions of hardworking immigrants, to spread economic prosperity to the interior of the country, and to develop a large class of conservative farmers who would have acted as a moderating influence on the radicalism that infected Argentinean politics in later years.

Thus, despite the fact that Argentina could show much evidence of impressive economic growth and progress, a closer look into many areas of Argentinean life could also uncover numerous signs of weakness. Because Argentinean nationalists recognized this, they tended to have two views of themselves as a people. They found much to support their desire to regard themselves as a successful national collectivity and at the same time, they saw disturbing problems that made them unsure of their success.

Argentina's ambivalent state of self-perception—whether the country should identify itself as successful or unsuccessful, as a "have" or a "have-not" nation—was particularly evident during the Perón era. Have-not nations are usually distinguishable by their serious economic problems such as low-productivity economies and indebtedness to foreigners. They tend to associate themselves with something called the Third World, are frequently heard to accuse the haves of exploitation, and invoke the theory of imperialism to make their case. While the most obvious general feature of the have-nots is their national weakness, that of the haves is their national strength. Have nation-states enjoy strong economies, possess lots of money, and commonly use this money to make foreign investments, to distribute loans, grants, and charity abroad, and to build powerful military machines in order to impress other countries. Their economic and military strength allows them, intentionally or unintentionally, to exert considerable influence over the weaker have-nots. Because Perón's Argentina was in an intermediate zone between have and have-not, at one time or another the country managed to display the characteristics of both kinds of nations. It was when Argentina was playing the role of a have nation that it most clearly revealed its ambition to be recognized as a world power.

One reason Perón dared to dream of great power status for his country was because he sprang from an environment where this was talked about all the time—the Argentinean military. Many of Perón's fellow officers believed it was Argentina's destiny to dominate the South American continent. German influence among these officers was very strong, and they were inclined to look to Germany with its militaristic traditions as a spiritual home and a model for their own country. During World War II Argentinean military men showed themselves sympathetic to German aims and vastly impressed with the initial German successes. In 1943 the military lodge to which Perón belonged distributed to its members the following circular that described in detail their own vaunted hopes for conquest:

> Comrads! The war has shown that it is no longer possible for countries to defend themselves standing alone. . . . The age of the Nation is slowly being replaced by the age of the Continent. Yesterday the feudal manors united to form the Nation and today nations unite to form continents. This is the lesson of the war. Germany is realizing a titanic effort to unify the European continent. The largest and best equipped nation ought to direct the destiny of each continent in formation. In Europe, this will be Germany. In North America, the nation in command will for a time be the United States. But in South America there is currently no nation strong enough to assert hegemony without a challenge. Our mission is to make possible our unquestioned hegemony.
>
> This ambition is immense and demands sacrifice, but the fatherland cannot be forged without total sacrifice. The titans of our independence sacrificed well-being and life itself. In our time Germany has given a new sense of heroism to life. These will be our models. In order to accomplish the first step that will enable us to make Argentina strong and great, we will have to seize power. Never could a civilian comprehend the greatness of our ideal; civilians must be eliminated and be given one sole mission: Work and Obedience.

Once power is conquered, our mission will consist of making us strong, stronger than all the other nations united. It will be necessary to arm ourselves, overcoming all difficulties, fighting against every internal and external obstacle. The struggle of Hitler in peacetime and in war will serve as our guide. Alliances will be the first step; we already have Paraguay and we will have Bolivia and Chile. Together these four nations will be able to exercise pressure on Uruguay and then it will be easy to attract Brazil due to its form of government and the large groups of Germans that live in the country. Our hegemony will be a glorious one, without precedent, brought into being by the political genius and heroism of the Argentinean army.[96]

Hitler's "heroic" little war did not turn out as planned, but Perón, who assumed power right after the war, saw no reason to abandon his own dream of great power domination. One important reason why he was able to do this was because he had plenty of money with which to work. During the course of World War II Argentina had built up hundreds of millions of dollars in unpaid credits, and Perón inherited this engorged public purse when he came to power. It was these surplus funds that made it possible for Perón, more than any other leader in Argentinean history, to attempt to achieve for this country the status of a great power.

The first move that Perón made toward great power status was, of course, to strengthen the Argentinean military. Perón not only poured money into the Argentinean military but demonstrated a fondness for highly visible, highly prestigious military weapons. One of the more spectacular projects was the construction of jet airplanes. At great expense Perón imported hundreds of highly skilled German technicians and engineers to help him in this task; and Argentina became one of the five countries in the world to produce its own jet aircraft.[97] Even more spectacular but less successful was the development of an Argentinean atomic bomb. The Austrian scientist who was in charge of this project turned out to be a complete fraud, but he fooled Perón long enough for the Argentinean leader to make the dramatic announcement to an astonished world that Argentina was on the brink of becoming the world's fourth nuclear power.[98]

Another method Perón used to project a great power image was to demonstrate Argentina's economic power to the world. Because great powers are not supposed to be economically dependent on other countries, Perón moved to eliminate the more obvious signs of economic dependencia. Drawing upon his ample treasury reserves, Perón wasted little time in paying off Argentina's foreign debt and nationalizing the politically sensitive banking, communications, and transportation sectors of the economy. And because economically powerful countries are also noted for their ability to make foreign loans, Perón jumped into the business of international finance by extending credits to such countries as France, Finland, Czechoslovakia, Portugal, and Spain. Soon Perón was publicly bragging that Argentina was one of the world's three creditor nations.[99] Perón also became interested in making investments abroad, particularly those kinds of investments that would secure for Argentinean industries supplies of raw materials. Despite charges of "economic imperialism" thrown back at him, Perón attempted to secure agreements from Chile, Bolivia, and Paraguay giving Argentina the right to develop new sources of raw materials in those countries in exchange for favored access to them.[100]

Knowing that one of the more conspicuous characteristics of great powers was their ability to dispense foreign aid to needy countries, Perón was also ready to play that role to the hilt. Whenever a natural disaster would occur in some corner of Latin America, Perón's wife Eva, who was the head of the state-supported Eva Perón Foundation, would rush in planeloads of supplies to the suffering population. On occasion Eva was even moved to send foreign aid to the poor in Western Europe and the United States.[101] Even more dramatic than Eva's acts of charity was the announcement by the Peronist delegation to the 1948 Havana Trade Conference that Argentina was prepared to establish a multibillion-dollar foreign aid fund to assist Latin American development. Later at a press conference in Caracas, a high Argentinean official urged the immediate creation of an inter-American bank and promised that Argentina would provide most of the financial backing. Still another Argentinean representative on a different occasion publicly announced that Argentina had set up the machinery of a "little Marshall Plan" and was ready to begin helping its Latin American neighbors.[102]

Nothing much came of these spectacular promises, but the reason why Perón made them was because he loved to act as if he were the head of a great power and a have nation. Perón's failing, however, was that he did not carefully consider whether he had the means to put his programs into action. As things turned out, Perón rapidly ran through his substantial foreign currency reserves due to profligate government spending. When these funds were depleted, the Argentinean dictator discovered he could afford neither grand armies, nor atomic arsenals, nor foreign aid, nor foreign credits, nor foreign investments, nor, for that matter, his own country's economic independence. Argentina, in fact, was definitely showing some of the signs of a have-not nation, and Perón's awareness of this was reflected in the *other* side of his foreign and domestic policies.

Since Perón, like other Argentinean nationalists, could not help but perceive Argentina as in some sense a have-not nation, it should not be surprising that accusations of imperialism were among his most repeated political war cries. Perón was especially emphatic about denouncing economic imperialism. At international conferences, he attacked the free trade theories of the West as exploitative and exhorted less developed nations to follow Argentina's example and build high tariff barriers to protect their new industries. In taking this position he was, of course, tacitly admitting that Argentina shared many of the same problems as nonindustrialized, have-not nations. Some of Perón's most important domestic programs also resembled those commonly associated with underdeveloped countries, such as five-year plans of forced industrialization, heavy state intervention in the economy, and the selective nationalization of foreign enterprises. Perhaps Perón's most prominent policy that suggested a have-not national identity for his contry was the famous "Third Position" taken in international affairs: Perón's Third Position was very similar in inspiration to the political slogan Third World currently in vogue because it expressed Argentina's determination to be politically, economically, and culturally independent of the Western and Soviet worlds. In fact, in his later exile years, Perón specifically acknowledged that his "Third Position" stand was a forerunner of the "Third World" idea so avidly embraced by underdeveloped countries today.[103]

Owing in no small measure to the ruinously incompetent and opportunistic leadership of Juan Perón, the years during and following his administration have not been kind ones for Argentina. Because of this, Argentineans who years ago used to boast that "Latin America's border stops at the Argentine" are today more likely to lament that Argentina has become "Latin Americanized." A greater blow to Argentinean national pride can scarcely be imagined.

At least one problem about Argentina's national identity, however, has been solved. Argentineans are no longer ambivalent. They know who they are. Only memories of the good days remain, as the Argentinean intellectual Jorge Paita reflected, "Yes, vaguely we remember that we had been told that we were a young country, a rich country, a country full of promise."[104] Sarmiento's plea "Let us be the United States!" has gone unheeded. Once-strong hopes of being recognized as an advanced nation-state have been shattered beyond redemption. When the aging Perón returned to power in 1973, he could no longer speak of Argentina as a have nation, a creditor nation, an independent nation, or a nation destined to become a great power. Instead, Argentina was unequivocally an "underdeveloped" country, an "exploited" country, and a "Third World" country.[105] In defining themselves to themselves, Argentinean nationalists today are, for the most part, resigned to placing their country in the ranks of the less successful and powerful nation-states.

While Argentineans have become over the years less ambivalent about their national identity and more certain of their Third World status, Brazilians show signs of moving in the opposite direction. Since the middle of the 1960s, Brazilians have witnessed their country undergoing impressive, and in some years, spectacular economic growth. This process has gone far enough for Brazilians to start acting as the engineers of a South American economic powerhouse. Brazilian credit managers have felt sufficiently wealthy to extend loans to South American nations like Uruguay, Chile, and Bolivia. Brazilian government and business leaders have channeled huge amounts of capital into foreign investments such as oil exploration and road construction in Ecuador; coal development in Colombia; industrial and pipeline enterprises in Bolivia; cattle ranches, sugar refineries, banks, insurance companies, and the world's largest hydroelectric complex in Paraguay. Brazilians have also become involved in military assistance missions and foreign aid projects, not to make money but to win prestige and influence in other South American countries.[106]

This growing Brazilian strength has enabled Brazil to displace Argentina as the most powerful nation in the area, and like Argentina of old, to give vent to its great power yearnings. For example, Argentina in its mightier days used to toy with the idea of annexing Paraguay, Uruguay, and Southern Brazil, and at the very least, wanted them as subservient border states.[107] Beginning in the 1970s, Brazil started to establish itself as South America's most feared aggressor. Uruguay, in particular, owing to its small size and proximate location, has come to be very sensitive to the cold shadow of Brazilian power. Reports have it that Brazil was ready to send troops into Uruguay if the leftist candidate there had won the 1972 election. And although the Brazilian-favored candidate won, Brazilian interference was still not over. When the new president was threatened by a general strike in 1973, the Brazilian government rushed in supplies and loans to shore up their man. Some Brazilians are already predicting that Uruguay will soon be little more than a client state of their country.[108]

Again similar to Argentina in past years, another important signal of Brazil's great power ambitions is its expensive armaments program. This project consists of modernizing the weaponry of the Brazilian military and making the country as self-sufficient in arms as possible.[109] It has developed to the point where Brazil is now actually exporting sophisticated hardware items like armored vehicles and jet fighters to Third World countries.[110] By far the most ominous feature of this drive is Brazil's determination to display atomic muscles. The key to this plan is an agreement with West Germany to purchase eight atomic power plants, which would include the technology necessary to manufacture atomic weapons. Brazilian leaders, of course, repeatedly reaffirm their passion for "fraternal coexistence," but in the next breath, they add that Brazil is "conscious of its place in history" and must be free to respond with "agility" to changing international circumstances.[111] Also quite discomforting are the facts that the Brazilian military leaders who began the nuclear program refused to sign the Nuclear Nonproliferation Treaty and that they allowed a controlled press to push the nationalistic line that if other nations have atomic weapons, then Brazil should have them also.[112] Even if Brazil had no realistic defense anxieties (and in 1977 Argentina announced that the country had developed the capacity to produce atomic weapons[113]), most diplomats familiar with the area assume that for reasons of prestige alone Brazil would strive to join the elite group of world nuclear powers.[114] It is, unfortunately, not merely a possibility nor even a probability but a virtual certainty that in a few years Brazil will have—The Bomb.

As a consequence of their expanding economic, military, and political strength, Brazilians have slowly been edging toward an ambivalent national identity. Brazilian nationalists have long been accustomed to regarding their country as a poor, vulnerable Third World nation and, in reaction, have generally clung to a typically Third World outlook that has featured pious outrage against "oppressors" and "imperialists." Now their lives have been complicated by the fact that some things in their country have been going well, and that their increasing power and influence have caused other Latin American peoples to hurl at them the same charges of imperialism normally absorbed by advanced nation-states. Obliged to stand up under namecalling such as "Colossus of the South," "miniimperialists," and "subimperialist power," they have lost some of their inclination to view themselves as a weak, exploited Third World people. And how do most Brazilians react to the fact that accusations of imperialism are now turned against them? A Brazilian diplomat answered precisely this question:

> When someone speaks to me of tortures and repression in my country, I am uneasy and nervous because it touches me. But when they accuse me of being an imperialist, it is like asking me how many women I made love to last week. I will say no, no, and deny it—but I am secretly flattered.[115]

Nationalization

The great majority of Latin American countries, of course, cannot realistically entertain the hope of great power status. For the smaller nations of the continent, a more plausible means of striving for a positive national identity is through a political process called nationalization.

The politics of nationalization have, in Latin America, assumed different forms. Usually Latin American governments have "nationalized" productive resources; that is to say, they have seized income-producing property from foreigners and have transferred the rights of ownership to themselves. Latin American governments have also "nationalized" the "labor" of their countries; that is, they have made it difficult for foreign residents and immigrants to make a living and by so doing compete with the native-born in economic activities. Still other governments have "nationalized" their "culture"; or more concretely, they have restricted the availability of the cultural creations of foreign countries such as songs or films in order to enhance the appeal of those produced at home.

The importance that Latin Americans attach to their nationalizations can be extraordinarily high, particularly when Latin American governments take control of the prominent citadels of foreign economic power. Juan Perón, for example, in order to emphasize the exceptional historical significance of his nationalization efforts, delivered his "Declaration of Economic Independence" on the same sacred ground and on the same hallowed date that the founders of Argentina declared their political independence from Spain in 1816.[116] In similar fashion, Mexicans regard a 1938 expropriation of American and British oil interests as one of the three great "Revolutions" in their history, comparable in importance to their independence from Spain and their much-acclaimed "social revolution" of the early twentieth century.[117] Other Latin American nations such as Peru and Bolivia have made their statement about nationalizations by designating the day they expropriated a major foreign concern as their "Day of National Dignity."[118]

As might well be suspected, despite all the stirring rhetoric that soars above the festivities commemorating days of "National Dignity," often the forces behind nationalizations are considerably less than idealistic. Because nationalizations frequently result in a quick surge of popularity, politicans are sorely tempted to score political gains from them, even if in the long run the expropriations are not in the best interests of the country. Latin American political leaders also find nationalizations useful because state takeovers of private industry increase the number of government jobs available to them to pass out to loyal supporters. On the other side of this relationship, the sizable and often influential group of people who aspire to bureaucratic state employment, particularly if they belong to the party of the government in power, generally favor an enlargement of the public sector because this improves their chances of securing the kinds of positions they desire.

Although nationalizations are usually intended to render some benefit to the national economy, it is obvious that they can also cause economic harm. The first problem that Latin Americans encounter when they confiscate foreign investments is that they run the risk of discouraging further investments from the centers where the greatest advances in economic productivity are being made. Latin Americans cannot give the impression that they will unpredictably seize anything they want, whenever they want, and expect the industrialized nations to share with them their skills and technology. Another problem Latin Americans must face when they nationalize is whether they can operate the expropriated enterprise as efficiently as the foreigners did. Even if the foreigners were guilty of carrying "excess profits" out of the country, a nationalization will accomplish no economic good if the savings are gobbled up in mismanagement, corruption, favoritism, and bureaucratic parasitism.

The harm caused by nationalizations can be psychological as well as economic. On the surface the purpose of nationalizations is to eliminate foreign exploitation, but in a deeper sense, their purpose is to eliminate the manifestations of dependencia that convey to Latin American nationalists the unwelcome message of foreign superiority. The difficulty, however, with expropriating enterprises that have grown to be conspicuous symbols of foreign power is that if a nationalization does not work out well, it will tend to reinforce the already widespread feeling among Latin Americans that they cannot do anything as well as foreigners. To take an example, some years ago when the water system in Montevideo was owned and operated by a private British firm, water was cheap and dependable and repairs on the pipelines were quickly executed. After the company was nationalized, water grew more expensive in relation to other goods, and maintenance on the system declined. This, of course, was not lost upon Uruguayans, who were quite capable of noticing the price and dependability of the water they were consuming; and a nationalization that was intended to be a symbol of national independence became instead a symbol of national incompetence. Nationalizations with similar results are very common in Latin America, and they do far more to weaken than to bolster a people's sense of national self-esteem.

Nationalizations are even more psychologically damaging when Latin Americans recognize that the principal motivation behind them was not dedication to the national interest but devotion to individual self-interest. One example of nationalization legislation where cynical opportunism is easily detected by Latin Americans is the "nationalization-of-labor" laws. This kind of legislation, which crops up from time to time in Latin America, is designed to prevent immigrants from outdistancing the natives in economic pursuits by depriving all foreign-born of the right to hold certain jobs or to own a business. For example, in the 1940s a president of Panama by the name of Arnulfo Arias issued a number of laws that dispossessed thousands of shopholders (most of them Chinese) from their small businesses. These measures not only were very popular among the improvident urban rabble but enabled Arias to redistribute the expropriated loot to "authentic" true-blue Panamanians who also happened to be his most useful supporters. Panamanians, of course, were perfectly aware of the game Arias was playing, and one newspaperman reflected the thinking of many of them when he exploded one day in his column:

> Why don't we work the way the foreigners do? We continue speaking against foreigners, laborer or businessman, who take over all the business that should be in the hands of the sons of the country; we raise our voices against him who dedicates most of his time fulfilling his duties, performing a job of some kind or attending to his commercial obligations and ends up by making some money after years of constant struggle.
>
> We criticize whoever raises himself from a humble position and succeeds in holding a notable position that the Panamanian should occupy. We live embittered by the well-being of the foreigners who get it by dint of hard work, and right now we are yelling because the Chinese have again taken over the grocery stores and prevent native elements from running them. We should be ashamed of ourselves for this crying which shows only our lack of working capacity, our laziness and our negligence.
>
> What happened to those stores, those bars, that passed to Panamanian hands because of an arbitrary and unjust command? How many Panamanians sold them back to their previous owners and how many still have them? The Panamanian, it is painful to confess, is no good for any job that requires steady application and responsibility, that separates him from the bar, cock fights, and horse races. In a word, he can't pull himself from this waste of time and money that forces him to abandon his store, his business, or his job.
>
> Certainly with such a mode of living no one can make a fortune, no one can prosper.
>
> But the foreigner, laborer or businessman, is different. He does his daily duty, works, struggles and after some years of incessant work, he realizes a fortune, and with it tranquility.
>
> Why can't we emulate him?[119]

Although nationalizations are inevitably accompanied by loud and fervent demonstrations of nationalist pride, it is clear that actions that aim to weaken foreign power and influence within a country will not, in themselves, bring about a positive national identity. Nationalizations may in some circumstances help a people acquire a more satisfying national self-image, but they may also have prescisely the opposite effect. What is important in this issue of positive national identity is not how effectively a nationalization reduces foreign influence but whether by doing so it also reduces the feeling of inferiority to the foreigners under attack.

Ultimately the only realistic way Latin American reactive nationalists may realize a sense of equality with foreigners is through real achievement of their own. They may move to shackle the progress of industrious immigrants with tyrannical legislation, but they will think more highly of themselves if they successfully compete with them in economic pursuits. They may choose to wage war against "cocacolonization" by confiscating the local Coca-Cola Company, but they will have a greater feeling of accomplishment if they create a brew they like better than Coca-Cola. They may try to overcome "mental colonization" by banishing foreign culture from the country, but they will experience more pride if they produce forms of cultural expression their countrymen prefer to those originating abroad. Latin American reactive nationalists, in other words, will achieve a positive national identity not by expelling foreigners but by matching the accomplishments of foreigners and by so doing, eliminating the indignity of dependencia.

Although a negative national identity can be a difficult psychological burden for Latin American nationalists, it is also a potentially very constructive force in Latin American society because it creates in nationalists a hunger for reform and modern progress. All over Latin America, nationalists can be heard expressing an almost lyrical view of modernization, the likes of which has not been popular in the West for some time. With grand gestures and vivid rhetoric, nationalist leaders place before their audiences a romantic vision of energetic Latin American peoples constructing great citadels of productive industry, seeding vast acres of life-giving land, penetrating dense, dark forests and spanning cloud-shrouded mountains with roads and bridges, inventing ingenious machines that harness the forces of nature, divining long-hidden secrets in the sciences, making enduring contributions to the arts, and, in general, advancing in heroic strides toward an ever-higher level of "civilization."

But if modern progress is the cherished goal of Latin American nationalists, what do they feel they must do to bring it about? The current dominant intellectual fashion is to blame the existence of "backwardness" and underdevelopment" on certain "reactionary" interest groups who have organized the "system" to their own advantage, and therefore to find the solution to underdevelopment in the redistribution of power and wealth to other more "progressive" groups in society. However, away from the public view, in the everyday conversations and remarks of Latin Americans, an older intellectual tradition lives on, for in more relaxed, informal social situations Latin Americans tend to attribute their developmental problems not just to entrenched elites but also to entrenched values and behavior patterns. So prevalent is this outlook among Latin Americans that even those who insist the underdevelopment in a general sense is caused by oligarchies and imperialists often talk in terms of modernization-impeding values when discussing specific, concrete problems that obviously contribute to underdevelopment. In other words, they simply compartmentalize the abstract theory they pick up in classrooms and in political harangues and do not allow it to influence the common-sense judgments they make about what they observe in their ordinary daily lives.

It is hardly surprising that contemporary Latin American reactive nationalists are reluctant to assign to their people, in a formal and public way, the main responsibility for the poverty and exploitation in their own countries. How difficult it can be to exist in the same cold, comfortless intellectual world as the adoptive nationalist Francisco Bulnes, who sternly warned Latin Americans that they first had to change themselves before they could hope to change their society:

> The ambitions of Europe and the United States are not the real enemies of the Latin peoples of America: there are no more terrible enemies of our welfare and independence than ourselves. . . . our traditions, our history, our morbid inheritance, our alcoholism, and our education harmful to the development of good character.[120]

If reactive nationalists accepted such a view, they would have to consider the possibility of their own failure as a people; and Bulnes left no doubt as to what an ardent Latin American nationalist like himself could think of failure:

> If we do not know how to save ourselves, history will write on our tomb the same epitaph that the Persians put on the tomb of the vanquished Babylonians: *Here lie those who did not deserve this land, not even to bury themselves in.*[121]

PART II
The Pursuit of
Collective Strength

6
TOTALITARIAN
IDEOLOGIES

The painful sense of national failure felt by Latin American nationalists inevitably caused them to look for ways to make their countries equal to the most advanced nations in the world. The first obvious step was to build up their economies. Nationalists commonly dreamed of launching modernization movements where the entire population was devoted to the single overriding goal of catching up with the West. The problem with the ideas espoused by modernization-minded nationalists was that these ideas often took on a totalitarian or semitotalitarian character. We can see today that this fact has enormous implications for the future. As of this writing the only government in Latin America that successfully exerts totalitarian control over its people is in Cuba. But if the modernization ambitions of nationalist elites easily lead to the point where they advocate totalitarian ideas, then we are likely to see more violently antidemocratic, anti-Western totalitarian regimes in the years ahead.

To explore this theme, we must first determine what totalitarianism is. For the purposes of this book, totalitarianism may be described as a theory of state and society that advocates that government should have no limitations whatsoever on its power. Totalitarianism can occur anywhere, but the historical record shows it is most likely to take root in Third World countries. The reason for this is that these societies are most likely to produce political elites with a passion for rapid modernization, and this passion can easily become so important that the elites crave unlimited government power to achieve their ends.

Although totalitarianism in contemporary times is most likely to spring up in Third World countries, it initially appeared in the more backward regions of Europe. Because of their proximity to the advanced countries, nationalists in these regions were the first to become acutely aware of their relative "backwardness" and the first to use totalitarian government power in an effort to catch up. (As we shall see at the end of this chapter, the one exception to this was the Meiji revolutionaries in nineteenth-century Japan.)

Nationalists who harbored such ambitions found it necessary to create political ideologies that would justify such an enormous expansion of government power. The two most important of these ideologies were Italian Fascism and Bolshevik Marxism-Leninism. The major purpose of this chapter is to present the components of these ideologies so that we will be able to recognize totalitarian tendencies in Latin American political movements no mater what name they may be found under. To do this we shall first concentrate on Italian Fascism, which is a far more sophisticated and logically consistent ideology than Marxism-Leninism. We shall next examine Marxism-Leninism, which since the end of World War II has been the ideology most likely to be chosen by Third World nationalists to justify a totalitarian state. Because of the special significance of Marxism-Leninism to contemporary Latin America, we shall briefly examine Marxism-Leninism's strengths and weaknesses as a modernization ideology, in part by comparing it to the most successful of all modernization ideologies—Japanese Shintoism.

ITALIAN FASCISM

To examine the important components of Italian Fascism effectively, it would be best to look first at the social and psychological conditions in Italy before the Fascist era, for it was in reaction to these conditions that the Fascist ideology was created. In pre-Fascist Italy, the most obvious social problem the country had to face was that of widespread poverty. Italy, to be sure, could boast a few bright spots in its economic picture. Milan, for example, was the leading textile center of Europe, and Genoa was the busiest port in the Mediterranean. But successes such as these were limited in number and were concentrated in the "European North" while the "Mediterranean South" continued to languish in a premodern age. Italy as a whole could not produce enough to sustain its large population, and millions of Italians were forced to uproot themselves and to emigrate to distant shores. Owing to its low level of production, Italy compared poorly with leading European countries in the indices of well-being. On the eve of World War I, Italy's per capita income was less than half of Britain's and no higher than that of Russia, a country looked upon by Western Europeans of the times as wild, semi-Asiatic, and chronically backward.

Italy also suffered from considerable political problems. Italy was not totally unified until 1870, and after it was, national leaders found the country an exasperating place to rule. The Italian parliament proved to be less a legislative body than an arena for interest groups to gather and collide. The bloated state bureaucracies were also impossible to control, weakened as they were by the familiar bureaucratic vices of overstaffing, favoritism, and corruption. Most important of all, the Italian population as a whole was difficult to govern. The Italian people, although theoretically united under the same flag, were deeply divided by geographical barriers, cultural and language difficulties, and seemingly irreconcilable self-interests. In the South insurrectionary bands roamed the hills and half-ruled over extensive areas. In the deep South the infamous Mafia exerted the most effective control over the ignorant peasants and villagers. In the North turbulent masses, recently arrived in the cities, were undergoing the wrenching experience of early industrialization. From one end of the land to the other much of the population was illiterate, inexperienced in the art of self-government, low in public spirit, and hostile to public authority. In the years immediately preceding the Fascist rise to power, the people, burdened as they were by postwar depression, unemployment, and national debt, grew especially ungovernable: striking urban workers disrupted industries and vital services; political factions brawled in the streets; peasants seized land in the countryside; tenant farmers refused to pay rents; the rural unemployed burned crops and destroyed livestock.

Italy's failure to mature into a prosperous and orderly nation-state was matched abroad by its failure to weigh heavily in international affairs. Not since the glorious days of the Renaissance had Italy, or any part of Italy, been respected as a European power. For Italian nationalists, it seemed paradoxical and intolerable that Italians who were capable of producing so many individual geniuses in virtually every field of human endeavor were obliged to hang their heads in shame because of their inability to act as a united people. Their gifted sons rocked the world with their discoveries and creations; yet collectively, Italians did nothing. Not only was "Italy" more a "geographical expression" than a country, but the "Italian people" was more a vision than a reality. Italians seemed contentious, easily swayed by passion, irrational, hot tempered, and if lovable and exuberant, not to be taken seriously by the nations that decided world destiny.

The two most spectacular ways Italy could have demonstrated its national strength to other countries would have been to have built a colonial empire and to have excelled at making war. It was, however, precisely in these areas that Italy's failures bordered on the disasterous. Italian nationalists longed to compete successfully with the British and French in the race for colonies in North Africa; and recalling the days of Roman eagles and trumpets, felt they possessed a God-given destiny there. But the Italians were forced to accept a humiliation when the French established a protectorate over the heavily

Italian area of Tunisia. Still more humiliating was a battle that took place in 1896 in which the Italian colonial army in Ethiopia was routed —not by the French or British—but by Ethiopians. Historians interested in the decline of the West have taken special note of this battle because it marked the first time that a European nation-state had been defeated in a test of arms by an nonwhite people. As for Italians, it left a grievous wound in their national pride, a wound which Mussolini was to exploit with adroitness some 40 years later.

For Italian nationalists, the consequence of the perceived failings of Italy as a nation-state was a national inferiority complex vis-à-vis the most successful countries of Europe. Italians were heard to call themselves the "Negroes of Europe" or to inflict upon themselves smarting witticisms: "Thank god for the Spaniards. . . . If there were no Spaniards the Italians would be the last people on earth." Massimo d'Azeglio, a Piedmontese marquis and prime minister described his nationalist shame in the following manner:

> With foreigners I experienced a sensation of humiliation so painful that from their friendship came to me more bitterness than satisfaction. I was ashamed of being an Italian! . . . The cold behavior of the English—the tranquil and self-confident pride that could be seen on their countenances—looked as if they were intended for me, to make me feel my inferiority, to make me understand that when a nation is the prey of anybody that takes it, when it allows all sorts of people from the four quarters of the world to come to it to amuse themselves, just as hunters migrate to regions where the game abounds, then those who belong to such a nation can be tolerated among foreigners, but cannot be considered their equal, ever.[1]

It was within the context of these social and economic conditions that Italian Fascism was born. Italian Fascism is unquestionably the most widely misunderstood major political phenomenon of modern times. This has much to do with the fact that Mussolini led his people into World War II and that his enemies, both the Soviets and the Western democracies, chose to define Fascism to suit their own propaganda ends. It has not been until relatively recently that a small number of academic figures have laboriously dug through the myths surrounding Italian Fascism and have convincingly revealed it to be a prototype of ideologies very common in the contemporary Third World.[2] In the spirit of this work, the word "fascism" in this book will be a generic term used to identify a distinct body of interrelated ideas similar to those that appeared under the banner of Italian Fascism several decades ago. Readers are cautioned to divest themselves of all ways the word "fascism" may be used today and to imagine themselves in the early 1920s, when the term was a fresh one in European politics.

One of the key features of Italian Fascism is a pronounced elitism. Elitism is by no means unique to fascism. In fact, Mussolini was a convinced elitist even in the early years of his career when he considered himself a Marxist, not a Fascist revolutionary. Elitism is a social theory that maintains that the majority of people in each society are passive and apathetic; that social and economic power, even in democracies, is largely controlled by activist minorities and elites; and that all social change, including revolutionary change, is brought about by elites. Mussolini applied these insights to the revolutionary situation in Italy and, notwithstanding his great respect for Marx, concluded that Marx was mistaken in his belief that the "masses" would carry out their own revolution. Instead, Mussolini believed the masses by themselves would never achieve a sufficient level of "revolutionary awareness" and that the revolution would come about only if small groups of enlightened revolutionaries committed themselves to the task.

An important aspect of Mussolini's elitist conception of revolution was his idea that moral convictions and ideological beliefs could stir human beings to action. Once again Mussolini was influenced in his thinking by critics of Marx who rejected the Marxist notion that all moral or ideological motivation in human beings was ultimately traceable to economic causes. Mussolini was more than willing to accept the importance of economic advantage in spurring human beings, but he also believed that both elites and masses could be motivated by convictions and ideas which could not be explained in terms of underlying economic factors. Since Mussolini's elitist view of history prompted him to believe that elites always formulated the specific content of moral ideas and then passed them on to the masses, his outlook on revolution closely resembled the Sorelian idea that socialist elites had to dedicate themselves to a similar mission among the proletarian masses of Europe. Unlike Marx, who thought that a proletarian revolutionary consciousness among the masses was the automatic result of capitalist industrial development, Mussolini adopted the position that the masses would never become conscious of their need to make a revolution without the guidance of an elite with superior judgment and vision.

Owing to the social and economic conditions that reigned in the Italy of Mussolini's day, Italian revolutionaries found an elitist view of revolution very easy to form. This was, in large measure, due to the extremes found within the Italian class system, not just the extremes of wealth but, more importantly, extremes of culture. Because of their level of education and generally bourgeois backgrounds, revolutionary leaders and intellectuals belonged in a cultural sense to that class that looked down upon the illiterate, impoverished lower orders. Although these revolutionaries had great sympathy for the masses, or at least the *idea* of the masses, they tended to feel that the great unruly conglomeration of humanity below them lacked sufficient enlightenment, cohesiveness, and purposefulness to be capable of action that would be beneficial to themselves as a group. At the heart of the elitist idea is the conviction that the elite knows what is best for the masses even better than the masses themselves.

A second major characteristic of Fascist ideology is a vigorous nationalism. Even in the days when Mussolini disagreed with Marx over whether majorities or minorities were the real catalysts of social change, Mussolini still identified himself as a socialist in the Marxist tradition because he believed that the essence of Marxism was class struggle. Mussolini had great faith in Marx's idea of class struggle because of certain basic assumptions he himself made about human beings and human communities: Mussolini regarded people as by nature social animals who could only realize their full potential within the context of some form of human community. Reasoning that a common sense of exploitation was a more powerful cohesive force than a common sense of nationality, Mussolini was convinced that the most viable "natural" community of his day was economic class and not, as others contended, the nation-state. He believed that the community of European workers spanned the artificial barriers of nation-states and made the lines drawn by geographers irrelevant. In Mussolini's view, nationalism could never be the prime motivating force of the European proletariat.

Mussolini's opinion that internationalist class sentiment among the workers had to be stronger than nationalist loyalty was certainly a plausible idea, for it was reasonable to assume that the impoverished workers in the various industrialized countries would feel they had much more in common with each other than with their bourgeois "countrymen" who broke up their strikes and smashed their labor unions. Mussolini's opinion, however, was still just a theory, and that theory was put to a conclusive test at the outbreak of World War I. Before the war Mussolini and other socialists contended that the workers would never fight against their brother workers in other countries because they knew that their real enemies were their capitalist overlords at home. But then World War I ignited and the workers, instead of throwing up barricades and protesting the war, eagerly enlisted in their respective national armies and marched off to engage one another in mortal combat. The war, in short, clearly demonstrated that European workers were more loyal to a community based upon a common language, culture, and territory than they were to one based upon a common sense of class oppression.

Mussolini viewed the lessons of World War I with astonishment. As an elitist he was aware that he needed an emotional sentiment that would energize and unify the masses and enable the elite to guide them to desired ends. He thought that he had identified that sentiment with class loyalty; but then he saw that when the masses were forced to choose sides in the war, they responded more to national than to class solidarity. Mussolini began to argue openly with his fellow socialists that they had to recognize the reality of nationalist emotion.[3] From there it was but a short road to where Mussolini and other like-minded socialists abandoned their old party and formed a new one. They called their fledgling organization the Fascist Party and described their movement as a *national* socialism.

By national socialism Mussolini meant that he was just as concerned about worker problems as before but now these problems would be solved in a national, not an international, context.[4] This soon led to the pronouncement of a third major feature of Fascist ideology—productionism. Traditional socialists had always concerned themselves with redistributive justice, and their tactic of class warfare was based upon the assumptions that first, society produced plenty of wealth and second, the workers were not getting their fair share. The Fascists, in contrast, contended that a good part of the workers' problem in Italy was that the country did not produce enough to redistribute; and so in order to realize the socialist objective of economic well-being, they had to meet the nationalist objective of greater production. Fascists were quick to add that they would not allow the workers to be exploited even while they were inciting them to produce. Unhappy workers, after all, would never be productive workers, and a nation torn apart by class war would never be strong and united. Thus, Mussolini and his "national" socialists saw an essential interdependency between nationalist and socialist aims.

An important aspect of Mussolini's nationalist outlook was his stand on international relations. This stand was very similar to that commonly assumed by Third World leaders today. Through the Fascist perspective, the world was divided into two groups, the "rich and the proletarian nations," and Italy was on the wrong side of that division.[5] The satisfied "rich" nations, a few of whom like England and France had carved out huge world empires for themselves, were striving to maintain the status quo and were, therefore, in fundamental opposition to the hungry "proletarian" countries like Italy. This basic theme of rich and poor nations, with the rich exploiting the poor, grew to be a prominent part of the official Fascist outlook on international relations; and in the 1930s it led to efforts on the part of Italy to create an alliance of have-not "proletarian" countries against the wealthy "plutocratic" powers.[6]

Yet while the first to protest the "imperialism" of other nations, Mussolini was quick to advocate a frank imperialism of his own. The apparently ambivalent position in international morality stemmed from Italy's intermediate standing in the hierarchy of nations.* Italy was the weakest of the European powers but was still a power, one of the Big Four of World War I. Mussolini regarded a colonial empire as a sign of a vigorous people who possessed the strength to "expand economically and spiritually."[7] Mussolini's aggressive, high-risk foreign policy during the late 1930s and early 1940s was intended to demonstrate to the world that Italy under Fascism had finally arrived as a first-rate power.

Still another major feature of Fascist ideology was statism—the advocation and justification of an all-powerful, all-intrusive state government. Fascist leaders felt that such a government was necessary in order to carry out and coordinate the enormous task at hand, that is to say, the transformation of a geographical expression into a modern nation-state, an undisciplined conglomeration of people into a disciplined community, a poor country into a rich country, and an important national entity into a respected world power.

The challenge to the Fascist ideologues was to create an ideology that would bestow legitimacy upon a government that recognized no government constraints when carrying out its revolution. To be sure, this was no easy intellectual task, for Italy was part of European civilization and for some time Europe had been moving toward the idea that governments were legitimate only insofar as they represented the "will of the people." The most logical and straightforward kind of political structure to translate this principle into reality is representative democracy, where citizens are allowed to vote for their own government leaders. An important part of liberal democratic theory is that democratic leaders have only limited authority over the people they rule. Citizens are regarded as possessing certain "inalienable rights" that governments cannot infringe upon without the consent of the governed.

It was against this enormously influential tradition that the Fascists pitted their ideology. The first intellecutal hurdle the Fascists had to overcome was to explain that even though their leaders were not chosen by ballot, they still represented the will of the people more than democratically elected leaders did. Secondly, because the Fascists

---

This ambivalence was not unlike that of Argentina under Perón (see pp. 195–200). However, in significant contrast to what has transpired in Argentina, Italy's postwar "economic miracle," its status as one of the world's leading industrial powers, its membership and participation in the European Common market, and the general weakening of nationalistic feeling within the have nations of Europe have diminished the problem of the national inferiority complex in contemporary Italy to the point where the concept is no longer of much analytical value when evaluating the country today.

believed they could not carry out their program without violating democratic inalienable rights, their ideology had to justify theoretically *unrestricted* state power where the individual possessed no moral barricade behind which to hide from intrusion by the state.

Liberal democratic and Fascist political theorists created vastly different political ideologies because their purpose for creating their ideologies was vastly different. Liberal democrats developed their ideas because they were deeply troubled by the age-old proclivity of governments to abuse their power. In reaction against this, liberal democrats attempted to construct a moral outlook that identified the use of government power in most areas of the citizens' lives as illegitimate. Fascists, on the other hand, were deeply troubled by the collective weakness and poverty of the Italian people. Rather than fearing government power, they wanted to remove all restrictions on government power because they felt that only a strong and completely unfettered central government could carry out the sweeping reforms they saw as necessary in Italian society. The two starting points could not have been further apart, and only by understanding this can we see why two political theories, both ostensibly conceived with the "good of the people" in mind, could have arrived at totally opposite viewpoints regarding the state.

Liberal political theorists began their philosophic defense of the individual citizen by first focusing on the individual in isolation from the rest of society and then by surrounding him with moral safeguards designed to protect him from the power of the state. In more specific terms, they held that every individual was born with a series of inalienable rights that afforded him the liberty to do what he saw fit without interference from government authorities. According to their logic, the individual achieved a maximum condition of freedom when no state or social constraints on individual behavior existed at all.

Only after the idea of the absolutely unfettered individual was considered, did the classical liberals bring the notion of state and society into the picture. The liberals theorized that at some point in the evolution of man, individuals living in a primitive state of maximum freedom discovered that they could realize certain advantages by coming together and forming *societies* of individuals. To do this they had to agree on a series of rules and laws and set up a government authority to enforce them. They were, in other words, willing to cede a certain amount of their previously unrestricted freedom to a government entity in return for the benefits of living in a human society. But notice the emphasis of a political philosophy where the individual is considered before the formation of a society and a state. The individual begins by possessing absolute freedom, and when the individual enters into a social arrangement, he surrenders only a portion of it to the state. The individual has ceded to the government the right to intervene in only a sharply limited area of his life. Most of the individual's activities continue to be of a kind that the government cannot rightfully curtail.

Fascist political theorists began their discussion of individual and state by attacking the liberal democratic position. One argument they used was that the idea of freedom contained in classical liberalism was refuted by its own internal logic. Because of their fear of government oppression, the champions of classical liberalism tended to view freedom as the absence of government restraint.[8] Through the liberal point of view, individuals living in a stateless society would be free to run about in unbounded, joyous liberty. But as the liberals also admitted, life in this kind of society could be nasty, brutish, mean, and short because individuals were also free to run over each other. So, in order to protect themselves from themselves, they agreed to a code of rules and law as well as to the establishment of a government mediator. The logic of classical liberalism holds that the state of perfect freedom would be the absence of any law, and yet the same theory depicts individuals making a social contract in order to secure freedom from the tyranny of anarchy. Implicit in the liberal model itself is the denial that freedom really does exist in an environment devoid of social and government constraints.

The Fascist critics also argued that the liberal notion of freedom as an absence of constraint was an entirely debased conception of the idea of liberty. They contended that the freedom of the individual to do anything he desired, cling to any point of view he wanted, right or wrong, could not, in any elevated sense, be freedom. Such pure arbitrary caprice reduced human relations to the law of the jungle with the strong triumphing over the weak. In order for people to be civilized, not savage, they had to recognize restraint in their behavior. But since the definition of right and wrong behavior emerged from a social consensus on rules and law, people could raise themselves from their subhuman condition only by participating in the agreed-upon norms and mores of society. In the ideal sense, rules were established not for the enslavement of people, but for their survival, security, and further development. Thus, the Fascists concluded, people did not lose but actually gained their freedom by agreeing to abide by the covenants of a law-governed society.

With criticism such as this, the Fascist political philosophers shifted the focus of their theoretical concern away from the individual to the society or collectivity itself. The liberals in their speculations had deliberately enhanced the importance of the individual by making him the creator of society. The Fascists, on the other hand, emphasized how society was actually the creator of the individual because without society, the individual could exist only in an animal-like state. The Fascists believed, in fact, that whatever value the individual had was due to his membership in the collectivity. Through the Fascist perspective, the collectivity towered above the individual in strength and importance. The collectivity could endure for centuries, growing richer and more brilliant with age, while the individual quickly exhausted his energies and expired. The collectivity was an almost mystical entity that simultaneously embodied the past, present, and future of a people. The collectivity was the repository of the precious spiritual patrimony of the past, and its mission was to transfer that heritage to those living in the present. The collectivity also performed the vital social task of connecting the peoples of yesterday and today to the yet unborn generations of tomorrow. Far more than a simple "contract" between individuals, the collectivity possessed an existence of its own and in an important sense was greater than the sum of all its parts. For the Fascists, the collectivity was like an organism, a living "whole" from which the parts that made it up derived their function and meaning.

Once the Fascists had established the vital social role of the collectivity, they were ready to elevate the government to a similar level of importance. They did this by identifying the nation-state as the collectivity within which Italians were to develop their spiritual values. They then argued that the nation-state needed a specific institution to carry out this humanizing task, and they identified the state government as that institution. Regarding the state Mussolini wrote:

> The keystone of the Fascist doctrine is the conception of the State. . . . The State as conceived and built up by Fascism, is a spiritual and ethical entity for securing the political, juridical and economic organization of the nation, an organization which is the expression of the spirit in its origin and growth. The State guarantees the safety of the country at home and abroad, and it also safeguards and hands down the spirit of the people, elaborated through the ages in its language, its customs and its faith. The State is not only the present; it is also the past and above all the future. Transcending the individual's brief spell of life, the State stands for the inherent conscience of the nation. . . . The State educates its members to citizenship, makes them aware of their mission, urges them to unity; its justice harmonizes their divergent interests; it hands down to future generations the conquests of the mind in the fields of science, art, law and human solidarity.[9]

To the Fascists, the state was not in conceptual terms a necessary evil, a natural antagonist that had to be watched lest it abuse its power. Rather, it was a vital part of a civilized society, a "spiritual and ethical entity" without which the individual could not develop his higher spiritual nature. The state was an ongoing organic entity that lived beyond the short lifespans of individuals and carried out the civilizing task of transmitting the culture's spiritual heritage from generation to generation. Like the national collectivity, the state was simultaneously past, present, and future: it bestowed upon the people the lessons of the past, helped them to realize themselves in the present, and led them into the future. The state's very definition was so bound up in service to the nation that state and nation became virtually synonymous with each other.

Once the state was raised to a high level of importance by identifying it with the national collectivity, Fascist thinkers moved on to the critical question of the individual's relationship to the state. The Fascists maintained that the will of the state must on all occasions take precedence over the will of the individual. An important element in the Fascist justification for this was a well-established principle of political theory, recognized even by liberal democrats, that the state can legitimately interfere with what an individual wants to do if his *immediate* self-interest (what he wants to do now) and his *ultimate* self-interest (what would be best for him in the long run) do not coincide. The classic illustration of this is when the state prevents a suicidal individual from killing himself on the assumption that he is temporarily blinded by passion and cannot see his own real self-interest as well as state authorities. This idea that an individual's immediate and ultimate self-interests could be different and that the state could evaluate them better than the individual was pushed to an extreme by the Fascists, who claimed that a select minority of exceptional individuals could see what was best for the masses more clearly than the masses themselves. The Fascists maintained that just as in the arts and sciences, politics also produced occasional geniuses and that these geniuses were more capable than the general run of men of divining the ultimate interests of the people. Such a point of view appears most plausible in a society where collectively the masses seem to be more a conglomeration than a community and who, in their blind pursuit of immediate self-interest, often do seem to be acting to their own long-term disadvantage. The Fascists contended that their *Duce* was a man gifted with rare political genius and was thus most qualified to lead the masses out of the wilderness toward where they really wanted to go.

Fascist reasoning along these lines led inexorably to conclusions that favored a totalitarian organization of society. When society was described as an organism, the whole, that is, the collectivity, became more important than the sum of all its parts. Compared to the collectivity the individual was small and dependent, for without the collectivity the individual could not hope to realize his potential worth. Next, the collectivity most appropriate for the time was identified as the nation. The individual developed himself as a human being insofar as he participated in national life and contributed to the nation's development, which in Fascist Italy meant sacrificing personal self-interests to the collectivistic cause of modernization and national greatness. For the individual there was no escape from this duty to the nation. He had no inalienable rights that afforded him moral protection against the state's insistence on reminding him of his duties. He had, in fact, not the smallest private corner of this life where the state could not legitimately enter. As the Fascist theorist Giovanni Gentile aptly declared, in Fascist Italy "there is nothing really private . . . ; there are no limits to State action."[10]

Indeed, the state not only possessed the right to intrude into every nook, crevice, and cranny of society, it had a moral obligation to do so. It was the Fascist view that the masses were mired in a desperate materialism yet at the same time longed to realize the spiritual side of their human nature. Fascists boasted that their government was "integral," or whole, because unlike other political leaders, they concerned themselves with the spiritual as well as the material needs of the people. The Fascists sought to do this by making their political movement not just a movement but also a secular religion. Fascist leaders were very open about the "religious" character of Fascism and unabasedly referred to their ideology as *La Fede* (The Faith). In the preamble of the Fascist constitution they announced, "Fascism is not merely a grouping of Italians on a definite program to be realized, but is above all a faith."[11] Fascist leaders urged their supporters to follow the "Ten Commandments of Fascism," and required them to recite from memory prayers like the following:

> I believe in the genius of *Il Duce* and our Lord Fascism,
> I believe in the Communion of the martyrs of Fascism,
> Lord, thou who lightest every flame,
> Lord, thou who rulest every heart,
> Revive in me each day
> My passion for Italy.[12]

The Italian Fascists placed enormous importance on their task of converting the Italian people to their "spiritual" cause. Mussolini, in fact, maintained that the most significant characteristic of the Fascist Revolution was not the political or structural changes but the "high moral tension" he believed the movement had infused into the Italian population.[13] The Fascists frankly aimed at forging the Italian people into a single "moral unity," where they all believed ardently in the same moral ideals. The objective was not only to meet the spiritual needs of the people but to induce them to act together in the service of nationalist and Fascist goals. The Fascist elite hoped to use mass devotion to Fascist ideals as a means of transforming the Italian nation from a flaccid, faction-ridden collectivity into what Mussolini called a "granite block of a single national will."[14]

The passion of the Fascist ideologues for "moral" and national unity and the horror they experienced at the sight of the divisiveness allowed by Italian-style democracy were important factors that led them to create a state that was almost the antithesis of a liberal democratic state. The classical liberals had labored mightily to fence in the state with moral restrictions. Fascist theorists, using the same tools of political philosophy, tore these down and declared their state to be "totalitarian," one that acknowledged no moral limits to its right to reform and reshape society. Holding power in this totalitarian state were, not elected officials who were supposed to respond to the immediate demands of the masses, but leaders blessed with special insight who recognized and worked for the ultimate interests of the masses.

The end result of this effort was a justification of a totalitarian dictatorship. By a series of identifications, the will of the leader became the will of every member of society: the totalitarian equation began with the collectivist identification of the individual with the nation; then the nation was identified with the state; and lastly, the state was identified with the Party leaders or leader. In the ideal totalitarian society the leader and the people were pictured as enveloped in the same "moral unity": they shared the same ideals and aspirations to such an extent that the masses obeyed the directives of the state elite as if they were their own. Far from the individual being swallowed up by the state, Gentile insisted that the "individual swallows the State."[15] For the Fascists the word *totalitarian* was a boast, a word that expressed their own particular vision of a humanistic social order.

The problem with the totalitarian view of the good society was that it required an impossible-to-realize utopia where every member of society felt himself a member of the predominant political faith. In a society where such unanimity does not exist, totalitarianism only enhances the psychological well-being of the believers. Nonbelievers, those hostile or simply indifferent to the government-sponsored cause, have no right of privacy against the intrusion of these insistent ideals upon their lives. Nonbelievers find themselves and their children exposed with no legal defenses to a state that wishes to "teach," "persuade," "socialize," or "brainwash" the entire population (the term chosen depends upon the point of view) to where it makes up a homogeneous "moral unity."

The fact that there were those who resisted the Fascist version of the way, the truth, and the light scarcely diminished the enthusiasm of the Fascist zealots. The Italian Fascists were possessed by the spirit of reactive nationalism, and to them the overriding preoccupation was not tolerance for divergent viewpoints but the solution of problems that kept Italy from becoming a leading nation-state. The feelings that ardent Fascist believers had toward nonbelievers were something like those that religious missionaries have commonly demonstrated toward the heathens they have tried to convert: they looked down upon the unenlightened from a position of moral superiority and at the same time loved them enough to dedicate their lives to their uplifting. But the Fascists loved the unconverted, not for what they were, but for what they could become. Mussolini was very frank about this. To him the Italian people were a "mass of precious materials," that required "smelting, purifying, and working," and that, with the help of a leader who possessed the "delicate touch of an artist," could be transformed in a wonderous "work of art."[16] Mussolini's feelings about the Italian people when they resisted his artistry were also very clear:

> When the masses are like wax in my hands, when I stir their faith, or when I mingle with them and am almost crushed by them, I feel myself to be part of them. All the same, there persists in me a certain feeling of aversion, like that which the modeler feels for the clay he is moulding. Does not the sculptor sometimes smash his block of marble into fragments because he cannot shape it to represent the vision he has conceived? Now and then this crude matter rebels against the creator![17]

But if the artist had succeeded in molding the clay to the shape he desired, what would the final masterpiece have been like? The raw material the Fascist leaders worked with was the Italian people, and they talked continuously of changing the Italian people into something they called "new men." The idea of new men was a direct reaction against what they perceived to be the decadence, disunity, and ungovernability of the Italian population. The Fascists understood that the strength and prosperity of a nation was primarily dependent on the character of the people that made it up, and they felt that Italy had long been weak because Italians were incessantly clashing among themselves and bleeding their society dry with their uncivic behavior. For this reason the Fascists aimed, in the words of Alfredo Rocco, for the "radical transformation of the mind and character of the Italian people. Thus after centuries of indiscipline and idleness, Italy will be able once more to become a great military and warlike nation."[18]

If one word were used to describe the Fascist new men, it would be *soldiers*. Fascist literature was filled with military metaphors, starting with the Fascist Constitution, which stated unequivocally:

> Fascism is a Militia at the service of the Nation. Its objective: to realize the greatness of the Italian people. From its origins, which are mingled with the renaissance of the Italian conscience and with the will to victory, until the present, Fascism has always regarded itself as in a state of war: first to overthrow those who thwarted the

> will of the nation, and today and always, to defend and develop the
> power of the Italian people.[19]

Fascists described their movement in the terminology of a military
campaign because it was this language that best expressed their idea
of a well-functioning totalitarian society. The Fascist elite wanted,
even in peacetime, the Italian masses to be mobilized, tense, alert, and
unified, as if their nation were at war. The hoped that all Italians, including the women and children, would come to think of themselves as
soldiers in a solid phalanx of humanity working together and advancing triumphantly toward national goals. The Fascist elite was
especially attracted to the idea of the Italian people as one vast army
because soldiers are conditioned to obey the orders of their superiors
reflexively, and the elite wanted the people to close ranks behind the
strategy they planned for national development. Fascist leaders were
also enamored with the idea of this army being the most formidable
kind of army—one animated by faith and enthusiastic belief in the
righteousness of its struggle. When Mussolini at his oratorical spectacles exhorted the mammoth crowds below him to *"Credere,
Ubbidire, Combáttere"* ("Believe, Obey, Fight"), he visualized not just
trained mercenaries but truly aroused warriors who were as excited
about his objectives as he was. At these stupendous displays of
uniform mass emotion, the General and his soldiers did appear to be of
one faith and will. It was Mussolini's totalitarian ambition that when
he sent down the order for Italian workers to "produce," these loyal
"troops of labor" would throw themselves into their jobs as if they
were "fighting" in a national crusade.

The goal of the Italian Fascists in reorganizing Italian society along
totalitarian lines was to make Italy a highly unified and industrialized
country and, ultimately, a powerful nation-state. As such,
totalitarianism is an extreme manifestation of some very
distinguishable Western European ideas. The essence of the modern
nation-state idea is greater and greater internal unity, greater and
greater collective strength, and if this is taken far enough, it can only
lead to a totalitarian society. Furthermore, the idea of rapidly expanding economic growth that had excited the imagination of Europeans
since the early Industrial Revolution grew to be nothing less than an
obsession under the Fascists. That such quintessentially Western ideas
should have achieved their greatest emphasis in the decidedly anti-
Western Fascist movement is actually quite understandable. The
Fascists were so completely preoccupied with the collectivist objectives
of modernization and national unity that they were willing to sacrifice
concern for the individual in order to attain them in the shortest possible time. Because their priorities were exclusively nationalist and not
democratic, the Fascists renounced the particular humanism of the

Western democracies even as they sought to learn the secrets of their enormous power.

Although Fascist totalitarianism is a definite child of European civilization, it is an ideology that grew up on the periphery of Europe in a country that was relatively underdeveloped and weak. For this reason the moral outlook it espouses, once it is shorn of the label "Fascism," tends to be very attractive to modernizing elites in Latin America and in other less developed areas of the contemporary Third World. Underlying Fascism is an involved sociology that explains the elitist, nationalist, statist and productionist sentiments that are frequently cherished by Third World leaders and intellectuals. Fascist political philosophy sanctions the dictatorships of revolutionary rulers and accomodates their elitist passion to transform the values and attitudes of the masses and to push them into the twentieth century. Fascism approves of charismatic, semideified leaders, obedient masses, and sweeping moral crusades where the "rights" of individuals are not allowed to hinder progress toward nationalistic ends. Fascist totalitarian ideas, in short, justify moral precepts that are well suited to the ambitions of highly nationalistic revolutionary leaders in underdeveloped countries who wish to subordinate everything to the success of a state-led modernization movement.

THE IDEOLOGY OF MARXISM-LENINISM

Another modernization ideology that has had enormous impact on the twentieth century is Marxism-Leninism. Marxism-Leninism is a strange ideology in that it originated as a system of ideas known as classical Marxism, still claims to be based on classical Marxism, and yet has evolved into something almost totally different. Marxism-Leninism has, in fact, evolved into an ideology very similar to Italian Fascism.

The term *classical* or *orthodox* Marxism refers to the ideas on economics and revolution developed by Karl Marx during his mature years as a scholar. Classical Marxism is dramatically different from Italian Fascism. Italian Fascism, we recall, is elitist, statist, nationalist, and productionist. Classical Marxism is definitely not elitist because Marx believed that the development of industrialization in Europe would inevitably produce, first, a numerical majority of proletarians and, secondly, a "revolutionary consciousness" among those proletarians so that they would be aware of their need to overthrow their capitalist oppressors. In other words, Marx's concept of revolution depended upon a majority of citizens rising up and toppling the ruling class, not upon a small elite of professional revolutionaries. Nor was classical Marxism productionist because Marx assumed that the of wealth in an advanced industrial society was one of equitable distribution and not production. Nor was Marxism in any sense nationalistic because Marx believed that the primary loyalty of workers was to class, not nation. And lastly, Marxism was not statist. Marx believed that the government was created by one class to oppress another and that in his revolution the state would "wither away" and disappear.

Classical Marxism was not suited to either Italy or Russia owing to the fact that Marx wrote his ideas to explain conditions in advanced industrial societies while Italy and Russia were at the time semideveloped countries. Mussolini and Lenin adopted classical Marxism in their early years because both had a burning desire for revolution in their respective countries and Marxism was the leading protest ideology of the day. Mussolini, however, quickly became a revisionist Marxist and then totally broke with Marx to become a "national socialist," or Fascist. Lenin, particularly after he acquired power in 1917, was forced to make similar revisions but for personal reasons never wanted to admit he had veered from the orthodox Marxist path. Lenin, therefore, simply changed the content of his ideology while retaining the name. This process was continued under Stalin, who, in his own words, "creatively developed"[20] Marxism-Leninism into an ideology that was essentially an inarticulate version of the Fascist ideology that was simultaneously developing in Italy.

Lenin's first departure from classical Marxism took place in 1901 when he wrote an article indicating he could no longer assume that the workers would inevitably become aware of their need to make a workers' revolution. Lenin had learned by this time that workers, no matter how pure their proletarian experience, were not as revolutionary minded as Lenin's small circle of professional revolutionaries, which was made up mostly of middle-class intellectuals. Lenin, therefore, concluded that the workers were capable only of a "trade union" consciousness and that the true bearers of proletarian consciousness were certain select members of the "bourgeois intellegencia."[21] Lenin's position was incorrigibly elitist: a tiny, self-selected minority consisting of individuals who considered themselves blessed with special insight had to bring its message to the proletarian masses. It was this elite and not the workers themselves who knew what was best for the working class.

The Bolsheviks grew even more strongly elitist after they came to power and were confronted with the need to build up the Russian economy. These Marxist revolutionaries found themselves in the incongruous position of being at the head of a socialist revolution in a country where Marx had said socialism was impossible because of Russia's poverty and backwardness. Stalin was obliged to resolve this dilemma by announcing the Russian Revolution was genuinely Marxist because the Bolsheviks would build up the Russian economy to the point where the Marxist version of a socialist society was possible. Stalin began lecturing the Bolshevik leaders that the "decisive, exceptional" factors in creating socialism in Russia were their courage and dedication and not the "objective conditions" emphasized by Marx.[22] Fascists in Italy were saying essentially the same thing when they expressed the view that a small group of determined individuals could alter the course of history, even economic history.

Stalin's thesis of "socialism in one country" was as obviously productionist as it was elitist. It was, in fact, the same kind of productionism that was being proclaimed in Fascist Italy—that productionist and socialist goals were to be striven for within the context of the nation-state. Both the Bolsheviks and the Fascists held that socialist distributionist justice was impossible without first building an adequate industrial base. The major difference between their respective positions was that at the far end of the Bolshevik rainbow was a hazy vision of a nationless-stateless society made up of friendly producers' cooperatives.

Another important element that was eventually incorporated into Soviet Marxism-Leninism was statism. Before Lenin came to power he took the orthodox Marxist position that only a weak "semi-state" would be necessary to rule after a socialist revolution, and that even this impotent state would immediately "begin to wither away" after the victory of the socialist revolutionaries.[23] Lenin was intellectually a radical democrat, but both intellectually and emotionally he craved what he called "unity of will" between the revolutionary elite and the masses. Lenin felt that this unity of will was consistent with his belief in a weak government because he was certain that the exploited majority would voluntarily follow the guidance of their revolutionary saviors. When this did not take place, Lenin was forced to reverse his position and reluctantly admit that "coercion" and a strong state were necessary to achieve the unity the revolution needed.[24] After Lenin's death Stalin was quick to take up the same banner and boast that the Soviet Marxist-Leninists would construct the "mightiest and strongest state power that has ever existed."[25]

Perhaps the most incongruous feature of an ideology that claims to be based on Marxism is nationalism, but the Soviet Marxist-Leninists learned to sing praises to the Fatherland with a devotion second to none. Lenin never explicitly accepted nationalism, but Stalin was in power much longer than Lenin and like the Fascists knew the importance of a moral ideal that could stir up the masses and direct them toward collective ends. The Fascists judged the great moral force of their time to be devotion to the nation, a sentiment which Marxists were supposed to regard as inferior in potency to internationalist class loyalty. Stalin, however, sensed that the idea of the fatherland had an enormous impact upon the Russian masses; and because of this, he announced to the Russian workers that they too had a "fatherland" which they could "defend" even in peacetime by building up its industrial strength:

> In the past we had no fatherland, nor could we have one. But now that we have overthrown capitalism and power is in the hands of the working class, we have a fatherland and we will defend its independence. Do you want our socialist fatherland to be beaten and lose its independence? If you do not want this, you must put an end to its backwardness in the shortest possible time and develop genuine Bolshevik tempo in building up its socialist system of economy. There is no other way.[26]

The commitment here was obviously to the nation and not to the international class of proletarians. Whether Stalin's goal was the construction of the economy or the defeat of the Germans, nationalism was the collective emotion he relied upon to mobilize the Russian masses. Stalin's performance in international politics is still another indication of his dedication to the principle of national egoism. Both in his frantic prewar switching of alliances and in his postwar drive for control of Eastern Europe, Stalin was plainly pursuing Russian national interests and not those of an international proletarian class. The fact that Stalin supported the Third International and continuously professed internationalist sentiments can scarcely be used to counter the evidence of Bolshevik nationalism. It might be remembered that the Italian Fascists, who were unequivocal about the primacy of national loyalty, also sponsored their own "Fascist International" made up of have-not "proletarian" countries whose purpose was to challenge the "Holy Alliance of plutocratic Western nations."[27] As was the case with Fascist Italy, the rhetoric of internationalism was very loud in Stalin's Russia, but the enduring reality was always the nation.

Many of the views that Stalin expressed over the years, despite their "Marxist-Leninist label," were so traditionally nation oriented that they could have passed for those of the first serious modernizer of Russia, the seventeenth-century czar Peter the Great. Like Peter, Stalin's attention was fixed upon the West, and what he wanted most from the West was the secrets of its power. Again like Peter, Stalin passionately desired to build up Russian national might both to protect his country from the depredations of foreigners and to engage in great power chauvinism of his own. As if trembling with the spirit of the old czar, Stalin harangued the Russian people:

> To slacken the tempo would mean falling behind. And those who fall behind get beaten. No, we refuse to be beaten! One feature of the history of old Russia was the continual beatings she suffered

for falling behind, for her backwardness. She was beaten by the Mongol khans. She was beaten by the Turkish beys. She was beaten by the Swedish feudal lords. She was beaten by the Polish and Lithuanian gentry. She was beaten by the British and French capitalists. She was beaten by the Japanese barons. All beat her— for her backwardness. . . .

We are fifty or a hundred years behind the advanced countries. We must make good this distance in ten years. Either we do it, or they will crush us.[28]

The Marxist-Leninists of Russia, like the Fascists of Italy, were keenly aware of the backwardness of their country and the consequent humiliations suffered at the hands of stronger peoples. Both movements sought to overcome their weakness in the space of a few decades with massive developmental efforts that took on the markings of national crusades. Both ideologies recognized in such an endeavor the "decisive, exceptional" importance of modernizing elites infused with single-minded determination and will. Both ideologies stressed, through a facile series of substitutions, that these self-appointed elites spoke for the "ultimate will" of the people: The Marxist-Leninists proclaimed that the "proletariat" represented the "people," the Party the proletariat, and the leader the Party. The Fascists, no less agile, identified the "people" with the "state," the state with the Party, and the Party with the charismatic Mussolini. Neither ideology would admit to any limitation of state authority over the people. Indeed, it was the state's sworn duty to mold the people into a vast army of "new men" dedicated to the nationalistic mission of collective strength and equality with the "capitalists" or "plutocratic" powers. The "revolutionary" values that both regimes attempted to instill into their "new men" were emphatically collectivist and productionist, and were an obvious reaction against the factious indiscipline and economic privation that characterized life in the old society.

Owing to a chance set of historical circumstances, orthodox Marxism, which was designed for advanced industrial societies, underwent a strange evolution in the wilds of primitive Russia. For their own reasons Lenin, the leader of the Russian Revolution, deified Marx, and his Bolshevik successors deified Lenin. Thus, neither Lenin nor those who followed him wanted to admit, even after it became logically absurd for them not to do so, that there was scarcely any Marxism left in their brand of "Marxism-Leninism." Instead, the original ideas of Karl Marx had to be "creatively developed," and what they were "creatively developed" into was an ideology that A. James Gregor has called an "ideologically inconsistent fascism—an involuntary fascism—a fascism in spite of itself."[29]

TOTALITARIAN IDEOLOGIES AND THE THIRD WORLD

Given this overview of the origins of totalitarianism, we may now discuss the impact of Fascism and Marxism on Latin America and the Third World. To do this, we might first recapitulate the social and psychological conditions that gave rise to both ideologies. In the decades prior to the Bolshevik and Fascist revolutions, a handful of Western European nations had made the most extraordinarily rapid progress in virtually every area of human endeavor the world had ever seen. Almost all the other countries around the world were left behind in the wake of these advances and therefore by comparison were relatively backward, secondary centers of culture. However, it was the peoples in the periphery of Western Europe, because of their physical proximity to the advanced centers, who first became acutely aware of their condition of "backwardness" and who first developed a reaction against it. The Bolshevik and Fascist revolutions were two of those reactions. Both the Bolshevik and Fascist revolutionaries were ashamed of their national weakness and were afraid of being exploited by the newly industrialized great powers. Both groups of revolutionaries devised a strategy of using unlimited state power to direct a massive national effort of forced modernization.* The Fascists used an ideology called Fascism to justify to themselves and to others this extraordinary concentration of state power and the usurpation of individual rights. The Bolsheviks used Marxism-Leninism, which was inferior to Italian Fascism in terms of intellectual sophistication but which served essentially the same purpose—the justification of the totalitarian state.

By the time the Bolsheviks and Fascists gained power, the same psychological conditions that helped give rise to their movements also existed in the relatively backward areas of the world. Because the

---

*Nazi Germany is the only example of an advanced industrial country that has adopted totalitarianism. This exception, however, may point out the validity of the general observation that totalitarianism is most likely to be adopted by peoples in underdeveloped countries who see themselves as downtrodden and backward. In the years preceeding the Nazi rise to power, Germans had undergone the trauma of defeat in a major war, forced reparations to foreign powers, the greatest inflation in history, and the greatest depression in history. The economic deprivation suffered by millions and the overall sense of national disgrace and decline made the German people receptive to a regime that advocated not a movement of national modernization but a great collective movement of national *recovery*. The German example is particularly disturbing because it reveals the possibility of a totalitarian regime coming to power in an advanced industrial country that has the capacity to do great harm.

revolutionaries in other lands shared many of the same problems as the Bolsheviks and Fascists, a considerable number were attracted to the same solutions and the ideological justifications for those solutions. Almost immediately after the appearance of the Bolsheviks and Fascists upon the international scene, Marxist and Fascist parties began to spring up, like spontaneous growths, around the backward regions of the world. The protest ideology chosen by a particular political group depended upon the country it was in and the circumstances involved. The Bolsheviks had come to power in a country that was an Asian as well as a European presence; and somewhere amid the faceless masses of China, a young university student named Mao Tse-tung read about the Russian Revolution and in 1920 embraced Marxism-Leninism. In areas within the reach of Italian influence such as Latin America or some of the poorer European countries, fascist parties became politically prominent. After World War II the term *fascism* became discredited because Mussolini miscalculated and allied himself with the side that lost the war.* Since that time modernizing revolutionaries with totalitarian ambitions have avoided the fascist label and have instead tended to choose Marxism-Leninism as a name for their modernization ideology.

Because Marxism-Leninism has emerged as the dominant totalitarian modernization ideology of our time, it would be useful to take a closer look at this ideology to examine its strengths and weaknesses. The most important advantage of adopting a Marxist-Leninist ideological identity is obvious and needs little comment: the Soviet Union and China are Marxist-Leninist countries with a large amount of aid to dispense, and they are more likely to direct that aid to revolutionaries who belong to the same ideological family.

A less obvious advantage is that revolutionaries who have chosen a Marxist-Leninist ideological identity have a better chance of creating enemies among Western countries. This may not seem like much of an advantage, but if totalitarian modernizing leaders did not have real enemies, they would have to pretend that they existed, for as Fidel Castro once observed,

---

*It is important to keep in mind that Mussolini sided with Hitler because he thought the Germans would win the war, not because Fascists and Nazis had a similar ideology. Although many observers tend to lump German Nazism and Italian Fascism together, the two ideologies are actually quite incompatible because the Nazi elite believed the most "natural" community of people was race, not nation. If the Nazis had succeeded in reorganizing Europe along racial lines, they would have eliminated the nation-state which was something absolutely essential to Fascism.[30]

> The Revolution needs the enemy; the proletariat does not flee from the enemy, it needs the enemy. To develop himself, the revolutionary needs his antithesis, which is the counterrevolutionary.[31]

The reason why totalitarian modernizing leaders feel a need for outside antagonists is because they want their entire nation to be emotionally mobilized as if it were at war, and war requires enemies. Totalitarian leaders realize that the masses are never so moved by public spirit, dedicated to group unity, and subservient to collective ends as when their country is at war. They also know that people are willing to work the hardest and expect the least in return when they feel their country is threatened by outside forces. Totalitarian leaders love the unifying spirit and productive energy conjured up by war, and so they attempt to convince their people that their homeland is at war even in peacetime. A Marxist-Leninist identity helps them in this regard because Western powers often react with (usually ineffectual) displays of hostility to communist countries. This lends credibility to the contention of Marxist leaders that their country is, in effect, in a state of war and that their people must defend themselves by producing more, sacrificing more, and forming a united front under one national leader.

The most obvious weakness of the Marxist-Leninist ideology is the negative effect this ideology has on efficient economic organization. This problem stems from the fact the Marxism-Leninism contains the elements of two distinct and not always compatible revolutions, one a socialist revolt against capitalism and the other a nationalist revolt against economic and military backwardness. Owing to Marxism's anticapitalist origins, Marxist-Leninists are inclined to equate integrity and piety with opposition to any technique of economic management that is characteristic of capitalist countries. The difficulty with this is that many of these techniques are the most effective ever devised for building and managing an economy, and any ideological prejudice against them has the effect of impeding the nationalistic goal of rapid modernization.

Perhaps the economic technique that most offends Marxist-Leninists is individual profit making. But profit making can serve a vital function in the economic life of a society; and when Marxist-Leninists forbid its practice, they are giving up a formidable economic tool. The reason for this is that the single most important factor in the economic development of a country is the quality and quantity of its economic leaders, and the profit system is the best method yet devised for selecting these leaders. The profit system allows any individual in society, however obscure, to dream, to aspire, to step forward with a new idea and to prove its worth by making a profit. The profit system, in other words, allows those with courage and vision to choose themselves as economic leaders. In contrast, the Marxist-Leninist system relies upon state bureaucrats to perform this task; and state bureaucrats cannot select individuals with the rare qualities it takes to be top-rate managers or innovators as effectively as these individuals can select themselves. Thus, when Marxist-Leninists allow themselves to act upon their antiprofit fetish, they deprive their society of one of its primary economic resources—the ambition and creativity of its potential economic leaders.

Another point of socialist morality that has proven disastrous is the hostility of Marxist-Leninists to decentralized free markets and their preference for centralized planning. This means that the decision-making power as to what is produced, how much is produced, and for whom goods or services are produced is concentrated in the hands of a few state planning officials rather than spread out among large numbers of independent businessmen. In the early stages of modernization, this system can work reasonably well so long as the planners focus their attention and resources on a few comparatively simple economic tasks such as the construction of certain heavy industries, the mechanization of agriculture, and the production of critical commodities like steel, coal, and oil. The problem involved in central planning are felt much more acutely later on after the basic industrial foundation has been laid and the economic structure on top of it grows increasingly complicated and involved. To cite an example of how complicated managing a modern economy can be, in 1965 a single U.S. industry, railroads, required 43 *trillion* separate prices.[32] According to one Soviet expert, the task of planning his country's industrial output in 1964 was 1,600 times more complex than in 1928 when the first Five-Year Plan was inaugurated.[33] The central planning system is structured so that it swamps its administrators with detail they cannot handle. This inevitably causes planners to make mistakes and this, in turn, contributes to the proverbial ineffiency of Marxist-Leninist economies.

Profit making and decentralized free markets also serve another vital economic function in that together they allow consumers to communicate to producers about their ever-changing needs and desires. Let's say, for example, that collectively consumers decide they want more sweet potatoes and fewer cabbages. In a free market with its constantly fluctuating prices and profit margins, producers would notice that the profits in sweet potatoes were going up while the profits in cabbages were going down. Farmers would then be able to respond to this information by shifting resources from one commodity to the other. In a centralized system, prices are not free to go up or down and so cannot automatically send a signal to the producers. Consumers, therefore, would have their needs met less efficiently. This is not to say, of course, that a decentralized free market works as well in practice as it does in theory, but what is certain is that it is a vastly more effective economic technique than anything the Marxist-Leninists have designed to replace it.

It is obvious that an adequate treatment of this subject would take up a volume in itself, but we can see even from these brief comments that at least part of the reason why Marxist-Leninist regimes have not been economically successful is that their ideology prejudices them against using efficient economic techniques. As such, the Marxist-Leninist ideology does not serve its adherents well because it does not give them the freedom to pursue most effectively their objectives of modernizing their country and raising the standard of living of their people. Marxism-Leninism, in other words, has the ironic effect of inhibiting the Marxist-Leninist "national socialists" from achieving both their nationalist and socialist goals.

The strengths and weaknesses of Marxism-Leninism as a modernization ideology might be better appreciated by comparing it to the most successful modernization ideology of all—Japanese Shintoism. It is well known that Japan has been the only country that has moved from a condition of complete economic backwardness into the small circle of advanced industrial nations. What is not well known is that Japanese revolutionaries managed this extraordinary feat by setting up what amounts to a totalitarian state, by designing a totalitarian ideology to justify it, and by successfully exerting totalitarian control over the population. To understand this, we must go back to the origins of the Japanese revolution in the nineteenth century.

The Japanese modernization movement was a classic example of a people revolting against their own national weakness. Until the middle of the nineteenth century, the Japanese had dealt with the outside world by refusing to deal in any fashion with foreigners. Then in 1853 American warships appeared in Japanese waters and forced the Japanese government to establish commercial relations on unfavorable terms. Some Japanese began to conclude that the only way their people could protect themselves was to become the equal of foreigners. In the late 1860s a group of Japanese, sometimes known as the Meiji revolutionaries, overthrew the government in power and launched what we can clearly see today was a movement of forced modernization. The Meiji revolutionaries felt that in order for them to modernize their country they had to rid their people of all the "absurd customs"[34] that were causing them to live in the feudal past. They also believed that a powerful state would be necessary to bring about this reform, a state so powerful that it wielded totalitarian control over their people.

The Meiji leaders were well aware that they needed an ideology that would justify this kind of government and this kind of massive intrusion into the lives of their people. Fortunately for them, they had no

Marxist-Leninist models to follow at that time; and so they turned to their own history, dug deep, and resurrected a decrepit Japanese institution called the Imperial Court and an ancient religion of obscure origins called Shinto. The Imperial Court was an institution that in ages past had wielded great power in Japan but had long been weak and isolated from mainstream Japanese society. The Meiji leaders took the Emperor and his family and once again placed them at the apex of the Japanese social hierarchy. They then took the Shinto religion, which in ancient times was a simple pantheism, and completely transformed it into a revisionist religion that exaulted the position of the Emperor. In modern Shinto the Emperor was not just an object of veneration but of worship. The Emperor was nothing less than a god in human form. Once the Emperor was invested with divine authority and the idea was accepted by the Japanese people, the Meiji leaders were able to legitimize their sweeping social reforms by simply claiming that they were acting in the name of the Emperor.

Shinto was a religion that also functioned as a political ideology, and an important purpose of Shinto was to bring about the same "unity of will" that Lenin longed for. While Lenin proclaimed that in Marxist-Leninist Russia millions had to "subordinate their will to the will of one,"[35] the Meiji leaders declared that the Japanese subjects had no will apart from the will of the Emperor. Dr. Shinkichi Uesugi, a professor of law at the Imperial University of Tokyo, expressed this idea with unwavering clarity:

> Subjects have no mind apart from the will of the Emperor. Their individual selves are merged with the Emperor. If they act according to the mind of the Emperor, they can realize their true nature and attain the moral ideal. This is the fundamental relationship existing between the Japanese people and their Emperor who is the descendant and extension in time of the Great Deity (*Amaterasu Omikami*). The organizing will resides inherently in the Emperor and apart from the Imperial mind there exists no organizing will.[36]

The totalitarian rulers in both Bolshevik Russia and Meiji Japan proposed the unity-of-will idea in order to foster national unity and collective strength. The only substantial difference between the two positions was that while one used faith in history to justify unity, the other used faith in Shinto.

The Bolsheviks and the Meiji leaders both successfully used their respective ideologies to inculcate a similar passion for unity of will in a special group of people the Bolsheviks called *revolutionary cadres*. Revoluntionary cadres are an indispensable part of any successful totalitarian modernization movement. Revolutionary cadres are the ardent believers in the revolution and are those most willing to follow the dictates of the modernizing elite. Revolutionary cadres must be numerous enough—perhaps 2 to 4 percent of the population—to be placed throughout the government bureaucracy and at the grass-roots level of society in villages, on city blocks, and on factory floors. Revolutionary cadres are vitally important because they are the connecting link between the leaders and the people and make totalitarian control over the people possible.* The Meiji leaders recruited their revolutionary cadres mainly from the class of samurai warriors, who had a strong tradition of loyalty to their feudal lords. The Meiji elite, in a brilliant stroke, abolished the class of feudal lords and transferred the loyalty of the samurai to the Emperor. The Bolshevik Marxist-Leninists recruited their revolutionary cadres from everywhere and ran them through an intense indoctrination process. The point to be made here is that both the secular faith of Marxism-Leninism and the religious faith of Shinto had the power to inspire a sufficiently large minority of the population to make totalitarian control over the majority possible.

As a modernization ideology Shintoism and Marxism-Leninism obviously had much in common, but the great advantage that Shintoism had over Marxism-Leninism was that it encouraged its adherents to be pragmatic rather than dogmatic over economic issues. Shintoism did not formally espouse pragmatism but was simply neutral on the subject of how an economy ought to be organized. Unlike Marxism-Leninism, Shintoism had no distant anticapitalist origins and therefore put no socialist dogma between the modernizing leaders and their objectives of developing their economy and enhancing the well-being of their people. The Meiji leaders were free to take advantage of useful capitalist techniques such as individual profit making, decentralization of authority, and determination of prices by a market mechanism. They were also free to use state power to foster economic growth when they felt that private entrepreneurship was not strong enough to carry out a task. The Meiji rulers were, in fact, free to use any mix of state planning and market-oriented techniques that they thought necessary without violating Shinto ethics.

The major lesson to be learned from this comparison of Shintoism and Marxism-Leninism is that Marxism-Leninism has serious deficiencies as a modernization ideology. Shintoism was specifically designed as a modernization ideology and therefore was perfectly suited to the needs of a modernizing elite. Marxism-Leninism was adapted from an ideology that was designed for an anticapitalist revolution in a postindustrial

---

*Mussolini, it might be noted, failed to develop a vigorous system of revolutionary cadres and therefore failed to develop a firm totalitarian grip on the Italian people. In Mussolini's Italy, the totalitarian state was more an avowed aspiration than a reality.

society. The result has been that although in some respects the Marxist-Leninist adaptation has been useful to Marxist leaders, in other respects it has severely hindered them from achieving their ends of rapid modernization and economic prosperity for their people.

The overview of totalitarian modernization ideologies presented in this chapter is sufficient preparation for us to move on to the subject of totalitarianism in Cuba. As we shall see, contemporary Cuba easily fits the description of a totalitarian society. The significance of this is that totalitarianism in Cuba is a direct result of the social and psychological conditions discussed in the earlier chapters of this book—conditions that to one degree or another are found all over Latin America.

7

CUBAN
TOTALITARIANISM

Cuban totalitarianism is the result of a reaction against certain social and psychological conditions that Cuban nationalists found intolerable. The most fundamental of these conditions was a negative national identity. This negative national identity was largely the product of Cuban nationalist shame over economic, cultural, and political dependencia (see pp. 108–21) and also over the high levels of exploitation found within the Cuban conglomeration (see pp. 100–5). In more specific terms, Cuban totalitarianism is a tool used by a highly nationalistic political elite to eliminate the indignity of dependencia and to turn a chaotic conglomeration of people into a more orderly, less exploitative community.

During the armed struggle phase of their revolution, the Cuban rebels declared that they intended to solve the problems causing dependencia and exploitation by using democratic means. Most of the rebels, including Castro, were probably sincere in this promise; but when they came to power, they soon realized that the fight against their adversary Batista was the easiest part of their revolution; for once Batista was out of the way, they discovered through experience that dependencia could be defeated only by doing battle against a far more formidable enemy—the values and customs of the Cuban people. In time the Cuban leaders began to use language that reflected their aspirations for value reform. They began to speak of a "New Cuban Man," a "new consciousness," a "proper way of thinking among the people."[1] Fidel Castro frankly stated:

> Certainly the conquest of power was not the most difficult task regardless of how difficult that phase may have seemed. . . . The most difficult task was the one that came later. The most difficult task was the task in which we are engaged today: the task of building a new country on the foundations of an underdeveloped economy, the task of creating a new consciousness, a new man on the ideas which had prevailed practically for centuries in our society.[2]

240

In other discourses as well, the Cuban commander has drawn the battle lines very clearly:

> Today we aren't fighting against men—if anything against ourselves: . . . we are fighting against the past which remains with us today . . . old ideas . . . old selfish habits . . . old habits of thinking and ways of viewing everything.[3]

Once the Cuban leaders decided their battle against dependencia could not succeed without reforming the values of the people, they could not live up to their promise to implement their reforms democratically. For in order to carry out their program of value reform, they had to exert an extraordinary degree of control, of very undemocratic control, over the lives of their people.

Democracies are suitable only for peoples who are satisfied with what they are. Democracies allow their citizens the freedom to pass on their values from generation to generation. Individuals in democracies are, to be sure, "socialized," "educated," "molded" and "indoctrinated" —but this is done by parents, pastors, teachers, in short, by the society at large. The government does not have the dominant or centralizing role.

In Cuba the revolutionary leaders could not allow this kind of freedom because they were not satisfied with what their people were. It was their perception that Cuban society did not instill in its citizens sufficient levels of civic and economic virtue. Thus, they felt that they as modernizing leaders had to assume the task of accomplishing what the broader society failed to do. Convinced of their mission, they launched what they called a "Battle Against the Past," and in the process the individual lost any private area where the state recognized it could not intrude. In this society crippled by a weak spirit of civic virtue, the collectivity became everything, the individual nothing, and the state unlimited in power and thoroughly totalitarian.

TOTALITARIANISM AND VALUE REFORM

The Cuban thinking on totalitarianism and value reform was clearly revealed by Che Guevara in a famous book called *Socialism and Man in Cuba*. The starting point for Guevara's ideas was a profound aversion for certain features of the old society. Guevara maintained that the Cuban Revolution had to "compete fiercely with the past" and triumph over it. The term *past* was a euphemism for the unacceptable behavior patterns of the Cuban people, who had acquired these habits as part of their cultural legacy.

Guevara's dissatisfaction with the values of the ordinary Cuban meant that his attitude toward the "individual" in the new Cuba had to be very different from that of liberal democratic theorists. Liberal democrats placed the individual at the center of their political philiosophy and sought to structure government and society so as to enhance the individual's freedom to be whatever he wanted to be. Guevara, on the other hand, realized that to allow the individual the freedom to remain as he was and to pass on his values to the next generation would be disastrous for Cuban nationalist goals. In his philosophical essay, therefore, Guevara had to "define the individual" in considerably less flattering terms:

> I believe that the simplest approach is to recognize his [the individual's] unmade quality: his is an unfinished product. The flaws of the past are translated into the present in the individual consciousness and constant efforts must be made to eradicate them.[5]

Because Cubans carried around "flawed" values inherited from the past, those values had to be reformed. The Cuban masses could not be expected to do this on their own, however, because they could "see only by halves." Guevara explained that it was, on the one hand, the duty of those with unimpaired vision, the revolutionary leaders, to lead the masses out of the darkness and, if necessary, to subject them to "incentives and pressures of some intensity" to induce them to cooperate. It was, on the other hand, the duty of the semiblind multitudes to follow "the vanguard, composed of the Party, the most advanced workers, the advanced men who move along bound to the masses and in close communion with them." Guevara's attitude toward the Cuban people was typically elitist in that he was dissatisfied with what they were yet fascinated with what they might become. To him the Cuban people were flawed yet nonetheless precious because they were the "basic raw material of our work," the "malleable clay with which the new man . . . can be formed."[6]

If Mussolini had been alive at the time that Guevara was writing his essay, he would have instantly understood what Guevara was trying to do, for both leaders shared the same dream of imposing totalitarian "unity of will" on their people and using their collective energy to achieve nationalist goals. The ambitions of the two revolutionaries were so close, in fact, that they were inclined to express their ideas using similar metaphors and phrases—such as the notion of the political "artist" "molding" human "clay" into the "New Men" of the "revolutionary" "New Society." And like Mussolini, Guevara was also partial to using the military metaphor to describe his deeply held totalitarian dream:

> Thus we march forward. Fidel is at the head of an immense column—we are neither ashamed nor afraid to say so—followed by the

best party cadres and right after them so close that their great strength is felt, come the people as a whole, a solid bulk of individualities moving towards a common aim.[7]

The general outlines of the value system the Cuban leaders are seeking to instill in their people are quite clear. In general, revolutionary leaders favor those values or morals that, first, increase the productive capacity of Cubans and, secondly, increase their sense of public responsibility. The Cuban leaders are sometimes heard to say that their finished product, the "New Cuban Man," will be a splendidly different moral animal from the "capitalist" species that has flourished in the West. If successful their value reform will certainly be revolutionary in the Cuban context, but their New Cuban Man will hardly constitute a novel addition to the human race. In fact, by contemporary Western standards, the Cuban value reform harks back to the past more than it explores a bold new future. The New Cubans that the Cuban government is trying to create might be best understood by describing them as possessing an old-fashioned Protestant work ethic, an old-fashioned American achievement drive, and an old-fashioned Prussian sense of public responsibility.

If one were to peruse the printed works of Fidel Castro, Karl Marx, and Benjamin Franklin with a special eye for their ethical concerns, one would find that all three authors display a fondness for moralizing but only two emerge as spiritual cousins. Unlike the German dialectician, the Cuban revolutionary and the American codifier of early middle class virtues reveal a preoccupation with good productive work habits, community spiritedness, and personal self-discipline. Fidel Castro, in fact, sometimes sounds like a walking edition of *Poor Richards's Almanac.*

> If you ask us now what is the fundamental thing in our revolution, we would answer without hesitation that it is work. . . . Our country is presently ruled by the spirit of work and the virtues of the citizens of this country, their revolutionary spirit, are measured by their spirit of work.[8]

With young Cubans, the New Men of tomorrow, Castro does not bother with Marxist dialectics but rather gets down to basics:

> We must struggle so there won't be any delinquents in the future; we must struggle so there won't be any loafing, laziness, lies, parasitism, lack of loyalty, or lack of solidarity with others in the society of the future.[9]

The fact that many of Franklin's "bourgeois" aphorisms could fare so well in "socialist" Cuba should not really be surprising. These ancient bits of hoary wisdom reflected qualities of national character that were crucial in the economic development of the advanced countries; and the Cuban leaders, in an insight as old as Latin American nationalism (see pp. 149–53), are aware that their people must adopt similar economic virtues. So the spirit of the old Protestant ethic and the old Puritan sobriety stalks contemporary Cuba, eagerly encouraged by the modernizing elite. Greatly celebrated are ethical notions that encourage production and restrict consumption, notions such as the inherent virtue of untiring activity; work as a value in itself; thrift and foresight, moderation and self-control; the early-to-bed, early-to-rise routine; and the evils of selfish indolence, conspicuous consumption, frivolous consumption, vain obsession with personal appearance, and self-indulgent, decadent sensuality.

The Cuban version of the Cromwellian Puritan Revolt has gone considerably beyond the state of voiced ideals. Like an angry god seeking repentance and reform, the Revolution has hurled bolts of moral lightning upon the wicked dens of sin. Prostitution in Cuba has been greatly reduced, with the pimps and whores swept from the streets, the fallen women ejected from their lairs and packed off to perform socially useful labor. Havana's famous gambling casinos have been silenced, the bloody spectacle of cockfighting eliminated, and the unegalitarian practice of tipping, once considered morally repugnant in early America, effectively discouraged. Bars and nightclubs have been placed on limited hours, and for a time Castro closed all of them down, thundering from the pulpit, "There is no reason for us to foster drunkenness. What we must foster is the spirit of work!"[10] Lest anybody miss this message, Cubans have lost that leisurely, enervating two-hour lunch-siesta period and are expected to adjust to a no-nonsense half-hour break. They have also been deprived of their national lottery, an omnipresent corruption of the old society that much more than religion was the opium of the urban poor. Justifying this action in terms that would have pleased a Calvanist grandmother, Castro warned his flock that a lottery promotes

the idea of solving one's problems by luck and not by work. And what we must point out to the people is that their work, their sweat, their efforts are the only things that will permit them to enjoy the goods they need; they are the only things that can make the people prosperous . . . To try to solve one's problems through luck is not a virtue.[11]

As if searching for an appropriate fashion to symbolize the drab, steady discipline of a society at work, the Cuban leaders have taken a strong position on popular apparel and appearance, fostering the wholesome, well-scrubbed, clean-cut look. They have busied themselves with campaigns against erotic styles such as miniskirts and tight, thigh-hugging pants, and superfluous, nonutilitarian plumage like streaming long hair, sideburns, and of all things—beards. To replace these interests they have given Cuban youth the motto *Estudio-Trabajo-Fusil* (Study-Work-Rifle) as well as a behavior code that stresses such quaint old virtues as respect for parents and teachers. Those who have not conformed to the norm laid down by the elite have not fared well in revolutionary Cuba. One example of a nonconformist group was the unkempt, unwashed Cuban "hippies" who proliferated in Cuban cities a few years ago. These rebellious youth preferred to rhapsodize to foreign rock music and to obsess about clothing styles than to concern themselves with work, school, or the broader national mission of reconstruction. In revolutionary Cuba the hippies were regarded as stricken with "sickness" (*la enfermidad*) and were contemptuously ridiculed as "the little sick ones" (*los enfermitos*).[12] Using another metaphor Castro has called the "undisciplined idle young" of Cuba a "parasitic virus."[13] A more lengthy and specific example of official criticism can be seen in the following piece of revolutionary propaganda:

> The young boys [of Havana] think that the new man is one who wears tight pants. One sees how these illmannered brats talk back to their parents and how they act in their homes, on the streets, and in the schools. They are disrespectful and use improper language. . . . Perhaps not so many of them have taken up their little guitars after Fidel spoke about them, but there are many left. They wear tighter pants every day and they let their hair grow longer until they look like girls. We could say that these are the new men of a bankrupt universe. They are the ones who like to sing and dance to modern music. . . . What do they call modern music? A Yankee rhythm which is imported so that they can dance their epileptic dances? They themselves say that they are sick, and they are. They need to be cured. They need a radical cure. The coffee plantations are waiting. The mini-skirt, a type of urban bikini, is another of the styles we import with the greatest shamelessness. It is temptation in the middle of the street. . . . Is that the new world? Is that the human being of the coming third world so heralded by the intellectuals? No! . . . Lack of respect and lack of clothes are not qualities which will characterize the new man.[14]

A time-tested political maxim holds that politics makes strange bedfellows, but even to the observer aware of this, it is still not without considerable astonishment that some of Cuba's most fervent support in the West has emerged from its own rebellious counterculture. Those who once taped posters of Che Guevara to their bedroom walls most likely belonged to segments of the "do-your-own-thing" generation—a loose fraternity of young people who matured in the postwar years and who learned to disdain numerous economic virtues, to regard most forms of work as spiritually deadening, and to glory in resisting conformity to the dominant national culture.

The appearance of these groups within liberal Western societies has meant, among other things, a weakening of the cultural homogeneity that had long helped these developed countries excell in collective endeavors. But while the politically minded among them were cheering on the Cuban revolutionaires, the Cuban revolutionaries were condemning equivalent "fashions, customs, and extravagant behavior" that threatened to loosen the imposed conformity of Cuban life.[15] In response to the sharp questions of a young American visitor, a Cuban justified such policies with this argument:

> A uniform pattern had to be chosen. That pattern could have been long hair and moustache. That one wasn't chosen. We chose to have short hair and no moustache. . . . Without a uniform way of life, we'd have anarchy, a total chaos.[16]

And what would happen if those outrageous symbols of Western anticonformist protest, those seditious manes of long, streaming, glistening hair, appeared in Cuban schools? "We could cut it," crisply replied a Cuban teacher.

> We work in collective groups, and it's important for the students to be similar. Otherwise, we'll have controversies, and that wouldn't be correct. If we permit one student to be different in dress, hair, or behavior, what can we expect from the rest? We have to create similarity among the students and form them with a collective philosophy. That is a basic tenet of Communism.[17]

In these voices the Revolution expresses its preoccupation with uncontrolled *individualismo*, *viveza*, and national disunity that so troubled the Cuban past. This modernization movement will simply not allow Cuban youth to splinter into hostile subnational groupings, nor will it grant them the freedom to choose "alternative lifestyles," whether they may be experiments in hedonistic self-indulgence, revolutionary protests, or exotic forms of spiritual "self-realization." The Cuban Revolution is jealous of other claims upon the loyalty of its youth and will not tolerate "self" centered lifestyles, "do-your-own-thing" philosophies, or "counterculture" activities that do not contribute to the collective tasks of the nation-state.

While the presence of revolutionary puritanism makes modernization in Cuba to a certain extent Westernization, Cuban teaching on public responsibility renders the comparison, after a certain point, less valid, for the ethic of public responsibility taught in Cuba is quite different from that which prevails in the West. It is, in fact, decidedly collectivistic and militaristic in character.

The Cuban definition of civic responsibility is the result of the Cuban nationalist perception that collective tasks, namely the war on *dependencia*, are overwhelmingly important. When the collective task is all-important, the individual is very unimportant. This makes the Cuban version of civic responsibility quite different from the Western idea of a person balancing his individual rights against an awareness of his social responsibilities. Owing to its collectivist emphasis, the Cuban spirit of civic responsibility is much like the ethos dominating a military encampment. In military life collective objectives are so critical that there can be no concern for the individual rights of the combatants. For soldiers there is only duty. Thus the public virtues favored by the Cuban elite are precisely those of soldiers engaged in war: duty, discipline, unity, self-sacrifice, loyalty, and obedience to hierarchical authority. In the last analysis, it is appropriate that Commandante Fidel Castro does not outfit himself in austere Puritan black but continues with just what he's wearing—rugged army green.

The objective of the modernizing leaders in Cuba is to transfer their collectivist and productionist values to the rest of the population. To accomplish this they use techniques that liberal democrats would regard as political indoctrination or mass brainwashing. The Cuban revolutionaries, looking at the same techniques, call them "social education."[18] The shift in wording is the result of a distinct perspective, not an attempt to obscure an ugly reality with a euphemism. The Cubans take no pains to conceal from the outside world what amounts to a totalitarian aspiration. Their First National Congress on Education and Culture was only reasserting an accepted ideal when it issued the resolution, "We reaffirm the need for maintaining the monolithic ideological unity of our people and the battle against any form of deviation."[19]

The most obvious technique that the Cubans use to inculcate revolutionary values ("revolutionary consciousness") in the Cuban population is saturation propaganda. One of the first principles of saturation propaganda is that the political elite never allows the ideas of others to compete with its own. Thus, in the Cuba of Fidel Castro only one truth is permitted—the revolutionary truth. The revolutionary truth has enemies enough—the innumerable manifestations of the stubborn "Past"—without allowing opposition parties or hostile media. Instead, every conceivable instrument of propaganda is pressed into the service of the revolutionary forces, who never cease their proselytizing efforts to rescue more souls from the darkness of the "Past." In fact, the Cubans are often heard to say that their society is "one huge school." The formal education system, of course, supports the "truth"; so do the powerful organs of modern mass communications, the most admired Cuban personalities, the public spectacles of nationalistic adoration as well as many less obvious devices of saturation advertising. For example, when Castro delivered an important speech entitled, "Angola was an African Bay of Pigs for American Imperialism," the title suddenly appeared overnight on walls all over the cities and countryside; thousands of meetings "spontaneously" erupted in support of the Prime Minister; and when any Cuban lifted to his ear a telephone receiver to make a call the operator answered, "We support Fidel's statement, Good Morning."[20] The "truth" exhorting revolutionary consciousness settles like a thick fog over contemporary Cuba, and there is scarcely a corner in the land where its presence does not intrude.

An even more effective method of inculcating revolutionary values in the people are mass revolutionary organizations. If revolutionary values were taught only through the media and classrooms, they would tend to remain abstract ideals to be admired but not practiced by the people. The revolutionary leaders need some way of transmitting these values to the people so they become part of their daily routine. They accomplish this by mass revolutionary organizations which encourage people to assimilate revolutionary values by putting them into action. For example, these organizations teach people the value of manual labor and cooperative endeavor by setting up local projects where people can pick up a shovel and work together for a common end. This system also affords revolutionary leaders a means of finding other committed revolutionaries, for only by deeds, not words, can the true extent of commitment be known; and Cuban leaders eagerly recruit those who demonstrate the most dependable "revolutionary consciousness" and place them in positions where they can carry on the teaching process.

The Cuban leaders realize that the success of their value reform program depends upon whether Cubans become what the leaders call "integrated" into the revolutionary process. The best way they have of integrating Cubans is to have them become members of at least one revolutionary organization. The Cuban leaders have applied considerable moral and financial pressure to achieve this end and as a result have managed to get the great majority of Cubans to join at least one approved association. In Cuba those who refuse to become involved are derisively called *nonintegrados* (people who are not integrated)—a term of contempt that not many are willing to bear.

"Integration" into the value reform process begins at an early age in Cuba when Cuban leaders gather up the nation's children and place them in an extensive network of compulsory state schools. The most effective method these schools have of teaching revolutionary values is to require the children to put these values into practice. The objective of the schools is to transform these values into firmly embedded habits before the students graduate from the system. Thus, students "learn" the value of cooperation by cooperating together, the value of manual labor by performing manual labor, the value of producing green vegetables by producing green vegetables. Cuban schools place considerable stress on teaching productive virtue and so have work-study programs on every level. For example, many primary school pupils are required to tend daily the vegetable plots that they planted a short distance from their classrooms. Secondary school and university students generally labor in more demanding tasks such as the picking of coffee, the planting of citrus fruit trees, or the design and manufacture of furniture. And when the season for hacking and sweating arrives, students, professors, and administrators are sent out from the cities to the tropical wilds of rural Cuba, where in Castro's terms they "discover underdevelopment" by sweltering in the sugar cane fields for a month or two.[21]

The best environment the Cuban leaders have to teach collectivistic military values is the military itself or organizations set up along military lines. This is one reason why the Cuban leaders maintain large armed forces. It is the main reason why they have established so many paramilitary organizations that the country sometimes appears to be a garrison state.

Cubans receive their first taste of military-style education at the tender, pliable age of five. Virtually all schoolchildren belong to a little league military organization called the *Pioneros* (Pioneers).[22] Hardly out of diapers these juveniles are climbing into blue and white uniforms, snapping off smart salutes, and marching from class to class with their own version of the German goosestep. Like good little soldiers, they are trained to briskly attend to their "duties": one keeps the blackboard clean, another oversees the first aid kit, while still another waters the flowers every day. Drilled into them is a pattern of ideological responses which they can swiftly shoot back upon command:

"Where was Che [Guevara] born?"—"Argentina."

"Where was Che assassinated?"—"Bolivia."

When the teacher enters the classroom, the Pioneros do not great her with a cheerful "good morning" but with a hardy "Seremos como Che" ("We will be like Che"). In addition to heroes to emulate, the Pioneros have been provided with enemies to despise. The following is a stanza from a song those uniformed toddlers sing to lighten their day:

> If you want to buy a donkey,
> You should bear in mind
> That only 90 miles away
> There is a donkey President![23]

The teaching of collectivist values continues in a grown-up organization called the Cuban Armed Forces. Once male Cuban youths graduate from school, they are required to serve three years in the armed forces or in labor brigades organized in military fashion. This is a phase in the education of these Cubans that is designed to reinforce the outlooks and values taught them from their earliest years.

Cuban leaders have found that military training is an excellent way of fostering the collectivist outlook where the needs of the collectivity (the nation-state) are seen as far more important than the needs of the individuals that make it up. The spirit of collectivism begins to impress itself upon the individual from the moment he steps into his uniform and disappears into a sea of olive green. Homogeneity and uniformity are enforced to an exacting degree: a blizzard of regulations ensures that "uniforms" are worn in uniform fashion, right down to the cock of the hat; no significant differences in personal grooming are tolerated; not a button, a medal, a ribbon, can be a fraction of an inch out of place. Such uniformity presents an impressive image of monolithic unity on the parade grounds, but the individual is lost in its midst. In a sense, however, he is also found, for he discovers a positive identity, a pride in being part of such an imposing collective entity.

Military training is also an effective way to teach Cubans the need for "unity of will." The military, of course, teaches soldiers unity of will or disciplined cooperation so that they can work closely together to overcome a common enemy. The Cuban leaders want their people to develop the same habit so that they can work together to achieve common national goals.

Still another collectivist value that the Cuban leaders recognize as fostered by military training is obedience. In military life, of course, obedience training is very important because soldiers can work effectively together to meet a common foe only if they have been trained to unquestionably accept orders from leaders who direct the movements of the entire collective body. So essential is this training that soldiers are often ordered to perform patently absurd tasks such as "spitshining" their shoes to a mirrorlike reflection. The army is not as interested in looking-glass shoes as it is in habituating its troops to carrying out even tiresome, pointless orders with reflexive obedience. Those famous, ridiculous marching drills enforce the same ethic. Although such spendid phalanxes are hardly useful on the modern battlefield, soldiers march with spitshined shoes left, right, forward, and backward, responding as precision machines to the commands of a driver whether or not such turns and reverses make any sense to them at all.

Castro's attempt to reform the values of the Cuban people through military-style education has inevitably resulted in the militarization of Cuban life. The most obvious sign of this is the enormous size of the Cuban military establishment. Considering absolute numbers alone, without even counting the people's militia, the little island of Cuba supports more fighting men than any other country in Latin America, including Brazil, which has ten times the population.[24] In terms of the percentage of the population involved, the Cuban forces rank with the largest in the contemporary world; and in relative size they are comparable to the Prussian armies under Frederick the Great.[25]

In addition to its great size, the Cuban military establishment has a strong psychological impact on Cubans because of the prominent role it plays in Cuban life. To begin with, the most popular leaders in Cuba are also military leaders and are constantly seen hurrying about the Cuban countryside in fatigues or uniforms. One of Cuba's best-known weekly magazines, *Verde Olivio* (Olive Green), is compiled and published by the army. Singers, orchestras, and various sports teams from the armed forces attract large, enthusiastic crowds. The military's most conspicuous activities, however, take place on the all-important economic fronts. Literally waves of soldiers are sent into the sugar fields during harvest season to spearhead "machete charges." Special military teams are trained to operate and maintain tractors, bulldozers, and other heavy machinery for land reclamation and road building. The Che Guevara Trailblazer Brigade, made up of soldiers and officers from the Rebel Army, has taken the military model one step further by using Soviet tanks to clear new acreage. The Air Force frequently flies in support missions for aerial spraying of pesticides and fertilizers. The French agronomist René Dumont repeatedly used the term "militarization" to describe the organization of Cuban agriculture he saw during the late sixties.[26]

Hardly a corner of Cuban life, then, escapes the pervasive influence of the military spirit. Everywhere, it seems, soldiers, militia, women, and children are marching. The militarization process, however, does not mean that the Cuban elite is constantly preparing the people to wage war. What it definitely does mean is that the elite is inculcating in the people collectivist virtues that place exceptional value on the willingness to perform social duty and on the willingness to abide by the decisions of the political authorities in the interpretation of that duty.

The revolutionary values of collectivism and productionism are also cultivated in other Cuban social organizations besides the schools and armed services. Unlike the educational and military institutions, many of these are voluntary, or at least voluntary in appearance. Their numbers make up a lengthy list and their purposes are varied. But they all have in common the intention to "integrate" the individual into the Revolution, to teach him a new attitude, to stimulate him into practicing his ideals so that the energy from these efforts may be siphoned off and directed toward the collective goals of the Revolution. At least in a formal sense, almost everybody is integrated into some organization, with many people belonging to several revolutionary groups. The women are organized, the workers are organized, the Communists are organized, the Young Communists, the children, the students, the artists, the athletes.

The most prominent and important of these organizations in revolutionary Cuba is by far the largest. This is an association made up of many small units called *Comités de la Defensa de la Revolución*, or Committees for the Defense of the Revolution (CDRs). The aggregate membership of these CDRs totals in the millions. In fact, 80 percent of all Cuban adults over 14 years of age are said to belong.[27] The CDRs are basically a network of grass-roots community service organizations located in villages, in collective farms, in housing complexes, and on urban streetblocks. The Cuban government depends heavily upon them to carry out many of those small unglamorous yet vital revolutionary tasks that translates the rhetoric of revolution into reality. For example, the CDRs take the lead in vaccination campaigns, checkups for breast cancer, and blood donation solicitation. They send thousands of workers to the sugar fields as volunteer hands and thousands more to the schools as unpaid teachers. They endure the tedious footwork involved in census taking and statistics gathering. They organize projects such as the cleaning of streets and vacant lots, the nocturnal patrolling of cities to thwart crime, and the collecting of scrap paper, cardboard, metals, and bottles. With mass participation these humble efforts can sometimes add up to significant contributions. An example of this is the case of old bottles, where in the first half decade of the 1970s CDR members collected 355 million glass bottles worth 18 million dollars.[28] In addition to assisting the movement with its more substantive needs, the CDRs are also involved in cosmetics—in making sure that the Revolution always shines with a pretty face. When the time arrives to distribute a new load of revolutionary posters or to bedeck the neighborhood gaily for a revolutionary holiday, these groups are at the forefront of the activity. And if foreign observers have ever stopped to wonder how those large enthusiastic crowds ever turned out to cheer wildly for some Mongolian socialist they never before knew existed—they must look to the CDRs, who are behind this rather remarkable bit of magic as well.

The CDR system is invaluable to the Cuban elite not because the majority of Cubans belong but because a sizable minority are extremely dedicated. In 1970 the Cuban leaders estimated their hard-working, trusted CDR activists to be around half a million.[29] These zealots make up the bulk of the Cuban modernization movement's revolutionary cadres (see pp. 237–38). They are the true believers of the Revolution, people whose ambitions and sense of personal positive identity are intimately bound up in the success of their national crusade. In basically the same spirit as religious missionaries, they seek to heat up the surrounding swarm of lukewarm humanity with the fire of their own enthusiasm. Their main job is to bring an ever-larger number of Cubans into the revolutionary fold and to help the Cuban elite teach them revolutionary values.

It is vitally important to the Cuban elite that the CDR activists are counted not in the hundreds but in the hundred thousands. Because they are so numerous, they are able to operate on every street block, in every apartment complex, and in every small village all over Cuba. CDR activists use peer-group pressure to push their lukewarm coun-trymen closer to the revolutionary models of good workers and good soldier-citizens. They are effective because while Cubans can easily ig-nore the appeals of a radio broadcast for revolutionary sacrifice, they cannot as readily ignore the appeals of a CDR member who is both a neighbor and influential leader in the community. People in any culture have a tendency to conform to socially approved behavior while suppressing their "antisocial" inclinations because of who may be watching and listening. Through the CDRs the Revolution has eyes and ears everywhere, watching and listening for deviations from the revolutionary morality and "monolithic ideological unity" the modernizing elite seeks to impose. In the words of one American reporter, Cuba has become a "neo-Orwellian society" where "it is not Big Brother who watches you but the more benevolent eye of your next door neighbor."[30]

The CDR system of neighbors watching neighbors is an essential part of Fidel Castro's ambition to exert totalitarian control over the Cuban people. Even if Castro had an absolute monopoly over the use of force and the most sophisticated "Big Brother" technology, he would not be able to fashion a totalitarian society without a large following to carry out his orders judiciously. Castro never had the advantage of ruling over a people with an already-established tradition of obedience to public authority. Nevertheless, Castro has over the years managed to establish relatively effective totalitarian control over his people by converting a sizable group of Cubans into dedicated believers in his revolutionary cause. In a feat of political artistry that would have im-pressed Benito Mussolini, Castro has performed as a kind of political guru, inspiring a passionate, quasireligious commitment from a minority of the population that is large enough to influence the daily lives of the less committed majority.

The relationship that exists between Castro and his revolutionary cadres might be considered a living embryo of the totalitarian dream—a "unity of will" between the leader and the people. In fact, the cadres are frequently referred to in Cuba as the *vanguardia*, the vanguard Cubans, the prototypes of the New Men who will one day make up the entire human material of the "New Cuba." When en-thusiasts are imbued with revolutionary *conciencia*, (consciousness) they become much like their revered leader, in a vital sense an extension of him—his passions, his beliefs, his morals, his nationalistic faith. The unity is not only of "will" but of outlook, and more importantly, of emotion. The realization of these strong bonds means that the cadres are likely to conduct themselves in their daily lives as Fidel would want them to, that they are likely to follow his orders as if they were their own.

The CDR system that Fidel Castro has built up in Cuba provides him with two major assets in his drive to reform the values of his people. To begin with, it gives Castro a training ground where Cubans can internalize revolutionary values by actually putting them to practice. Secondly, it provides Castro with a large number of revolutionary cadres that make it possible for him to carry out his value reform even in the most remote corners of Cuba.

The Cuban CDR system and the spirit that enlivens it are the critical elements that make Castro's totalitarian dictatorship distinct from the more traditional developmental dictatorships in Latin America. The high political figures that direct these other announced modernization drives cannot avoid demanding profound and painful changes from their peoples; and when running against the grain of embedded customs and values, their elitist initiatives encounter especially fierce resistance. Although they may presume to describe their efforts as "revolutionary," they find their lines of authority breaking down, their commands losing potency in proportion to the distance they travel from their point of origin. (We have seen an example of this in an earlier description of the frustrated reforms within the Colombian school system see pp. 96–98). But Castro, through his hundreds of thousands of revolutionary cadres, has in a sense multiplied himself many times over, enabling his authority to remain strong on the many levels of Cuban society as if he himself were there. It is as though his person were brought down from the distant mountaintop of popular charismatic heroes to be present on every street corner dutifully collecting useful scraps and old bottles. For a leader to be able to mold large numbers of followers, and ultimately an entire people, in his own image is the final fulfillment of the totalitarian urge.

ECONOMIC DEPENDENCIA

We have seen that the Cuban leaders have imposed totalitarian value reform upon the Cuban people because they believe that such a reform is necessary to overcome dependencia and exploitation in their society. Perhaps the most basic of the Cuban nationalist objectives is the elimination of economic dependencia because more economic prosperity can help the leaders achieve their other aims. To achieve economic independence, of course, the Cubans do not have to be completely independent from the world economic system. Dependencia is a nationalist psychological burden that has come about as a result of too much strength on one side of the exchange between peoples and too much humiliating weakness on the other. Thus, the Cubans will overcome economic dependencia when they honestly consider themselves the equals in terms of productive ability of the most advanced peoples on earth. Our next question might be how the Cuban strategy for bringing about this increase in economic productivity has worked.

Castro unquestionably has had many things working in his favor in his drive for economic development. He had a good idea in substituting a "communist" work ethic for a "Protestant" work ethic because Cuban culture lacked strong prestige patterns that encouraged assiduous saving, hard work, and creative productive endeavor. Castro also accomplished the difficult task of capturing the loyalty of thousands of revolutionary cadres to help him spread his productionist gospel. In addition, Castro managed to convince the Soviet Union to provide Cuba with several times more foreign investment capital per capita than was available to any other country in Latin American.[31] Yet Despite all these advantages, Cuban economic performance has been dismal. In the same 25 years the Cubans have had, and with almost no outside help, the Meiji revolutionaries had moved their country well along the road to modernization and were on the verge of making Japan a great power. The Cubans, to be sure, have made considerable progress in certain areas of their economy such as the mechanization of the sugar industry and increases in citrus, fish, and egg production. Overall, however, the Cuban people are still collectively unproductive and as a consequence are still collectively poor. In addition, the Cuban economy depends heavily on a constantly increasing subsidy from the Soviet Union, which is hardly consistent with Cuban aspirations for nationalist dignity. In short, after many years and much struggle, the Cuban revolutionaries have not come close to their goal of economic equality.

The main problem for the Cubans has not been a lack of dedication and energy thrown into their task but the organization of their economy. The Cubans have suffered from the burden of socialist morality, which has undergone various interpretations over the years. The first socialist phase the Cuban revolutionaries plunged into was one in which they thought the problems of poverty could be solved by redistributing existing wealth and eliminating exploiters. This campaign caused hundreds of thousands of Cubans to flee from the island, many of whom were some of Cuba's most productive citizens. The high quality of the people whom the revolutionaries forced to emigrate to Miami during this period is suggested by the fact that the Miami

Cubans have become the only conspicuously successful Latin American colony in the United States. Needless to say, the combination of the redistribution of wealth and the persecution of Cuba's most enterprising people precipitated a drastic decrease in production. The Cuban revolutionaries soon realized that their "socialist" revolution had to be one of production, not of consumption.

The next phase the Cubans rushed into was one of overnight industrialization. During this period the Cubans were influenced by the terms-of-trade theory, which stated that their country was poor because its economy was based upon agriculture and not upon industry (see pp. 177–81). Acting upon this theory, the Cuban revolutionaries diverted resources away from sugar production and, with the help of Russian aid, began to construct the greatest number of factories in the shortest possible time. This turned out to be one of history's most expensive lessons in freshman economics. To the Cubans' amazement they discovered that the cost of importing the raw materials to make a product was sometimes more costly than simply importing the finished product itself. They had ignored the law of comparative advantage. Cuba was eminently well suited to sugar production, and the country could enjoy a higher standard of living by cultivating and exporting this commodity while importing what other countries produced most efficiently.

By the time the Cubans had assimilated the law of comparative advantage, they were ready to try a totally opposite strategy and push sugar production to the neglect of all other sectors of the economy. This campaign was called the Great Revolutionary Offensive and was similar to the Great Leap Forward attempted by the Chinese a few years earlier. During the Great Revolutionary Offensive, Castro exhorted his people to make every effort and sacrifice possible in order that Cuba could leap from underdevelopment to development in a short span of a few years. The culminating achievement of this drive was to be a record 10-million-ton sugar harvest in 1970. But this time the Cubans ignored the law of diminishing returns—that at a certain point far below ten million tons, greater and greater investment would be required to yield less and less sugar. The Cubans not only failed to reach their goal of ten million tons, but they severely damaged the rest of their economy striving to achieve it.

Castro's drive to reach the ten-million-ton harvest was the most radical period of his socialist economic experimentation. Castro, following the logic of socialist morality, decided to strive for the socialist goal of absolute income equality. He sought to accomplish this by rationing on the basis of "need" an ever larger share of Cuba's goods and services and by reducing the number of goods Cubans could buy with their money. Castro even announced that he planned to do away with the use of money altogether, calling it, in a fit of socialist pique, a "vile intermediary between man and the product of his labor."[32] Castro's plan to maintain labor discipline under these circumstances was to teach Cubans the moral necessity of working hard for the collectivity even if they could not see a connection between work and immediate benefit for themselves or their families. In other words, Castro set up a situation in the Cuban workplace where Cubans had little fear of punishment if they did not work, little fear of hunger if they did not work, and little hope for personal advancement if they did work. The only reason left for Cubans to drag themselves out of bed in the morning and labor hard at their jobs was that such social behavior was ethically correct.

While some Cubans did respond to Castro's "moral" incentives, a great many did not, and their example was profoundly demoralizing and easily contagious to those in the middle. During this radical socialist period, labor discipline collasped throughout Cuba. Workers in large numbers did not bother to show up on their jobs and those who did saw little reason to work hard. Even the American sympathizers Huberman and Sweezy, who normally toured socialist countries with ideological blinders, estimated that the agricultural labor force in Cuba was being used at only 50 percent capacity.[33] A time-loss study carried out by Cuban investigators in 200 separate enterprises reported that anywhere from one-fourth to one-half of an average workday was being wasted.[34]

The radical socialist phase of the Cuban Revolution ended in 1970 with the failure of the ten-million-ton harvest. Since that time Castro has heeded the advice of his Russian mentors and adopted the orthodox Soviet approach for organizing an economy. The Cuban economy has rebounded as a result of these reforms; but the problem is that although the Cuban leaders have put aside their radical socialist ambitions, they have still modeled their coutnry's economic system after the woefully inefficient Soviet system. Thus despite some efforts at decentralization, the Cuban economy is still overcentralized. Despite some experimentation with free market prices, a general system of self-adjusting free market prices does not exist. And despite a much-improved system of work incentives, these incentives still lack sufficient force to make workers perform to the best of their ability and to motivate managers to search restlessly for creative ways of increasing productivity. To even the casual eye, slack work discipline and haphazard economic management continue to be conspicuous features of Cuban economic life. If the Cuban leaders wish to tap the full productive potential of the Cuban people, ensure vigorous economic growth in future years, and eventually free themselves from dependence on Soviet aid, then they will have to modify the basic structure of the Cuban economy. That is to say, they will have to rely much more than they are presently doing on incentives based on individual self-interest, decentralized management, and prices determined by some form of market mechanism.

One of the worst effects of Cuban economic mismanagement over the years has been its negative impact on the Cuban value reform. We have seen that through the point of view of modernization, one of the weaknesses of traditional Latin American culture is the lack of social prestige associated with many forms of productive endeavor (see pp. 64–68). This has hurt Latin American economic growth because people in general have a basic hunger for social prestige as well as material reward. The Cuban revolutionaries have successfully used their totalitarian state power to modify prestige patterns in Cuba to the point where Cubans can gain real social prestige for being productive. But the Cuban leaders have also reduced the impact of their value reform by denying Cubans the material rewards. The genius of the Meiji revolutionaries in Japan was to shower productive people with social prestige and also to allow them to reap the fruits of their efforts. The Japanese, in other words, designed an incentive structure so that social prestige and economic benefits would work together rather than against one another. The Cuban revolutionaries, on the other hand, have been weighed down by socialist morality and were afraid they would create economic classes if they allowed productive Cubans to benefit from their increased productivity. During their radical socialist period, the Cuban leaders attempted to eliminate all income differentials and to depend almost entirely upon social prestige to motivate their people to be productive. Now they allow some differences in income, but the economic incentives in Cuba are still not strong enough to create the kind of economic leadership the country needs. The end result of this has been that while the Cuban revolutionaries have with their value reform gone a good distance in correcting a serious flaw of the old society, they have neutralized the positive effects of this by refusing to allow Cubans the right to enjoy the full material rewards of their hard work and creative ideas on how to increase productivity.

It is obvious that the revolutionaries in Cuba have not made the economic progress they hoped for, and consequently the standard of living of most Cubans is still quite low. Standard of living, however, does not tell the whole story. The Cuban revolutionaries have managed to give their people some substantial economic benefits not so much by increasing their consumption as by lessening a number of the problems that are normally part of being poor in underdeveloped countries. The poor in underdeveloped countries lead existences that are harsh—even brutal—for reasons that go beyond the fact that they have little to consume. The Cuban revolutionaries have used their totalitarian control over the population to remove some of this harshness and therefore have made poverty in Cuba easier to bear.

One of the most significant changes the Cubans have made to the character of poverty in Cuba is in security. Although the poor in Latin America are, by definition, living on the brink of poverty, they actually suffer more consistently from the element of insecurity in their lives than from real physical deprivation. The reason for this is that while they experience many days in which they know they have enough to-day, they can never rid themselves of a gnawing uncertainty about tomorrow. The Cuban Revolution has been able to eliminate much of this insecurity: Cubans know that they will always receive their basic necessities through a distribution system that rations available goods. Their medical needs are well attended to free of charge by an effective public health system that reaches the most remote corners of Cuba. They are never threatened by unemployment because the state makes certain that work is always available. Cubans, in short, are able to live in the confidence that society guarantees them the "basic minimum," which will not be blown away by changing economic winds. In terms of emotional well-being, therefore, the difference between coping with privation in the old and new Cuba is considerable. The poor of contemporary Cuba are still quite poor and yet are relieved of one of the great burdens of poverty—the disheartening day to day insecurity of what the morrow may bring. It must also be added, however, that the price Cubans pay for this economic benefit is high because this kind of economic security substantially weakens traditional work incentives, and the Cuban elite has to bolster work incentives by the practices of totalitarian control.

Narrowing cultural gulfs have also served to reduce the burden of being poor in Cuba. To understand this we have only to look at the situation in prerevolutionary Cuba. In those times the cultural gulf between the rich and the poor was so large that wealthy and poor people were almost like species brought up in different planets. The problem with this was that the poor not only saw themselves as different from the rich in education, speech, manners and dress but as "inferior." Cultural differences, in other words, had a damaging effect on the self-esteem of the poor. When the Cuban revolutionaries gained power, they set out to homogenize the population culturally because they recognized that cultural gulfs discouraged national unity. With youths they did this quite easily by running all young Cubans through the same educational system. Today Cuban youths, compared to those of prerevolutionary times, are beings of remarkable similarity. The revolutionary elite conspired to reduce the psychological distance between adult Cubans by regularly sending off the upper strata to the fields and factories to labor at the side of ordinary Cubans. Today the old Cuban axiom that soft hands never cross rough hands no longer applies. The result of this has been that the poor in Cuba are no longer so different from wealthier Cubans and therefore have no need to feel the same kind of inferiority. This ia an important point because one of the worst consequences of being poor in underdeveloped countries is the ruinous effects this sense of inferiority can have on people's fragile self-esteem.

Still another way the Cuban revolutionaries have managed to lessen the burden of being poor in their society is to use the totalitarian power at their disposal to reduce social exploitation. In highly exploitative societies, wealth assumes a special importance because it enables individuals to protect themselves against predators or to sustain their blows without grave damage (see pp. 41–42). Because the poor do not have money, those who live in this type of society are vulnerable to many forms of social exploitation. As the Cuban totalitarian state has expanded its capacity to regulate exploitative, antisocial behavior, money has relinquished some of its protective function and the need to possess it has become less urgent.

EXPLOITATION

The subject of exploitation brings up a vitally important aspect of the Cuban Revolution. We have seen that the reduction of exploitation in Cuba was a prime objective of the Cuban nationalists from the very beginning of their Revolution. The Cubans, however, could not eliminate exploitation by toppling a small group of wicked "oligarchs" from the pinnacle of society for the simple reason that most of the exploitation in Cuba was not caused by a handful of powerful Cubans but by millions of ordinary Cubans who exploited one another. Cubans exploited one another because they were motivated by a value system that, as described earlier (see pp. 99–105), is characteristic of conglomerations. Thus, in order for the Cuban revolutionaries to reduce exploitation, they had to modify the values that caused exploitation. To carry out this task the Cubans set up a totalitarian state and made the elimination of exploitative values and practices a central feature of their value reform.

The implications of the Cuban attack on exploitative values might be better appreciated if we make a distinction between *standard of living* and *quality of life*. Standard of living refers to the level of consumption that an individual enjoys. Quality of life refers to everything that affects an individual's overall well-being, including the number of goods and services he consumes. We have seen that the Cuban leaders have woefully mismanaged the economy and therefore have not been able to improve substantially the Cuban standard of living. Many observers have written off the Cuban Revolution as a failure because of the obvious economic failings. However, the Cuban leaders have successfully used their value reform to modify the values that encourage Cubans to exploit one another. Thus despite the fact that Cubans have not significantly raised their standard of living, they have been able to raise their quality of life in areas other than material consumption.

Liberal democrats will never accept the humanistic potential of totalitarianism as worth the price of the negative features of those types of societies. They do, however, need to understand the appeals of totalitarianism in order to understand its strengths. The Cubans developed a humanistic outlook very different than that of early American democrats like Thomas Jefferson partly because the type of exploitation they were concerned with was very different. The Cuban revolutionaries did not concern themselves, as did the American revolutionaries, with protecting their people from exploitation by the state because they felt that a far more compelling challenge in Cuban society was to prevent their people from exploiting each other.

One practical result of this difference in outlook between Cubans and liberal democrats is that the type of social control that prevails in Cuba is very different from that found in well-ordered, democratic countries. In these latter countries people have acquired economic and civic virtues as part of their cultural legacy, practice those virtues out of habit, and need little encouragement from the state to make them do so. In Cuba people did not inherit comparable values, and so the state imposed a substitute of social control that we may call *totalitarian social control*. Common to both types of social control is the fact that the antisocial attitudes and actions of individuals are curtailed in some way by pressure from the community. What distinguishes them is that within one cultural environment the behavior of the individual is regulated by the people at large responding to established social mores, while within the other the individual's behavior is regulated by political activists responding to revolutionary social mores decreed by the political elite.

It is the regulation of the individual by political authority, not social convention, that disturbs those with liberal democratic sentiments. In the conflict between democratic and totalitarian ideals, two kinds of humanism are in evidence—that which focuses upon the value of orderly, disciplined communities and that which focuses upon the danger of unrestricted state power.

The appeal of both democratic and totalitarian humanism is very real and sometimes can even be found pulling within the same human being. This is clearly seen in the writings of Joe Nicholson. Nicholson is an unusually perceptive American journalist who, during his extensive traveling and interviewing in Cuba, visited a place called *Districto* (District) José Martí. Districto José Martí at that time was a newly constructed building complex of about 50 thousand inhabitants and was populated by Cubans with relatively high *conciencia*. Nicholson described the district as a neat, well-run, peaceful community with many inexpensive social services available owing to the amount of volunteer work performed by the people. These residents had originally come from shabby areas Americans would call slums, and so their new homes were similar to "urban renewal" enterprises constructed for slumdwellers in the United States. Nicholson contrasted the Cuban housing project with its American counterparts, which all too frequently have swiftly degenerated into a sorry state. Instead of graffiti on the walls, glass on the sidewalks, garbage in the alleys, and crime in the corridors and streets, Districto José Martí radiated "tenant pride in their cultivated gardens, careful maintenance and immaculate cleanliness."[35]

How was this miracle accomplished? José Chavez, the administrator of Districto José Martí, was probably not attuned to American sensitivity to civil liberties when he blurted out his enthusiastic response. His words reveal an unapologetic devotion to the idea of value reform and the necessity of Cubans to conform to values promulgated by the political elite. "We bring them [the slumdwellers] first as volunteers," Chavez explained, "to clean the streets and work the gardens. After they move here, they are educated through the CDRs and the district's educational councils. . . . We maintain our buildings with the residents' volunteer work. We hold meetings of volunteers in the parks and in the buildings. We educate through these activities. That is why our people are incorporated [integrated]. Each building has a CDR, a chapter of the Federation of Cuban Women, and a neighborhood council. The neighborhood council has five members, a president, and specialists in education, gardening, organization, and propaganda. These groups work constantly to educate the tenants. We in Cuba say, 'No man can escape from them.' . . . The capture of them!" exaulted Chavez as he gave vent to his unalloyed elitism. Then, more subdued, he warned, "If we didn't do this, we would lose all this." At this point Nicholson writes that the administrator "waved at the walls and ceiling and out the window toward the gardens."[36]

The interview continued as Chavez, without a hint of discomfiture, began to reveal the details of the community's system of social control. Nicholson records this:

> Chavez, proud of the carefully orchestrated educational program, added, "Each apartment has a file." He paused to lift several family dossiers from a filing cabinet for me to examine, "Besides the apartment and furniture contracts, the file contains any criticism from the neighborhood council or any infractions." The first file showed—the attention to detail would have made J. Edgar Hoover turn enviously in his grave—that a resident named Compañera Afelia Forneya García, of block 1, apartment 2, had allowed water to overflow and damage the garden outside her apartment at 6 P.M.,

July 14, 1970. "On this day water came out into the garden and spoiled the said garden," read the typed notes in the slip, one of about a dozen sheets of paper in Mrs. Garcia's dossier. (Chavez said the infraction would have been more serious if the water had been soapy.) The sheet was a standard form: below the space for remarks were four boxes on successive lines, each beside an infraction: "hanging out clothes"; "throwing of water and other things"; "keeping animals in the apartment"; "damaging the gardens"; "alter or damage in any method interior or exterior of apartment." Mrs. Garcia's sheet had circles around the boxes indicating "throwing of water and other things" and "damaging the gardens." Asked how the case was resolved, Chavez referred me to a handwritten note on the back of the sheet. "She said it was because she was cleaning her windows," he read, "and logically the water ran down."

Reading a second personal dossier, I found the Compañera Carmen Gallego had committed a "public scandal," and been referred by Chavez's office to the Popular Tribunal—the local court. (Chavez said that the referral decision was made by the neighborhood council which considers all cases and refers the more serious ones to the court.) She was sentenced to fifteen days of work in the project gardens. "She was fighting in the streets with another woman," Chavez explained.[37]

"Let me demonstrate to you the kind of control we have here," continued the administrator, and he proceeded to outline thorough methods designed, according to Nicholson, to "weed out undesirables, including homosexuals and alcoholics" before they ever have a chance to move into the Districto. And once desirable citizens are rewarded with admission into the housing project, it appears difficult for them to acquire personal as well as social vice. For example, the residents of Districto José Martí receive only a strictly rationed quantity of liquor so that, in the judgment of one of the tenants, "there isn't any real possibility someone could become an alcoholic." The heart of this entire interview could be expressed in a single confident sentence by José Chavez: "Our struggle is to educate people to live correctly.[38]

Nicholson's remarks are worth some pause and reflection because they are authored by an American who has traveled extensively in Latin America as well as in Cuba, and drawing upon this broad experience, has become plainly sympathetic with the humanistic advances of the Cuban Revolution. And yet, being a product of American culture, he could not help but be torn by the appeals of democratic humanism as well.

Cuba's ideal socialist community had a handful of disturbing aspects: personal dossiers, investigations of private lives, inculcation in the correct political ideas, compulsory or near compulsory membership in political organizations, evictions based on personal habits or beliefs . . . the big brother scrutiny made me wonder if there was any privacy and individuality.[39]

There is actually no need to wonder. Because the Cuban Revolution is reacting against the ruinous exploitation caused by the socially uncontrolled behavior of individuals and the lack of genuine community life, the rights of the collectivity in the new Cuba take complete precedence over the rights of the individual. In specific terms, this means that the Cuban state does in fact what Italian totalitarianism advocated in theory: it recognizes no area of "privacy" it cannot enter and no aspect of "individuality" it cannot touch.

State-imposed social control, then, has a lengthy reach in Cuban society, and its encroaching presence is likely to be felt anywhere within the radius of national life. We have previously noted this intervention in the working lives of the Cuban people. The state has pronounced work a social duty and has taken away the "right" to be nonproductive.[40] According to Cuban revolutionary morality, freedom from poverty is an essential building block of a humanistic society, and so refusal to work must be construed as a form of social exploitation. Included among the post-1970 reforms was a plan to keep a lifetime file of the work performance of every single laboring Cuban; and since Cuba is now receiving computer technology from the Soviet Union, we can expect that these records will eventually be digested and systematized by Big Brother leviathans.

Totalitarian social control is used in Cuba to teach civic as well as economic virtue. The main method the state has to accomplish this is to encourage Cubans to contribute voluntary labor to the common good. This kind of control the state has over Cubans is humanistic in the sense that when day care centers are organized, playgrounds built, people vaccinated, streets cleaned, and gardens planted, the overall quality of life tends to be enhanced.

The strengthening of civic virtue in Cuba has also brought to the people important psychological benefits. In my own conversations with ordinary citizens in revolutionary Cuba, I was struck by their distinct mood of being able to influence in a positive way their own lives and their own communities. If they wanted to build a concrete home for themselves with the help of neighbors, to plant flowers along the street in front of their home, or to discipline the individual next door who was making too much noise at night—all this they could do through existing community organizations. Conspicuously absent was that feeling I so frequently encountered among the poor of other Latin American countries of everything and everybody around them being out of their control, of remorseful despair at changing anything, of bitter cynicism about human nature, of bleak hopelessness as they looked to the future. The anthropologist Oscar Lewis encountered this same transformation of mood when he returned to a Cuban slum he had studied prior to the Revolution and was able to talk to some of the same families he had known before. "It was clear," wrote Lewis, "that the people were still desperately poor, but I found much less of the despair, apathy, and hopelessness which are so diagnostic of urban slums in the culture of poverty. They expressed great confidence in their leaders and hope for a better life in the future. The slum itself was now highly organized, with block committees, educational committees, party committees. The people had a new sense of power and importance."[41]

Greatly contributing to this optimistic outlook is the fact that the Cuban leaders have been able to use the control they have over the population to moderate aggressive social behavior. The unity-minded revolutionary leaders are, needless to say, implacably opposed to the values of individualismo and viveza, which reduce societies of people to conglomerations of contending individualities. In the words of Fidel Castro:

> The sentiment of human confraternity is not possible ... in a society in which reigns the law of the strongest, the slyest, the most vivo, in a society where individualismo and egoismo predominate, where each man is abandoned to his fate. . . [42]

Revolutionary ethics in Cuba are also designed to discourage the artful practices of "rising" in status at the expense of others and tearing others down whether or not their ascents are legitimate (see pp. 23–24). Individuals, to be sure, are encouraged to excel in the new Cuba and are awarded status for their efforts; but collectivist ethics lay heavy stress on the ideas that increased social prestige must be the result of genuine social contributions and that such rises in status derive their value from the fact that they afford the successful, not personal advantage, but a greater opportunity to enhance the common good. This is the reason, for example, that Cuban Olympic champions consistently treat us to seemingly wooden, self-effacing speeches declaring that they have worked hard to excel not for themselves, but for the "good of the people" or the "glory of the Fatherland" or the "advancement of the socialist cause."[43] The collectivist emphasis works to keep the successful humble and, at the same time, to discourage the envy reflex against socially useful activities, for as long as achievements that bring status are legitimized by their purpose of "serving the people," any manifestation of the envy reflex would be condemned as an attack against the "people" itself. The entire thrust of revolutionary morality seeks to prevent Cubans from dispersing their collective energy in every direction either by scrambling over each other in order to "rise" or by desperately holding each other down. It seeks to control and channel this energy so that individuals will cooperate so that the people as a whole will rise together. This is a classically totalitarian moral vision: the focus is entirely upon the collectivity in which the individual, for his own good, exists only to serve.

A good illustration of how the Cubans have learned to deal with socially disruptive behavior can be seen in their approach to the problem of common crime. Cuban authorities make the credible claim that they cut their country's crime rate in half during the first decade of the Revolution and have kept it at a low rate ever since.[44] The Cubans were able to do this because they used their increased control over the population to turn conglomerations of people into communities. In conglomerations perpetrators of antisocial acts operate quite freely amid crowds of indifferent people. In communities citizens are more civic minded and make more of an effort to identify malefactors and bring them to justice.

In Cuban communities CDR committees are in the forefront of the fight against crime. One way that CDR leaders discourage crime is to solicit volunteers to patrol the streets at night.[45] Another way, and perhaps the most effective, is to pay close attention to everything that goes on in their small jurisdictions. A worker from Varadero, for example, once triumphantly unveiled a television set in his home and invited his friends to enter and partake of his good fortune; his neighborhood CDR leader, however, was well aware that he could not afford such an item, so he informed the police, who quickly discovered that the set was stolen.[46]

Effective policing, of course, must be backed up by a flexible judicial system that is capable of handling and dispensing justice on any and every variety of social infraction. There are two reasons why: First, certainty of punishment is an effective deterrent to crime, a much greater one than sheer severity irregularly applied. Secondly, it is very important that even small offenders be dealt with by the judicial process and administered fair penalties because this tends to discourage the growth of incipient criminality.

A comparison of the justice measured out by the courts in the United States and Cuba helps illustrate this point. By democratic civil libertarian standards, the judicial system in Cuba is seriously deficient because it cannot protect the individual against arbitrary state authority. As a practical matter, however, this limitation is not very meaningful to the vast majority of either country because most Cubans and Americans are not inclined to become involved in the kinds of exotic, especially political, "crimes" that would cause the intervention of high executive officials in the judicial process. People are generally far more concerned about the smaller yet nevertheless aggravating injustices that inflict pain upon their daily existences. But

American courts are frequently too weighed down with major crime to process the lesser offenses against society. The American court system is also very expensive and time consuming, and people can afford to use it only to redress their most serious grievances. The American Bar Association admits this is the reason why 65 percent of Americans employ the services of a lawyer only once in their lifetimes.[47] While the citizens of the United States are provided more constitutional shelter from political oppression than Cubans, they possess much less protection against the lower-order injustices that are much more likely to cross their lives. While this incapacity is not terribly important in America's stable, low-crime communities where the occurrence of social aggression is not a major problem, it constitutes a serious inadequacy of justice in the more socially chaotic inner city neighborhoods.

The disparity between the two judicial systems in ability to deliver ordinary, plebian justice is due, in great measure, to differences in formal institutions. The Cubans have created organizations called "popular tribunals" to handle their society's accumulation of small complaints. These houses of justice are set up to take care of the lesser exacerbations of life: petty theft, vandalism, sanitary violations, family quarrels, fights with neighbors, excessive noise, or even something as minor as swearing in front of children. This type of structure is particularly crucial if people are not organized into orderly communities and have to deal efficiently and fairly with many eruptions of social aggression.

The reason why poor Cubans can afford such extensive judicial machinery while rich Americans cannot, is that they keep their overhead low. The "people's courts" are bereft of expensive pomp and majesty. They consist of any reasonably sized room that happens to be vacant in the evenings, a few rude benches, and three judges who are workmen by day and volunteer arbitrators by night. The judges are selected from each local community by the Party and CDR committee and approved (or rejected) by the people through a secret ballot. They are not schooled in law nor familiar with crabbed legal jargon. Nor do they have to be because all they need is common sense and resolve to be fair. Take, for example, the case of the rowdy customer at an ice cream parlor who dumped his ice cream on the head of a waitress. It hardly required the holder of a law degree graced in silk robes to pass sentence on this ill-tempered sort—ten consecutive Sundays washing dishes at the parlor in order to "appreciate the problems of serving other people." Another actual "punishment" consisted of obliging a man who drank too much to go to school and earn a sixth-grade diploma. Still another delinquent was incarcerated—ordered to remain in his apartment every evening and all weekends for two weeks. His "jailers" were his neighbors who contributed to community social control by making sure he observed these sanctions.[48]

It cannot be said that these punishments are terroristic and leave the Cuban citizenry quaking with fear. Yet they are an integral part of the totalitarian control that the elite exercises to reshape human customs and behavior. The state seeks to confront lesser acts of social agression with justified sanctions, thereby discouraging wrongdoers from not only continuing their misdeeds but escalating their antisocial truculence into more ruinous crimes.

One further factor that should be considered in evaluating the quality of life in a poorly regulated society is fear. The physical harm inflicted upon people living in a human conglomeration is bad enough, but the invisible effects of fear and uncertainty upon their emotional well-being is also very destructive. In fact, for most participants in this type of society, anxiety and apprehension over what might happen is more harmful than what actually does happen. Few of those accustomed to life in stable communities can appreciate the exhausting emotional burden that victims carry throughout their days in a culture without *confianza* (trust), where the intentions of all strangers and most acquaintances are suspect, where even seemingly innocuous words and gestures must be scrutinized for hidden offense. With details such as these in mind, it becomes less difficult to understand the humanistic aspects of a totalitarian campaign that aims to temper the kind of immediate, pervasive exploitation characteristic of populations with weak mechanisms of social control.

Just as it is helpful to examine the role of genuine "communities" in controlling social exploitation, it is also instructive to study how the reduction of social exploitation greatly assists in the formation of genuine "communities." A central feature of the Cuban Revolution has been a deliberate, hard-fought campaign against the traditional forms of exploitation that have long kept the Cuban people divided amongst themselves.

Within Cuban society one of the most exploited groups of human beings were women. The primary reason for this was that many Cuban men were motivated by the macho complex (see pp. 35–39). The Cuban revolutionaries came to recognize the ethic of male supremacy as one of the social ailments of the old society that had to be overcome. In a speech to the Cuban Federation of Women, Fidel Castro enthusiastically embraced the cause of "woman's equality," flatly predicting that just like the idea of private property, the idea of women as property would be exorcised from Cuban society.[49]

In certain limited areas the revolutionary elite could make immediate, decisive advances in curbing the harm wrought by machismo. For example, by virtually abolishing prostitution and domestic service, they were able to free thousands of women from these often-humiliating social roles as well as eliminate occupational structures that, by their nature, encouraged abuse.

In general, however, machismo was an attitudinal problem resistant to the quick thrusts of revolutionary action. Its hold upon the people was, in Castro's terms, the result of "an old culture, old habits, old concepts, old prejudices"[50] that would not easily give way before the pressure of state initiative. The government, therefore, dug in for a long battle, regularly drawing from its arsenal the weapons of legislation, revolutionary prestige, education, and propaganda.

Since the modernizing elite sought to expand the labor supply whenever possible, they were especially interested in cutting the cords of tradition that tied potential female workers to their kitchen sinks. To many Cuban husbands the notion of a working spouse was nothing less than anathema; but the government countered this with fusillades of propaganda about their revolutionary duty, a network of day care centers to manage the children, and a liberal policy of paid maternity leave for expectant wives.[51]

Many women, especially lower-class women, benefited from another government initiative that encouraged legal matrimonial ties. In just ten years the rate of marriages in Cuba increased 176 percent,[52] allowing many women a degree of security and regularity that had eluded them in the pattern of life of the old society.

The state, however, was concerned not only about the quantity of marriages but about their character as well, for this state was totalitarian—willing and anxious to penetrate the most private affairs of families, ready to influence even details such as who washed the dishes at night. Government authorities began by rewriting the old statutory "family code" that dated back to colonial times and implicitly recognized the male as lord and master. The new legislation went so far as to impose upon the Cuban husband the legal obligation to assist with the household chores.[53] Helping around the home may not seem an especially radical proposition by American standards, but within Cuban culture it is nothing less than revolutionary because Cuban men often feel emotionally threatened by such symbolic admissions of female equality.

Given the deep emotional roots of machismo, it is not surprising that even the most vigorous value reform has not broken this kind of exploitation but only loosened its grip. Behold, for example, the frenzied scene inside a Havana theater while a propaganda film attacking the practices of machismo was being shown. The movie depicted a university student explaining to an interviewer how he helped his wife with the housework. Incensed by this outrageous notion, almost the entire audience exploded into a chorus of jeers, insults, whistles, and condemnations. "Liar! Fag!" the men hollered as the documentary showed the couple washing dishes and serving coffee to each other. One or two women in their midst tried to applaud, but their weak cheers were drowned out by male hooting and laughter.[54] Little wonder that when Elizabeth Sutherland devoted a chapter of her book on Cuba to the condition of women in that country, there was both a ray of hope and a sigh of sadness in her title, "The Longest Revolution."[55]

Another painful form of social exploitation that divided Cubans in the prerevolutionary society was discrimination based upon racial characteristics. A strengthened totalitarian state forcefully attacked this value, just as it did machismo, and its partial success is understandably perceived by many Cubans as a humanistic improvement in the culture.

The easiest citadels of racism to conquer were those relatively few corners of Cuban society—a number of luxury hotels, restaurants, social and sporting clubs—that had previously excluded blacks under any circumstances. In general, however, Cuban racial discrimination, conforming to the broad Latin American pattern (see p. 22), was not so clearcut and rigid. Negroes faced difficult but not impassible barriers; they could overcome the liability of race and rise quite high in social prestige by doing very well in acquiring the other status determinants such as wealth, power, education, or a respected profession.

The Revolution improved upon this situation by making it easier for Cuban blacks to enhance their educational and occupational prospects, and indirectly their social prestige. The new rules of job advancement nullified the advantage of wealth and the disadvantage of race. The sole criterion was usefulness to the tasks of national reconstruction, a substantially more promising situation to Negroes at the bottom of society.

But racial discrimination still exists in revolutionary Cuba. The ruling elite has successfully confronted institutional and occupational racial bias, but the reflexive habit among the Cuban people of raising or lowering status on the basis of racial characteristics is something considerably more difficult to alter. Those who betray such attitudes are often quickly put on the defensive by the aggressive revolutionary egalitarianism that dominates the country. Nevertheless, this kind of discrimination persists in subtle forms—a casual phrase, an off-color joke, an uneasy glance at a white woman on the arm of a black man. The emotional depths from which this springs can be appreciated by regarding the undisputed suzerainty of Caucasian standards of beauty. Even among Cuban blacks, coarse, kinky hair, broad, flat noses, and thick Negroid lips are not favored. Elizabeth Sutherland found herself observing with disappointment that an issue of Cuba's leading magazine for women contained not a single dark face among the 48 pages of fashion photographs and drawings.[56] Government posters and billboards also reflect a rather mild form of discrimination by disproportionally featuring the all-Caucasian look to represent the typical Cuban.

In one further respect the position of the Negro in Cuba should be considered, and whether this is "bad" or "good" would be a subject of lively debate. Dark-skinned Cubans, like all Cubans, live within the womb of a totalitarian culture. Cuban blacks are eagerly embraced as first-class Cubans and are exhorted to be "proud" of being Cuban, but they are not allowed to be black or to be "proud" of being black. As in any totalitarian society, it is the elite that makes the basic decision on group identity and defines the nature of the collectivity within which the individual may locate a spiritual home. The elite has judged (not the blacks) that racial discrimination no longer exists, that "blackness" is irrelevant, and that a group identity based on race makes about as much sense as a group identity based on height. What does matter is nationality, and the elite has created a strong nationalist identity for the Cuban Revolution. And nothing is allowed to exist outside this Revolution. This Revolution is very jealous. Its passion is homogeneity and monolithic unity. The Revolution would never permit a black identity, nurtured by antagonism to whites, to divide the nation. It would be as intolerant of "Afros" and "cornrows" and all these hairstyles symbolize as it is to long hippie hairdos and all they symbolize (see pp. 244–46).[57]

It is obvious that exploitation is a vital subject to explore when discussing totalitarianism in Cuba. In the first place the existence of exploitation and the desire of a nationalistic elite to eliminate it were important reasons why the elite chose to build up a totalitarian state. The revolutionary leaders felt that Cubans were victims of a value system that encouraged them to exploit one another; and they also felt that a powerful totalitarian state would be necessary to reform those values effectively.

Our discussion of exploitation has also revealed one of the great advantages of totalitarianism. We have seen that the Cuban leaders have failed in their objective of raising the Cuban standard of living; and because of their mismanagement, they have brought much economic hardship upon the Cuban people. The Cuban revolutionaries, however, have been able to retain the support of most of their people in part by using their totalitarian power to modify the values that caused Cubans to take advantage of one another. By so doing they have raised the Cuban quality of life even while they have failed to raise the Cuban standard of living.

This does not mean, however, that the Cubans can continue their poor economic performance indefinitely. The reason for this is that the younger generations without memories of the old society will tend to take the Revolution's humanistic advances for granted and will, therefore, place more importance on increasing their standard of living. This, in fact, is the darkest cloud that hangs over the Cuban Revolution, for sooner or later the leaders will be in a position where they can significantly raise the quality of life in Cuba only by providing more economic benefits. The dilemma for the Cubans is that despite the fact that they have this problem looming on the horizon, they have institutionalized economic inefficiency in their country by modeling their economy after the Soviet system.

The implications of this for the future of totalitarianism in Cuba are also very ominous. Although it has always been true that a significant number of Cubans would flee their homeland if given the chance, the majority have over the years received enough material and nonmaterial benefits to support the revolutionary regime. This has allowed the Cuban elite to exert totalitarian control over the population without extensive use of coercion. If, however, continued economic failings should eventually cause the majority of Cubans to lose faith in the Revolution, then the elite will have to rely much more on the oppressive techniques of totalitarian control than they do at present.

CULTURAL DEPENDENCIA

Another feature of Cuban life that the Cuban Revolution resolved to change was cultural dependencia. Cultural dependencia offended nationalist sensibilities because it meant that Cubans preferred foreign culture to their own. This to the nationalists was simply another aggravating reminder of Cuban national weakness and inferiority. In order to overcome cultural dependencia, the nationalists had to overcome the imbalance of cultural exchange between Cuba and the primary centers of culture. They could not do this by forcing foreigners to accept their culture, so they set out to accomplish their task by purging foreign culture from their land. Today Cuba is remarkably free from the foreign words, expressions, fads, fashions, products, entertainment forms, and media gimmickry that characterize other Latin American countries.

In order to contrast the cultural situation in Cuba with that of an ordinary Latin American country like Mexico, we might follow the progress of an American reporter as he terminated his lengthy stay in Cuba and departed for Mexico. At Havana's José Martí International Airport he noticed only one sign, a small banner that read, "Yankee Bandits Out of Vietnam." As his plane approached the runway at Mexico City and the landscape grew larger and more distinct, a far different scene loomed large before his eyes:

A skyline dominated by massive billboards along the airport runway greeted us in Mexico: "Beefeater Gin for a Perfect Martini"; "Marlboro"; "Pepsi"; "Enjoy Coca-cola"; "Nescafe Symbol of Friendship"; "Holiday Inn Host to the World."[58]

Upon disembarking and proceeding to the center of the city, the journalist found himself ready for a bite to eat. Off to the side was a Colonel Sanders Kentucky Fried Chicken emporium with the "Finger Lickin' Good" slogan translated to read, "It will make your fingers good to lick." The reporter passed up the Colonel's kitchen and the chance to lick his fingers and instead, from a nearby streetcorner vendor, asked for a taco. The vendor sold only hot dogs.

The American visitor then continued his walk down one of Mexico's most glittering avenues, Paseo de la Reforma.

The paseo's store windows displayed Maxwell House instant coffee; Hershey bars; Aunt Jemima hotcakes; V-8 vegetable juice; Campbell's black fried beans; Gordon's distilled dry gin ("the soul of a good cocktail"); Ballentine's finest scotch whiskey; Toastmaster air conditioners; Hoover vacuum cleaners; Aqua Velva; Max Factor lipstick; and Del Monte canned tropical fruit—from the U.S.

Mexicans were lining up at a movie theator to see Jacqueline Susann's *The Love Machine*. The kiosk in front of the theater displayed Spanish editions of *Readers Digest; All You Ever Wanted To Know About Sex**But Were Afraid To Ask*, explained by Dr. David Reuben; and a selection of comic books, including Woody Woodpecker (translated as the Crazy Bird), Tarzan of the Apes, Mickey Mouse, Donald Duck, Batman, and Dennis the Menace.[59]

It might be noted that owing to the nature of cultural dependencia, totalitarian power is only of limited usefulness in redressing the imbalance of cultural exchange. The Cuban totalitarian leaders can vigorously purge from their society the kind of pervasive foreign cultural influence mentioned above. What they cannot do is use their power to force Cubans to create a national culture that will be imported by other countries around the world. Because of this, the need to overcome cultural dependencia cannot be regarded as potent a reason for the Cubans to adopt totalitarianism as the need to solve the problems of national poverty and exploitation.

POLITICAL DEPENDENCIA

Another vitally important objective of the Cuban Revolution was the elimination of political dependencia. Before the Revolution, Cubans had experienced considerable interference by Americans in their internal affairs. On several occasions Americans had intervened militarily, and on numerous other occasions Americans used the threat of force to influence the policy of Cuban political leaders.[60]

The interest of Americans in Cuba was primarily strategic. Americans felt they needed to keep a watchful eye on Cuba and sometimes to intervene because Cuban political life was violent and corrupt and the leaders who dominated Cuban politics were often too weak to maintain order or too irresponsible to pay back the loans they had contracted in Europe. This led to situations where European lives, property, and financial interests in Cuba were sometimes in jeopardy. European powers were known to rectify situations such as these by sending in troops; and the Americans feared that some European government might take advantage of this to set up a permanent military presence on this island. This, of course, would threaten U.S. security interests; and so the Americans took it upon themselves to act as a stern guardian toward Cuba in order to prevent any situation that might precipitate a European intervention.

The result of this was that the Cuban reaction against political dependencia was not only against Americans but also against themselves—that is to say, against Cuban national weakness. The Cuban nationalists were well aware that their impotent military could not extract a high enough price from the Americans to act as a deterrent. More importantly, the Cubans knew that they were too weak and disorganized as a people to create a stable political environment that would have made the American interventions unnecessary.

The most obvious way for Cubans to overcome political dependencia is to acquire enough strength as a people to prevent foreigners from intervening in their internal affairs. Ironically, a second way is to become so collectively strong that they can project their influence abroad. On the surface it may seem strange that one way the Cubans can overcome political dependencia is to become involved in the internal affairs of other peoples. We have seen, however, that political dependencia for the Cubans is not simply a political condition; it is also a psychological burden created by an awareness of their national weakness. To overcome this psychological burden, the Cubans need to prove to themselves that they are growing collectively strong, and the most dramatic way of demonstrating collective strength is by wielding power among other peoples.

Given the passion of the Cuban nationalists for collective strength, it was obviously advantageous for them to impose totalitarian control over their people. During the early decades of the twentieth century, Americans had been able to invade and occupy Carribean countries with only a handful of troops because the Latin Americans were not united in opposition to these invasions. Some Latin Americans opposed the interventions, some welcomed them, and the great majority were indifferent. The whole thrust of Cuban totalitarianism is to unite the people into a "monolithic ideological unity" where the followers think like the leaders, especially when it comes to foreign interventions. Because the Cuban people are now highly politicized and conditioned to the value of obedience, it is much more difficult for foreigners to impose their will upon Cuban leaders. Likewise, totalitarian control over the people makes it easier for the Cuban revolutionaries to project Cuban power abroad vigorously, especially when they feel the need to engage in costly military commitments.

Another asset Castro has effectively used in his drive for political independence has been his own remarkable political skills. Castro's first step toward political independence was to reduce American influence in Cuba; he acheived this by allying himself with the Soviets. Then Castro had to undergo a series of maneuvers to prevent the Soviets from having too much influence in Cuban affairs. There are those who say that Castro has simply switched dependency from one great power to another. Castro obviously has to work within the constraint of his need for Soviet aid; but as we shall see, the Cuban leader's foreign policy is virtually incomprehensible unless we understand his passion for maximum political independence from any great power.

As mentioned, Castro's first step in his effort to achieve political independence was to come to grips with the United States. Needless to say, Castro was highly suspicious of the "Colossus of the North" that for decades had wielded enormous influence in Cuba. The Americans, in turn, were highly suspicious of Castro who engaged in inflammatory leftist rhetoric and had known communists among his followers. It is possible that herculean statesmanship on both sides could have produced a new understanding between the two countries and prevented a rupture of relations. Neither side, however, was willing to go very far to accommodate the other. There is a weighty literature that explores the diplomatic give and take during these critical months, and well-researched and well-documented accounts have come to totally opposite conclusions on who deserves most of the blame for Castro's decision to ally himself with the Soviets. What is clear is that fairly early in the affair the Americans decided to organize an invasion, and that Fidel Castro knew of these plans by the summer of 1960, and by then any chance of the two parties reaching an accord had ended. Castro intensified his efforts to get the Soviets involved; and after the failure of the American-sponsored Bay of Pigs invasion, the Soviets willingly moved in to fill the vacuum.

Now the Cuban nationalists had a new dependency problem on their hands. They had kicked out the Americans but could only do so by opening the door to the Soviets. For a short period the Cuban leaders were apparently naive enough to believe that the Soviets were pouring in foreign aid out of a sense of international socialist duty.

Their eyes were soon opened by an especially sobering event called the Cuban Missile Crisis. In October of 1962 the Soviet Premier, retreating before an American ultimatum, agreed to withdraw Soviet missiles from Cuba. The entire negotiation took place between the Soviet Union and the United States. The Cubans were never consulted. It was obvious that the Soviets were preoccupied exclusively with their own interests and that the wishes of the Cuban leaders did not matter.

The Cuban Missile Crisis taught the Cuban revolutionaries two important lessons: first, that the Soviets had their own national interests which did not necessarily coincide with those of the Cubans; and secondly, that the Soviets were capable of foresaking fellow communists in the pursuit of those interests. The Cubans grew even more suspicious of the Soviet Union when, after the missile crisis, the Soviet leaders began a policy emphasizing cooperation over confrontation in their dealings with the United States. The Cubans, in fact, felt caught in a squeeze between the two superpowers. Their close association with the Soviet Union ensured the unremitting hostility of the United States while it failed to give them an absolute guarantee of their security. After 1965 this position was felt with increasing discomfort. American troops had invaded the Dominican Republic and were pouring into Vietnam, signaling a tougher, more bellicose anticommunist foreign policy. The Soviet response to these "imperialist aggressions" seemed unadmirably restrained. Indeed, the Soviet Union continued to push forward with its policy of eased relations with the United States. The Vietnam War, following quickly in the wake of the missile crisis, reinforced Cuban fear that the Soviet Union was capable of sacrificing its communist allies.

The Cubans communicated their displeasure with the Soviet Union by acts of defiance and displays of independence. Given the critical importance of Soviet aid in sustaining the economy, the extent to which they were able to demonstrate their sheer cussedness was remarkable. The Cubans refused to recognize the Soviet Union as the ultimate interpreter of Marxism-Leninism and even intimated that the "Cuban Way" was producing a superior species of socialism. On economic and foreign policy matters, they freely ignored the advice of their patrons and regularly aired their disagreements through public pronouncements such as the following:

> We proclaim it to the world: this Revolution will never be anybody's satellite or yes-man; it will never ask anybody's permission to maintain its own position either in matters of ideology or on domestic or foreign affairs.[61]

The Cubans periodically reinforced their thinly disguised verbal taunts with calculated diplomatic rebuffs. To an important meeting of communist parties in Bucharest at which the Soviets hoped to line up support against Peking, the Cubans declined to send a representative. To the epic fiftieth anniversary celebration of the Russian Revolution, the Cubans contributed only a low-level official. At the United Nations they roundly denounced the Nuclear Non-Proliferation Treaty and became the only non-Asian communist country to refuse to sign the Soviet-American accord. At home the Cuban leadership purged, arrested, and sentenced to jail important members of the pro-Soviet faction of the Cuban Communist Party.[62]

Perhaps the most aggravating point of contention between Castro and the Soviets was over the issue of continentalism. Continentalism is actually an extension of Cuban nationalism. It refers to the frustrated dream of Latin American nationalists, dating from Bolivar, to unify the entire continent and build upon this unity one of the great nations of the world. Latin American continentalism resembles the character of nationalism prevalent among the German people before the unification of their country in the nineteenth century. German nationalists longed for political unity because only with this reform could they collectively stand as tall as the French and British peoples. Latin American nationalists often reveal a similar ambition—that Latin Americans would one day form themselves into a huge continental union that would possess the power and strength to secure for their people a respected place in the world.

Continentalism was a logical policy for Castro to pursue at this time because he felt that Moscow's commitment was unreliable and therefore he needed to find more dependable allies. Castro could think of no group of people more dependable than Latin American revolutionaries who were inspired by the same spirit of reactive nationalism as he and who were rebelling against the governments of other Latin American countries. Castro actively supported guerrilla movements all over Latin America with the hope not only of finding allies but of encouraging his allies to come together and form a continental union.

Castro's efforts to foment revolution in other Latin American countries placed the Soviets in an awkward predicament. The Soviets were skeptical of the possibilities of armed revolution in Latin America and preferred to extend their influence in Latin America by increasing diplomatic and commercial relations with existing governments. But since they were supporting the Cubans, who were conspiring to overthrow these very regimes, in effect one tentacle of Soviet foreign policy was struggling against the other. Castro was enraged at the Soviet Union's eagerness to collaborate with Latin American "reactionaries" and publicly excoriated their policy. At a major international conference he challenged, "if internationalism exists, if solidarity is a word worthy of respect, the least that we can expect of a state in the socialist camp is that it refrain from giving any financial or technical aid to these regimes."[63]

With the advantage of hindsight, we can now observe that an important turning point in Cuban-Soviet relations took place in the distant forests of Bolivia. After witnessing failure after failure of guerrilla uprisings within Latin American countries, the Cubans sent their best man, bearing their highest hopes, into the Bolivian jungles. Yet even a well-equipped, well-trained guerrilla band led by the legendary Che Guevara was easily wiped out by Bolivian rangers. The whole concept of guerrilla warfare, as outlined by Guevara and Régis Debray, was thrown into doubt. Cuba, it appeared, could not train and assist handfuls of guerrilla warriors and expect these to overthrow the established governments on the mainland. Unable to influence events by the device of armed insurrection, there was no reason why the discredited strategy should any longer be a contentious issue between Cuba and the Soviet Union.

While these difficult lessons were slowly settling upon the reluctant Cubans, the Soviets were turning the economic screws—not drastically, but enough to cause some sharp pain and much anxiety over the future. The combination of defeats abroad and undependable Soviet assistance convinced Castro that the most viable route to political independence was for the Cubans to refocus their attention back home and concentrate on quickly building up the Cuban economy. The Cubans' idea was that a strong economy would reduce their dependency on Soviet aid and this, in turn, would reduce the leverage that the Soviets had over them. It was at this time that Castro announced the Great Revolutionary Offensive (see p. 256) in which Cubans were to make a heroic, all-out effort to modernize the Cuban economy rapidly. In a major speech launching the drive, Castro explained the political reasons behind the massive campaign:

> Great is the task that faces us! A people that is not willing to make the effort has no right even to utter the word "independence," no right even to utter the word "sovereignty"! Let us struggle bravely, among other reasons, to minimize our dependence on everything from abroad. Let us fight as hard as possible, because we have known the bitterness of having to depend to a considerable extent on what we can get from abroad and have seen how this can be turned into a weapon, how, at the very least, there is a temptation to use it against our country. Let us fight for the greatest independence possible, whatever the price![64]

In order to achieve the fast economic growth that he hoped for, Castro knew that he needed Soviet aid; and to secure this aid, he was willing to placate the Soviet Union with a more pro-Soviet foreign policy. This strategy became a long-term one after the failure of the Great Revolutionary Offensive. Castro at this point realized that Cuban modernization would take years of effort, and for this he needed years of reliable economic backing from the Soviet Union. This brings us to the present stage of Cuban-Soviet relations. Whatever disharmony may exist between them and the Soviets, the Cubans feel obliged to mute their disagreements and trumpet their "solidarity" with their Soviet benefactors.

With regard to the new Soviet-Cuban relationship, however, the more things change, the more they remain the same. Despite Castro's "solidarity" and close cooperation with the Soviet Union, nationalism and continentalism are as alive as ever in Cuba. Castro, in fact, has told his Cubans that Latin American unification is not simply a matter of fulfilling hallowed tradition but rather has become a "vital necessity" in political and economic terms for the contemporary Latin American states. The Castroite vision of the world of tomorrow is a "world of great human and economic communities," and without integration into one of these, "no small country will have even the slightest chance of advancing." According to Castro, the place of Cuba in this world is clear: "We think that one day we will be politically and economically integrated with the rest of the people of Latin America."[65]

When Castro talks about his vision of the future, it cannot be said that the Soviet Union holds an especially vaunted position. Castro the navigator has made it clear that he has put his craft into a Soviet harbor only for temporary refuge, and he impatiently awaits favorable winds that will take him back to the continent where he really belongs. Castro has carried out this maneuver because integration, according to the navigator, "will take time. We can't make plans based on an integration that could take 10, 15, 20, 25, 30 years—this last for the most pessimistic. Meanwhile, what do we, a small country surrounded by capitalists and blockaded by the Yankee imperialists, do? We integrate ourselves economically with the socialist çamp!" However the Cuban Odysseus does promise his crew, "When the hour of revolution arrives in the rest of Latin America, we will integrate ourselves with the rest of Latin America."[66] Castro leaves no doubt that only when his vessel leaves its Soviet berth and sails for home will the fundamental nationalist idealism vitalizing the Cuban Revolution achieve its ultimate fulfillment.

Another way Cubans have of demonstrating their national strength both to themselves and to other peoples is to project their power abroad. The Cubans have chosen to do this by selecting themselves as leaders in the Third World movement and by becoming involved in the affairs of Third World countries. The most common method the Cubans have used to assert their leadership in the Third World has been to send an array of advisory missions to an astonishingly large number of underdeveloped countries. Cubans technical missions, at times with personnel numbering in the hundreds, have labored in Third

World countries like Vietnam, Laos, Congo-Brazzaville, Guyana, and Jamaica. In Guinea, Cuban instructors have established a "Marxist" center for African seekers of ideological enlightenment. Cuban military advisers have been active in Algeria, Libya, South Yemen, Guinea, Congo, Tanzania, Equatorial Guinea, Guinea Bissau, Sierra Leone, Mozambique, and Madagascar as well as other "emerging" nations. In the October War of 1973, 500 Cuban tank experts fought alongside Syrian troops. After 1975 Cuban involvement overseas reached the massive-intervention level. In a coup that amazed Western foreign ministries, 20,000 Cuban troops slipped across the Atlantic, took sides in the Angolan civil war, brought a "Marxist" faction into power, and opened the door to waves of Cuban medical, agricultural, industrial, and education specialists in charge of keeping the Angolan economy together.[67] A short time later thousands more Cuban troops joined Ethiopia in a territorial dispute with Somalia and helped push the Somalis back across their own borders.

Perhaps the most dramatic way that the Cuban nationalists have magnified their country's influence abroad has been to take advantage of their relationship with the Soviet Union, play upon the more aggressive side of Soviet great power ambition, and elicit Soviet help in their favorite foreign policy endeavors. This was almost certainly the case in Angola, where the Cubans decided independently of the USSR to send in large numbers of combat troops and soon afterward convinced the Soviets to support them*.[68] The Cubans were able to do this even though Angola was a low-priority area for the Soviets and the project jeopardized one of their high-priority diplomatic efforts—eased relations with the United States.

The avowed reason for Cubans to become so involved in the Third World is that they are dedicated to the international socialist cause. The real reason, however, is that the Cuban radical nationalists wish to announce to the world that Cuba is no longer a weak and impotent nation-state. It is ironic that Castro has sent troops to the same part of the world as Mussolini did, for the prize sought by both dictators is esentially the same. Mussolini wished to demonstrate that Italy for the first time since the Renaissance had arrived as a world power; and Castro wishes to demonstrate that Cuba, which has never been an important nation-state, is now a significant force in international affairs.

---

*Because Castro was the one who took the initiative in Angola, it is obvious that the notion that the Cuban army is acting as a proxy fighting force for the Soviet Union is not very useful. The Soviets were responsible for persuading Castro to send his troops to Ethiopia; but Castro's refusal to use his army to help the Ethiopians crush the Eritrean rebellion shows that it is Castro, not the Soviets, who makes the decisions on how the Cuban army is used.[69]

The place where Castro would really like to project Cuban power is, of course, Latin America. Victories in Africa afford Castro international prestige, but they do not allow him to fulfill his nationalist-continentalist ambitions. Africa, however, is a useful testing ground for a new strategy that Castro has obviously had much success with. During the 1960s Castro relied mainly upon guerrilla warfare to influence events in Latin America, and that policy not only failed but failed miserably. In Angola Castro has experimented with a new tactic and has learned that a substantial contingent of Cuban troops can turn the tide of battle in a civil war. Castro will undoubtedly be keeping his eye out for similar situations in Latin America.* For as we have seen, Fidel Castro regards Latin Americans as his people and is convinced that Latin American integration is his brightest hope for belonging to a great national community that is free from political dependency on any large power.

If we were to sum up the results of the Cuban struggle for political independence, we can see that in some respects the Cubans have done well while in others they have not. One of the most important points to be made about this struggle is that the Cubans have been helped considerably by their totalitarian control over the population. Because of this control, Castro is capable of uniting the entire people behind him in opposition to any foreign intervention. This makes it considerably more difficult for the Americans to invade Cuba, for the price they would have to pay to subdue the island would be much higher than was the case in prerevolutionary times. Castro's totalitarian control also makes it more difficult for the Soviets to influence events in Cuba (as they have done in other Third World countries) by playing one rival political faction against the other. In Cuba there is only one faction to play with. The Soviet leaders have little respect for anything except power, and there can be no doubt that they respect the power Fidel Castro has over his people.

Another advantage that totalitarian power has given Castro is that the Cuban people will support him in costly foreign policy endeavors. Castro feels that a dramatic display of military prowess abroad will have a positive effect on his people, who have long thought of themselves

---

*The American invasion of Grenada sent a clear signal to the Cubans that the United States might be willing to use force to oppose Cuban military intervention in El Salvador. Castro, however, is aware that the American willingness to use armed force varies from administration to administration. The Cubans have admitted that they sent troops to Angola only after they had decided that the Americans, who were still suffering from a post-Vietnam disillusionment with military interventions, would not do the same.

as collectively weak. Normally peoples are willing to support their leaders in foreign policy adventures so long as the sacrifices they have to make are not too great. Because of his totalitarian grip on the people, Castro has been able to carry out protracted warfare in Africa that has been costly both in terms of lives and money. Any other government in Latin America that had become bogged down in a similar quagmire would have been toppled from power long ago.

In addition to his totalitarian power, Castro has also used his consummate diplomatic skills to help him overcome political dependencia. By a series of deft maneuvers Castro was able to take his country out of the American sphere of influence and realign it with the Soviet Union. Once he had committed the Soviet Union to protect his Revolution from the United States, he could then use simple geopolitical realities to protect his country from the Soviet Union. Cuba has a big advantage over East European countries like Poland and Czechoslovakia in that it cannot easily be invaded and reduced to the status of a hapless satellite, for not only is Cuba thousands of miles away from the Soviet Union, but it is also situated in the middle of the Caribbean, which the Americans consider for defense purposes their own private lake.

Castro has also increased his freedom of action from the Soviet Union by putting himself in a position where the relationship is not completely one-sided and the Soviet Union needs him just as he needs the Soviet Union. Castro's aid to the Soviet Union is almost entirely ideological and political. Castro has acquired enormous prestige in the Third World because of his vigorous stand against the West and he has used this to help the Soviet Union. Castro has made the argument to Third World nationalists that they can adhere to their policy of nonalignment and yet at the same time regard the Soviet Union as their "natural ally." Castro has also attacked the Chinese "three worlds" theory which states that Soviet "hegemonism" is as much a threat to the Third World as Western imperialism. The battle that the Soviets are waging in the Third World is largely one of ideas; and because Castro is accepted as a prominent spokesman for the Nonaligned Movement, he is the Soviet Union's most effective ally for voicing their point of view. Indeed, under these circumstances it is advantageous for the Soviet Union not to make Cuba a subservient client state like Poland, for then Castro would lose his influence as a Third World leader.

Despite the successes the Cuban revolutionaries have experienced in their fight for political independence, they have some long-term problems that will be difficult to overcome. These problems stem mainly from the poor performance of the Cuban economy. Up to the present Castro has done very well at getting substantial economic aid from the Soviets while holding Soviet influence in Cuba's internal affairs to a minimum. If, however, the Cuban leaders do not succeed in developing the economy and become permanently dependent on a large Soviet subsidy, they may in the future find it much more difficult to keep the Soviets at bay. This danger will undoubtedly grow more acute once Fidel Castro disappears from the scene and Cubans can no longer use his international prestige and political genius as resources. In the long run the only effective guarantee for Cuba's political independence is for the country to become economically strong. The problem for the Cubans is that waste and inefficiency are so firmly institutionalized that the propects for the Cuban economy are not very bright.

TOTALITARIANISM AND THE RADICAL NATIONALIST REVOLT

If the Cuban Revolution were to be reduced to its essence, it would best be described as a reaction by radical Cuban nationalists against national weakness. In more specific terms it was a revolt against two manifestations of that weakness—dependencia and exploitation. In order to help them in their revolutionary struggle, the Cuban nationalists chose a form of government that we have described as totalitarian. The Cubans chose to build up a totalitarian state because they felt that only by reforming the values of the people could they achieve their aims and that only with totalitarian control over the population could they bring about value reform.

It is important to recognize that the origins of totalitarianism in Cuba can be traced to a combination of specific social conditions, namely, Cuban national weakness and the negative national identity Cuban nationalists suffered as a result of that weakness. Cuban totalitarianism, in other words, sprang from seeds indigenous to the island and has flourished on a soil well suited to its growth. Western observers can make no greater error than to assume that totalitarianism in Cuba is mainly due to the scheming of a perverse minority and is somehow "alien" to the Cuban or Latin American spirit.

Cuban totalitarianism can also be regarded as a logical, understandable development within a much broader continental nationalist tradition, for totalitarian value reform in Cuba is a direct descendant of a considerably older Latin American nationalist ambition that yearned to raise the Latin American countries to the level of the European by rendering the Latin American masses less like Iberians and Indians and more like the most advanced Europeans. The Cuban "Battle against the Past" is but a contemporary expression of the hope of nineteenth-century nationalists who, in the language of the day, sought to "shake the people from their habits of lethargy," their "gross, indolent customs," their "immorality," by "regenerating" the masses, by "moralizing," by "civilizing," by "Europeanizing" the masses (see pp. 152–54).

Times have changed, however, and similarities in aspiration do not mean similarities in strategy. Many earlier Latin American nationalists thought of solving their countries' "backwardness" by "whitening" the population, by drowning out the "past" (the Iberian and Indian heritage) with waves of European immigration. This idea once swayed statesmen, academics, editors, and even poets in Latin America who used to talk extravagantly about the "blond European youth" toiling in the countryside and to speak of them as "heroes of labor."[70] Contemporary Cuban nationalists, in contrast, employ a modernization strategy that entails taking the dark-skinned multitudes native to their own land and, through the techniques of totalitarian control, reshaping them into authentically Cuban "heroes of labor."

The nationalist dream of a country peopled by labor heroes has a long history in Latin America, and totalitarianism is the means that the Cuban Latin Americans have chosen to try to translate their vision into a concrete national reality.

8

THE TOTALITARIAN
IMPULSE IN LATIN AMERICA

One of the most important lessons we can learn from the Cuban Revolution is that because the social and psychological conditions that exist in Cuba can also to one extent or another be found in other Latin American countries, then it is probable that some nationalists in these countries will, like the Cubans, aspire to build up a totalitarian state in order to help them solve their social problems. The best way to reveal the presence of totalitarian ambition or totalitarian tendencies in Latin American nationalists is to examine the ideological movements in which they become involved. Ideological labels are in themselves not reliable indicators of whether a group of nationalists harbor totalitarian ambition. As we shall see in this chapter, those who overtly espouse democracy may show real potential for developing into totalitarians while those who espouse Marxism-Leninism may not. What we need to do is to go beyond superficial labeling and examine the fundamental character of a nationalist movement in order to see if it has some of the same characteristics as Italian Fascism or Cuban Marxism-Leninism.

THE TOTALITARIAN IMPULSE: LATIN AMERICAN FASCISM

As a start to this discussion, it would be useful to focus our attention on two political movements that have frequently been described as "fascist." The first of these is Brazilian Integralism, which flashed through the Brazilian sky like a brilliant comet during the 1930s, and the second is Argentinean Peronism, which dominated political life in Argentina for ten years after the Second World War and for three years during the 1970s. The Integralist movement never succeeded in its bid for power, and the Peronist movement lacked the quality of leadership needed to achieve its ends; but both produced enough polemical and ideological writing to reveal essentially the same radical nationalism and ambition for totalitarian social control that are so evident in revolutionary Cuba. Although the Integralist and Peronist parties described themselves as anticommunist and, as we have seen, were commonly identified as fascist, both the spirit and the content of their ideological statements are very compatible with the kind of society that is actually being realized in Marxist-Leninist Cuba.

The most obvious point of comparison between Cuban Marxism-Leninism and the two Latin American fascisms is their touchy, combative, highly emotional nationalisms. Plinio Salgado, leader of the Integralists, and Juan Perón, leader of the Peronists, were easily a match for Fidel Castro when they let their nationalism roar. As in Marxist Cuba, the Integralist and Peronist nationalisms were reactive in nature: they literally seethed with antiforeign sentiment, and the character of their ideals was deeply influenced by the social problems of cultural, economic, and political dependencia.

To emphasize their freedom from cultural dependencia, both movements insisted upon their "intellectual independence" from foreign ideas and inspiration. Perón boasted that to attain Argentinean objectives, "we don't need to depend upon foreign theories or methods . . . it is enough for us to be Argentineans and nothing but Argentineans."[1] As if to prove his point, Perón promulgated legislation that was specifically designed to curb the prevalence of foreign cultural norms (see p. 187). Salgado, for his part, regularly flaunted the Integralist doctrine as "original, genuinely Brazilian, with its own philosophy, a clear wisdom distinguishable from the confusion of the contemporary world."[2] Although Salgado never came to power, he promised that if he did he would "suffocate cosmopolitanism, snobbism, imitations of foreign customs" and, in general, the Brazilian culture of imitation that so rankled his nationalist soul.[3]

The Peronist and Integralist ideologies were held aloft by still another essential pillar called economic independence. Both movements employed a style of rhetoric that could be readily mistaken for one of Castro's harangues. In their respective views, Argentina and Brazil were "economic colonies," tributaries of imperialist exploitation," "enslaved" by "international monopolists" and by a domestic "semi-feudal oligarchy" that was "mortgaging the wealth of the country to foreign greed."[4] The ever-valiant Juan Perón proclaimed himself "ready to die, should it be necessary to obtain our economic independence" and pledged to "cut off my hands" before ever reaching out for a foreign loan.[5]

The subject of political independence was aired with oratory no less spirited. Peronist and Integralist leaders demonstrated the same keen sensitivity as have the Cuban revolutionaries over the prospect of foreign political influence compromising their national sovereignty. Repeatedly they launched slashing verbal attacks on what they called the insatiable "imperialist" appetites of the great powers. The Peronists carefully used the phrase "Third Position", which was meant to warn the superpowers that the Argentineans intended to steer a "third" course in international politics "between capitalism and communism." In later years Perón claimed that his term "Third Position" expressed the same passion for political independence that the more famous phrase "Third World" does for underdeveloped peoples today.[6] Salgado never invented a catchword to embody this feeling but was just as adept at revealing its character and depth:

> Brazilians! We Integralists do not have to strive to satisfy foreigners! We don't allow here orders from abroad, neither from Stalin, Hitler, Mussolini, nor Trotsky. We are independent. We are dignified. We are self-reliant. We are free.[7]

While political, economic, and cultural independence were fairly broad nationalist objectives, they might all be summed up in one much larger. Both the Integralists and Peronists frequently referred to this as *grandeza*—national "greatness" or "grandeur." The deep thirst of these revolutionaries for grandeza is not easily appreciated by those without parched throats from more self-confident cultures. The winning, grandeza would have meant victory over the national inferiority complex that pained the nationalist heart and that both Salgado and Perón singled out as an enemy to destroy.[8] It would have meant an end to the days when their weak, divided, and unproductive peoples were but an "appendage of mediocre importance to the history of Civilization."[9] It would have meant national self-respect, the realization of a positive national identity. With reason then, Perón never tired of stressing, "Our people, we catagorically affirm, are filled with a legitimate longing for greatness."[10] Likewise Plinio Salgado promised that he would never rest until Brazil was "the first nation of the world."[11]

Since the possibility of grandeza would have been far greater with continental integration, Integralism and Peronism had their respective continentalist visions. We have seen that when Argentina was at its strongest, Perón thought of achieving this by overshadowing other Latin American nations (see pp. 196–99). In his declining years, as his country declined with him, he grew more realistic and called for Latin American political unity on the basis of equality rather than hegemony.[12] Salgado, conscious of Brazil's weakness as well as its potential, indicated that his mind was open to either way of achieving the "dream of Bolivar."[13]

The Integralists and Peronists declared their intention of pursuing national "greatness" by means strikingly similar to those chosen by the Cuban Communists. Their writings and speeches suggested essentially the same kind of "revolution" the Cubans have found necessary to implement—a radical transformation of the values and customs of the people. Very much in Latin American tradition, these Brazilian and Argentinean revolutionaries spoke with eloquence and passion of a "national rebirth," a "national resurgence," a "restoration of the spirit," a "rejuvenation of the Nationality," a "spiritual renovation."[14] Rebelling against the decrepitude of the old society, they dedicated their "renovating crusade" to the formation of a "New Society," a "New Civilization," a "New Fatherland," the basis of which would have been "New Men."[15]

Again exhibiting a style that has long been common among Latin Americans, missionaries from both political causes interpreted the need for a change in values as a need for a change in morality. Juan Perón pledged his energies to the "moral betterment" (mejoramiento moral) of the masses and promised his revolution would bring about the "moral recuperation of the Argentinean people."[16] To Perón the connection between this and national "greatness" was only too evident. It was his reading of history that nations drew their collective vigor from the collective morality of their populations. "The defects of societies," Perón once lectured, "are often not due to the lack of capacity of their rulers but to the absence of morality among men. . . . The great peoples of world history have always been the most virtuous. . . . We understand that the health of the nation depends upon strengthening materially and morally the people that make up our country."[17]

Integralist leaders repeated this same basic lesson to their own following. Their explicit command, "Make a revolution in yourselves first," carried with it the implicit message that Brazilians caught in old value patterns sustained the old society and only by becoming "New Men" could the "New Society" come into being.[18] Again and again revolutionary theoreticians stressed the idea that the most crucial revolutionary battles that Integralists had to fight were not with external enemies but with themselves:

> The Integralist Revolution is principally directed at ourselves. It is a movement of liberation. Each one liberates himself from himself. It is a movement of humanity. Each one strives to recognize and correct himself. It is a movement of patriotism. Each one seeks to live a life that will enhance social harmony and national happiness. . . . If this Integralist movement hopes to save our Brazil, if it hopes to make a Great Nation, the objective of the supreme ambition of man, make sure, Integralists, that we recognize the fundamental causes of the evils that humiliate our Fatherland and struggle to fight them, not only those that we see around us, but much more importantly, those that exist within us.[19]

As is the case in revolutionary Cuba, the virtues singled out for special emphasis by the Integralist and Peronist Revolutions were those best suited to the needs of a modernization movement. To begin with, there were the values that spurred greater national production. The Integralists vowed to transform every Brazilian worker into a "hero of the new Fatherland."[20] The Peronists exhorted, "Remain faithful to the watchword of the movement: Produce! Produce! Produce!"[21] Daily the Peronist press carried stories of courageous mechanics who toiled for 106 consecutive hours, valiant brewery workers who labored for 221 hours, intrepid metal workers who labored for 224 hours; and faithfully reported along with such feats of heroism were telegrams of congratulations from Juan and Eva Perón.[22]

As in Cuba, however, the most respected movement virtues were those which contributed to the spirit of national solidarity—a unified, disciplined, military-style collective effort on the part of every member of society. Ideologists of both camps railed against factious political sects, contentious economic interests, and the "absurd," "excessive" individualismo of their peoples.[23] They viewed their respective societies as confused collections of individuals and interest groups, a lamentable situation that rendered impossible a unified drive toward "greatness." Moved by disgust with national divisiveness and by a vision of national unity, revolutionary propagandists eulogized virtues that fostered collective cohesiveness and strength—virtues that were characterized by unmistakable martial hues. Recoiling from their perceptions of social indiscipline, they regarded discipline as the "soul" of their "renovating" movements. To ensure discipline, they felt no moral imperative more vital than unquestioning loyalty and obedience to the political hierarchy.[24] For example, every Integralist "soldier of the Fatherland" was required to make a sacred oath of obedience to this "commander-in-chief" Plinio Salgado. One Integralist leader explained that by this solemn act, "we commit ourselves to sacrifice personal interests, ambitions, and inclinations for the success of a great cause."[25]

The revolutionary program of value reform advocated by the Integralist and Peronist leaders clearly revealed their elitist sentiments. When the masses are felt to be deficient in essential values, those individuals who long to "regenerate" the morals of the multitudes can scarcely help but regard themselves as beings of a special order. Salgado called these chosen ones "pioneers, apostles, evangelists, revolutionaries," who possessed no less a mission than the resurrection of the nation.[26] Perón described himself as selected by a "decree of destiny" to lead Argentineans from the wilderness. His wife Eva compared his ascent to power with the coming of Christ and wrote in the preface of her book, " Perón was and is a gigantic condor that flies high and sure among the summits and near to God."[27] The dramatic heights of the precipices upon which these revolutinary elitists were capable of perching themselves is suggested by the following passage from the memoirs of Juan Perón:

> The country was alone. It was off its course, unguided and without a compass. All had been handed to foreigners. The people, lacking justice, were oppressed and incapable. Foreign countries and international forces submitted them to a dominion not far removed from colonial oppression.
>
> I realized that it could all be remedied.
>
> Little by little it dawned on me that it was I who could remedy it.
>
> From that moment my country's problem came to be my own problem.
>
> I solved it by deciding on the revolution.
>
> This decision was "my aid to destiny."[28]

The presumption of these elitists was that they, placed by destiny upon such majestic peaks, could better discern realities than the masses huddled in the valleys below. Not only did they regard themselves as men gifted with insight but they also saw themselves as revolutionaries burdened with duty. It was this mission that prompted the Peronist leaders to describe their state as a "great molder of character" dedicated to "molding" the "moral progress" of the people.[29] A similar spirit stirred the Integralist elite who advocated a similar revolutionary task, "to transmit to the people a clear concept of the truth," to "form a new consciousness in the mass," to produce a "disciplined people conscious of its destiny."[30]

A distinguishing feature of the plans of both groups of revolutionaries to turn factious conglomerations into disciplined communities was the awareness that the project required far more cohesive energy than could be generated by sweet reason alone. Both movements, to be sure, developed abstract ideological justifications for their actions designed to persuade the minds of thoughtful men. But the leaders understood that if their doctrines were to inspire widespread, passionate commitment, they had not merely to convince human intellects but to serve human emotional needs as well. The revolutionary elitists observed with keen interest that side of men that discovers happiness in becoming dedicated to a cause higher than themselves, and they recognized that this capacity of human beings for sacrifice could be tapped as readily by a political crusade as by a religious revival. The Integralists, therefore, regarded *Integralismo* as not just a "doctrine" but a "lofty ideal, an absolute faith."[31] Likewise the Peronists insisted that *Peronismo* without "faith" was not *Peronismo*.[32] Peronist party cadres were instructed to think of themselves as not so much "teachers" but "preachers." To these cadres Perón lectured, "Doctrine is not just taught but inculcated. It is not directed only at the understanding of men but at their souls. It is not sufficient to understand doctrine; it is necessary to understand it and feel it."[33] Followers who "felt" the doctrine were those who derived emotional gratification from participation in the movement; converts with such emotional needs were highly prized by the revolutionary elites because it was from these that anything could be asked.

Inducing these hopes of exploiting the potential of the masses for belief in secular faiths was the familiar nationalist hunger for "unity of will." Salgado openly dreamed of an "extraordinary unity of thought and emotion" among Brazilians, a "majestic unanimity," a "prodigious communion that realizes the stupendous miracle of a single national aspiration."[34] The Peronists craved the same reward—a vast national homogeneity of revolutionary beliefs and heightened emotional feelings. For them the idea of a "sacred union of all Argentineans" meant that Argentineans would be more than citizens sharing common territory and culture but "coreligionists" sharing a "collective" or "Peronist soul."[35] In more concrete terms the "sacred union" meant that "each man in the mass [would] think and feel within the doctrine with the same intensity as each one of his leaders."[36] The fulfillment of this essentially totalitarian ambition would have resulted, of course, in enormous collective strength—a great human mass united in thought, emotion, and aspiration with its directing elite. It would have meant the realization of Perón's "basic objective," "national unity," and possibly the realization of his "great ambition," the "aggrandizement of the Argentine nation."[37]

Just as similarities suggest an essential compatibility between Peronist and Integralist Fascism and Cuban Marxist-Leninism, this notion may also be appreciated by examining their supposed differences. Both Integralism and Peronism paraded anticommunist banners, so these differences should logically have been substantial. Several of the objections to communism, however, were based on the assumption that communists adhered to certain basic tenets of classical Marxism; and for the Cuban Communists, this assumption does not hold.

We have seen how the revisions of Marx's works intensified with the Revolution in Russia and how since then so-called "Marxist revolutionaries" in backward lands continued to alter, invert, or simply ignore the teachings of Marx to the point where there are few "Marxists" left among them. Latin Americans were no exception to this trend to transform Marxism from social theory to revolutionary symbol. José Carlos Mariátegui, most frequently cited as the continent's most eminent "Marxist" thinker, admitted that the "true disciples" of Marx were "revolutionaries stained with heresy"; that is to say, the "true" followers were the followers who refused to follow.[38] As part of this tradition, Fidel Castro's Marxism has been rendered even more flexible by the fact that the Cuban leader has apparently little knowledge of the original theoretical system. Unlike the manuscripts of Lenin and Mussolini, Castro's writings and speeches reveal little familiarity with the basic Marxist texts. In fact, Castro's brother Raúl confessed to Herbert Mathews that when he and Fidel plowed into the dense Germanic prose and abstruse reasonings of *Das Capital*, neither one of them lasted more than three chapters.[39] This has afforded Castro the freedom to make of "communism" whatever he wants to, and he has chosen to identify a "communist revolution" with the revolution he holds next to his heart.[40] But this revolution is nationalist, productionist, elitist, and totalitarian—the kind of revolution best articulated and justified by the Italian Fascist ideology.

Because Cuban-Marxist-Leninism shares with Integralism and Peronism a comparable perspective on revolution, Cuban Marxism is not vulnerable to the anti-communist arguments of the two Latin American fascisms. Salgado, for example, frequently criticized Marxist theory for its reductionist "materialism," for describing the "consciousness," the ideas and ideals of men, as mere by-products of economic forces; and because of this, he charged communists with neglecting the "spiritual" side of human nature and ignoring the role of elitist willpower in shaping human history.[41] The Cubans, however, conceive of their revolution as a project of determined elites infusing the masses with "consciousness" *(conciencia)* and the masses, in turn, marching heroically together in order to build a new stage of economic development. Far from overlooking the spiritual needs and potential of men, the Cuban state recognizes the obligation of cultivating in the masses the ideals of nationalism and public virtue *(conciencia communista)*. Indeed, the inculcation of conciencia in the masses is so similar to Integralist ideas that the Cubans at times refer to their "New Man," their well-rounded finished product of the future society, as the "Integral Man."

Integralists and Peronists criticized communism even more stridently for the fact that communist ideals seemed to run directly counter to nationalist ideals. To these Latin American fascists, adherents of communism appeared to be both culturally and politically dependent; that is to say, they appeared to rely on a "foreign" ideology and to follow the advice, and even the orders, of a foreign power. However the Cuban "Communists" have amply demonstrated a passion for national independence by deliberately mapping out an allegedly unique, original "Cuban Road" to socialism and by carefully striking a balance in their relationship with the Soviet Union between the maximum political independence and the maximum economic assistance.

Integralists and Peronists reserved, perhaps, their most energetic anticommunist rhetoric for the communist idea of class warfare. Both parties maintained that little good would result if the "bourgeois" class ruling in its own self-interest were replaced by a "proletariat" class ruling in its own interest. Instead they advocated a revolution that would unite and not divide the country and a government that would rule in the interest of the whole nation and not of any particular group. In place of class conflict they proposed class "collaboration" in order to promote what they termed the "harmony" or "equilibrium" of all conflicting social claims.[42]

The class collaboration idea in Marxist Cuba has an interesting history because it even appeared in the pre-Marxist mountain manifestos when the rebels endorsed "solidarity and harmony" rather than warfare and liquidation among classes.[43] Did the Cubans abandon this ideal after their conversion to "communism"? Did the class of "proletarians" within this "communist" revolution fare as they should have according to the Marxists' scripts?

With their rise to power the Cuban leadership found itself confronted by a social situation far different from the one that incited Marx to take up his revolutionary advocation. To begin with, the group of laborers that most closely resembled Marx's definition of "proletariat," the unionized urban workers, were not a majority but a minority in Cuba. Secondly, these Cuban wage earners were not suffering from an unjust distribution of wealth; their slice of the national income was greater in only three developed Western countries, Great Britain, the United States, and Canada.[44] The Cuban proletariat was, in fact so well equipped with parasitic privileges mandated by previous populist regimes, that as a class they constituted not the exploited but the exploiters (see pp. 80–84). Therefore, when the revolutionary leaders assumed their new commands, the demands of a reasonable social justice forced them to *reduce* the proletariat's share of wealth and power mainly by depriving them of their right to strike, a weapon they had used irresponsibly, selfishly, and with devastating effectiveness. It was by subduing the proletariat, then, that those who called themselves "champions of the proletariat" fulfilled their original nationalist pledge of "solidarity and harmony" among the classes.

The nationalist objective of "class collaboration" did not mean to Salgado and Perón, anymore than it does to Castro, that their regimes could not be socialistic and favor the disadvantaged classes. The Integralists and Peronists, in fact, argued that the spirit of national unity and national cooperation could not grow in a climate poisoned by class antagonism, and that socialism was not only compatible with nationalist goals but absolutely essential to them. Their stormy meetings and demonstrations blazed with inflammatory, have-not, radical socialist rhetoric: they attacked the "domestic oligarchy," the "foreign monopolists," the "privileges of property," "capitalism," "liberalism," and "imperialism"; they defended the proletariat, the peasantry, and the poor in general; promised to install directed economies and five-year plans; and vowed to "Brazilianize" or "Argentinize" the economy and culture.[45]

The pronounced socialism in the Integralist and Peronist ideologies existed side by side with a vibrant nationalism. Theoreticians from both movements enunciated the principle that all group interests were subservient to the national interest, and because they regarded long-term class and national interests as essentially harmonious, they described their revolutions as a fusion of socialism and nationalism.[46] The Cuban elite is, of course, no less nationalistic, and they too have made it plain that no group interest may overrule their interpretation of what is good for the nation as a whole. Régis Debray, a "Marxist" intellectual very much in favor with the Cubans, has been willing to acknowledge both the nationalistic and socialistic elements in "Fidelism" and has explicitly identified the Cuban Revolution as a fusion of nationalism and communism.[47]

Aside from comparing voiced ambitions, ideological positions, and political actions, another method of judging the similar character of the movements in question is to listen to what they have to say about each other. With regard to Integralism, this is not possible, for the movement died long before the Cuban Marxists came to power. Peronism, however, is a different story because of the astonishing longevity of its leader Juan Perón. In 1973 Argentina opened its doors to the Second Coming of the Man of Destiny, and for three years the Peronists once again ruled the land. It was during this period that the Peronists had a chance to regard the Cubans and the Cubans to ponder the Peronists.

For the Second Coming the Peronists brought with them the same ideology, the same style, and the same aspirations that had sustained them in their first years of power. But at that time their movement was considered by outside observers as a form of fascism. Until the Nazi death rattle grew so loud as to be undeniable, Perón and the group he consorted with did little to discourage the word "fascist" as a label for their ideas. Perón hailed Mussolini as the "greatest man of our century" and his military lodge described the Axis effort as "heroic." Cordell Hull, the United States Secretary of State, publicly criticized Argentina as fascism's headquarters in the Western Hemisphere. A former Undersecretary of State, Sumner Welles, denounced Perón as a "fanatical fascist." An American Ambassador to Argentina reported home that the Perón regime could be described only as "Fascist and typically Fascist." United States Representative John F. Coffee opposed Argentina's admission to the United Nations on the basis that "we dare not let them into the society of free peoples, they are still

Fascists." Books published in the United States bore such titles as *Argentina: Fascist Headquarters* and *The Nazi Underground in South America*. So accepted was the image of a "fascist" Perón that *Time Magazine* could flatly and without controversy declare, "Perón operates a state essentially modeled on the classic Nazi-Fascist pattern."[48]

The rise and return of Juan Perón afforded more contemporary analysts as unusual opportunity to observe just how much spiritual kinship exists between a war-era fascism and a "Third World" totalitarian modernization movement. During the 1960s when Perón began to see his reemergence into Argentinean politics as a possibility, he dusted off his ideological weapons and brought them up to date with the world events occurring around him. He correctly diagnosed the emotions behind his "Third Position" concept as fundamentally the same as those that propel the "Third World" movement. He still remained anticommunist, but his anticommunism was still directed at the Soviet Union, the communist version of an "imperialist" superpower, and at the servile, dependent followers of the Soviet propaganda line. As for independent Third World communists, he praised the sacrifice of Che Guevara and offered kind words to the "leftist" terrorists operating in Argentina. Far from condemning the communisms of the have-not nations, he boasted that he was a "precursor" to Mao Tse-tung in China and Fidel Castro in Cuba.[49]

And how did Fidel Castro, the man who vowed death to all fascists, respond to such compliments? With compliments of his own. Castro hailed the Peronists as a "progressive" political force, and he directed the Cuban propaganda machinery to lavishly cheer their triumph. To cement the new accord, he dispatched his highest ceremonial emissary, President Dorticós, to personally deliver warm Cuban embraces and profuse sentiments of eternal solidarity.[50] Régis Debray elevated these honeyed diplomatic phrases to a more intellectual plane when he specifically identified Peronism as a "variant of Fidelism" and sharply criticized the "sectarian" anti-Peronist communists who allied themselves "with reactionary forces against Peronism."[51]

TOTALITARIANISM AND LATIN AMERICAN DEMOCRACY

The Peronist and Integralist movements are significant in the context of this essay not so much in what they accomplished as in what they intended. Integralism never reached the summit of power, and Peronism was too afflicted with corruption and opportunism to inspire the kind of "moral recuperation" envisioned in its rhetoric. Their ideologies and their voiced aspirations, however, do plainly reveal the presence of the totalitarian impulse in important Latin American political movements well before this insistent urge was finally realized in revolutionary Cuba.

But the totalitarian impulse can also be seen attempting to express itself elsewhere in Latin America in far less conspicuous areas of the continent's political life. There are many convinced democrats from Western lands who would acknowledge the totalitarian ambitions of Latin American fascism and Cuban Marxist-Leninism and would place their hope in those movements that espouse democracy and openly praise the concepts of social pluralism, individual rights, and the moral limits of state power. But before these Western liberal democrats too quickly select champions and choose sides in Latin American politics, they should remember that Lenin on the eve of the Russian Revolution was not only a democrat but a radical democrat, advocating (probably sincerely) a progressive reduction of state authority until it shriveled away and disappeared. The case of Fidel Castro provides an even more relevant example. Castro, we recall, began his revolutionary career as an announced democrat, and most observers both sympathetic and unsympathetic have concluded that Castro did not plan from his Sierra Maestra haunts the direction he took after his ascent to power. What most likely happened to Castro was that he came to realize that he could not carry out his battle against dependencia and exploitation without reforming the values of the people and he could not conduct an effective value reform program within the framework of a democratic society. With these precedents in mind, then, it is reasonable to consider whether avowedly democratic political movements in Latin America harbor tendencies toward totalitarian methods and viewpoints.

An investigation of this sort requires the selection of democratic movements that have engaged in considerable self-examination and through their writings have revealed much about themselves. One of the most extensive ideological and polemical literatures ever elaborated in Latin America was produced by an ostensibly democratic movement called *Aprismo*. Founded in Peru during the 1920s by Victor Raúl Haya de la Torre, Aprismo has over the decades generally been accepted by Western observers[52] for what it claimed to be: an intensely nationalistic movement dedicated to various degrees of socialistic reform within a democratic society. The strongly voiced democratic platform of Aprismo promised decentralization of government authority, a vigorously pluralistic political life, and a full range of inalienable individual rights for each and every Peruvian.

Apristas, the proponents of Aprismo, were socialists in the sense that they felt the state should not merely ensure the political freedom of its citizens but provide for their economic well-being as well. In pursuit of this, they advocated commonly structuralist reforms that varied in emphasis in different periods but that overall proposed the redistribution of at least some power and wealth from the Peruvian "oligarchy" and foreign "imperialists" to the more disadvantaged and "exploited" sectors of the population. As part of their task of "social justice," Apristas promised that their government would organize a "planned economy" that would meet the material needs of the people by encouraging economic modernization.

In addition to structural change, Aprista leaders were very aware of the necessity of value reform, and they greatly stressed this to their membership. They spoke of a Peru mired not just in a political, social, and economic crisis but in a "moral crisis" as well.[53] They claimed their revolution was a reaction against a "country of vice, corruption and sin."[54] Within their own circles they singled out specific values and attitudes and attacked them unrelentingly. Peru, they lamented, was a country "sick" with "skepticism," "pessimism," "hedonism," "sensuality," "apathy," "viveza," "opportunism," "spiritual flabbiness," and "mental colonialism."[55] In a typical passage one leader condemned the social vice of individualismo as

> our tropical idiosyncrasy . . . our undisciplined Hispanic-American rebelliousness . . . that does not comprehend, without hatred and envy, authority and direction. The result of this is that all unity of action is difficult among ourselves. It is important, therefore, to react against these defects, these weakeners of our political strength, by fighting them without truce.[56]

The Apristas responded to what they regarded as Peru's moral turpitude with a cry for "spiritual renovation." "Aprismo," they declared, "means renovation," and they claimed moral strength to be the dimension of their movement that most distinguished it from ordinary political parties. The Apristas insisted that they were producing "new men" (again that recurrent term) who were bearers of a "new moral attitude," living examples of an "authentic moral renovation."[57]

But "new men" and "moral renovations" are not made by reason alone. Aprismo was deeply immersed in the mood of a religious revival. Participation in the movement was regarded as not just a political statement but a whole way of life—a religious vocation. While Aprista ideologues sometimes argued that their doctrine was "scientific," they more frequently called it a faith—an "Aprista Faith" (Fe Aprista). A stanza of the most popular Aprista anthem joyfully expressed this notion when it exhorted Peruvians to "embrace" Aprismo "the new religion" in order to "conquer the coveted redemption."[58]

Like other revolutionary ideologies that acknowledged the critical need for value reform, Aprismo readily succumbed to the elitist interpretation of mass leadership. At the center of this "new religion" stood the majestic figure of Victor Raúl Haya de la Torre. To the Apristas Haya was "Chief and Teacher," "comrade and guide," "brother and friend."[59] Far more than a political leader, Haya was held to be nothing less than a spiritual "redeemer."[60] One Western observer, lost amidst a huge Aprista multitude rendering homage to Haya on his birthday, gave this report that captured well the attitude of Aprista political converts toward their charismatic leader:

> I remember clearly one night in Lima when it was Haya's birthday. We all stood in the square waiting for Haya to appear at midnight. Tens of thousands of Apristas stood in the square, in the darkness, while candles burned and a loudspeaker announced every few minutes, as if the Apocalypse were imminent: "Ten minutes to midnight"... "Five minutes"... "Two minutes."
> Then "Great teacher of our heart ... brother and teacher ... our beloved leader. . . " Precisely at midnight, Haya arrived. He was standing in an open car with his right arm raised, as if in salute or blessing. The ocean of faces was whitecapped with a hundred thousand waving handkerchiefs and the voices shouted themselves hoarse: "Happy birthday, Victor Raúl. Happy birthday, Victor Raúl."[61]

While never minimizing the importance of his own earthly mission, Haya also exalted the role of his Aprista followers. The Aprista Party consisted of chosen disciples who shared with him his elitist burden: "We feel upon our shoulders the cross of redeeming old Peru from her sins." Haya ceaselessly lectured the faithful about their "apostolic mission," their "civilizing mission." Apristas, he solemnly declared, were destined to be the "Saviors of Peru."[62]

The Aprista leaders realized that before the rank and file could fan out across Peru and "save" their countrymen, the apostles-in-training had first to unreservedly embrace the "Aprista Faith" themselves and to become "new men" by undergoing the rigors of a fundamental moral transformation. To infuse this new meaning and instill these new values into the Party members, the elite employed the usual techniques: intense instruction in Aprista doctrine, obligatory and often very painful self-criticism sessions, and demands that the converts "prove" themselves by toil, sacrifice, and suffering. They also showed themselves aware of the usefulness of persecution and hardship imposed by a common enemy in wielding followers together into a highly charged emotional unit. This preparation and training was meant to cultivate and fortify values that would fuse the individuals of the Party into "one solid column" capable of decisive "unity of action," its cohesiveness sustained by a common belief in, and feeling for, a revolutionary doctrine.[63] The leaders understood homogeneity to be more important than numbers; and they threatened with expulsion all Party members who did not demonstrate the correct attitude or en-thusiasm.[64] (One of those Haya de la Torre purged from the Party was his own brother.)

Reinforcing their indoctrination process were efforts by the Aprista leaders to insulate their followers from the corrupting influence of the unconverted sector of the population. Apristas attempted to achieve for themselves as great a degree of self-sufficiency as possible—intellec-tual, social, emotional, and even economic. Toward this end they established their own schools, newspapers, publishing houses, social and recreational centers, cafeterias, stores, and shops. And in order to put distance between themselves and the outsiders who did not par-ticipate, Apristas had their own distinctive style: their own slogans, salutes, songs, anthems, heroes, celebrations, flags, marches, symbols, emblems and ways of greeting and saying farewell to one another. By means such as these, Party members lived in a somewhat closed en-vironment filled with helping hands, critical eyes, and reminders that they were not merely Peruvians but "new Peruvians" and were expected to conduct themselves as such.

In the overall revolutionary strategy of the Aprista leadership, the notion of moral regeneration assumed an importance that can hardly be exaggerated. The ambitious Aprista blueprint revealed three broad but closely interrelated stages. The initial task was for the revolu-tionary elite to work upon the receptive minds and emotions of Party members, to shape their viewpoints with Aprista doctrine and to swell their hearts with "Aprista Faith." The second phase required using these earnest followers as a weapon to win political power. With this triumph completed, the third and most difficult state of the Aprista revolution had only just begun. The Aprista elite displayed con-siderable insight in recognizing (before they ever came to power) that the implementation of the social revolution they envisioned required the support of a virtual army of dedicated revolutionary cadres. This kind of human material scarcely existed within the impossibly lethargic state bureaucracy, so the Aprista leaders had to produce within their own Party the substantial number of obedient zealots the future Aprista state would need. For this reason Haya de la Torre described his Party not only as a "school of morality" but also as a "state within a state"; he regarded the "new men" developing within the Aprista ranks as "half a million potential leaders," a kind of revolu-tionary bureaucracy in exile. The "half million" were assigned the mis-sion of moral "vanguard" to millions of Peruvians, the prototypes of the "new men" who would populate the revolutionary society to come. More importantly, the "half million" were to provide the elite with the vital lines of authority they would need to extend the revolution throughout the country until the same "new moral attitude" that in-spired the Aprista party had spread and aroused all Peru.[65]

What was the nature of this moral spirit that was to vitalize Peruvian national life? Since the Aprista leadership demanded that Party members practice this morality, the vague craving for a national "moral rejuvenation" was articulated into a specific ethical code.

Once again the puritanical injunctions of sobriety, austerity, and self-discipline were drilled into a Latin American revolutionary grouping: Apristas were told to abstain from drinking, smoking, swearing, gambling, card playing, coca chewing, philandering, or dancing that "stimulated sexuality"; Apristas were taught the value of punctuality, honesty, self-criticism, and diligent study (but not the questioning) of the thoughts of Haya de la Torre; Apristas were reminded to look neat, stay clean, exercise regularly, brush their teeth, and go to bed early.[66]

The most applauded virtues of the Aprista code were those which tended to strengthen unity within the Party and toughen it for collective action: steadfast loyalty, reflexive obedience, iron discipline, generous self-sacrifice. The kind of people the Aprista leadership wanted their "new men" to be is very evident in the following passage, where Haya de la Torre describes the qualities it takes to become a "good Aprista".

> [Only like this! *ONLY LIKE THIS!*, understanding and making others understand: fusing the faith of our leader and our faith into one harmoneous *INTEGRAL PART* in which everyone cooperates; transcending, overcoming mentally and physically everything from an individual point of view and daily excelling in contributions, giving more and more to the common cause, feeling oneself and knowing oneself responsible and capable of more and more—in this manner one will come to be a *GOOD APRISTA*.[67]

Aware that these cherished collectivist values resembled military values, Aprista leaders regularly embellished their moral teachings with military metaphors. Apristas were "good soldiers" "fighting" in the thick of battle and as good soldiers they must learn how to "obey." In an essay written in 1932, Haya went so far as to compare his 500,000 Apristas who would one day "command" seven million Peruvians with the 100,000 German officers who "command[ed]" five million German troops.[68]

Even from this brief discussion of key features of the Aprista movement, it should be evident that a judgment of Aprismo should be based not only upon the Party's formal statements but also on whether these are compatible with its other enunciations. Haya de la Torre's comparison of the Aprista Party with the officer corps of the stiffly authoritarian German army is an indication of how sorrowfully unfit Apristas were, had they ever laid their hands on the levers of political power, to preside over a democratic society. The elite ran the Party hierarchically, like a military operation, glorifying above all else the stern ethic of obedience. This hardly constitutes the kind of training and life experience from which defenders of individual liberties and democratic diversity are likely to spring. However admirable might have been the ideals that the Aprista general staff was trying to instill in the "soldiers of APRA (Aprista Party), they certainly were not democratic ideals.

Nor did other positions taken by Aprista leaders bode well for the idea of government by the explicit consent of the governed. Haya de la Torre frequently displayed his rank elitism by reiterating the principle that "our Party is the people itself and whoever opposes our Party opposes the people."[69] Apristas were a self-selected minority who identified their own will with the will of the "people," whether the people liked it or not. When combined with ambition for state power, this elitism readily produced an amalgam called statism. The Aprista leaders regarded their Party as a "state within the state," and by their logic, it also represented the "people."

The statist idea, of course, is utterly antithetical to the democratic idea. Democratic idealism respects the masses for what they are; statist idealism hopes to "mold" them into something they are not. Democratic idealism justifies arming the people with inalienable rights to act as a shield against the state; statist idealism justifies the state controlling the people in order to permit it to "mold" their character in a manner it choses to believe is in their best interest. Democratic idealism begins with a concern for the individual, and because the individual occupies the very center of democratic political theory, he is constantly kept in sharp focus; statist idealism begins with a concern for the collectivity, and because the collectivity resides at the center, the individual is easily lost from view. In Aprismo the individual was simply "annulled." According to one leading ideologue,

> Every action, every opinion of a soldier of APRA is *subordinated* to the factor of discipline to the extreme where an *Aprista* personality is annulled in favor of the great interests of the Party.[70]

It appears, then, that just below the surface of the Aprista movement, strong undertows ran counter to professed democratic sentiments. One conclusion to be drawn from this is that no matter what the Apristas maintained and no matter how sincerely they maintained it, they were not credible democrats. The activities, attitudes, and aspirations of Apristas point to something more: their pronounced elitism, their party structure, their value reform, their spirited secular religion, their ambitions for a "fusion of faith" between leaders and followers—all suggest their receptiveness to a revamping of society along totalitarian lines.

An even less likely place for the totalitarian impulse to reveal itself was within the Chilean Christian Democratic movement, which enjoyed a reputation as one of the great democratic strongholds in Latin America. While there were always some doubts about Haya de la Torre, the opinion on Eduardo Frei, the leader of the Christian Democrats, was virtually unanimous. His style literally radiated conviction, and to hear him speak was usually enough to dispel any reservations. Frei was enthusiastically backed by the American embassy, his campaign funded by the CIA, his regime bolstered by generous foreign aid from Americans anxious to see his experiment in democratic reformism a success. Around the world Frei was the darling of liberal democrats. On a state visit to Western European capitals, he was toasted with exceptional honors. Writers and journalists wished his experiment well. The editor of the famous American magazine *Look* wrote an entire book on Frei's movement and, borrowing a phrase from Lincoln, called it democratic Latin America's "Last Best Hope." And as if this were not enough to suggest a democratic commitment, it should finally be mentioned that Eduardo Frei ruled—democratically—for six years in Chile and finished his term by constitutionally turning over power to his elected opponent.

The question is, then, not what Christian Democracy was but what it might have been. Over the course of many years Frei and his supporters expended considerable intellectual energy articulating their viewpoints and ideas, and together they compiled a voluminous literature and elaborated an extensive ideology. Delving deeply into something they called the "Chilean reality," these thinkers disclosed much about the character of their nationalism, their particular perception of their social problems, their hopes and aspirations, and the means by which they intended to achieve political ends.

A perusal of Eduardo Frei's works of social criticism quickly introduces a Chilean who was not just a democrat but also a fervent nationalist intensely concerned with the national problems of Chile. The tone of his nationalist feeling betrayed not confidence but distress. Frei perceived his "Fatherland" as an underdeveloped country, a poor relative, and one wanting in status in the family of modern nation-states. Furthermore, Frei recognized that the trends of his time were in the wrong direction, that Chile had been slipping steadily downhill for decades, and that unless something were done to arrest and reverse this process, his country was running the "risk of entering a permanent decadence that spotlights our failure as a nation."[71] In short, Frei's sense of nationalist identity showed the same passion for equality and longing for national self-respect that pervades the nationalisms in other underdeveloped Latin American cultures.

At the base of Frei's proposals for national revival was his analysis of what was wrong with Chile. Frei saw structuralist constraints (see

p. 5) as factors and therefore recommended "structuralist reforms such as land redistribution, worker participation in industry, and a cooperative organization of society.

But the Christian Democratic leader was never one to believe that the simple shifting of power and wealth from certain social groupings to others would by itself perform the necessary miracles. He also recognized the crucial importance of value reform. To Frei this improvement in mass customs and values was absolutely fundamental, and he agreed with the insight of another author who maintained "that a social renovation is not possible except by men who have morally renovated themselves" ("se hayan renovado moralmente ellos mismos").[72] Frei complained of Chilean "decadence" and attributed it to "defects" in the Chilean national character. Listing them off he blamed "poor work habits," "fatalism," "duplicity," "lack of honesty," "loss of nationalistic spirit," an insipid cosmopolitanism among the more affluent classes, and a ridiculous preoccupation among these same groups for securing white-collar employment ("empleomania").[73] In a typically Latin American gesture, he pointed to Chile's immigrants who "begin with no capital yet prosper rapidly," relying on "initiative, dedication to work, sobriety, the spirit of enterprise."[74] Chileans had to be taught the "basic fundamental virtues" that were the indispensable instruments of immigrant success: "frugality, love of work, punctually, orderly, disciplined lives, self-confidence, sobriety."[75] Frei argued that his country was poor in natural resources, that Chile's "primary resource" was people, and that the development of the nation depended mainly upon the positive qualities of these people. To this future president of Chile, the modernization of the country was basically a "problem of will" (problema de voluntad),[76] a united, determined effort on the part of the Chileans themselves. The implications of this were inescapable, and it was a serious and somber Eduardo Frei who warned his countrymen, "Only we can save ourselves."[77]

In his insistence on the moral reform of the Chilean masses, Frei betrayed elitist sentiment that is so much a part of the Latin American experience that its appropriateness is hardly questioned. Latin American nationalists of all political hues have long been susceptible to the temptation to "love the people" while holding the masses in low regard; and Frei, the Christian Democratic nationalist, was one more reformer in the mainstream of this tradition. Frei's view of social elites was that they were at once inevitable, necessary, and justified so long as they were "founded on service" to the people.[78] But who was to determine ultimately what form of "service" the people needed—the "people" or the elite? Frei strongly believed the masses were carriers of value and attitudinal "defects" and that their customs and habits had to be "improved." The masses were obviously not making the decision to bring about these essential changes on their own, and so they existed to be acted upon. It was the "historical mission" of the elite to perform this "service" for the people, because the minority saw the interests of the "people" more clearly than the majority. "Nothing," contended Frei, "can be worse for a people not to recognize in time the conductors [*conductores*] and minorities who know the correct way."[79]

According to Frei the "people are waiting for the hand to lift them up and awaken their potential energies."[80] The means to this end was a political faith that the movement would inspire in its following. "The masses," said Frei, "more than concrete solutions crave hope, more than reasonable arguments are anxious for a faith that lifts them up and purifies them in its flame."[81] This Frei construed as part of the elitist burden—to bring to the masses the spiritual meaning that they could not find for themselves.

Frei's political faith had, of course, profound political implications. The Christian Democratic leader observed with some alarm that well-intentioned governments had existed before in Latin America and that their reforms had as much enduring effect as pebbles thrown into a pond. Reformist governments needed mass support, and the masses could only be aroused and galvanized into unified action by inflaming their hearts with loyalty and passion that went far beyond what reason alone could muster.

A Christian Democratic political faith was also necessary to combat the movement's enemies on their own terrain. Quoting similar insights of Henri de Man and Jacques Maritain, Frei specifically identified communism as a form of secular religion. His conclusion was that

> To oppose them [the communists] it is necessary for us also to have an impassioned faith [*fe apasionada*] that multiplies itself in the thousand activities of men, that blossoms in the most hidden corners of their lives, that with its mystique generates poets, martyrs, apostles, propagandists, technicians, possessed by a spirit and a vision aflame with a unique, final, absorbing way of thinking.[82]

Frei clearly intended that the Christian Democratic ideology be infused with the same revolutionary spirit that made the early Christians grateful for the opportunity to throw themselves before the lions. But over the Christian Democratic horizon lay not a heavenly but an earthly vision of an apocalypse as perfect as the Marxist—a "new society," a "new civilization," a "new age," a "new world," a land of tranquility, fraternity, abundance, and justice brought about by the "coreligionists" of the Partido Democratico Cristiano.[83]

Obviously the Christian Democratic elite had before them a good distance to travel, and they quite naturally looked upon a strong central government as a vehicle to carry them there. Frei, in fact, stood in awe of the power of the "modern state" whose potential force "can't even really be estimated."[84] He showed himself enormously impressed by the productive miracles wrought by the governments of leading nation-states and before World War II made no attempt to suppress his admiration for the "battle of wheat" in Italy, the rearmament of Germany, the industrialization of the Soviet Union, and the New Deal recovery in the United States.[85] To Frei these lessons meant that the economic modernization of Chile need not wait for a class of entrepreneurs to bestir itself to action; the state could take the lead. But for the state to meet this and other social challenges, government had to be strong and vigorous. "There is no oppression more terrible," insisted Frei, "than the suffering of a people when those who ought to command don't or when the government abdicates its right and responsibility to exercise authority."[86] With evident satisfaction Frei declared the liberal laissez-faire concept "dead"—too unsuited to modern times.[87] "The immense complexity of modern life demands unity of action, a single direction, because any other way will foment petty dictatorships in the unions, the parties, the administration, the economy, the committees." "Men are too vile," he added, "their egoisms and passions too violent not to require a hierarchy that insures order and punishment."[88]

At the same time, however, that Frei the revolutionary was marveling at the possibilities of the potent modern state, Frei the democrat was warning against the reach of the modern "omnipotent state."[89] While the latter concern seemed to strengthen in emphasis after World War II, the protection of the individual from state power was always a central preoccupation of Frei's social thinking. To avoid the danger of an "omnipotent" central government, he proposed the classical safeguard of institutionalized pluralism; a dispersal of power among municipal governments, regional governments, and "intermediate" economic groups such as professionals' guilds and workers' syndicates. Frei also strongly supported the full array of democratic rights and freedoms designed to defend the individual from too much interference by the state.

Without question the Christian Democratic ideological system combined the best of all possible worlds. It provided the state with enough power to transform an entire nation and people, and yet it provided the people with enough power to protect themselves from the state. But was the combination workable? The central government could indeed be capable of decisive action and the individuals and social groups under it could indeed be autonomous provided that these individuals and social groups, out of a sense of civic virtue, were willing to collaborate with the central government in what Frei used to describe as "our common destiny."

This high degree of social collaboration, of course, presupposed within Chilean national culture a considerable uniformity of shared values, beliefs, emotions, and ambitions that would induce Chileans to think, feel, and act alike and inspire them to work together to build a greater Chile. It is this hope for a vast cultural uniformity conducive to realizing a national vigor never before seen in Chile that exposes in Christian Democracy emotional roots similar to those that fed Latin American totalitarian movements. With these movements, Christian Democracy shared a craving for "unity of action" on a national scale. With these movements, Christian Democracy stressed collaboration among individuals, classes, and interest groups in pursuit of goals shaped by nationalist passion.

Beyond this common nationalist impulse, however, Fascism, the ideology of totalitarianism, and Christian Democracy departed drastically. Fascists justified trampling on democratic liberties in order to achieve uniformity, collaboration, and their final vision of "monolithic unity." Christian Democrats, on the other hand, were committed to preserving those very democratic liberties, and their government had to achieve uniformity, collaboration, and "unity of action" without transgressing the democratic limitations placed on government.

This, indeed, was a formidable challenge. Democratic pluralism enabled subnational "petty dictatorships" and interest groups to resist collaboration with the central government, thereby thwarting a national "unity of action." Democratic inalienable rights enabled individuals to resist value reform and a national cultural uniformity. For example, "vile" individuals in Christian Democratic Chile possessed the inalienable right to regard manual labor with contempt, evaluate Chilean culture with a cosmopolitan sneer, and hold a host of other attitudes antithetical to those of the highly nationalistic modernizing elite.

"Vile" men and "petty" dictators could, of course, be refashioned by value reform and the Christian Democracts were fully aware of the increasingly effective methods available to governments of persuading the minds and manipulating the emotions of the masses. The conquering of minds and hearts was, in fact, the hope to which the Christian Democratic revolutionaries clung in order to bring about the necessary social collaboration within a democratic society. Yet here too they were constrained by their own espousal of democratic liberties. Mass persuasion to modernization-encouraging values and mass conversion to a single political faith most readily take place in an atmosphere where the population ceaselessly breathes in one and only one point of view. The Christian Democratic commitment to freedom of speech and freedom of expression ensured that the masses were exposed to many. The Christian Democratic truth was but one among many truths furiously competing with one another, sowing confusion and division among the masses, and frustrating any dream of transforming Chile into a nation of willing collaborators.

The Christian Democrats were fond of describing their movement as a "Revolution in Liberty." Given the nature of the kind of revolution they wished to see, the sweeping moral reform, the single political faith, the "unity of action," their slogan, Revolution in Liberty, contained elements that were sharply hostile to each other. The Christian Democrats handled the tension within their ideology the only way they could—by ignoring it. However, when the helm of political power fell into their hands and problems demanded specific decisions, they were forced to make a choice between "revolution" and "liberty." They chose "liberty."

Although the ideas and ideals of Christian Democrats harbored tendencies that if left unchecked could have led to totalitarianism, they never allowed such inclinations to exert themselves within the world of practical politics. They stayed within the confinements imposed by democratic institutions because they lived in an unusual Latin American country with time-honored democratic traditions, and because their leader Frei was, by all accounts, a sincere democrat. Tradition and sincerity were, no doubt, reinforced by the fact that they had no other road to travel. The Chilean army, which reserves the right to stray from the democratic path only to itself, would have blocked a Christian Democratic move in the same direction.

Christian Democrats, then, never came close to totalitarianism. Then again, neither did they come close to their central revolutionary objectives. In fact, despite all the excitement stirred up in Western capitals, their government amounted to little more than just another ineffectual democratic regime. With considerable fanfare they succeeded in instituting some structural reforms, but they failed in the far more difficult task of value reform. They encouraged more Chileans to participate in the mainstream of national life, but this only swelled the ranks of the demanders. Their "Revolution in Liberty" raised expectations and stimulated appetites but did little to inculcate the spirit of discipline and self-sacrifice needed to satisfy the hunger. With more vociferous organized interest groups clamoring for a larger slice of an inadequate national pie, Frei's popularity declined so drastically that he could not even keep the peace within his own party of squabbling "coreligionists." Rather than transforming the unruly Chilean conglomeration into an orderly, cohesive national community, the Christian Democratic elite only aggravated its condition to the point where it became more intractable, more unmanageable, and more ungovernable than ever.

The totalitarian urges within Christian Democracy never developed beyond their first incipient stages, but the fact that they appeared in this kind of movement at all is an indication of how common they are in Latin American political life. The impulse to totalitarianism has revealed itself again and again in Latin America because a particular combination of political, economic, social, and emotional circumstances in that society have favored it. To date this impulse has matured to fruition only in "Marxist-Leninist" Cuba, but it also can be seen in one form or another in Latin American fascisms, "democratic" Aprismo, and even in Christian Democracy. It is reasonable to conclude, therefore, that for future Latin American revolutionaries filled with ambition to reform the values of the masses and to push their countries into the first league of nation-states, the totalitarian alternative will continue to be a forceful allurement and a recurring temptation.

TOTALITARIANISM AND LATIN AMERICAN MARXISM

We have seen in a previous chapter that the most common ideology contemporary Latin American nationalists use to justify totalitarian ambition is Marxism-Leninism. We should not take this to mean, however, that all Latin American revolutionaries who espouse Marxism-Leninism necessarily have totalitarian designs, for just as onlookers cannot be sure that professed Latin American democrats will not eventually evolve into totalitarian elitists, they cannot be sure that professed "Marxists" will. Observers should bear in mind, therefore, that it is hazardous to make ready assumptions about future political behavior simply on the basis of a "Marxist" ideological label because a "Marxist" label alone does not provide us with much information as to what a "Marxist" will do.

An understanding of this point might be approached by once again reviewing the old antagonism between the structuralist and value interpretations of national poverty. In the original Marxism, designed for advanced industrial civilizations, the social problem of poverty was explained primarily in terms of the "structure" of power and wealth within society, and the solution was found primarily in the redistribution of power and wealth from the "exploiting" to the "exploited" sector of the population. We have seen, however, that revolutionaries who called themselves "Marxists" came to power in underdeveloped countries only where the real needed revolution was one of production and not of distribution, and that this revolution of production demanded a revolution in people's values as well as in social structure. The result was that over the years "Marxism" evolved from a doctrine that explained the inevitability of massive redistribution into what one Cuban leader has called a "doctrine for transforming Man."[90]

The term "Marxism," then, circulates in contemporary Latin America with this ambiguous heritage. Latin American Marxists who, like the Cuban elite, feel they have to "transform" the values of the masses are those most likely to aspire to totalitarian control over the masses. Other Latin American Marxists, however, who believe that a Marxist revolution means little more than simple redistribution, do not need a totalitarian grip on the masses to achieve their ends and will therefore be less apt to strive for totalitarian social control.

Latin American Marxists who have not yet been chastened by the responsibilities of office are likely to find the structuralist translation of Marxism most appealing. It is only after they have tried shifting the levers of political power and have experienced the inevitable failure of purely structuralist reforms that they are more prone to revise their Marxism into a doctrine justifying totalitarianism. The reasons for the initial attractiveness of a structuralist emphasis are several. To begin with, the assumption that revolution is largely a matter of redistributing wealth and power has the advantage of avoiding uncomfortable questions about deficiencies in economic virtue. Secondly, it is a viewpoint that inspires optimism and emboldens revolutionary ambition; through its reasoning the revolution appears deceptively simple, a matter of vanquishing enemies, seizing power, and implementing redistribution measures—all of which are possible with a preponderance of armed force. Lastly and perhaps most important of all, the structuralist explanation of mass poverty is an excellent theoretical edifice for accommodating a very basic feeling of moral outrage that is very easily brought on by the social inequalities of Latin America. There the rich live so conspicuously well, the poor so conspicuously poorly; and to make matters worse, the privileges of the wealthy do not usually seem justified by the special contributions they make to society. The idea of prying open the cupboards of the greedy rich and distributing bread to the outstretched hands of the grateful poor affords considerable moral pleasure to those who are offended by the brutal extremes in living conditions found in Latin America. In short, the exclusively structuralist analysis of underdevelopment allows an idea of revolution that is elegantly simple, readily attainable, and thoroughly virtuous.

The strong appeal of the structuralist approach to understanding underdevelopment is suggested by the fact that even the Cubans, in the initial phase of their Revolution, were swayed by its charms. The first revolutionary actions the Cuban leaders took when they came to power were redistributionist reforms, such as the confiscation of farmlands, the nationalization of industries, and the declaration of a populist celebration. The latter revolutionary "advance" consisted of providing free social services, freezing rents, mandating price controls, and raising salaries an estimated 23 to 30 percent.[91] Jean Paul Sartre, perhaps, best caught the spirit of this early period when he wrote how he had asked Castro what he would do if his people asked him for the moon; Castro calmly replied that he would give it to them.[92]

Cubans are sometimes heard to refer to that delightful interlude when the meek were inheriting the earth and the moon as a *pachanga,* a festive dance in the rumba tradition. For a time spirits ran high, but then came the hangover. The country suffered a precipitous decline in production, and the Cuban leaders were confronted with the hard reality that they could not distribute what they didn't produce. The Revolution lurched from a distributionist to a productionist emphasis, and Castro began speaking of an ongoing Revolution that had yet to conquer the "Moncada of old ideas,"[93] that is to say, the attitudes and values that held back Cuban progress.

Another Latin American Marxist leader who fell victim to revolutionary structuralist ideas—and with far more serious results—was Salvador Allende of Chile. A crucial difference between Salvador Allende's "Marxist" revolution and that of Fidel Castro was that the entire duration of Allende's rule resembled the brief consumptionist phase that took place in Cuba. It was as if once the Chilean version of the Cuban pachanga began, it never stopped until the country collapsed from weariness.

Allende's idea of a "Marxist" revolution never ventured far beyond the notion of redistribution. The Chilean Marxist willingly listened to a group of economists who theoretically demonstrated how production would automatically expand once demand was increased by a revolutionary policy of redistribution. With his mind put at ease by a paper solution to production, Allende was free to follow the populist tuggings of his heart, which he identified as Marxist idealism. Allende made it plain to the Chilean people that his revolution meant not toil and sacrifice but *vino tinto y empanadas* ("red wine and meat pies"). Allende's Marxism was quite literally a pie-in-the-sky Marxism.

Allende's great socialist redistribution scheme basically entailed the shifting of purchasing power and productive power from one social group to another. His administration channeled purchasing power into the hands of Chilean workers by legislating wage increases (an average of 50 percent),[94] by regulating prices, and by sopping up the pools of unemployed with a sponge-like government bureaucracy. Allende's government extended its control over Chile's productive power (referred to by the Chilean left as the "means of production") by launching a zealous program of state expropriations and nationalizations. The latter course of action was sustained by a moralistic belief in the sinfulness of private control over income-producing property and by the audacious assumption that such usurpations would not result in lower production.

The famous land reform effort under Allende was one part of this enthusiastic policy of shuffling productive resources. Allende's predecessor, Eduardo Frei, had also drawn up a land redistribution plan; but Frei had proceeded with a measured gait, trying to maintain agricultural output by confiscating only large farms with poor production records.[95] Allende, however, was a far more dogmatic member of the redistributionist faith; being piously convinced of the inherent superiority of state and cooperatively-owned property, he greatly outstripped the Frei program and, in the process, brought into the "reformed" area some of the best managed agricultural estates in the country.[96] Although Allende had manfully predicted increased agricultural output, his helter-skelter agrarian appropriations resulted in production declines that worsened with every season.[97]

Redistribution within the industrial sector was also carried out by massive nationalizations: in less than three years Allende increased the percentage of state-controlled industry from 50 percent of the total to 80 percent.[98] As was the case with agriculture, the nationalization of Chilean industry precipitated many problems that discouraged efficient production. Both actions unleashed political antagonisms that forced many talented managers to leave their jobs and sometimes even to flee the country. They also frightened off private and foreign investment; and owing to the slim profit margins earned by nationalized industry, the state lacked the funds to fully compensate for the loss of investment capital. Socialist intellectuals, however, were most surprised at the severe weakening of labor discipline encouraged by the nationalization policy. Workers who found their places of employment publicly and not privately owned, producing for people and not for profit, did not behave as proud toilers freed from alienation. Instead of standing solidly behind Allende's government, which claimed to represent their interests, many workers took advantage of the breakdown of the old order and grew increasingly resistant to all types of authority, including state authority. The frequent refusals to follow orders, the vilification of plant managers and engineers, the poor maintenance and willful sabotage of machinery, the escalating corruption and absenteeism, the spreading practice of half or three-quarter working days, the repeated occurrence of socially paralyzing strikes—all were signs of how workers had become increasingly politicized and mobilized but had increasingly moved out of the control of the politicizers and mobilizers.[99] Needless to say, all these problems had a negative impact on Chilean industrial performance. During Allende's stay in power, Chile's crucial copper production expanded only slightly despite the opening of several new mines attributable to investments carried out by the Frei administration.[100] After the first year of Allende's stewardship, overall industrial production began a steady decline that did not cease until the final blood-smeared overthrow.[101]

Very little grasp of economics is needed to see the disaster inherent in Allende's "Marxist" revolution of redistribution. Infused with populist fervor, his government deliberately generated demand by raising salaries and creating jobs.* Expanding demand could only be satisfied with expanding supply. To some extent this supply could be provided by foreign producers: in one year Allende's government gobbled up the country's 343 million dollars in foreign exchange and in three years increased the country's indebtedness by 36 percent.[103] In the main, however, expanding supply depended upon what Chileans could do for themselves; and the other side of the Allende revolution, the redistribution of producing power, weakened the country's ability to produce.

When a government allows or urges its citizens to try to consume more than they produce, it brings upon them an affliction called inflation. Unable to make Chileans increase production, Allende could only attempt to live up to his promises of increased consumption by printing and passing out money unbacked by real goods and services. The Chilean leader tried to mitigate the inflationary effects of his drastic expansion of the money supply by placing legal limits on price rises. But since demand for goods greatly exceeded available supplies, Chileans were forced to waste their time in endless queues—waiting, for example, as long as six or seven hours to buy bread. It used to be possible for workers to spend the day lounging in line, sell half of what they got on the black market, and thus earn more money than they could at their job.[104] Eventually well over half the economic activity in the country was conducted outside the law.[105] While the inflation rate with controlled prices was toward the end of the Allende years a brisk 323 percent, in the unregulated black market it was closer to 2,000 percent.[106] It was here in this "illegal" marketplace while trying to obtain goods unavailable elsewhere, that Chileans were most likely to make the bitter discovery that whatever gains they may have initially realized had been wiped out, and that their real wages were actually lower than when the whole uproar began.[107]

In the long run Allende's pie-in-the-sky Marxism only made meat pies and red wine more difficult to acquire. It was because a redistributionist revolution alone cannot bring about basic Latin American nationalist objectives that Fidel Castro disagreed with Allende's interpretation of what a "real" Marxist revolution should be. "Marxism," Castro insisted, "is a revolution of production; Allende's was a revolution of consumption."[108] After Castro's own redistributionist experiment, the Cuban leader guided his Revolution beyond simple nationalizations and primitive populism to a newer phase of

---

Often these jobs were shamelessly unproductive. For example, 4,000 additional workers were added to the original staff of 18,000 at the *El Teniente* copper mine in 1971 with no significant increase in production.[102]

value reform and totalitarian control. Instead of a revolution that mobilizes and politicizes the masses and attempts to distribute to them what they do not produce, the "Marxist" Revolution in Cuba has come to mean a movement that mobilizes and politicizes the masses and attempts to forge them into a disciplined human community capable of producing what they need.

There are many more revolutionaries in Latin America with the same ideological identity as Fidel Castro and Salvador Allende, some of whom might in the future climb to the pinnacle of political power in their respective countries. Complicating any judgment as to what these "Marxist" malcontents might do with political power is the fact that they are still in the conspiratorial stage of their struggle and are apt to be less sure of what kind of "revolutionaries" they are than are those others sobered by the experience of ruling a nation. In light of this, and after observing how two different "Marxist" leaders have produced two different "Marxist" revolutions, it would be understandably hazardous to assume, simply on the basis of their professed ideology alone, that those who classify themselves as "Marxists" are consciously committed to a totalitarian reorganization of society.

The safest significant generalization that may be rendered about Latin American Marxist revolutionaries is that they will probably exhibit the behavior characteristics of Latin American reactive nationalists. This is quite likely true even for those Marxist parties in Latin America that have close ties with the Soviet Union. For years these peculiar political sects have been accepting Soviet subsidies and slavishly adhering to the Soviet political line; and because of these questionable activities, they have justly merited the suspicion that if they ever came to power they might be more concerned with Soviet interests than with those of their own country. These Marxists, however, claim to be loyal nationalists and surmount the problem of their two loyalties by denying that the interests of a "Marxist" Soviet Union and a "Marxist" country in Latin America could ever be at odds. Intellectuals who are unfettered by the responsibilities of governing a nation can afford to rationalize inconsistencies in theoretical positions with no ill effects; but if the destiny of their fatherland ever fell into their hands, they could very well find themselves propelled by inner emotions, self-interests, and political forces to respond as reactive nationalists would in defending their country against Soviet efforts at political dominance.

Marxist revolutionaries moved by reactive nationalism will, of course, act to overcome dependencia, especially economic dependencia. Their ideas of what causes underdevelopment will certainly be influenced by the structuralist perspective that, as we have seen, has displaced the value explanation for underdevelopment among Latin American intellectuals. A structuralist analysis might lead future

Marxist leaders to a combination of reforms that can be realized without a totalitarian hold on the masses. Like Allende they might believe a revolution to be a populist celebration and move to redistribute purchasing power. Or they may concentrate more on redistributing productive power, which would probably result in state control of the "means of production" or in some degree of worker management of production centers.

However, just as the structuralist approach to underdevelopment thrives in academic and political circles in Latin America, the less systematically articulated value approach thrives in the streets—appearing and reappearing in the ordinary conversations of the people. If purely structuralist reforms fail to overcome the manifestations of dependencia that so enrage reactive nationalists, and if the masses do not spontaneously respond as expected by the modernizing elite, then the latent notion of value reform is likely to press forward for the attention of the revolutionary planners. If revolutionary leaders began to consider the necessity of transforming the values of the people, they could, in turn, very easily acquire elitist yearnings for totalitarian control of the people who have to be changed. The "Marxism" of Latin American "Marxists" can, then, conceivably develop into various forms of a structuralist revolution, a totalitarian revolution, or any combination of these alternatives—all under the name of "true Marxism."

While the conclusion of these observations is that Marxism and totalitarianism should not be regarded as synonymous, they should nevertheless be recognized as very compatible. We have seen how the nature of underdevelopment and the character of nationalism in Latin America have come together and produced a climate favorable to the growth of totalitarian ambition. Those who call themselves Marxists are generally not resistant to this urging because intellectually few if any are sincerely committed to the idea of a democratic dispersal of power. In addition, many have already become emotionally conditioned to a totalitarian way of life by their submission to the rigors of a party discipline that stresses unquestioning unity of thought, feeling, and action.

The compatibility of Marxism and totalitarianism also works in the opposite direction. If nationalist Marxists are receptive to the idea of totalitarianism, then non-Marxist nationalists are at least inclined to be receptive to the idea of Marxism, for once a Latin American modernizing elite has decided on a program of value reform employing the techniques of a totalitarian modernization movement, among the revolutionary instruments they require is an ideological justification that is infused with a quasi-religious mystique. As the Cuban elite has discovered[109] and others are likely to, Marxism-Leninism is in essence a secular religion that can be used to incite an entire people into a Holy War against underdevelopment and other forms of national weakness.

Epilogue

A relatively short time ago, roughly 200 years, European society took its first tentative steps into the Industrial Age. This proved to be a most remarkable phase in man's development owing to its many achievements and the astonishing speed in which those achievements appeared. It was as if all human progress up to that point had proceeded at a crawl and then suddenly, somehow, took off in upward flight. There had been nothing like it in the entire history of the human race. Production climbed to heights undreamed of before. Stunning scientific discoveries and spectacular technological breakthroughs followed each other in rapid succession. Diseases once thought unconquerable fell before the advances of modern medicine. Famine, once thought inevitable, became a relic of the past. And as European society increased in wealth and provided more security of life, it grew more humane; Europeans gradually came to believe that practices and institutions of a previous age, such as torture, slavery, debtors' prisons, and capital punishment for petty crimes, were both unnecessary and "barbaric." At the end of the nineteenth century, Europeans could look at their first few decades of modern progress with justified pride. As they strode resolutely into the twentieth, they could scarcely have been more confident.

Changes of this magnitude however could not take place without causing some problems; and Westerners were to grow more aware of them as the twentieth century wore on. One of the more serious of these was their relationship with the great mass of "backward" people left behind in the modernization process. These peoples greatly admired the spectacular Western achievements, but along with their admiration they developed a pronounced anti-Western hostility. In part this hostility was due to the fact that Westerners sometimes misused the considerable military and economic power at their disposal. By and large, however, negative feeling toward Western countries was due much more to the enormous impact of their example on other peoples than to their abuse of them. It was this example that caused peoples around the world to think of themselves as distinct nationalities, created in them a desire for a positive national identity, and saddled them with the problem of achieving it. Because nationalists in backward lands were distressed by their perception of their countries as "backward," they ardently searched for ideas that would allow them a more positive interpretation of their national experience. By far the most popular of these ideas was the theory of imperialism, which shifted the blame for national poverty from the underdeveloped to the developed countries and afforded those who felt themselves "exploited" a certain sense of moral superiority over the "exploiters." The arguments sustaining the theory of imperialism were never very strong, but since the idea served the emotional needs of nationalists and was endlessly repeated as unquestionable truth, it came to be widely believed.

The spirit of antiimperialism has proven itself to be a political force of enormous consequence in the twentieth century. The West began to be harassed by antiimperialist sentiment as early as 1917 when Communist revolutionaries in Russia vowed to overthrow every "capitalist-imperialist" government in the West. Soon afterward Fascist rulers in Italy launched their own crusade and for over two decades shook their fists at the "plutocratic-imperialist West." Shintoist leaders in Japan cranked up still another anti-Western campaign during the 1930s. This particular flowering of antiimperialism was somewhat unusual in that ever since the Russo-Japanese War of 1905, the Japanese had generally come to think of their country as a powerful and successfully industrialized nation, not one oppressed by more advanced countries. Political and economic developments in the thirties, however, severely shook Japanese confidence, and the military leaders who grabbed power in that period revived an earlier form of suspicious, anti-Western nationalism that had characterized Japan during the decades it was struggling to modernize.[1] When the Japanese reactive nationalists embarked upon their war of conquest in the Pacific, a major theme of their propaganda was that they were leading an antiimperialist war of the East against the West.

Reactive nationalist antiimperialism became an even more conspicuous feature of twentieth-century life with the emergence of countries that make up what is known today as the "Third World." The so-called "awakening of the Third World" is, in essence, a development where larger and larger numbers of people in the underdeveloped countries have become aware of their national identity and have come to regard that identity as important to their own sense of self-esteem. Third World nationalism was once mainly confined to the literate elites, but gradually it sifted to the broader population, and by the end of World War II it had built up sufficient force to burst into the open and force itself upon the attention of Westerners. Observers in the West were inclined to view the phenomenon as a longing for independence, a reaction against colonial rule, but it was actually much more than that. The mere existence of a powerful, prosperous, and creative West threatened the self-esteem of reactive nationalists; and so when they protested against the West, they were also protesting its superior position in the hierarchy of civilizations. It was for this reason that antiimperialist passion in colonial countries did not subside after the countries won their independence. The reactive nationalists simply substituted one set of grievances for another, claiming that their people were "exploited" by everything from foreign investments to foreign rock and roll.

The entry of Third World countries as active participants in the international system is, for the West, one of the most ominous developments of the postwar era. Westerners usually see any potential problems Third World nations may cause in terms of whether they ally themselves with the two communist superpowers. But the harm Third World countries can inflict upon the West goes considerably beyond this. There was once a time when Western nations could ignore the reactive nationalist passion of backward peoples because they were weak. Westerners only had to pay attention to an underdeveloped country if, like Japan or China, it became militarily or economically powerful. Today conditions in the world have changed, so that countries that produce very little and assemble sorrowful, undisciplined armies can nonetheless have a substantial impact upon Western peoples. Present trends are even more threatening than present conditions, for this ability of the weak to harass the strong will grow more pronounced in the foreseeable future.

Historians of some future era will probably point to the last quarter of the twentieth century as a period of fundamental and critical change in the relationship between the Third World and the West—one where certain Third World countries acquired the power to exert tremendous influence over the lives of Western peoples. This shift in power began in 1973 when a few oil-producing Third World countries formed an oil cartel and accumulated billions of dollars of surplus "petrodollars." By doing this they put themselves in a position to upset the delicate financial system of the West by shifting massive sums of money from bank to bank or from country to country. Ironically, even poor countries acquired substantial leverage over Western financial institutions during this period by borrowing hundreds of millions of the petrodollars that the oil-producing states had deposited in American and European banks. Today, often these poorer countries cannot afford to repay their loans; and many economists fear that several large defaults could cause major banks to fail, which, in turn, could precipitate a financial panic the world has not seen since the Great Depression. It may, of course, not be in the economic self-interest of Third World countries to play havoc with the world's financial system; but we have seen that radical reactive nationalists, should they ever gain power in key Third World countries, may be more interested in carrying out their radical nationalist "mission" than in maintaining a stable world order.

Another way that weak Third World countries can intimidate the strong is through nuclear weapons. The nuclear era in the Third World began in 1974 when India exploded an atomic bomb. Since that epochal year several other Third World countries have started their own nuclear programs, and it is only a matter of time before they acquire either nuclear weapons or the ability to quickly manufacture them when they perceive the need. Today, building a crude atomic bomb is so simple that even Third World terrorists are capable of doing it.[2] This means, of course, that radical leaders of weak Third World countries or even tiny bands of terrorists without much popular support are capable of using nuclear blackmail as a weapon against the West.[3]

Because Third World nations are becoming increasingly important to the West, it is necessary to recognize and understand the kinds of political values likely to dominate their societies. The most conspicuous of these values, of course, is a highly emotional anti-Western reactive nationalism. We have seen that there are actually two sides to Third World reactive nationalism, admiration of the West and hostility toward it. Privately, Westerners are apt to encounter the admiration, sometimes to an embarrassing degree. Publicly, they are likely to witness hostility, though even there a political leader may try to curb the more excessive manifestations of anti-Westernism if he receives aid from the West or if his enemies are trying to stir up reactive nationalist passion in order to gain political power. Whether expressed openly or not, anti-Western reactive nationalism is a potent political force in Third World countries and will remain so as long as nationalists there perceive their societies as secondary centers of culture.

The conditions of poverty and backwardness in the Third World that fire the flames of reactive nationalism also encourage the acceptance of other political values that when grouped together and carried out to their logical consequences are plainly totalitarian. Third World nationalists are anxious to catch up economically with the advanced countries and so are inclined to emphatically embrace productionism as a value. In order to bring about rapid economic change, these nationalists realize that the modernization-impeding values of their peoples must drastically change. All over the Third World are groups of sincere nationalistic elites who are dissatisfied with the masses as they are and who dream of using state power to shape them into something they are not. Since they wish to accomplish this within a short period of time, they cannot waste too much tender concern over the rights of individuals. To these elitists, duty to the collectivity is the transcending value.

Because totalitarian control over masses of people is so difficult to achieve, totalitarian societies are relatively few while totalitarian ambition is widespread. We have seen the totalitarian urge revealing itself in Latin American fascist, Marxist-Leninist, and even "democratic" ideologies. A. James Gregor has identified it in various African socialisms.[4] The totalitarian urge may be found either in secular political ideologies such as Islam or Shintoism that serve as political ideologies. The people who adhere to these different belief systems may consider themselves bitter ideological enemies, but this does nothing to change the fact that they all have in common advocacy of totalitarian political values.

It is possible for totalitarian elites to use their control over the masses either to the benefit or to the detriment of their people. On the one hand, totalitarian social control can serve genuinely humanistic ends when it is used to reduce the kinds of exploitation that are characteristic of conglomerations and to foster productionist discipline in people who are not able to provide themselves with an adequate standard of living. The modernization elite in Meiji Japan is the best illustration of a totalitarian government that was responsive to the needs of its people. The revolutionary leadership in contemporary Cuba is another example of a totalitarian elite that has brought a considerable amount of good to the general population. On the other hand, totalitarian social control can be used to perpetuate the most horrendous crimes. Totalitarian regimes in the Soviet Union, Germany, Cambodia, and China have been responsible for the greatest genocides of the twentieth century.

While totalitarian governments are capable of enhancing the well-being of people in the countries they rule, a distinction must be made between this kind of behavior and what they are likely to do abroad. Totalitarian states have an inherent tendency to be aggressive and expansionist in their relationships with other nations. This is partly due to the military ethos the elites deliberately foster to instill in the masses a militaristic social discipline. Children grow up absorbing the tales of intrepid war heroes and marching in military formation. Citizens celebrate their most important national holidays staring open-mouthed at tanks and rockets in military parades. The people are told time and time again that their enemies are everywhere and ready to spring. The whole atmosphere of totalitarian societies glorifies the military way of life, tempts leaders to use the weapons they so eagerly accumulate and display with pride, and conditions followers to the idea of armed struggle. Another factor contributing to the aggressiveness of totalitarian regimes is that as leaders of relatively unsuccessful nation-states,[5] they are possessed by a special need for achieving significance in world affairs. The quickest and surest way of commanding the attention and respect of other nations is to build an impressive military machine. Deep hunger for world prestige is a vitally important reason why the leaders of the Soviet Union literally subordinate everything in the national life of the USSR to the maintenance of a first-class military; why Fidel Castro has sent his best troops into the wilds of Africa; or why the "Teacher-Leader" of Libya, Colonel

Muammar Qaddafi, has turned his country into a weapons arsenal and is avidly seeking an "Islamic atomic bomb."[6]

One further aspect of totalitarianism that Westerners should never lose sight of is that totalitarian political values are completely antithetical to democratic values. Although the West is hated by totalitarian reactive nationalists more for its status as a primary center of culture than for its democratic ideals, the fact that the West is democratic gives it a special mission; for when the West defends itself from totalitarian aggression, it is fighting not just to survive but to preserve a rich democratic humanism. The West is, in fact, something of an island in this final quarter of the twentieth century. It is surrounded by hundreds of millions of people who are living under fully developed totalitarian regimes as well as by Third World peoples mired in social conditions that readily inspire those motivated by nationalistic ideals to entertain totalitarian ambition.

It is important that Westerners not only be committed to defend democratic values but have a clear and specific idea of what that commitment entails. To begin with, Westerners should not expect that in order to demonstrate their faith in their form of government, they have to engage in a crusade to spread democracy around the world. In the past some Western leaders have used foreign aid and even armed force to pressure weak Third World nations into accepting democratic institutions. But formal democratic institutions are worthless if people are not willing or able to use them for their intended purpose. Nor are they particularly humanistic if they allow individuals and organized groups to trample over one another in unbridled pursuit of self-interest. The efforts of Westerners to further the appeal of democracy around the world should, in the main, be restricted to ensuring that self-government functions well in their own societies and by so doing providing an example for all those who wish to see, that the system can work. It was precisely the example of successful democratic government in the most advanced nations on earth that had an enormous influence on the gradual maturation of democratic institutions in Japan in the early twentieth century. Were it not for the economic crisis of the 1930s and the rise of totalitarian militarists to power, Japan might have evolved politically to approximately where it is today without a war and an American occupation.

The most obvious step Westerners can take to protect their democratic way of life from the totalitarian states is to maintain a strong military. Democracy has already come close to being snuffed out once in this century. In 1939 it remained alive in only 10 out of 27 European countries; soon after the Second World War began, it died almost everywhere on the continent. With totalitarian Germany and totalitarian Japan waging war on opposite ends of the earth, democracy was saved from extinction only by American power. It is one of the mocking ironies of history that because America possessed a superior power, even the peoples of the vanquished nations are today better off living in democratic societies than they would have been had their own leaders won the war.

Military preparedness is not only a question of piling up military hardware but of psychological factors as well; and one of the most important of these is the will to use power when necessary to deter aggression. Westerners have sometimes failed the test of will because they do not think and react the same way as their totalitarian adversaries and consequently have had trouble understanding their motivations. By their very nature totalitarian societies are highly militaristic, and this brings out the aggressive side of national collectivities. Totalitarian leaders vary greatly in the degree of caution they exercise, but they all have in common an ardent desire to extend their influence over other peoples by whatever means possible. This passion can be especially pronounced if the leaders are part of a people traditionally afflicted with a negative national identity and are, therefore, eager to "prove" themselves at the international level. Given these kinds of motivations, a foreign initiative of a totalitarian state may not at all be "rational" in the sense of its helping to secure a vital national interest. It may be nothing more than a way of demonstrating national vigor. If this is the case, then Western leaders cannot count on a totalitarian state stopping at any point except when confronted by countervailing force.

Another psychological factor that greatly influences the ability of Westerners to deter the aggressive impulses of totalitarian states is the confidence they have in themselves and in their own mission. Totalitarian elites are able to build up élan in their people by strictly controlling the circulation of ideas within their society and thereby effectively regulating what people believe. In the West citizens are exposed to many different points of view, and whether they choose the beliefs that help them maintain their way of life depends upon their awareness of their responsibility to preserve the democratic values that others before them have worked so hard to realize. Unfortunately, in recent years the West has spawned a large number of critics and a rather sizable audience of listeners who lack this sense of responsibility. Abandoning the crucial virtue of self-restraint, they have carried criticism of their own societies to a point bordering on narcissistic masochism. For example, with regard to their relationship with the newly emerging Third World, they are willing to believe, or at least to meet halfway, the political lie of communist and Third World countries that the West is systematically "exploiting" underdeveloped peoples, that the producers of wealth are responsible for the poverty of the nonproducers. To make matters worse, some of these critics are easily charmed by totalitarian governments of the "left" and prefer to focus selectively on the positive accomplishments of those regimes while deliberately ignoring their implacable hostility to democratic values. Westerners who engage in excessive guiltmongering are doing a great disservice both to themselves and to future generations, for by manufacturing fictions and conjuring up self-doubts, they diminish the pride people take in their democratic heritage and undermine their resolve to defend it. Benito Mussolini used to contend that the great antagonism of the twentieth century, the one that dwarfed all others in significance, was the conflict between totalitarianism and democracy. Today that struggle is still going on, and yet there are many in the West who are scarcely aware of it.

Westerners have one further challenge in their defense of democratic humanism that is quite obvious but merits repeating: they must take special care to guard against the weakening of their traditions of civic virtue. Because the original theoreticians of democracy were preoccupied with restricting the power of the state, democratic theory places almost exclusive emphasis on the liberties, or "rights," of individuals. In the real world, however, democracy has only worked well where people were willing to strike a judicious balance between their individual rights and their responsibilities to the collectivity or society. A constant danger inherent in any democracy is that individuals or associations of individuals will lose their sense of restraints and demand rights that do harm to the society at large. Such rights may be political or economic. Individuals or interest groups may gain so many political rights that the government is not able to curb their antisocial or exploitative behavior. They may also win so many economic rights that the government can meet them only by printing money. The intemperate distribution of rights in a democratic society can lead only to the kind of social chaos where democratic institutions are more harmful than helpful to the enrichment of human life. At this point state authorities will be able to step in, wield arbitrary power, and still be welcomed by the majority of the people. The citizens of Western countries are in a position to contribute on a daily basis to the preservation of democratic humanism by maintaining sufficiently high standards of civic responsibility. If they succeed in this, they will continue to offer peoples less favored by history a palpable example demonstrating that the democratic alternative is both possible and practical. If they fail, then the flame of democratic humanism will die in Western societies, and the light may not be rekindled anywhere in the world for centuries.

NOTES

PREFACE

1. Carlos Rangel Guevara, *Del buen salvaje al buen revolucionario* (Caracas: Monte Avila Editores, C.A.), p. 21.

CHAPTER 1

1. Juan Bautiste Alberdi, *Escritos póstumos de J. B. Alberdi*, vol. 1 (Buenos Aires: Imprenta Europa, Moreno y Defensa, 1895), p. 1.

2. This observation is an impressionistic one gained from considerable personal experience bolstered by regular but random questioning. For various reasons, to confirm it by survey research would be difficult but not impossible. Survey research by Myron Glazer among Chilean university students indicates the values outlook is widespread even in that sector of society where one would expect the structuralist approach to be strongest. See Myron Glazer, "Student Politics in a Chilean University," in *Students in Revolt*, ed. Seymour Martin Lipset and Philip Altback (Boston: Houghton Mifflin, 1969), pp. 441–42. A survey conducted by the Brazilian Aparecida Joly Gouveia in his own country among secondary schoolteachers shows the predominance of explanations of underdevelopment relating to values. See Aparecida Joly Gouveia, "Education and Development: Opinions of Secondary Schoolteachers," in *Elites in Latin America*, ed. Seymour Martin Lipset and Aldo Solari (New York: Oxford University Press, 1967), pp. 500–1.

3. Gunnar Myrdal, *Asian Drama: An Inquiry into the Poverty of Nations*, vol. 3 (New York: Twentieth Century Fund, 1968), pp. 1539–48, 1859–1919; Simon Kuznets, "Notes on the Study of Economic Growth," *Items* (Social Science Research Council), vol. 13, no. 2 (June 1959): 13–17; Benjamin Higgens, *Social Aspects of Economic Growth in Latin America*, vol. 2 (Paris: UNESCO, 1963), pp. 178–79; Everett E. Hagen, "Research on Economic Development: Turning Parameters into Variables in the Theory of Economic Growth," *American Economic Review*, vol. 50, no. 2 (May 1960): 625; Bert F. Hoselitz, *Sociological Aspects of Economic Growth* (Glencoe, Ill.: Free Press, 1960), p. 24; Michel Debeaurais, "The Concept of Human Capital," *International Social Science Journal*, vol. 14, no. 4 (1962): 661–62.

4. Gunnar Myrdal, Simon Kuznets, L. K. Sadie, Everett Hagen, Bert Hoselitz, and Theodore Schultz (who has concentrated on Latin America) are among the better-known critics.

CHAPTER 2

1. Alexis de Tocqueville, *Journey to America: (Notebooks)*, ed. J. P. Mayer, trans. George Lawrence (London: Faber and Faber, 1959), p. 263.

2. Stanislav Andreski, *Parasitism and Subversion: The Case of Latin America* (New York; Schocken Books, 1966), p. 57; Carlos Octavio Bunge, *Nuestra America*, 6th ed. (Buenos Aires: Casa Vaccaro, 1918), pp. 188–89. Observations on the absolute power of estate lords have been made by many generations of travelers to Latin America; see, for example, Rev. C. Fletcher and Rev. D. P. Kidder, *Brazil and the Brazilians*, 9th ed. (Boston: Little, Brown, 1879), pp. 521–22.

3. Jorge Juan de Ulloa and Antonio de Ulloa, *Noticias Secretas de América*, (Buenos Aires: Ediciones Mar Oceano, 1953), p. 238.

4. Gilberto Freyre, *The Masters and the Slaves* (New York: Knopf, 1946), pp. 75–76, 392–96.

5. T. Lynn Smith, *Brazil: People and Institutions*, 4th ed. (Baton Rouge: Louisiana State University Press, 1972), p. 483.

6. Charles Darwin, *Journal of Researchers into the Natural History and Geology of the Countries Visited during the Voyage of the H.M.S. Beagle round the World under the Command of Capt. Fitz Roy, R.N.*, vol. 1 (New York: Harper and Brothers, 1864), 302–3.

7. De Tocqueville describes this attitude well; see Alexis de Tocqueville, *Democracy in America*, vol. 2, trans. Henry Reeve, ed. Phillips Bradley (New York: Vintage Books, 1945), pp. 172–77.

8. William S. Stokes, *Latin American Politics* (New York: Thomas Y. Crowell, 1959), p. 8.

9. From Caetano Alberto Soares, *Memoria para melhorar a sorte dos nossos escravos lida na sessão geral do Instituto dos Advogados Brazileiros no dia 7 de Septembro de 1845* (Rio de Janeiro, 1847), p. 4; quoted in Stanley J. Stein, *Vassouras: A Brizilian Coffee Country, 1850–1900* (Cambridge, Mass.: Harvard University Press, 1957), p. 133.

10. Indeed, this attitude is strong even today; see Victor Villanueva, *Hugo Blanco y la rebelion campesina* (Lima: Librería-Editorial Juan Mejia Baca, 1967), p. 31.

11. Leslie Byrd Simpson, *Many Mexicos* (Berkeley: University of California Press, 1962), p. 232.

12. Freyre, *Masters and Slaves*, p. 428.

13. A. Alvarez, *La creación del mundo moral* (Buenos Aires: La Cultura Argentina, 1915), p. 212.

14. Andreski makes this same point in Andreski, *Parasitism and Subversion*, pp. 25–26.

15. James Marvin Lockhart, *Spanish Peru, 1532–1560: A Colonial Society* (Madison: University of Wisconsin Press, 1968), pp. 210–11; de Ulloa and de Ulloa, *Noticias secretas*, p. 201; Magnus Mörner, *Race Mixture in the History of Latin America* (Boston: Little, Brown, 1967), p. 27.

16. Mörner, *Race Mixture*, pp. 55–56.

17. Ibid., p. 57.

18. Jorge Juan de Ulloa and Antonio de Ulloa, *A Voyage to South America*, trans. John Adams (New York: Knopf, 1964), p. 217.

19. For a discussion of mestizos and mestizo insecurities see Eric Wolf, *Sons of the Shaking Earth* (Chicago: University of Chicago Press, 1959), pp. 233–43.

20. Fletcher and Kidder, *Brazil and the Brazilian*, p. 134.

21. Thomas Ewbank, *Life in Brazil* (New York: Harper and Brothers, 1856), p. 184.

22. Jacaré Assu, *Brazilian Colonization from an European Point of View* (London: Edward Stanford, 1873), p. 99.

23. The middle classes developing in Europe were obviously very different from the "middle classes" in Latin America for those in Latin America were greatly influenced by the aristocratic value system.

24. Vernon Parrington, *Main Currents in American Thought: The Colonial Mind, 1620–1800* (New York: Harcourt, Brace & World, 1927), pp. 7–11.

25. Andreski, *Parasitism and Subversion*, pp. 31–32.

26. De Tocqueville, *Notebooks*, p. 262.

27. Matthew Josephson, *The Robber Barons* (New York: Harcourt, Brace, 1934), p. 9.

28. Andreski, *Parasitism and Subversion*, p. 26.

29. Francisco Bilbao, *La América en peligro* (Santiago de Chile: Ediciones Ercilla, 1941), pp 151–52.

30. Ibid., p. 151.

31. This perspective is similar to that of Maxwell Maltz, except that Maltz uses the term *positive self-image*; see Maxwell Maltz, *Psycho-Cybernetics* (New York: Pocket Books, 1960).

32. The term *national character* that historians of Europe find so convenient for their purposes, is obviously not a perfect fit for the Latin American situation, for the continent is not a "national" unity in the political sense. When viewed in its global context, however, Latin America can be treated as a cultural entity, and it is to this that the phrase "Latin American national character" refers.

33. Stokes, *Latin American Politics*, pp. 1–9; John Gillin, "Ethos Components in Modern Latin American Culture," *American Anthropologist*, vol. 57 (June 1955): 496.

34. Parrington, *Main Currents*, p. 361.

35. Seymour Martin Lipset, *The First New Nation* (New York: Basic Books, 1963), p. 95.

36. Kaspar D. Naegele, "From De Tocqueville to Myrdal: A Research Memorandum on Selected Studies of American Values,"

Comparative Study of Values: Working Papers No. 1 (Oct. 1949), pp. 37–38.

37. T. W. Adorno, Else Frenkel-Brunswik, D. J. Levinson, R. N. Sanford, *The Authoritarian Personality* (New York: Harper & Row, 1950), pp. 413–15.

38. The best piece of research on the race question in a Latin American country can be found in Charles Wagley, ed., *Race and Class in Rural Brazil* (Paris: UNESCO, 1952). In this book, see especially Ben Zimmerman's essay "Race Relations in the Arid Sertão."

39. Stokes, *Latin American Politics*, pp. 13–24. Stokes, an old Latin American hand, devoted a chapter to these. See also Payne's observations of Colombian society in James L. Payne, *Patterns of Conflict in Colombia* (New Haven, Conn.: Yale University Press, 1968), pp. 28–33.

40. Colloquialisms are used to express the same idea, for example, the Spanish phrases *hacerlo menos* (to make one less), *traer abajo* (to bring down), or *dejar colgado de la brocha* (an expression that envokes the image of a house painter whose scaffold is knocked out from under him, thereby "leaving him to hang on his paintbrush").

41. Carlos Delgado O., "An Analysis of 'Arribismo' in Peru," *Human Organization*, vol. 28, no. 2 (Summer, 1969): 134.

42. Gerado Reichel-Dolmatoff and Alicia Reichel-Dolmatoff, *The People of Aritama* (Chicago: University of Chicago Press, 1961), p. 447.

43. Oscar Lewis, *Life in a Mexican Village: Tepoztlán Restudied* (Urbana: University of Illinois Press, 1963), p. 54; George M. Foster, *Tzintzuntzan: Mexican Peasants in a Changing World* (Boston: Little, Brown, 1967), pp. 194–211, 312–13, 318.

44. Lewis, *Life*, pp. 294–95; Reichel-Dolmatoff and Reichel-Dolmatoff, *People of Aritama*, pp. 396–405.

45. Reichel-Dolmatoff and Reichel-Dolmatoff, *People of Aritama*, p. 396.

46. Ibid., 446; Foster, *Tzintzuntzan*, p. 155.

47. Foster, *Tzintzuntzan*, p. 154.

48. Reichel-Dolmatoff and Reichel-Dolmatoff, *People of Aritama*, p. 448.

49. Foster, *Tzintzuntzan*, pp. 142–43.

50. Reichel-Dolmatoff and Reichel-Dolmatoff, *People of Aritama*, p. 442.

51. Lewis, *Life*, p, xvii. Here Lewis refers to the "poor quality of inter-personal relations among the villagers" and criticizes the reluctance of some outsiders to come to terms with this despite the evidence. See also George M. Foster, "Interpersonal Relations in Peasant Society," *Human Organization*, vol. 19, no. 4 (Winter, 1960–61): 174–78. For a Peruvian study see Ozzie G. Simmons, "Drinking Pat-

terns and Interpersonal Performance in a Peruvian Mestizo Community," *Quarterly Journal of Studies on Alcohol,* vol. 20, no. 1 (March 1959): 104–5.

52. Foster, "Interpersonal Relations," p. 135.

53. Lewis, *Life,* pp. 287–97, passim.

54. Quoted in Linda Martin, "The 'Colorful' Indians of Peru: In Truth, a Sad Story of Neglect," *New York Times,* Dec. 3, 1972, Sec. 10, p. 23.

55. Lewis's two families are an example of this; see Oscar Lewis, ed., *Pedro Martinez: A Mexican Peasant and His Family* (New York: Random House, 1964), p. xlix.

56. Roger S. Greenway, *An Urban Strategy for Latin America* (Grand Rapids: Baker Book House, 1973), p. 24.

57. Nicolás Sanchez-Albornoz, *The Population of Latin America,* trans. W. A. R. Richardson (Berkeley: University of California Press, 1974), pp. 246–50, passim.

58. George J. Beier, "Can Third World Cities Cope?" *Population Bulletin,* vol. 31, no. 4 (Washington, D.C.: Population Reference Bureau, 1976), p. 9.

59. Penny Lernoux, "Paraguayan Aborigines Face Destruction," *Washington Post,* June 14, 1977, p. A13.

60. William W. Stein, *Hualcan: Life in the Highlands of Peru* (Ithaca, N.Y.: Cornell University Press, 1961), pp. 233, 228.

61. "Cowboy's Retrial Near in Colombia," *New York Times,* Jan. 7, 1973, p. 20.

62. Pedro María Morante, *Los felicitadores* (Caracas: Tipografia Garrido, 1952), p. 5.

63. Ibid., pp. 8–9.

64. Delgado, "Analysis of 'Arribismo,'" p. 135.

65. Wolf, *Sons,* p. 240.

66. Samuel Ramos, *Profile of Man and Culture in Mexico,* trans. Peter G. Earle (Austin: University of Texas Press, 1962), p. 66.

67. Orlando Fals-Borda, *Peasant Society in the Colombian Andes: A Sociological Study of Saucio* (Gainesville: University of Florida Press, 1955), p. 208.

68. Ramos, *Profile,* pp. 71–72.

69. Octavio Ignacio Romano V., "Donship in a Mexican-American Community in Texas," *American Anthropologist,* vol. 62, no. 6 (Dec. 1960): 972; Fals-Borda, *Peasant Society,* pp. 208–9; Lewis, *Life,* pp. 293–94.

70. Fals-Borda, *Peasant Society,* pp 211–13.

71. Aniceto Aramoni, "Machismo," *Psychology Today,* vol. 5, no. 8 (Jan. 1972), p. 71.

72. Wolf, *Sons*, p. 239.

73. Reichel-Dolmatoff and Reichel-Dolmatoff, *People of Aritama*, p. 164.

74. María Elvira Bermúdez, *La vida familiar del Mexicano*, (Mexico City: Antigua Librería Robredo, 1955), p. 52; the translation here is from Andreski, *Parasitism and Subversion*, p. 48.

75. James Bruce, *Those Perplexing Argentines* (New York: Longmans, Green, 1953), p. 167.

76. Arthur J. Rubel, *Across the Tracks: Mexican-Americans in a Texas City* (Austin: University of Texas Press, 1966), p. 84.

77. Lewis, *Life*, pp. 327–28.

78. Ibid., p. 322; Oscar Lewis, *A Study of Slum Culture: Backgrounds for La Vida* (New York: Random House, 1968), p. 164; Reichel-Dolmatoff and Reichel-Dolmatoff, *People of Aritama*, p. 189; Foster, "Interpersonal Relations," pp. 60–61; Fals-Borda, *Peasant Society*, p. 207.

79. Foster, "Interpersonal Relations," p. 131.

80. Bermúdez, *La vida familiar*, p. 53; see also Lewis, *Tepoztlán*, p. 56; Foster, "Interpersonal Relations," p. 63.

81. Oscar Lewis, *Tepoztlán: Village in Mexico* (New York: Holt, Rinehart & Winston, 1960), p. 56.

82. Bermúdez, *La vida familiar*, p. 56.

83. Andreski, *Parasitism and Subversion*, p. 11.

84. Oscar Lewis, ed., *The Children of Sanchez* (New York: Random House, 1961), pp. 232–33.

85. Lewis, *Tepoztlán*, p. 54.

86. For a representative case study see Richard W. Patch, *Life in a Callejon*, American Universities Field Staff Reports, West Coast South America Series (Peru), vol. 8, no. 6 (June 1961).

87. John Biesanz and Marvis Biesanz, *The People of Panama* (New York: Columbia University Press, 1955), pp. 286–87.

88. Bruce Van Voorst, "The Abandoned Children of Latin America," *Newsweek*, Aug. 6, 1974, p. 43.

89. Ibid.

90. Ibid.; see also Terri Shaw, "Survival in the Street," *Washington Post*, June 6, 1974, p. A31.

91. Humberto Rotondo, Javier Mariátegui, Pedro Aliaga L. Carlos García-Pacheco, "Estudio de Salud Mental," in José Matos Mar, *El valle de Lurín y el pueblo de Pachacamac* (Lima: Dept. of Anthropology, San Marcos University, 1964), pp. 232–48; see also in this regard Reichel-Dolmatoff and Reichel-Dolmatoff, *People of Aritama*, p. 450.

92. This classification was first introduced by Eric Wolf in Eric Wolf, "Types of Latin American Peasantry: A Preliminary Discussion," *American Anthropologist*, vol. 57, no. 3 (June 1955): 452–71. Wagley and Harris have used the terms *Indian peasant* and *mestizo peasant*

communities in place of Wolf's "open" and "closed" communities. These other terms, however, do not serve the purposes of this essay as well because peasants generally regarded as having the cultural characteristics of Indians can nonetheless be open community types; that is to say, they can be open to the value system of mestizo and creole culture; see Charles Wagley and Marvin Harris, "A Typology of Latin American Sub-cultures," *American Anthropologist*, vol. 57, no. 3 (1955): 428–51; also see Charles Wagley, "The Peasant," in *Continuity and Change in Latin America*, ed. John J. Johnson (Stanford, Calif.: Stanford University Press, 1964), pp. 21–48.

93. Melvin M. Tumin, "The Dynamics of Cultural Discontinuity in a Peasant Society," *Social Forces*, vol. 29, no. 2 (Dec. 1950): 136–37; Melvin M. Tumin, *Caste in a Peasant Society: A Case Study in the Dynamics of Caste* (Princeton, N.J.: Princeton University Press, 1952), pp. 142–48. Low expectations are an implicit, crucial feature in Erasmus's study of the Yaqui Indians of Northwest Mexico; see Charles J. Erasmus, "Cultural Change in Northwest Mexico," in *Contemporary Change in Traditional Societies*, vol. 4, ed. Julian H. Steward (Urbana: University of Illinois Press, 1967), pp. 3–131.

94. For a good brief discussion of this see Tumin, "Dynamics," pp. 137–41; also see Tumin, *Caste*, pp. 148–54.

95. Bruce, *Perplexing Argentines*, p. 28; Bruce here notes that how one "appears" in a discussion takes priority over the issue itself.

96. Delgado, "Analysis or 'Arribismo,'" p. 134.

97. Wade Green, "A Farewell to Alms," *New York Times Magazine*, May 23, 1976, pp. 36, 40.

98. Ibid.

CHAPTER 3

1. The term *entrepreneur* is used here in the broad sense and includes the creative managers as well as the founders of economic enterprises.

2. Warren Dean, *The Industrialization of São Paulo, 1889–1945* (Austin: University of Texas Press, 1969), p. 46.

3. Warren Dean, "São Paulo's Industrial Elite, 1890–1960" (Ph.D. diss., University of Florida, 1965), p. 43.

4. Seymour Martin Lipset and Reinhard Bendix, *Social Mobility in Industrial Society* (Berkeley: University of California Press, 1962), pp. 30–31; see also José Luis Imaz *Los que mandan* (Buenos Aires: Editorial Universitaria de Buenos Aires, 1964), pp. 138–39.

5. For a study that directly addresses itself to this point see Charles Erasmus, "Work Patterns in a Mayo Village," *American Anthropologist*, vol. 57, no. 2: 322–33.

6. Gerado Reichel-Dolmatoff and Alicia Reichel-Dolmatoff, *The People of Aritama* (Chicago: University of Chicago Press, 1961), p. 259.

7. Ibid., pp. 260–61, passim.

8. Ibid., pp. 262–63.

9. Lewis, for example, discusses similar work patterns in Oscar Lewis, *Life in a Mexican Village: Tepoztlán Restudied* (Urbana: University of Illinois Press, 1963), pp. 56, 111–12.

10. Arthur J. Rubel, *Across the Tracks: Mexican-Americans in a Texas City* (Austin: University of Texas Press, 1966), p. xxiii.

11. Octavio Ignacio Romano V., "Donship in a Mexican-American Community in Texas," *American Anthropologist,* vol. 62, no. 6 (Dec. 1960); 973.

12. Lewis, *Life,* p. 294.

13. William Madsen, *The Mexican Americans of South Texas* (New York: Holt, Rinehart and Winston, 1964), p. 23.

14. Rubel, *Across the Tracks,* pp. 88–89.

15. For other discussions of the envy reflex see George M. Foster, "Interpersonal Relations in Peasant Society," *Human Organization,* vol. 19, no. 4 (Winter, 1960–61): 174–78; Helmut Schoeck, "The Envy Barrier," in *Foreign Aid Reexamined: A Critical Appraisal,* ed. James W. Wiggins and Helmut Schoeck (Washington, D.C.: Public Affairs Press, 1958), pp. 90–110; Charles Erasmus, "Community Development and the Encogido Syndrome," *Human Organization,* vol. 27, no. 1 (Spring, 1968): 70–71.

16. Lipset's essay and bibliography are an excellent summation of the available research on the subject; see Seymour Martin Lipset, "Values and Entrepreneurship in the Americas," in *Revolution and Counterrevolution,* ed. Seymour Martin Lipset (New York: Basic Books, 1968), pp. 65–66. For a number of essays by leading economists see Peter Kilby, ed., *Entrepreneurship and Economic Development* (New York: Free Press, 1971).

17. William F. Whyte, "Culture, Industrial Relations, and Economic Development: The Case of Peru," (Mimeograph, 1966), pp. 5–6. This research was later published in William F. Whyte, "High-level Manpower for Peru," in *Manpower and Education: Country Studies in Economic Development,* ed. Frederick Harbison and Charles A. Myers (New York: McGraw-Hill, 1965), pp. 65–66.

18. Theodore Levitt would go even further than this; see Theodore Levitt, "Management and the Post-Industrial Society," *The Public Interest,* no. 44 (Summer, 1976): 72–75, 83–85.

19. Whyte, "Manpower."

20. Lipset, "Values and Entrepreneurship," p. 76.

21. Ibid., p. 78.

22. John Fayerweather, *Management of International Operations* (New York: McGraw-Hill, 1960), pp. 24–27.

23. Thomas C. Cochran, *The Puerto Rican Businessman* (Philadelphia: University of Pennsylvania Press, 1959), p. 108.

24. Ibid., pp. 91, 108.

25. Lipset, "Values and Entrepreneurship," pp. 77–78.

26. Emanuel de Kadt, "The Brazilian Impasse," *Encounter*, Sept. 1965, p. 57.

27. Ibid.

28. Albert Lauterbach, "Government and Development: Managerial Attitudes in Latin America," *Journal of Inter-American Studies*, vol. 7, no. 2 (April 1965): 209; Albert Lauterbach, *Enterprise in Latin America* (Ithaca, N.Y.: Cornell University Press, 1966), pp. 75–76; Lipset, "Values and Entrepreneurship," pp 79–80.

29. One of the best-known interpretations of these incentives is David C. McClelland, *The Achieving Society* (Princeton, N.J.: D. Van Nostrand, 1961).

30. "Sears, Roebuck in Brazil," *Fortune*, Feb. 1950, p. 151.

31. Cochran, *Puerto Rican Businessman*, p. 81.

32. Lipset, "Values and Entrepreneurship,"; Lauterbach, *Enterprise*, p. 75–76.

33. W. Paul Strassman, "The Industrialist," in *Continuity and Change in Latin America*, ed. John J. Johnson (Stanford, Calif.: Stanford University Press, 1964), pp. 172–74.

34. Harold R. W. Benjamin, *Higher Education in the American Republics* (New York: McGraw-Hill, 1965), p. 16.

35. Whyte, "Manpower," pp. 61–63.

36. Bert F. Hoselitz, *Sociological Aspects of Economic Growth* (Glencoe, Ill.: Free Press, 1960), pp. 151–52.

37. John Fayerweather, *The Executive Overseas* (Syracuse, N.Y.: Syracuse University Press, 1959), p. 93.

38. Everett E. Hagen, *On the Theory of Social Change* (Homewood, Ill.: Dorsey Press, 1962), p. 370.

39. Aaron Lipman, "Social Backgrounds of the Bogotá Entrepreneur," *Journal of Inter-American Studies*, vol. 7, no. 2 (April 1965), p. 234.

40. Stanislav Andreski, *Parasitism and Subversion; The Case of Latin America* (New York: Schocken Books, 1966), pp. 119–20.

41. Ibid., p. 119.

42. John Maynard Keynes, *The Economic Consequences of the Peace* (New York: Harper Torchbooks, 1920), pp. 18–21.

43. Lauterbach, *Enterprise*, p. 159.

44. Tomás Roberto Fillol, *Social Factors in Economic Development: The Argentine Case* (Cambridge, Mass.: MIT Press, 1961), p. 20.

45. Thomas C. Cochran, "Cultural Factors in Economic Growth," *The Journal of Economic History*, vol. 20, no. 4 (Dec. 1960): 518.

46. Neil McKendrick, "Josiah Wedgewood and Factory Discipline," *The Historical Journal*, vol. 4, no. 1 (1961): 51.

47. "What it Takes to Run a Big Country," *U.S. News and World Report*, Dec. 12, 1977, p. 69.

48. International Bank for Reconstruction and Development (IBRD), *Report on Cuba: Findings and Recommendations of an Economic and Technical Mission* (Washington, D.C.: International Bank for Reconstruction and Development, 1951), p. 168; see especially chaps. 44, 48.

49. For a good resume of this see Andreski, *Parasitism and Subversion*, pp. 125–51.

50. Andreski has coined the term *kleptocracy* to describe these governments; see ibid., pp. 62–69.

51. For figures and discussions see Edwin Lieuwen, *Arms and Politics in Latin America*, rev. ed. (New York: Praeger, 1961), pp. 149–50; Stokes, *Latin American Politics*, pp. 389–91; Andreski, *Parasitism and Subversion;* Frank Owen, *Perón* (London: Cresset Press, 1957), p. 250; Jack Anderson, "Politics Dilute Anti-Corruption Effort in Mexico," *Washington Post*, Aug. 24, 1984, p. E12.

52. Andreski, *Parasitism and Subversion*, pp. 12–15.

53. Ibid., p. 172.

54. Henry Foster, *Travels in Brazil* (1817); reprint edition edited and introduced by C. Harvey Gardiner (Carbondale and Edwardsville: Southern Illinois University Press, 1966), p. 20.

55. Thomas Ewbank, *Life in Brazil, or a Journal of a Visit to the Land of the Coca and the Palm* (New York: Harper and Brothers, 1856), pp. 184–85. Some armies in Latin America actually did support more officers than regular soldiers. For example, in 1901 the Venezuelan army had 4 top generals-in-chief, 28 generals-in-chief one step below, 1,439 ordinary generals, 1,462 colonels, 7,308 majors, 3,230 captains, 2,300 lieutenants, and 1,000 ensigns. Approximately three-quarters of the Venezuelan army at this time was made up of officers. See Fritz Epstein, "European Military Influence in Latin American" Washington, Library of Congress Photoduplication Service, 1961, pp. 44–45.

56. Andreski, *Parasitism and Subversion*, pp. 86–87; see also Payne's research method and statistics dealing with Colombia in James L. Payne, *Patterns of Conflict in Colombia* (New Haven, Conn.: Yale University Press, 1968), pp. 57–60.

57. Philip B. Taylor, *Government and Politics of Uruguay* (New Orleans, La.: Tulane University Press, 1960), p. 83.

58. Andreski, *Parasitism and Subversion*, p. 172.

59. Payne, *Patterns of Conflict*, pp. 65–67.

60. Andreski, *Parasitism and Subversion*, p. 91; Samuel Shapiro, "Uruguay's Lost Paradise," *Current History*, vol. 62, no. 366 (Feb. 1972), p. 100.

61. William S. Stokes, *Latin American Politics* (New York: Thomas Y. Crowell, 1959), p. 239.

62. James L. Payne, *Labor and Politics in Peru* (New Haven, Conn.: Yale University Press, 1965), pp. 3–26.

63. Stokes, *Latin American Politics*, p. 239.

64. Boris Goldenberg, *The Cuban Revolution and Latin America* (New York: Praeger, 1965), p. 109.

65. Paul N. Rosenstein-Rodan, "Why Allende Failed," *Challenge*, May-June, 1974, p. 12.

66. Frank Bonilla, *The Failure of Elites* (Cambridge, Mass.: MIT Press, 1970), p. 290.

67. Andreski, *Parasitism and Subversion*, p. 199.

68. IBRD, *Report on Cuba*, pp. 145–46, 395, passim.

69. Dudley Seers, ed., *Cuba: The Economic and Social Revolution* (Chapel Hill: University of North Carolina Press, 1964), p. 18.

70. IBRD, *Report on Cuba*, pp. 146, 392.

71. Ibid., pp. 143–51, passim.

72. See, for example, John Biesanz, "The Economy of Panama," *Inter-American Economic Affairs*, vol. 6, no. 1 (Summer, 1956): 15–17.

73. Andreski, *Parasitism and Subversion*, pp. 121–23.

74. Ibid., pp. 286–89; Shapiro, "Lost Paradise," pp. 99–100, passim.

75. Jonathan Kandell, "Some Argentines Turn to Prayer as Economic Crisis Deepens," *New York Times*, Aug. 13, 1975, p. 6; Juan de Onis, "Argentineans Learn to Live, Unhappily, with Inflation of 335%," *New York Times*, Jan. 8, 1976, p. 10.

76. *U.S. News and World Report*, Jan. 31, 1977, p. 46; Joanne Omang, "Latin Top Secret: Economic Statistic," *Washington Post*, April 12, 1977, p. A12. A 6,000 percent figure was given by the military government; some observers feel statistics in Latin America are most trustworthy when given just after a military coup because the new rulers don't have to exaggerate—the truth is shocking enough.

77. Lieuwen, *Arms and Politics*, p. 147.

78. Andreski, *Parasitism and Subversion*, p. 73.

79. Ibid.

80. Stokes, *Latin American Politics*, p. 112.

81. Marvin Howe, "Peru's Leaders Vow to Press Reorganization of the Nation's Life," *New York Times*, Jan. 15, 1974, p. 2; Joseph Novitski, "Andes Arms-Limit Meeting Postponed," *Washington Post*, Jan. 10, 1975, p. A16; Hugh O'Shaughnessy, "Little Peru Spends Big for Arms," *New York Times*, March 7, 1976, sec. 4, p. 4.

82. Andreski, *Parasitism and Subversion*, pp. 87–89.

83. K. H. Silvert, *On Civil Discourtesy*, American Universities Field Staff Reports, West Coast South America Series (Chile), vol. 4, no. 2 (March 1957), p. 5.

84. Ibid.

85. "Latin American Bureaucracy Makes Frustration an Industry," *New York Times*, Oct. 27, 1975, p. 10.

86. Interview in Jamaica, Aug. 1977.

87. *El Comercio* (Lima), July 20, 1968, p. 12.

88. Andreski, *Parasitism and Subversion*, p. 67.

89. Leonard Greenwood, "Survivors of Peru's Epic '70 Quake Ask Where the Aid Went," *Washington Post*, Aug. 2, 1976, p. A8.

90. James Pringle, "A Whiff of Scandal," *Newsweek*, Oct. 7, 1974, p. 56.

91. Biesanz, "Economy of Panama," p. 25.

92. Andreski, *Parasitism and Subversion* p. 65. This particular problem appears to be an enduring feature of Mexican life; see "Mexico Promises Corruption Drive, but Mexicans Wait and See," *New York Times*, Dec. 22, 1974, p. 12.

93. Ibid., p. 68.

94. *Ojo* (Lima), July 20, 1968, p. 1.

95. Francisco Gonzalez Pineda, *El Mexicano: psicología de su destructividad* (Mexico City: Editorial Pax-Mexico, 1968), pp. 80–81.

96. Hoselitz, *Economic Growth*, pp. 173–74.

97. Reichel-Dolmatoff and Reichel-Dolmatoff, *People of Aritama*, pp. 120–22.

98. H. A. Murena, "Notas sobre la crisis argentina," *Sur* (Buenos Aires), Sept.-Oct., 1957, pp. 6–7.

CHAPTER 4

1. Manuel Gonzalez Prada, *Horas de lucha*, 2d ed., (Callao, Peru: Tip. "Lux," 1924), p. 335.

2. V. Gordon Childe, *Man Makes Himself* (New York: Mentor Books, 1951), pp. 134–42. Originally published in 1936.

3. Augusto Salizar Bondy, *La cultura de la dependencia* (Lima: Instituto de Estudios Peruanos, 1966), pp. 10–11.

4. Robert J. Alexander, *Today's Latin America* (New York: Doubleday, 1962), pp. 203–16.

5. Seymour Martin Lipset, *Revolution and Counterrevolution* (New York: Basic Books, 1968), p. 91.

6. Ibid., pp. 90–91.

7. José Luis de Imaz, *Los que mandan* (Buenos Aires: Editorial Universitaria de Buenos Aires, 1964), pp. 136–39.

8. Lipset, *Revolution*, p. 90.

9. Arron Lipman, "Social Backgrounds of the Bogotá Entrepreneur," *Journal of Inter-American Studies*, vol. 7, no. 2 (April 1965), p. 231.

10. John Biesanz, "The Economy of Panama," *Inter-American Economic Affairs*, vol. 6, no. 1 (Summer, 1952), p. 9.

11. Thomas E. Weil, *Area Handbook for Venezuela* (Washington D.C.: GPO, 1970), p. 56.

12. David Chaplin, *Industrialization and Distribution of Wealth in Peru* (Land Tenure Center Research Paper No. 18, University of Wisconsin, July 1966), p. 24; William F. Whyte, "High-level Manpower for Peru," in *Manpower and Education: Country Studies in Economic Development*, ed. Frederick Harbison and Charles A. Myers (New York: McGraw-Hill, 1965), p. 46; Raymond Vernon, *The Dilemma of Mexico's Development* (Cambridge, Mass.: Harvard University Press, 1963), pp. 156–57.

13. Lipset, *Revolution*, p. 95. Lipset uses figures from Suzanne Keller, *The Social Origins and Career Lives of Three Generations of American Business Leaders* (Ph. D. diss. Department of Sociology, Columbia University, 1953), pp. 37–41.

14. Edwin Lieuwen, *Arms and Politics in Latin America*, rev. ed., (New York: Praeger, 1961), pp. 31–32, 153.

15. Examples of military dependencia prior to World War II are even more dramatic. For example, one German advisor served as Commander-in-Chief of the Bolivian army during the Chaco War (1932–35). Another, General Emil Koerner, was the most powerful military figure in Chile around the turn of the century and was given the authority to completely remake the Chilean army into the mirror image of the German. Koerner even had the boy scouts in Chile doing the German goosestep. See Fritz Epstein, "European Military Influence in Latin America" (Research paper, Library of Congress, Washington, D.C., 1941) pp. 116–24; for an overview of the entire continent see pp. 114–213.

16. The mystique of foreign advisors is so pronounced in Latin America that these advisors do not necessarily have to be experts. In Peru a young Peace Corps volunteer of my acquaintance with nothing more to his educational credit than a bachelor's degree in liberal arts was asked to join an elite national planning commission. Another, fresh out of Anglo-Saxon law school and barely able to speak enough Spanish to order a meal, worked at the cabinet level on an important piece of reform legislation.

17. F. Houtart and E. Pin, *L' Église a l'heur de l'Amérique latine* (Casterman, 1965), p. 153.

18. The intellectual historian Crane Brinton, for example, in his famous book *Ideas and Men* did not even list Latin America in the index. See Crane Brinton, *Ideas and Men* (New York: Prentice-Hall, 1950).

19. Julian Steward, "The Prominent Families of Puerto Rico," in *A Study in Social Anthropology*, ed. Julian Steward (Urbana: University of Illinois Press, 1956), p. 433.

20. Julio de la Fuente, "La civilización 'pocha' de Mexico," (Dec. 1948): 444, as quoted in Oscar Lewis, "Mexico since Cardinas," in *Social Change in Latin America Today*, ed. Richard N. Adams (New York: Vintage Books, 1960), pp. 296–97.

21. J. Serra, "The Brazilian Economic Miracle," in *Latin America: From Dependence to Revolution*, ed. James Petras (New York: John Wiley, 1973), pp. 126–27.

22. In Chile, for example, 65 percent of the television programs aired in 1971 were imported. See David J. Morris, *We Must Make Haste—Slowly* (New York: Random House, 1973), p. 268.

23. This comparison was made by averaging films advertised in recent random issues of *El Comercio* (Lima) and *The Philadelphia Inquirer*.

24. *Veja* (Rio de Janeiro), quoted in "Brazil: Filmmakers at the Ready," *Atlas*, March 1976, p. 36.

25. James Bruce, *Those Perplexing Argentines* (New York: Longman's Green, 1953), pp. 332–33.

26. A 1973 study by the Chilean Ministry of Education found that 60 percent of the country's high school students smoked marijuana. See Morris, *Make Haste*, p. 260.

27. Alberto Zum Felde, *El problema de la cultura americana* (Buenos Aires: Editorial Losada, S.A., 1943), p. 27.

28. Ibid., p. 33.

29. Ibid., p. 37, 41.

30. Childe, *Man Makes Himself*, p. 142.

31. Zum Felde, *Cultura americana*, p. 38.

32. Louis Mouralis, *Un Sejour aux Etats-Unis du Brésil* (Paris: Les Presses Universitaires de France, 1934), pp. 118, 137–38.

33. Plinio Salgado, *A quarta humanidade* (Rio de Janeiro: Livraria José Olympio-Editora, 1934), p. 179.

34. Zum Felde, *Cultura americana*, p. 34.

35. Quoted in Raul Damonte Taborda, *Ayer fué San Perón* (Argentina: Ediciones Gure, 1955), p. 44.

36. Rafael L. Trujillo, *Fundamentos y política de una régimen* (Ciudad Trujillo, D.R.: Editora de Caribe, 1960), pp. 6–7.

37. Salvador Allende, *Su pensamiento político* (Santiago: Empresa Editora Nacional Quimantu Limitada, 1972), p. 209.

38. Samuel Ramos, *Profile of Man and Culture in Mexico*, trans. Peter G. Earle (Austin: University of Texas Press, 1962), p. 9.

39. Leopoldo Zea, *Latin America and the World*, trans. Francis Hendricks and Beatrice Berber (Norman: University of Oklahoma Press, 1971), p. 9.

40. Tancredo Pinochet Le Brun, *Como construir una gran civilización chilena e hispanoamericana* (Santiago de Chile: Editorial "Asies," 1940), p. 98.

41. Helio Jaguaribe de Mattos, "A Succinct Analysis of Brazilian Nationalism," in *Nationalism in Latin America*, ed. Samual L. Bailey (New York: Knopf, 1971), p. 181.

42. Howard J. Wiarda, "The Methods of Control of Trujillo's Dominican Republic," Latin American Monographs, ser. 2, no. 5 (1968): 122.

43. Frederick B. Pike, *Hispanismo, 1898–1936* (Notre Dame, Ind.: University of Notre Dame Press, 1971), pp. 8–9.

44. Clarance H. Haring, *South America Looks at the United States* (New York: Macmillan, 1929), p. 62.

45. Ramos, for example, attributes much of the social behavior that is characteristic of hierarchical personalities to the national inferiority complex even though there have clearly been and continue to be many people in the rural areas of Latin America who display such behavior yet are too uneducated and too far removed from the centers of national life to be very concerned about the existence of foreign peoples.

46. "Argentina: Safety First," *Newsweek*, Feb. 9, 1976, p. 39.

47. "Argentina: There's No Tomorrow," *Newsweek*, Dec. 8, 1975, p. 44.

48. Quoted in Richard Fagen, "Mass Mobilization in Cuba," in *Cuba in Revolution*, ed. Rolando Bonachea and Nelson Valdés (New York: Doubleday, 1972), p. 213.

49. Giangiacomo Foà, "La piccola Italia del Sud America," *Epoca*, no. 28 (1971): 117.

50. Bruce, *Perplexing Argentines*, p. 14.

51. Mouralis, *Sejour*, p. 132.

52. Leslie Byrd Simpson, *Many Mexicos*, (Berkeley: University of California Press, 1962), p. 260.

53. Warren Dean, *The Industrialization of São Paulo, 1880–1945* (Austin: University of Texas Press, 1969), p. 11.

54. Bruce, *Perplexing Argentines*, p. 15.

55. These fears, for example, prompt contemporary Latin American intellectuals to protest still a remark made a century and a half ago by the German philosopher Hegel, who dismissed Latin America as an "echo of the Old World." They also are disturbed by the fact that Hegel completely ignored Latin America in his writings. See Leopoldo Zea, "El occidente y la conciencia," *Mexico y lo Mexicano*, vol. 14 (1959): 27–34.

56. *El Comercio* (Lima), Aug. 5, 1968, p. 1.

57. Fayerweather, for example, notes, "Such an apparently inconsequential matter as a native American earning a post in major league baseball in the United States has been seized on as a nationally publicized symbol of pride." See John Fayerweather, *Management of International Operations* (New York: McGraw-Hill, 1960), p. 210.

58. From *The Guiness Book of Olympic Records* (Middlesex, England: Penguin Books, 1972).

59. I covered the 1968 summer Olympic Games as a journalist, and I as well as other foreigners who were there at the time frequently encountered this sentiment.

60. Richard Patch, "A Hacienda Becomes a Community," *American Universities Field Staff Reports*, West Coast South America Series, (Peru) vol. 4, no. 11 (Oct. 1957), p. 5.

61. Wallace Kirkland, *Recollections of a Life Photographer* (Cambridge, Mass.: Houghton-Mifflin, 1954), p. 103.

62. Vincenzo Petrullo, *Puerto Rican Paradox* (Philadelphia: University of Pennsylvania Press, 1947), pp. 137–38.

63. Patch, *Hacienda.*

64. Pedro A. Villoldo, *Latin American Resentment* (New York: Vantage Press, 1959), p. 11.

65. Ibid.

66. Stephen Bonsal, "Greater Germany in South America," *The North American Review*, vol. 176 (1903): 61.

67. Wallace Thompson, *The Mexican Mind: A Study of National Psychology* (Boston: Little, Brown, 1922), pp. 291–92.

68. Harry L. Foster, *A Gringo in Mañana-Land* (New York: Dodd, Mead, 1924), p. 181.

69. Charles Darwin, *Journal of Researches into the Natural History and Geology of the Countries Visited during the Voyage of the H.M.S. Beagle Round the World under the Command of Capt. Fitz Roy, R.H.*, vol. 1 (New York: Harper and Brothers, 1864), pp. 190, 301.

70. Edward Alsworth Ross, *The Social Revolution in Mexico* (New York: Century, 1923), pp. 18, 7.

71. Charles M. Pepper, "The Spanish Population in Cuba and Porto Rico," *Publication of the American Academy of Political and Social Science*, no. 313 (1901): 169, 171–73, passim; Nevin O. Winter, *Mexico and Her People Today*, rev. ed., (Boston: Page, 1907), pp. 185–87; Reginald Lloyd, *Twentieth Century Impressions of Brazil* (London: Lloyd's Greater Britain Publishing, 1913), pp. 130–32.

72. Maturin M. Ballow, *History of Cuba and Notes of a Traveller in the Tropics* (Boston: Phillips, Sampson, 1854), p. 218.

73. Pepper, *Spanish Population*, pp. 177, 178.

74. Richard F. Behrendt, "The Uprooted: A Guatemala Sketch," *New Mexico Quarterly Review* (Spring, 1949): 28.

75. Edwa Moser, *The Mexican Touch* (New York: Duell, Sloan, and Pearce, 1940), pp. 143–45.

76. William Chapin, "Masters of the Plantation," *New York Times*, Dec. 3, 1973, sec. 10, p. 17.

77. Gunnar Myrdal, *Asian Drama: An Inquiry into the Poverty of Nations*, vol. 1 (New York: Twentieth Century Fund, 1968), pp. 14–16, 23.

78. Frank Tannenbaum, *Ten Keys to Latin America* (New York: Knopf, 1962), pp. 177–78.

79. Quoted in Herbert Cerwin, *These Are the Mexicans* (New York: Reynal and Hitchcock, 1947), p. 347.

80. William Madsen, *The Mexican Americans of South Texas* (New York: Holt, Rinehart and Winston, 1964), p. 22.

81. Oscar Lewis, ed., *The Children of Sanchez* (New York: Random House, 1961), p. 339.

82. Arthur J. Rubel, *Across the Tracks: Mexican-Americans in a Texas City* (Austin: University of Texas Press, 1966), p. xxiii.

83. Some Latin American women have had such bad experiences with macho behavior that they have adopted the extreme position of refusing to enter into marriage with a man of their own nationality. See John Biesanz and Marvis Biesanz, *The People of Panama* (New York: Columbia University Press, 1955), p. 296.

84. Lewis, *Children of Sanchez*, pp. 440, 431.

85. Ibid., p. 299.

86. Ibid., p. 232.

87. Oscar Lewis, *Pedro Martínez* (New York: Random House, 1964), p. 455.

88. Quoted in Francis Donahue, "Oil Age in Venezuelan Literature," *The Texas Quarterly* (Winter, 1968): 156.

89. Leopoldo Zea, "El occidente y la conciencia," pp. 11–12.

90. Octavio Paz, *The Labyrinth of Solitude: Life and Thought in Mexico*, trans. Lysander Kemp (New York: Grove Books, 1961), pp. 166–69, passim.

CHAPTER 5

1. Norman Macrae, "America's Third Century," *The Economist*, Oct. 25, 1975, p. 19.

2. Adam Smith, *An Inquiry into the Nature and Causes of the Wealth of Nations*, ed. Edwin Cannan (Chicago: University of Chicago Press, 1976), p. 16.

3. *Annual Register (1781)*, vol. 24 (London: J. Dodsley, 1782), p. 163.

4. D. Juan Bautiste Alberdi, *Organización politica y económica de la confederación argentina* (Buenos Aires: Imprenta de José Jacquin, 1856), pp. 36, 38.

5. Domingo F. Samiento, *Conflicto y armonías de las razas en América* (Buenos Aires: La Cultura Argentina, 1915), pp. 455–56.

6. José Victorino Lastarria, *La América*, 2nd ed. (Gante: Imprenta de Eug. Vanderhaeghen, 1857), p. 227.

7. Wenceslao Vial, *Observaciones a los escritos de M. Coucelle de Seneuil sobre la crisis económica, con un apéndice sobre la*

inmigración europea (Santiago: Imprenta del Ferrocarril, 1858), p. 8; José Ingenieros, "La formación de una raza argentina," *Revista de Filosofía*, vol. 1, no. 6 (Nov. 1915): 474; Alberdi, *Organización*, p. 37.

8. Lastarria, *La América*, p. 228.

9. See, for example, Tomás Iriarte, *Memoria sobre inmigración y línea de fronteras sobre los indios salvajes* (Buenos Aires: Imprenta del Estado, 1852), pp. 6, 18, 19.

10. Edmundo Correas, "Sarmiento and the United States," *Latin American Monographs* (Gainesville, Fla.), no. 16 (June 1961): 29–30.

11. And it was specifically European settlers they wanted, not Asians or Africans. As to which Europeans they preferred, this depended upon how concerned they were over the assimilation of the new settlers. The northern Europeans were recognized as the best producers, the Mediterranian Europeans as more easily assimilated. See Salvador Debenedetti, "Sobre la formación de una raza argentina," *Revista de Filosofía* (Nov. 1915): 417. Juan Bautiste Alberdi, *Escritos póstumos de Juan Bautiste Alberdi*, vol. 1 (Buenos Aires: Europa, Morenoy Defensa, 1895), pp. 73, 475–76; João Manuel Pereira de Silva, *Situacion Sociale, Politique, et Economique de L'Empire du Brésil* (Rio de Janeiro: B. L. Garnier, 1865), pp. 108–9. C. A. M. Mejer, *Los extranjeros en Sud América* (Lima: Imprenta El National, 1869), p. 30; Juan A. Alsina, *La inmigración en el primer siglo de la independencia* (Buenos Aires: Filipe S. Alsina, 1910), pp. 203–9.

12. Alberdi, *Organización*, p. 42.

13. Domingo Faustino Sarmiento, *Facundo, o civilización i barbarie en las pampas argentinas*, 4th ed. (New York: D. Appleton, 1868), pp. 7–8.

14. Ignaecio Domeyko, *Memoria sobre la colonización en Chile* (Santiago de Chile: Imprenta de Julio Belin i Cia., 1850), pp. 4–5.

15. J. de C. Fortinho, *Estudios sobre inmigración y colonización* (Montevideo: Imprenta de El Telegrafo Marítimo, 1877), p. 120.

16. Joaquin Villarino, *Estudios sobre la colonización i emigración a Chile* (Santiago de Chile: Imprenta Nacional, 1867), p. 170.

17. F. C., *De la inmigración en Chile* (Santiago de Chile: Imprenta de la República, 1868), p. 38.

18. Vial, *Observaciones*, pp. 6–7.

19. Villarino, *Estudios*, pp. 21–22.

20. Gino Germani, "The Nationalist Pivot," in *Latin American Radicalism*, ed. Irving Louis Horowitz, Josué de Castro, and John Gerassi (New York: Random House, 1969), pp. 327–28. For a more detailed breakdown of these figures see *Tercer censo national de la República Argentina (1914)*, vol. 8 (Buenos Aires: Talleres Gráficos de L. J. Rosso y Cia., 1916), p. 135. In another study Germani has corrected for the fact that the foreign population tended to contain a greater percentage of adult males than the Argentinean population, thereby

increasing the likelihood of greater economic participation. However, Germani's method of considering the "economically active sector" of the two populations does not substantially alter the basic picture of foreign ownership of industry and commerce far out of proportion to their "economically active" percentages. See Gino Germani, *Estructura social de la Argentina* (Buenos Aires: Editorial Raigal, n.d.), pp. 118–36.

21. Alberto Zum Felde, *Proceso intellectual del Uruguay y crítica de su literatura*, vol. 2 (Montevideo: Comisión Nacional del Centinario, 1930), pp. 88–89.

22. Victor Pérez Petit, *Rodó: su vida, su orba*, quoted in William Rex Crawford, *A Century of Latin American Thought* (Cambridge, Mass.: Harvard University Press, 1945), p. 79.

23. José Enrique Rodó, *Ariel* (Mexico City: Imprenta Universitaria, 1942), p. 78.

24. These terms are used by Keen in Benjamin Keen, ed., *Readings in Latin American Civilization* (Boston: Houghton Mifflin, 1955), p. 460.

25. Rodó, *Ariel*, p. 93.

26. Ibid., p. 127.

27. Alexis de Tocqueville, *Democracy in America*, vol. 2, trans. Henry Reeve, ed. Phillips Bradley (New York: Vintage Books, 1945), pp. 178, 444–45.

28. Rodó, *Ariel*, p. 106.

29. Zum Felde, *Proceso* (1941 ed.), pp. 242–43.

30. Tancredo Pinochet, *Como construir uan gran civilización chilena e hispanoamericana* (Chile: Editorial "Asies," n.d.), p. 38, see esp. pp. 30–38.

31. Military imperialism, of course, had been an issue before this time in Latin America, but only in Chile was economic imperialism an important social topic.

32. Charles Blackford Mansfield, *Paraguay, Brazil, and the Plate: Letters Written in 1852–53* (Cambridge: Macmillan, 1856), pp. 222–23.

33. James W. Wikie, ed., *Statistical Abstract of Latin America*, vol. 18 (Los Angeles: University of California Press, 1977), p. 301.

34. For a listing of these see *Situation in Cuba: Hearings before the Committee on Foreign Relations and the Committee on Armed Services, United States Senate*, 87th Congress, 2d sess. (Washington, D.C.: GPO, 1962), pp. 80–87.

35. Edwin Lieuwen, *Arms and Politics in Latin America*, revised. (New York: Praeger, 1961), p. 101.

36. Most bandit chasing was done by U.S. troops on the Mexican-American border.

37. Quoted in Arthur P. Whitaker, *The United States and South America: The Northern Republics* (Cambridge, Mass.: Harvard University Press, 1948), p. 163.

38. John W. Burgess, *Political Science and Comparative Constitutional Law*, vol. I (Boston: Ginn, 1890), p. 46.

39. Ibid., pp. 47–48.

40. Quoted in Henry Pringle, *Theodore Roosevelt: A Biography* (New York: Harcourt, Brace, 1931), pp. 282–83.

41. Quoted in Clarence H. Haring, *South America Looks at the United States* (New York: Macmillan, 1929), p. 6, and John Morton Blum, *The Republican Roosevelt* (New York: Atheneum, 1963), p. 128.

42. Blum, *Roosevelt*, pp. 131–32.

43. Quoted in Museo Social Argentina, *The Argentine Republic: Its Resources and Production* (Buenos Aires: Imprenta Kidd, 1931), p. 48.

44. *El Mercurio*, May 26, 1914, as quoted in Frederick B. Pike, *Chile and the United States, 1880–1962* (Notre Dame, Ind.: University of Notre Dame Press, 1963), p. 374.

45. Alfredo Colmo, *Los países de la America Latina* (Madrid: Hijos de Reus, 1915), p. 649.

46. For details concerning the occupation see Robert E. Quirk, *An Affair of Honor* (Lexington, Ky.: University of Kentucky Press, 1962), pp. 121–55.

47. Ibid., p. 154.

48. Stanislav Andreski, *Parasitism and Subversion: The Case of Latin America* (New York: Schocken Books, 1966), p. 278.

49. Quirk, *Affair of Honor*, pp. v–vi, 2–3.

50. "'Tuna War' Flares up Again in Ecuador," *Washington Post*, March 10, 1975, p. A3.

51. Jonathan Kandell, "U.S. Aid Embargo Strains Peru Ties," *New York Times*, April 18, 1973, p. 8.

52. Lawrence Stern, "U.S. Helped Beat Allende in 1964," *Washington Post*, April 6, 1973, pp. A1, 12.

53. Paul E. Sigmund, "Less Than Charged," House Subcommittee on Inter-American Affairs, *Hearings: United States and Chile during the Allende Years, 1970–1973* (Washington, D.C.: GPO, 1975), p. 662.

54. Ernesto "Che" Guevara, *Che Guevara* (Havana: Campamento 5 de Mayo, 1968), p. 35.

55. Jonathan Levin, *The Export Economies* (Cambridge, Mass.: Harvard University Press, 1960), p. 94.

56. Penny Lernoux, "Venezuela: On the Petroleum Merry-Go-Round," *The Nation*, Feb. 15, 1975, p. 168; Stephen Klaidman, "Venezuelan Candidates Run Hard, but Side-step Oil Issue," *Washington Post*, Dec. 1, 1973, p. A12, Karen De Young, "Venezula: Oil-Rich, Food-Poor," *Washinton Post*, July 17, 1977, p. A 18.

57. Quoted in Noel Grove, "Venezuela's Crisis of Wealth," *National Geographic*, Aug. 1976, p. 208.

58. Edwin L. Dale, "Idea of Growing Disparity in World Prices Disputed," *New York Times*, May 25, 1975, p. 1.

59. In 1959, for example, well over one-third of all U.S. investment in Latin America was in oil; see John P. Powelson, *Latin America: Today's Economic and Social Revolution* (New York: McGraw-Hill, 1964), pp. 146–47.

60. Dale, "Growing Disparity", pp. 1, 8; Jane Rosen, "U.N. Study Finds Poor Nations Not Hit by Price Rises," *Washington Post*, June 4, 1975, p. A23.

61. Kevin C. Kerns, "The Andean Common Market: A New Thrust of Economic Integration in Latin America," *Journal of Interamerican Studies and World Affairs* (May 1972); 225–49; for recent developments in Mexico where much U.S. investment is concentrated, see Richard Severo, "Mexico Planning Investing Change," *New York Times*, Jan. 2, 1973, p. 51, and Richard Severo, "U.S. Investors Accept Mexico's Policy," *New York Times*, Nov. 24, 1972, pp. 59–60.

62. Andreski, *Parasitism and Subversion*, p. 99.

63. Samuel Shapiro, *Invisible Latin America* (Boston: Beacon Press, 1963), pp. 14–15.

64. Edwin Lieuwen, *Petroleum in Venezuela* (New York: Russell and Russell, 1954), p. 29; Powelson, *Latin America*, p. 149; H. J. Maidenberg, "Caracas Now Its Own Boss," *New York Times*, Jan. 25, 1976, p. 28.

65. "Some Yankees Go Home," *Time*, Nov. 13, 1972, p. 91; H. J. Maidenberg, "Ecuador Is Finding Trouble Selling Oil," *New York Times*, Dec. 9, 1974, p. 57.

66. Andreski, *Parasitism and Subversion*, p. 99.

67. This appears true even for the large corporations in the tiny Central American "banana republics" that once had this kind of power; see H. J. Maidenberg, "New Rules, Harsh Life in Bananas," *New York Times*, May 11, 1975, sec. 3, pp. 1, 9.

68. Robert A. Bennett, "Mountains of Debt Pile up As Banks Push Foreign Loans," *New York Times*, May 15, 1977, sec. 3, p. 1.

69. Ibid.

70. Victor Raúl Haya de la Torre, *Pensamiento político de Haya de la Torre*, vol. 1 (Lima: Ediciones Pueblo, 1961), p. 97.

71. *Granma* (Havana), May 9, 1971, p. 2. Unless otherwise indicated, all citations from *Granma* will be from the weekly English edition.

72. Quoted in David J. Morris, *We Must Make Haste—Slowly* (New York: Random House, 1973), pp. 270–71.

73. Ricardo Rojo, *Mi amigo el Che* (Buenos Aires: Editorial Jorgé Alvarez, S.A., 1968), p. 159.

74. Tom Wells, "Mexico Ends Pepsi Generation," *Washington Post*, June 19, 1976, p. A16.

75. "Mexicans Seek Halt to Music 'Colonialism,'" *Washington Post*, Oct. 4, 1975, p. A4

76. Frank Le Van Field, Jr., "The Unique Political Influence of Juan Perón" (Ph. D. diss., Harvard University, 1958), pp. 71–73.

77. "Brazil: Filmmakers at the Ready," *Atlas*, March 1976, p. 35.

78. Morris, *Make Haste*, p. 271.

79. Ibid.

80. Ibid.

81. The logic of his argument was that socialist science, being superior to capitalist science, could prevent these natural calamities, and so imperialists were to blame because they kept socialists from gaining power.

82. For the Mexican critic Victor Alba's comments on Latin American scapegoating, see Victor Alba, *The Latin Americans* (New York: Praeger, 1969), pp. 314–17.

83. *Segundo censo de la república argentina, 1895*, vol. 2 (Buenos Aires, 1898), p. xlviii.

84. James Bruce, *Those Perplexing Argentineans* (New York: Longmans, Green, 1953), p. 11.

85. Ibid., pp. 10–11; "Brazil: Poor Man's Yankees," *Newsweek*, Aug. 20, 1973, p. 44.

86. Ingenieros, "Raza argentina," p. 479.

87. Quoted in Alcides Arguedas, *Pueblo enfermo* (Santiago de Chile: Ediciones Ercilla, 1937), p. 55.

88. Lewis Hanke, *Mexico and the Caribbean* (Princeton, N.J.: Van Nostrand, 1959), p. 72.

89. José Vasconcelos, *Aspects of Mexican Civilization* (Chicago: University of Chicago Press, 1926), p. 92; José Vasconcelos, *¿Qué es la revolución?* (Mexico City: Ediciones Botas, 1937), pp. 217–18.

90. José Vasconcelos, *Indología: una interpretación de la cultura iberoamericana* (Paris: Agencia Mundial de Librería, n.d.), p. 78.

91. See Ibid., pp. 65–108, for the heart of Vasconcelos's theory.

92. Hanke, *Mexico and the Caribbean*, p. 173.

93. Leslie Byrd Simpson, *Many Mexicos* (Berkeley: University of California Press, 1962), pp. 21–22.

94. José Clemente Orozco, *Autobiografía* (Mexico City: Ediciones Occidente, 1945), pp. 99–100.

95. Ibid.

96. Quoted in Alejandro Magnet, *Nuestros vecinos justicialistas* (Santiago de Chile: Editorial del pacífico, S.A., 1953), p. 136.

97. P. Nuñez Arca, *Perón: Man of America* (Buenos Aires: 1950), p. 70.

98. Virginia Lee Warren, "Perón Announces New Way to Make Atom Yield Power," *New York Times*, March 25, 1951, pp. 1, 8, 9, 10; "Fueron ampliadas los detalles sobre las experiencias atómicas," *Los Principios* (Cordoba, Argentina) March 26, 1951, p. 1; Raul Damonte, *Ayer fue San Perón* (Argentina: Ediciones Gure, 1955), pp. 52–56; Julio Rafo, *La razón de su huida* (Buenos Aires: 1955), pp. 20–22.

99. Robert J. Alexander, *The Perón Era* (New York: Columbia University Press, 1951), pp. 158–59.

100. Ibid., p. 184.

101. Maria Flores, *The Woman with the Whip: Eva Perón* (New York: Doubleday, 1952), pp. 196–97.

102. Alexander, *Perón*, p. 177.

103. Juan Perón, *La hora de los pueblos* (Buenos Aires: Ediciones de la Liberación, 1973), p. 32.

104. Jorge A. Paita, ed., *Argentina, 1930–1960* (Buenos Aires: Editorial Sur, 1961), p. 7.

105. Juan Perón, *Latinoamérica: ahora o nunca* (Montevideo: Editorial "Diálogo," 1967), pp. 13–15, 31, passim.

106. "Poor Man's Yankees," *Newsweek*.

107. Alexander, *Perón*, p. 186.

108. "Poor Man's Yankees," *Newsweek*.

109. Bruce Handler, "Brazil Seeks Arms Self-Sufficiency," *Washington Post*, July 9, 1975, p. A18.

110. Larry Rohter, "Brazil Stepping up Arms Output," *Washington Post*, Dec. 18, 1977, pp. A1, 34.

111. Handler, "Arms Self-Sufficiency."

112. Marvin Howe, "Brazilians Order Silence on A-Pack," *New York Times*, June 12, 1975, p. 11.

113. "The Atomic Club," *Parade*, Feb. 20, 1977, p. 16.

114. Joanne Omang, "Brazilian Diplomacy Making It a Major Latin Power," *Washington Post*, Nov. 2, 1975, p. A14.

115. Quoted in "Poor Man's Yankees," *Newsweek*.

116. Arthur P. Whitaker, *Nationalism in Latin America* (Gainesville: University of Florida Press, 1962), p. 51.

117. William S. Stokes, *Latin American Politics* (New York: Thomas Y. Crowell Co., 1959) p. 206.

118. Jonathan Kandell, "U.S. Aid Embargo Strains Peru Ties," *New York Times*, April 18, 1973, p. 8.

119. Yugurta, "Salpicaduras," *Panamá-América*, Sept. 17, 1947, quoted in John Biesanz, "The Economy of Panama," *Inter-American Economic Affairs*, vol. 6, no. 1 (Summer, 1952): ll.

120. Francisco Bulnes, *El porvenir de las naciones hispanoamericanas ante las conquistas recientes de Europa y los Estados Unidos* (Mexico City: Imprenta de Mariano Nava, 1899), pp. 281–82.

121. Ibid., p. 282.

CHAPTER 6

1. Quoted in Luigi Barzini, *The Italians* (New York: Bantam Books, 1964), p. 188.

2. The most complete and distinguished work on this subject has been done by A. James Gregor. Much of the material found in this chapter can be found in greatly expanded detail in the following books by Gregor: A. James Gregor, *Contemporary Radical Ideologies* (New York: Random House, 1968); A. James Gregor, *Fascism: The Contemporary Interpretations* (Morristown, N.J.: General Learning Press, 1973); A. James Gregor, *The Fascist Persuasion in Radical Politics* (Princeton, N.J.: Princeton University Press, 1974); A. James Gregor, *Ideology of Fascism* (New York: Free Press, 1969). The latter book is Gregor's most complete account of the evolution of the Fascist ideology and is especially useful for more detailed study.

3. Benito Mussolini, "La situazione internationale e l'atteggiamento del partito," in *Opera omnia de Benito Mussolini*, vol. 6 (Florence: La Fenice, 1953), p. 428.

4. Indeed, Mussolini had no choice but to be attentive to worker problems, for 40 percent of the Fascist party members were industrial and agrarian workers; see Gregor, *Contemporary Interpretations*, p. 36.

5. Benito Mussolini, "Atto de nascita del fascismo," in *Opera omnia de Benito Mussolini*, vol. 12 (Florence: La Fenice, 1953), p. 323.

6. For a discussion of this see Michael Arthur Ledeen, *Universal Fascism* (New York: Howard Fertig, 1972), pp. 104–32.

7. Mussolini, "Atto."

8. Classical liberalism should not be confused with contemporary American liberalism, which in its eagerness to have the government solve a wide range of social problems, is willing to entrust it with a substantial amount of authority.

9. Benito Mussolini, *La dottrina del fascismo*, 2nd ed., (Milan: Ulrico Hoepli Editore, 1939), pp. 45–46. It was actually Giovanni Gentile who wrote this section of the *Dottrina*; Mussolini was only the formal author.

10. Giovanni Gentile, *Genesis and Structure of Society*, trans. H. S. Harris (Urbana: University of Illinois Press, 1960), p. 179.

11. The text of this constitution can be found in Herbert W. Schneider, *Making the Fascist State* (New York: Howard Fertig, 1968), pp. 317–20.

12. Quoted in Max Gallo, *Mussolini's Italy*, trans. Charles L. Markmann (New York: Macmillan, 1973), p. 221.

13. Benito Mussolini, "Discorso per lo stato corporativo," in *Opera omnia de Benito Mussolini*, vol. 26 (Florence, La Fenice, 1953), p. 96.

14. Benito Mussolini, *Discorsi del 1925* (Milan: Edizione "Alpes," 1926), p. 106.

15. Gentile, *Genesis and Structure*, p. 179.

16. Benito Mussolini, "Per la storia de una settimana," in *Opera omnia de Benito Mussolini*, vol. 10 (Florence: La Fenice, 1953), p. 87.

17. Quoted in Emil Ludwig, *Talks with Mussolini*, trans. Eden Paul and Cedar Paul (Boston: Little, Brown, 1933), p. 126–27.

18. Quoted in Gallo, *Mussolini's Italy*, p. 220.

19. Schneider, *Making the Fascist State*, p. 317.

20. J. Stalin, "Report to the Eighteenth Party Congress," in *Problems of Leninism* (Moscow: Foreign Languages Publishing House, 1947), p. 635.

21. V. I. Lenin, *Selected Works*, vol. 1 (Moscow: Progress, 1970), p. 143.

22. J. Stalin, "Report to the Seventeenth Party Congress," in *Works*, vol. 8 (Moscow: Foreign Languages Publishing House, 1955), p. 374.

23. V. I. Lenin, *The State and Revolution* (Peking: Foreign Language Press, 1970), p. 20.

24. V. I. Lenin, "Immediate Tasks of the Soviet Government," in *Selected Works*, rev. ed., vol. 2 (Moscow: Progress, 1975), p. 610.

25. J. Stalin, "Report to the Sixteenth Party Congress." Vol. 12 (Moscow: Foreign Languages Publishing House, 1955), p. 381.

26. J. Stalin, "The Tasks of Business Executives," in *Problems of Leninism* (Moscow: Foreign Languages Publishing House, 1947), p. 356.

27. Quoted in Schneider, *Making the Fascist State*, p. 29.

28. Stalin, "Tasks."

29. Gregor, *Contemporary Radical Ideologies*, p. 164.

30. Ibid., pp. 171–214.

31. *Revolución*, Feb. 23, 1963, p. 5, quoted in Richard Fagen, "Mass Mobilization in Cuba: The Symbolism of Struggle," in *Cuba in Revolution*, ed. Rolando E. Bonachea and Nelson P. Valdés (New York: Doubleday, Anchor Books, 1972), p. 201.

32. Barry M. Richman, *Soviet Management* (Englewood Cliffs, N.J.: Prentice-Hall, 1965), p. 238.

33. Ibid., p. 241.

34. Joseph Pittau, *Political Thought in Early Meiji Japan* (Cambridge, Mass.: Harvard University Press, 1967), p. 11.

35. Lenin, "Immediate Tasks," p. 611.

36. Shinkichi Uesugi, *Kokutai Seika no Hatsuyō* (Tokyo, 1919), p. 58; quoted in Daniel C. Holtom, *Modern Japan and Shinto Nationalism*, rev. ed. (Chicago: University of Chicago Press, 1947; reprint ed., New York: Arno Press, 1963), p. 10.

CHAPTER 7

1. From a Havana Radio Broadcast, April 27, 1971; quoted in Jaime Suchlicki, *Cuba, Castro and Revolution* (Coral Gables, Fla.: University of Miami Press, 1972), p. 16.

2. From a speech delivered July 26, 1967; quoted in W. Raymond Duncan and James Nelson Goodsell, ed., *The Quest for Change in Latin America* (New York: Oxford University Press, 1970), p. 304.

3. Ibid., p. 305; and *Granma* (daily), July 2, 1970, p. 2.

4. Ernesto Che Guevara, *Che Guevara* (Havana: Campamento 5 de Mayo, 1968), p. 8.

5. Ibid., p. 7.

6. Ibid., pp. 11, 12, 22, 18, passim.

7. Ibid., p. 21. My own translation of this passage is an improved version of the Cuban one. In the original Spanish the first sentence reads, "Asi vamos marchando." See Ernesto Che Guevara, *El socialismo y el hombre en Cuba* (Havana: Ediciones "R," 1965), p. 56.

8. From a speech delivered July 26, 1967; quoted in Duncan and Goodsell, *Quest for Change*, p. 307.

9. *Granma*, Sept. 26, 1971, pp. 2–3.

10. Fidel Castro, *Major Speeches* (London: State I, 1968), p. 303.

11. Ibid., pp. 303–4.

12. José Yglesias, "Cuban Report: Their Hippies, Their Squares," *New York Times Magazine*, Jan. 12, 1969, p. 52.

13. Foreign Broadcast Information Service, "Daily Report: Latin America," July 29, 1963, p. 27.

14. Ibid., March 7, 1968, pp. 3–4; quoted in Richard R. Fagen, *The Transformation of Political Culture in Cuba* (Stanford, Calif.: Stanford University Press, 1969), p. 146.

15. Joe Nicholson, Jr., *Inside Cuba* (New York: Sheed and Ward, 1974), p. 201.

16. Joe Nicholson, Jr., "Inside Cuba," *Harper's*, June, 1973, p. 57.

17. Ibid.

18. Lee Lockwood, *Castro's Cuba; Cuba's Fidel* (New York: Macmillan, 1967), p. 126.

19. *Granma*, May 9, 1971, p. 4.

20. "Castro Resumes Attacks on U.S.," *New York Times*, May 11, 1976, p. 9.

21. For the observations of various authors and reporters see Terri Shaw, "Schools with Workshops, *Washington Post*, Dec. 31, 1974, p. A7; Ted Morgan, "Cuba," *New York Times Magazine*, Dec. 1, 1974, p. 103; Rolland Paulston, "Education," in *Revolutionary Change in Cuba*, ed. Carmelo Mesa-Lago (Pittsburgh: University of Pittsburgh Press, 1971), p. 387; Carl J. Migdail, "Castro's 'New Cuba,'" *U.S. News and World Report*, Oct. 28, 1974, p. 44.

22. According to a statement by Fidel Castro to the First Communist Party Congress, 99 percent. See *Granma* (daily), Jan. 4, 1976, p. 7.

23. Morgan, "Cuba," pp. 108–9, passim.

24. According to figures taken from John Paxton, ed., *The Statesman's Year-Book, 1975–1976* (New York: St. Martin's Press, 1975),

pp. 783–84, 847–48. Estimates of Cuban military forces vary considerably for the good reason that nobody outside Cuba knows for sure. According to figures given by the *New York Times* and Carmelo Mesa-Lago, *The Statesman's* estimates considerably underestimate the size of the Cuban forces. See "Cuba, Emulating China, Is Using Army to Spur Development in Many Key Sectors of Her Economy," *New York Times*, Dec. 8, 1972, p. 11; and Carmelo Mesa-Lago, *Cuba in the 1970's* (Albuquerque: University of New Mexico Press, 1974), p. 95.

25. "Emulating China," *New York Times*. Figures used for the Prussian calculation are taken from R. R. Palmer, *A History of the Modern World* (New York: Knopf, 1965), p. 204.

26. Rene Dumont, "The Militarization of Fidelismo," *Dissent*, Sept.-Oct. 1970, pp. 418–21; (The Cuban armed forces obviously have great potential to be a parasitic drain on the economy. This potential can be kept in check so long as they heavily channel their activities into economic projects and continue to receive costly armaments free from the Soviet Union.)

27. *Granma*, Jan. 4, 1976, p. 6.

28. "Vigilante Groups Celebrate in Cuba," *New York Times*, Oct. 12, 1975, p. 17.

29. Lowry Nelson, *Cuba: The Measure of a Revolution* (Minneapolis: University of Minnesota Press, 1972), p. 179.

30. Morgan, "Cuba," p. 110.

31. These are 1976 figures; see Carmelo Mesa-Lago, *The Economy of Socialist Cuba* (Albuquerque: University of New Mexico Press, 1981), p. 106.

32. Robert M. Bernardo, *The Theory of Moral Incentives in Cuba* (University, Ala.: University of Alabama Press, 1971), pp. 56, 120; Castro, *Major Speeches*, p. 275; and Carmelo Mesa-Lago, "Labor Organization and Wages," in *Revolutionary Change in Cuba*, ed. Carmelo Mesa-Lago (Pittsburgh: University of Pittsburgh Press, 1971), pp. 234–35.

33. Leo Huberman and Paul M. Sweezy, *Socialism in Cuba* (New York: Monthly Review Press, 1969), p. 143.

34. Mesa-Lago, *Cuba in the 1970s*, p. 36.

35. Nicholson, *Inside Cuba*, p. 170.

36. Ibid., pp. 168–71, passim.

37. Ibid., pp. 171–73, passim.

38. Ibid., pp. 172–73, passim.

39. Ibid., p. 174.

40. This is in sharp contrast to the immediate prerevolutionary administrations, which responded like weather vanes to the parasitic demands of "popular" interest groups like the urban labor unions. An incident that could be considered symbolic of political attitudes in the old society was while the framers of the Cuban constitution of 1940

solemnly pronounced work as the inalienable *right* of the individual, they firmly voted down a proposal to describe work as both an individual *right* and a social *duty*.

41. Oscar Lewis, ed., *La Vida* (New York: Random House, 1965), p. xlix.

42. Fidel Castro, *Educación y Revolución* (Mexico City: Editorial Nuestro Tiempo, S.A. 1974), p. 81.

43. Kenneth Denlinger, "Tate's KO One Indicator of Cuba's Emergence," *Washington Post*, July 30, 1976, p. D4.

44. Morgan, "Cuba," p. 110.

45. Terri Shaw, "Block Clubs Oversee Cuba's Daily Life," *Washington Post*, Dec. 30, 1974, p. A14.

46. Morgan, "Cuba," p. 110.

47. "How to Cut High Legal Fees," *U.S. News and World Report*, Aug. 2, 1976, p. 40.

48. For a description of these courts see Jesse Berman, "The Cuban Popular Tribunals," *Columbia Law Review*, vol. 69, no. 8, (Dec. 1969), 1317–54; and Lee Webb, "People's Courts in Cuba," unpublished manuscript, 1970).

49. *Granma*, (daily), Dec. 2 1974, pp. 2–3.

50. Quoted in Terri Shaw, "Status of Women in Cuba: Progress vs. Tradition," *Washington Post*, Jan. 26, 1975, p. B3.

51. Ibid.

52. José A. Moreno, "From Traditional to Modern Values," in *Revolutionary Change in Cuba*, ed. Carmelo Mesa-Lago (Pittsburgh: University of Press, 1971), p. 482.

53. Shaw, "Status of Women"; and Claude Regin, "Sex Equality in Cuba," *Washington Post*, Aug. 4, 1974, p. F10.

54. Shaw, "Status of Women."

55. Elizabeth Sutherland, *The Youngest Revolution* (New York: Dial Press, 1969), pp. 169–90.

56. Ibid., pp. 141–42.

57. For the experiences of a U.S. Negro with a "black consciousness" identity who lived in Cuba see John Clytus, *Black Man in Red Cuba*, (Coral Gables, Fla.: University of Miami Press, 1970), pp. 131, 158; see also Henry Mitchell, "Eldridge Cleaver at Exile's End," *Washington Post*, Sept. 1, 1976, p. B1.

58. Nicholson, *Inside Cuba*, p. 220.

59. Ibid., pp. 220–21.

60. For a discussion of this see John Edwin Fagg, *Cuba, Haiti and the Dominican Republic* (Englewood Cliffs, N.J.: Prentice-Hall, 1965), pp. 54–82.

61. *Granma*, March 19, 1967, p. 10.

62. For this conflict explained in greater detail see Leon Goure and Julian Weinkle, "Soviet-Cuban Relations: The Growing Integration,"

In Jaime Suchlicki, *Cuba, Castro and Revolution* (Coral Gables, Fla.: University of Miami Press, 1972), p. 151–52, and Edward Gonzalez, "Relationship with the Soviet Union," in *Revolutionary Change in Cuba*, ed. Carmelo Mesa-Lago (Pittsburgh: University of Pittsburgh Press, 1971), pp. 93–94.

63. *Granma*, Aug. 20, 1970, p. 5, passim.

64. Castro, *Major Speeches*, p. 277.

65. *Granma*, Aug. 6, 1972, p. 5, passim.

66. Ibid.

67. For some more informative journalistic reports see Angus Deming and Andrew Jaffe, "Castro's Peace Corps," *Newsweek*, May 31, 1976, p. 41; Stanley Karnow, "Castro Rejects Reconciliation to Fight for the Cause," *New York Times*, Dec. 14, 1975, sec. 4, p. 1; Francois Raitberger, "Cuban Role in Angola Seen Long," *Washington Post*, July 29, 1976, p. A20; Don Oberdorfer, "Cuba's Intervention in Angola Intrigues World Capitals," *Washington Post*, Feb. 18, 1976, p. A6; Hugh O'Shaughnessy, "Cubans Face Test in Angola," *Washington Post*, Dec. 21, 1975, p. F5; Winsome Lane, "Arrival of Cubans Stirs Controversy among Jamaicans," *Washington Post*, Aug. 8, 1976, p. A18; Jim Hoagland, "Cuba's Imprint," *Washington Post*, Feb. 29, 1976, p. A20; Rowland Evans and Robert Novak, "Castro Acts in Laos," *Washington Post*, April 9, 1977, p. A9. In 1977 estimates of the number of Cubans in Angola ran as high as 23,000; see "Cuban Buildup in Africa Alarming, Study Finds," *Washington Post*, Nov. 17, 1977, p. A6.

68. William M. Leo Grande, *Cuba's Policy in Africa, 1959–1980* (Berkeley: Institute of International Studies, University of California Press, 1980), p. 27.

69. Ibid., p. 43.

70. Leopoldo Lugones, "A los ganados y a las mieses," in *Obras poéticas completas*, p. 438; and *La Nación*, Feb. 17, 1893, p. 1; as quoted in Carl E. Solberg, *Immigration and Nationalism: Argentina and Chile, 1890–1914* (Austin: University of Texas Press, 1970), p. 26.

CHAPTER 8

1. Juan Perón, *Doctrina peronista* (Buenos Aires: Editorial Fidelius, 1947), pp. 56–57.

2. Plinio Salgado, *A quarta humanidade* (Rio de Janeiro: Editor José Olympio, 1934), p. 88.

3. Plinio Salgado, *O que é o integralismo* (Rio de Janeiro: Editor Schmidt, 1937), p. 132.

4. Juan D. Perón, *Perón expone su doctrina* (Buenos Aires, 1948), pp. 69, 135–55, passim; Juan D. Perón, *Latinoamerica: ahora o nunca* (Montevideo: Editorial "Dialego," 1967), p. 41; quoted in George

I. Blanksten, *Perón's Argntina* (Chicago: University of Chicago Press, 1953), p. 238; P. Nuñez Arca, *Perón: Man of America* (Buenos Aires, 1950), pp. 130–31; Salgado, *A quarta humanidade*, pp. 74–75.

5. Quoted in Blanksten, *Perón's Argentina*, p. 246.

6. Juan D. Perón, *La hora de los pueblos* (Buenos Aires: Ediciones de la Liberación. 1973), pp. 23–24.

7. Plinio Salgado, *A doutrina do sigma*, 2nd ed. (Rio de Janeiro: Editor Schmidt, 1937), p. 161.

8. Ibid, p. 180, Raúl Damonte Taborda, *Ayer fue San Perón* (Argentina: Ediciones Gure, 1955), p. 44.

9. Salgado, *A quarta humanidade*, p. 178.

10. Perón, *Doctrina peronista*, p. 37.

11. Plinio Salgado, *Despertemos a nacão!* (Rio de Janeiro: Editora José Olympio, 1935), p. 34.

12. Perón, *Hora*, pp. 109–11, 172.

13. Salgado, *A quarta humanidade*, p. 79; Salgado, *Doutrina*, p. 86; Elmer R. Broxson, "Plinio Salgado and Brazilian Integralism, 1932–1938" (Ph.D. diss., Catholic University, Washington, D.C. 1962), p. 27.

14. Gustavo Barroso, *O que o integralista deve saber* (Rio de Janeiro: Civilização Brasileira S. A., 1935), p. 9; Olbiano de Mello, *Concepção do estado integralista* (Rio de Janeiro: Schmidt-editor, 1935), p. 55; Plinio Salgado, *Cartas aos "camisas-verdes"* (Rio de Janeiro; José Olympio-editora, 1935), p. 203; Salgado, *Doutrina*, p. 63; Salgado, *Que*, p. 130; Perón, *Perón expone*, p. 16; Perón, *Doctrina peronista*, p. 27.

15. Salgado, *A quarta humanidade*, p. 143; Salgado, *Doutrina*, pp. 152, 112, 143; Mello, *Concepção*, p. 55; Barroso, *Que*, pp. 28, 33; Marvin Goldwert, *Democracy, Militarism and Nationalism in Argentina, 1930–1966* (Austin: University of Texas Press, 1972), p. 79; Perón, *Doctrina peronista*, p. 54; Raul A. Mende, *El justicialismo; doctrina y realidad peronista* (Buenos Aires: Guillermo Kraft, 1951), p. 160.

16. Partido Peronista, *Manuel del peronista* (Buenos Aires, 1948), p. 36; Perón, *Doctrina peronista*, p. 110.

17. Perón, *Doctrina peronista*, pp. 27, 53.

18. Salgado, *Cartas*, p. 135; Salgado, *doutrina*, pp. 18–19; Barroso, *Que*, p. 16.

19. Salgado, *Cartas*, pp. 131–32.

20. Barroso, *Que*, p. 28.

21. Perón, *Perón expone*, p. 169.

22. Maria Flores, *The Woman with the Whip: Eva Perón* (New York: Doubleday, 1952), p. 216.

23. Perón, *Doctrina peronista*, p. 56; Olympio Mourão, *Do liberalismo ao integralismo* (Rio de Janeiro: Schmidt-editor, 1935), p. 141.

24. Salgado, *Doutrina*, pp. 28–29; Partido Peronista, *Manuel*, pp. 194, 196; Juan D. Perón, *Conducción politica* (Buenos Aires: Escuela Superior Peronista, 1951), pp. 190–92.

25. Barroso, *Que*, p. 111.

26. Salgado, *Doutrina*, p.91.

27. Eva Perón, *My Mission in Life*, trans. Ethel Cherry (New York: Vantage Press, 1957), pp. 37–40, 24, preface.

28. Quoted in Ibid., p. 24.

29. Partido Peronista, *Manuel*, pp. 38–39; Perón, *Conducción polícica*, pp. 20–21.

30. Salgado, *A querta humanidade*, p. 90.

31. Barroso, *Que*, p. 57.

32. Partido Peronista, *Manuel*, pp. 198–99.

33. Perón, *Conducción politica*, p. 56.

34. Salgado, *Doutrina*, p. 37, see also pp. 178–79.

35. Perón, *Doctrina Peronista*, p. 191; Partido Peronista, *Manuel*, pp. 93, 98.

36. Partido Peronista, *Manuel*, p. 110.

37. Quoted in Blanksten, *Perón's Argentina*, p. 222.

38. José Carlos Mariátegui, "La agonia de cristianismo de Don Migual de Unamuno," in *Critica Literaria* (Buenos Aires: Editorial Jorge Álvarez, 1969), p. 126.

39. Herbert L. Mathews, *Castro: A Political Biography* (London: Penguin Press, 1969), p. 163.

40. See Gregor's chapter on Cuban Marxism in Gregor, *Persuasion*, pp. 260–321.

41. Salgado, *Que*, pp. 43–45; Salgado, *Quarta*, p. 117.

42. Mello, *Concepção*, pp. 48–53; Mourão, *Do liberalismo ao integralismo*, pp. 174–77; Salgado, *Doutrina*, p. 179; Barroso, *Que*, pp. 48, 51; Perón, *Perón expone*, pp. 260–61, 243–44, 292.

43. "Program Manifesto of the 26th of July Movement," in *Cuba in Revolution* ed. Rolando E. Bonachea and Nelson P. Valdés (New York: Anchor Books, 1972), p. 132.

44. Mesa-Lago, "Economic Policies and Growth," pp. 279–80.

45. Mello, *Concepção*, pp. 63–70, 95–99, passim: Barroso, *Que*, pp. 48–51, 200–1, passim; Salgado, *Que*, p. 132; Blanksten, *Perón's Argentina*, pp. 246–48, 289, 292; Perón, *Perón expone*, pp. 73–76, 121, passim.

46. Mello, *Concepção*, pp. 48–53; Perón, *Perón expone*, pp. 260–61.

47. Régis Debray, *Strategy for Revolution* (New York: Monthly Review Press, n.d.), p. 81.

48. Quoted in Blanksten, *Perón's Argentina*, pp. 276–80, passim.

49. Perón, *Hora*, pp. 23–24, 32.

50. *Granma*, June 3, 1973. Almost the entire issue is dedicated to the Dorticós visit.

51. Debray, *Strategy for Revolution*, ⁹p. 80, 54; see Gregor on this point in Gregor, *Persuasion*, pp. 309–10.

52. The best-known defender of this point of view has been the U.S. political scientist Harry Kantor; see Harry Kantor, *The Ideology*

and Program of the Peruvian Aprista Movement (Berkeley: University of California Press, 1953).

53. Manuel Seoane, *Páginas polémicas* (Lima: Editorial "La Tribuna," 1931), p. 12.

54. Victor Raúl Haya de la Torre, *Cartas de Haya de la Torre*, ed. Carlos Manuel Cox (Lima: Editorial Nuevo Dia, 1940). p. 11.

55. Seoane, *Páginas polémicas*, pp. 8–9; Rómulo Meneses, *Por el APRA: en la carcel al servicio del P.A.P.* (Lima: Editorial Cooperativa Aprista "Atahualpa," 1933), pp. 76–77; Haya de la Torre, *Cartas*, p. 77; Victor Raúl Haya de la Torre, *El pensamiento político de Haya de la Torre*, vol. 2 (Lima: Ediciones Pueblo, 1961), pp. 40–49; Victor Raúl Haya de la Torre, *Treinta años de Aprismo* (Mexico City: Fondo de Cultura Economica, 1956), pp. 14–15.

56. Meneses, *Por el APRA*, p. 89.

57. Seoane, *Páginas Polémicas*, pp. 10, 12–13; Manuel Seoane, *Nuestros fines* (Buenos Aires: Publicaciones del P.A.P., 1931), pp. 9, 12; Kantor, *Idealogy and Program*, pp. 64, 121–22.

58. Reproduced in Kantor, *Ideology and Program*, p. 133.

59. Haya de la Torre *Cartas*, dedication.

60. Ibid., p. 69.

61. Georgia Anne Geyer, *The New Latins* (New York: Doubleday, 1970), p. 72.

62. Haya de la Torre, *Cartas*, pp. 14, 32, 34.

63. Ibid., p. 60.

64. Edward C. Epstein, "Motivational Bases for Loyalty in the Peruvian Aprista Party" (Ph.D. diss., University of Illinois, 1970), pp. 55–61.

65. Haya de la Torre, *Cartas*, pp. 29–32.

66. Kantor, *Ideology and Program*, pp. 135–37, passim.

67. Haya de la Torre, *Cartas*, p. 32.

68. Ibid., pp. 30–31.

69. Ibid., p. 34.

70. Meneses, *Por el APRA*, p. 97.

71. Eduardo Frei Montalva, *La política y el espíritu* (Santiago de Chile: Ediciones Ercilla, 1940), p. 228.

72. Ibid., p. 134.

73. Eduardo Frei Montalva, *Chile desconocido* (Santiago de Chile: Ediciones Ercilla, 1937), pp. 80–85, 93–95, 110–11, 136, passim.

74. Ibid., pp. 109–10.

75. Eduardo Frei Montalva, *Aún es tiempo . . .* (Santiago de Chile, 1942), p. 50.

76. Ibid., pp. 77–79.

77. Ibid., p. 87.

78. Frei, *Política y espiritu*, pp. 188–89.

79. Frei, *Chile desconocido*, pp. 94–96; Frei, *Aún es tiempo*, p. 116;

Frei, *Política y espiritu,* pp. 188–89. *Conductores* was a favorite Peronist term for elite; see Perón, *Conducción política.*

80. Frei, *Aún es tiempo,* pp. 113–14.

81. Frei, *Política y espiritu,* p. 36.

82. Ibid., p. 35.

83. Edward J. Williams, *Latin American Christian Democratic Parties* (Knoxville: University of Tennessee Press, 1967), p. 230; Maximo Pacheco Gomez, *Principios fundamentales de la doctrina social cristiana* (Santiago de Chile: Imprenta Universitaria, 1947), p. 209.

84. Frei, *Chile desconocido,* p. 145.

85. Ibid., p. 59, 143–46.

86. Frei, *Política y espiritu,* p. 189.

87. Frei, *Chile desconocido,* p. 145.

88. Frei, *Política y espiritu,* p. 189.

89. Frei, *Chile desconocido,* pp. 162–64.

90. Quoted in Elizabeth Sutherland, *The Youngest Revolution* (New York: Dial Press, 1969), p. 94.

91. Figures calculated by Felipe Pazos; see Boris Goldenberg, *The Cuban Revolution and Latin America* (New York: Praeger, 1965), p. 210.

92. Jean Paul Sartre, *Sartre on Cuba* (New York: Ballantine Books, 1961), p. 135.

93. Speech delivered July 26, 1967; reprinted in Fidel Castro, *Major Speeches,* (London: Stage I; 1968), pp. 63–64.

94. Paul N. Rosenstein-Rodan, "Why Allende Failed," reprinted in House Subcommittee on Inter-American Affairs, *Hearings: United States and Chile during the Allende Years, 1970–1973* (Washington, D.C.: GPO, 1975), p. 614.

95. For an account of the Frei program see Robert R. Kaufman, *The Politics of Land Reform in Chile, 1950–1970* (Cambridge, Mass.: Harvard University Press, 1972), pp. 79–286.

96. Robert Moss, *Chile's Marxist Experiment* (London: Newton Abbot, 1973), pp. 81–97.

97. Estimates run as high as a 30 percent average yearly decline in production; see Jonathan Kandell, "The Junta Has Turned Chile into a Police State," *New York Times,* Sept. 15, 1974, p. 3. A good indication of the seriousness of the situation is shown by the fact that the consumption of food rose much more slowly than the need for food imports; see Moss, *Chile's Marxist Experiment* p. 93. See also Paul E. Sigmund, "Less Than Charged," reprinted in House Subcommittee on Inter-American Affairs, *Hearings: United States and Chile during the Allende years, 1970–1973* (Washington, D.C.: GPO, 1975), p. 663.

98. Moss, *Chile's Marxist Experiment,* p. iii.

99. Harry A. Landsberger and Tim McDaniel, "Mobilization as a Double-Edged Sword: The Allende Government's Uneasy Relationship

with Labor 1970–1973," reprinted in House Subcommittee on Inter-American Affairs, *Hearings: United States and Chile during the Allende Years, 1970–1973* (Washington, D.C.: GPO, 1975), pp. 618–30; Joseph Novitski, "Chile's Austerity Plan Hurts Poor," *Washington Post,* May 29, 1974, p. A11; Norman Gall, *Copper Is the Wage of Chile,* American Universities Field Staff Reports, West Coast South America Series, vol. 19, no. 3 (August, 1972): 5–7.

100. Sigmund, "Less Than Charged," p. 663. Kandell reports an absolute decline in copper production during the Allende years; see Kandell, "Junta."

101. Sigmund, "Less Than Charged"; Paul E. Sigmund, "Allende in Retrospect," reprinted in House Subcommittee on Inter-American Affairs, *Hearings: United States and Chile during the Allende Years, 1970–1973* (Washington, D.C.: GPO, 1975), p. 604. In Allende's second year, the rate of increase of industrial output began to drop; and in his third, it dropped in absolute terms from the year before.

102. Moss, *Chile's Marxist Experiment,* pp. 77–78.

103. Sigmund, "Less Than Charged," pp. 661–62.

104. Rosenstein-Rodan, "Why Allende Failed," p. 616.

105. Jonathan Kandell, "Argentina, Always Mindful of Chile, Still Took the Same Path," *New York Times,* April 1, 1976, p. 3.

106. Sigmund, "Allende in Retrospect," p. 608; Jeffrey B. Gayner and Lawrence D. Pratt, *Allende and the Failure of Chilean Marxism* Washington, D.C.: Heritage Foundation, 1974), p. 2; Gayner's black market figure was taken from Hermongenes Perez de Arce, "Testimony presented to the House Committee on Internal Security" (Washington, D.C., March 7, 1974), p. 2548. This figure is supported by a study conducted by the International Monetary Fund; see "Where Chronic Inflation Brings Bewildering Results," *U.S. News and World Report,* Sept. 2, 1974, p. 55.

107. Rosenstein-Rodan, "Why Allende Failed," p. 613; Sigmund, "Allende in Retrospect," p. 612; Ricardo Lagos and Oscar A. Rufatt, "Military Government and Real Wages in Chile: A Note," *Latin American Research Review,* vol. 10, no. 2 (Summer, 1975): 130–40. These two researchers record only a slight drop in real wages under Allende, but they do not make clear whether the prices used in their calculations were controlled or black market prices.

108. Quoted in Rosenstein-Rodan, "Why Allende Failed," p. 615.

109. One Cuban leader (discreetly left unnamed) confided to Herbert Mathews that Marxism in Cuba performed the function of a "mystical theology" (*una mística*); see Mathews, *Biography,* p. 284.

EPILOGUE

1. Delmer M. Brown, *Nationalism in Japan* (Berkeley: University of California Press, 1955), pp. 168–99.

2. The only difficult part is finding the plutonium, and stolen plutonium is available for sale on the international black market. See Lowell Ponte, "Atomizing the World," *Skeptic*, no. 14, p. 35.

3. It's also possible that a Third World government might use a terrorist group as a front in order to hide its participation in the plan. In this scenario the government would supply the weapon to the terrorists and they would make the public demands.

4. A. James Gregor, *Contemporary Radical Ideologies* (New York: Random House, 1968), pp. 277–317.

5. As previously mentioned, the partial exceptions to this were the reactive nationalist leaders of Germany and Japan who came to power at a very low point in their nations' fortunes.

6. Arnaud de Borchgrave, "Libya's Arms Depot," *Newsweek*, July 9, 1979, p. 43.

ABOUT THE AUTHOR

Jeffrey Barrett was born in Boston, Massachusetts, in 1944. Mr. Barrett is a graduate of The Johns Hopkins School of Advanced International Studies, where he studied economics and international relations. He has traveled extensively in Europe, Africa, and Latin America. In Latin America he was a Peace Corps volunteer stationed in Lima, Peru. While serving in the Peace Corps, Mr. Barrett organized community development projects in the poorer sections of Lima. Mr. Barrett has also worked in Latin America as a journalist.

Mr. Barrett currently lives in Washington, D.C., where he writes on subjects dealing with the Third World.